STUDY GUIDE

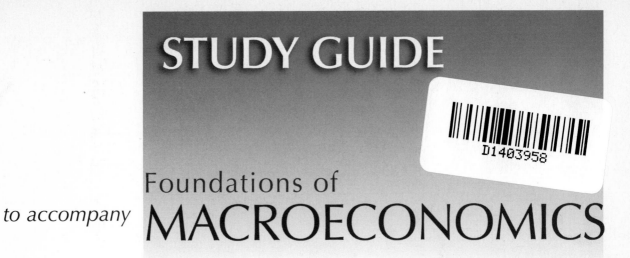

to accompany

Foundations of
MACROECONOMICS

Robin Bade

Michael Parkin

Mark Rush *University of Florida*

Neil Garston *California State University, Los Angeles*

Tom Larson *California State University, Los Angeles*

THIRD EDITION

Study Guide Multiple-Choice Questions Authored by
Ali Ataiifar, *Delaware County Community College*
Diego Mendez-Carbajo, *Illinois Wesleyan University*
William Mosher, *College of the Holy Cross*
Terry Sutton, *Rogers State University*
Cindy Tori, *Valdosta State University*
Nora Underwood, *University of Central Florida*

PEARSON

Addison
Wesley

Boston San Francisco New York
London Toronto Sydney Tokyo Singapore Madrid
Mexico City Munich Paris Cape Town Hong Kong Montreal

ISBN   0-321-36294-2

1 2 3 4 5 6 CW 09 08 07 06

Table of Contents

Your Complete Learning Package

■ The Complete Package

Your *Foundations of Macroeconomics* package consists of:

- Textbook
- Study Guide
- MyEconLab Access Kit

MyEconLab is a powerful and tightly integrated homework and tutorial system that puts you in control of your own learning. MyEconLab includes

- Practice Tests that let you test your understanding and identify where you need to concentrate your studying
- A personalized Study Plan that evaluates your test results and provides further practice
- Tutorial instruction that will guide you through the areas you have difficulty with
- eText—the entire textbook in Flash format with animated figures accompanied by audio explanations prepared by us and with hyperlinks to all the other components of the Web site
- Economics in the News updated daily during the school year
- Online "Office Hours"—ask a question via e-mail, and one of us will respond within 24 hours!
- Economic links—links to sites that keep students up to date with what's going on in the economy and that enable them to work end-of-chapter Web Exercises

Each new textbook arrives with a MyEconLab Student Access Card that unlocks protected areas of the Web site.

■ Checklist and Checkpoints: The Glue That Holds Your Tools Together

Each chapter of your textbook opens with a Chapter Checklist that tells you what you'll be able to do when you've completed the chapter. The number of tasks varies from two to five and most often is three or four. Begin by reviewing this list thoughtfully and get a good sense of what you are about to learn.

Each part of a chapter in the textbook, Study Guide, and MyEconLab Web site is linked directly to a Checklist item to enable you to know exactly what you're studying and how it will enable you to accomplish your learning objective.

Each part of a chapter in the textbook ends with a Checkpoint—a page that offers you a Practice Problem to test your understanding of the key ideas of the part, a worked and illustrated solution to the Practice Problem, and a further (parallel) exercise. The Checkpoints enable you to review material when it's fresh in your mind—the most effective and productive time to do so. The Checkpoints guide you through the material in a step-by-step approach that takes the guesswork out of learning. The Study Guide reinforces each Checkpoint by providing Additional Practice Problems. Use these if you're still not sure you understand the material or if you want to review before an exam.

The self-test questions in the Study Guide, the Study Plan Exercises on the MyEconLab Web site, and the chapter resources on the MyEconLab Web site are organized by Checkpoint so that you can maintain your focus as you work through the material.

■ Practice Makes Perfect

As you study, distinguish between *practice* and *self-test*. Practice is part of the learning process, learning by doing. Self-test is a check. It shows you where you need to go back and reinforce your understanding, and it helps you build confidence in your knowledge of the material.

The Checkpoint Practice Problems and Exercises, the end-of-chapter Exercises, and the Checkpoint Exercises in MyEconLab are designed for practice. The self-test questions in the Study Guide, the pre- and post-tests, and Study Plan Exercises in MyEconLab are designed to reveal your gaps in understanding and to target your final examination of the material.

■ Learn Your Learning Style

It is unlikely that you'll need to use all the tools that we've created all of the time. Try to discover how you learn best. Then exploit what you discover.

If you learn best by reading with a marker or pencil in your hand, you'll use the textbook and Study Guide more often than the other items. If you learn best by seeing the action, you'll often use the eText and MyEconLab tutorials. If you learn best by hearing, you'll use the eText audio explanations of the action in key figures. If you learn best by participating and acting, you'll often use the Study Plan Exercises.

■ Tell Us What Works for *You*

Please tell us the tools that you find most helpful. And tell us what you think we can improve. You can email us at robin@econ100.com or michael.parkin@uwo.ca, or use the Office Hours in your MyEconLab Web site.

Robin Bade
Michael Parkin
Ontario, Canada
October, 2005

Your Course and Your Study Guide

■ Introduction

My experience has taught me that what students want most from a study guide is help in mastering course material in order to do well on examinations. This Study Guide has been created to respond specifically to that demand. Using this Study Guide alone, however, is not enough to guarantee that you will earn an A or do well in your course. In order to help you overcome the problems and difficulties that most students encounter, I have some general advice on how to study, as well as some specific advice on how best to use this Study Guide.

Economics requires a different style of thinking than what you may encounter in other courses. Economists make extensive use of assumptions to break down complex problems into simple, analytically manageable parts. This analytical style, while ultimately not more demanding than the styles of thinking in other disciplines, feels unfamiliar to most students and requires practice. As a result, it is not as easy to do well in economics on the basis of your raw intelligence and high-school knowledge as it is in many other courses. Many students who come to my office are frustrated and puzzled by the fact that they are getting A's and B's in their other courses but only a C or worse in economics. They have not recognized that economics is different and requires practice. In order to avoid a frustrating visit to your instructor after your first test, I suggest you do the following.

■ Don't rely solely on your high-school economics.

If you took high-school economics, you have seen the material on supply and demand which your instructor will lecture on in the first few weeks. Don't be lulled into feeling that the course will be easy. Your high-school knowledge of economic concepts will be very useful, but it will not be enough to guarantee high scores on exams. Your college or university instructors will demand much more detailed knowledge of concepts and ask you to apply them in new circumstances.

■ Keep up with the course material on a weekly basis.

Skim the appropriate chapter in the textbook before your instructor lectures on it. In this initial reading, don't worry about details or arguments you can't quite follow — just try to get a general understanding of the basic concepts and issues. You may be amazed at how your instructor's ability to teach improves when you come to class prepared. As soon as your instructor has finished covering a chapter, complete the corresponding Study Guide chapter. Avoid cramming the day before or even just the week before an exam. Because economics requires practice, cramming is an almost certain recipe for failure.

■ Keep a good set of lecture notes.

Good lecture notes are vital for focusing your studying. Your instructor will only lecture on a subset of topics from the textbook. The topics your instructor covers in a lecture should usually be given priority when studying. Also give priority to studying the figures and graphs covered in the lecture.

Instructors differ in their emphasis on lecture notes and the textbook, so ask early on in the course which is more important in reviewing for exams — lecture notes or the textbook. If your instructor answers that both are important, then ask the following, typical economic question: which will be more beneficial — spending an extra hour re-reading your lecture notes or an extra hour re-reading the textbook? This question assumes that you have read each textbook chapter twice (once before lecture for a general understanding, and then later for a thorough understanding); that you have prepared a good set of lecture notes; and that you have worked through all of the problems in the appropriate Study Guide chapters. By applying this style of analysis to the problem of efficiently allocating your study time, you are already beginning to think like an economist!

■ Use your instructor and/or teaching assistants for help.

When you have questions or problems with course material, come to the office to ask questions. Remember, you are paying for your education and instructors are there to help you learn. Don't be shy. The personal contact that comes from one-on-one tutoring is professionally gratifying for instructors as well as (hopefully) beneficial for you.

■ Form a study group.

A very useful way to motivate your studying and to learn economics is to discuss the course material and problems with other students. Explaining the answer to a question out loud is a very effective way of discovering how well you understand the question. When you answer a question only in your head, you often skip steps in the chain of reasoning without realizing it. When you are forced to explain your reasoning aloud, gaps and mistakes quickly appear, and you (with your fellow group members) can quickly correct your reasoning. The Exercises at the end of each textbook chapter are extremely good study group material. You might also get together after having worked the Study Guide problems, but before looking at the answers, and help each other solve unsolved problems.

■ Work old exams.

One of the most effective ways of studying is to work through exams your instructor has given in previous years. Old exams give you a feel for the style of question your instructor might ask, and give you the opportunity to get used to time pressure if you force yourself to do the exam in the allotted time. Studying from old exams is not cheating, as long as you have obtained a copy of the exam legally. Some institutions keep old exams in the library, others in the department. If there is a class web page, check there—many instructors now post old exams on their class web pages. Students who have previously taken the course are usually a good source as well. Remember, though, that old exams are a useful study aid only if you use them to understand the reasoning behind each question. If you simply memorize answers in the hopes that your instructor will repeat the identical question, you are likely to fail. From year to year, instructors routinely change the questions or change the numerical values for similar questions.

■ Use All Your Tools

The authors of your book, Robin Bade and Michael Parkin, have created a rich array of learning tools that they describe in the preceding section, "Your Complete Learning Package." Make sure that you read this section because it makes sense to use *all* your tools!

USING THE STUDY GUIDE

You should only attempt to complete a chapter in the Study Guide after you have read the corresponding textbook chapter and listened to your instructor lecture on the material. Each Study Guide chapter contains the following sections.

Chapter in Perspective

This first section is a short summary of the key material. It is designed to focus you quickly and precisely on the core material that you must master. It is an excellent study aid for the night before an exam. Think of it as crib notes that will serve as a final check of the key concepts you have studied.

Additional Practice Problems

In each checkpoint in the textbook is at least one and generally more than one practice problem. These problems are extremely valuable because they help you grasp what you have just studied. In the Study Guide are additional Practice Problems. These Practice Problems either extend the Practice Problem in the text or cover another important topic from the Checkpoint. Although the answer is given to the additional Practice Problem, try to solve it on your own before reading the answer.

Following the additional Practice Problem is the Self Test section of the Study Guide. This section has fill in the blank, true or false, multiple choice, complete the graph, and short answer and numeric questions. The questions are designed to give you practice and to test skills and techniques you must master to do well on exams. Before I describe the parts of the Self Test section, here are some general tips that apply to all parts.

First, use a pencil to write your answers in the Study Guide so you have neat, complete pages from which to study. Draw graphs wherever they are applicable. Some questions will ask explicitly for graphs; many others will not but will require a chain of reasoning that involves shifts of curves on a graph. Always draw the graph. Don't try to work

through the reasoning in your head — you are much more likely to make mistakes that way. Whenever you draw a graph, even in the margins of the Study Guide, label the axes. You might think that you can keep the labels in your head, but you will be confronting many different graphs with many different variables on the axes. Avoid confusion and label. As an added incentive, remember that on exams where graphs are required, instructors often will deduct points for unlabelled axes.

Do the Self Test questions as if they were real exam questions, which means do them without looking at the answers. This is the single most important tip I can give you about effectively using the Study Guide to improve your exam performance. Struggling for the answers to questions that you find difficult is one of the most effective ways to learn. The adage — no pain, no gain — applies well to studying. You will learn the most from right answers you had to struggle for and from your wrong answers and mistakes. Only after you have attempted all the questions should you look at the answers. When you finally do check the answers, be sure to understand where you went wrong and why the right answer is correct.

Fill in the Blanks

This section covers the material in the checkpoint and has blanks for you to complete. Often suggested phrases are given but sometimes there are no hints—in that case you are on your own! Well, not really, because the answers are given at the end of each Study Guide chapter. This section also can help you review for a test because, once completed, they serve as a *very* brief statement of the important points within the important points within the checkpoint.

True or False

Next are true or false questions. Some instructors use true or false questions on exams or quizzes, so these questions might prove very valuable. The answers to the questions are given at the end of the chapter. The answer also has a page reference to the textbook. If you missed the question or did not completely understand the answer, definitely turn to the textbook and study the topic so that you will not miss similar questions on your exams.

Multiple Choice

Many instructors use multiple choice questions on exams, so pay particular attention to these questions. Similar to the true or false questions, the answers are given at the end of the Study Guide chapter and each answer references the relevant page in the text. If you had any difficulty with a question, use this page reference to look up the topic and then study it to remove this potential weakness.

Complete the Graph

The complete the graph questions allow you to practice using one of economists' major tools, graphs. If you will have essay questions on your exams, it is an extremely safe bet that you will be expected to use graphs on at least some of the questions. This section is designed to ensure that you are well prepared to handle these questions. Use the graph in the Study Guide to answer the questions. Although the answer is given at the end of the Study Guide chapter, do *not* look at the answer before you attempt to solve the problem. It is much too easy to deceive yourself into thinking you understand the answer when you simply look at the question and then read the answer. Involve yourself in the material by answering the question and then looking at the answer. If you cannot answer the question or if you got the answer wrong, the Study Guide again has a reference to the relevant page number in the text. Use the text and study the material!

Short Answer and Numeric Questions

The last set of questions are short answer and numeric questions. Short answer and numeric questions are classic exam questions, so pay attention to these questions. Approach them similarly to how you approach all the other questions: Answer them before you look at

the answers in the back of the Study Guide. These questions are also excellent for use in a study group. If you and several friends are studying for an exam, you can use these questions to quiz your understanding. If you have disagreements about the correct answers, once again there are page references to the text so that you can settle these disagreements and be sure that everyone has a solid grasp of the point!

FINAL COMMENTS

This Study Guide combines the efforts of many talented individuals. The authors of the Chapter in Perspective and many of the additional Practice Problems and answers are Neil Garston, from California State University, at Los Angeles, and Tom Larson, also from California State University, at Los Angeles. It was a pleasure to work with these fine scholars.

For the multiple choice questions, we assembled a team of truly outstanding teachers:
- Ali Ataiifar, Delaware County Community College
- Diego Mendez-Carbajo, Illinois Wesleyan University
- William Mosher, Assumption College
- Cynthia Tori, Valdosta State University
- Nora Underwood, University of California, Davis

I added a few multiple choice questions and wrote the fill in the blank, true or false, complete the graph, and short answer and numeric questions. I also served as an editor to assemble the material into the book before you.

The Study Guide and other supplements were checked for accuracy by a team of instructors. For previous editions, the team included:
- David Bivin, Indiana University-Purdue University
- Geoffrey Black, Boise State University
- Jeffrey Davis, ITT Technical Institute
- Ken Long, New River Community College

- Barbara Wiens-Tuers, Penn State University, Altoona
- Joachim Zietz, Middle Tennessee State University
- Armand Zottola, Central CT State University
- Harry Ellis, University of North Texas
- Kate Krause, University of Mew Mexico

A student who used this book also found errors that I did not catch. I think we owe this student a special thank you for her conscientious work and her initiative to report the errors. This student is

- Lisa Salazar-Rich, at Cal Poly Pomona

Jeannie Shearer-Gillmore, University of Western Ontario, checked every word, every sentence, every paragraph, and every page of the first edition of this book and many of the words, sentences, paragraphs, and pages of this edition. She made a huge number of corrections and comments. The easiest way to distinguish her work and mine is to determine if there is an error in a passage. If there is, it's my work; if there is not, it's her work.

Robin Bade and Michael Parkin, the authors of your book, also need thanks. Not only have they written such a superior book that it was easy to be enthusiastic about writing the Study Guide to accompany it, both Robin and Michael played a very hands-on role in creating this Study Guide. They corrected errors and made suggestions that vastly improved the Study Guide.

I want to thank my family: Susan, Tommy, Bobby, and Katie, who, respectively: allowed me to work all hours on this book; helped me master the intricacies of FTPing computer files; let me postpone working on our trains with him until after the book was concluded; and would run into my typing room to share her new discoveries. Thanks a lot!

Finally, I want to thank Butterscotch, Mik, Lucky, and Pearl, who sometimes sat on my lap and sometimes sat next to the computer in a box peering out the window (and occasionally meowed) while I typed.

We (all of us except the cats) have tried to make the Study Guide as helpful and useful as possible. Undoubtedly I have made some mistakes; mistakes that you may see. If you find any, I, and succeeding generations of students, would be grateful if you could point them out to me. At the end of my class at the University of Florida, when I ask my students for their advice, I point out to them that this advice won't help them at all because they have just completed the class. But comments they make will influence how future students are taught. Thus just as they owe a debt of gratitude for the comments and suggestions that I received from students before them, so too will students after them owe them an (unpaid and unpayable) debt. You are in the same situation. If you have questions, suggestions, or simply comments, let me know. My address follows, or you can reach me via e-mail at MARK.RUSH@CBA.UFL.EDU. Your input probably won't benefit you directly, but it will benefit following generations. And if you give me permission, I will note your name and school in following editions so that any younger siblings (or, years down the road, maybe even your children!) will see your name and offer up thanks.

Mark Rush
Economics Department
University of Florida
Gainesville, Florida 32611
November, 2005.

Getting Started

Chapter 1 defines economics, discusses the three major questions of *what, how,* and *for whom,* covers the five core economic ideas that shape how economists think about issues, defines the differences between microeconomics and macroeconomics, and examines methods used by economists to study the economic world.

■ **Define economics and explain the kinds of questions that economist try to answer.**

Economic questions exist because of scarcity, the point that wants exceed the ability of resources to satisfy them. Economics is the social science that studies the choices that individuals, businesses, government, and entire societies make as they cope with scarcity and the incentives that influence these choices. Economics studies how choices wind up determining: *what* goods and services get produced?; *how* are goods and services produced?; and *for whom* are goods and services produced? Economics also studies when choices made in someone's self-interest also serve the social interest. For instance, are the self-interested choices made about globalization and international outsourcing, use of tropical rain forests, and social security also promote the social interest about these issues?

■ **Explain the core ideas that define the economic way of thinking.**

The five ideas that are the core of the economic approach: people make rational choices by comparing benefits and costs; cost is what you must give up to get something; benefit is what you gain when you get something and is measured by what you are willing to give up to get it; a rational choice is made on the margin; and choices respond to incentives. A rational choice uses the available resources to most effectively satisfy the wants of the person making the choice. The opportunity cost of an activity is the highest-valued alternative forgone. The benefit of a good or service is the gain or pleasure it brings and is measured by what someone is willing to give up to get the good or service. Making choices on the margin means comparing all the relevant alternatives systematically and incrementally to determine which is the best choice. A choice on the margin is one that adjusts a plan. The marginal cost is the cost of a one-unit increase in an activity; the marginal benefit is the gain from a one-unit increase in an activity. Rational choices compare the marginal benefit of an activity to its marginal cost. Microeconomics studies choices made by individuals and businesses. Macroeconomics studies the national economy and global economy. Statements about "what is" are positive statements; statements about "what should be" are normative statements. Economists are interested in positive statements about cause and effect but determining causality can be difficult because usually many things change simultaneously. So economists often use the idea of *ceteris paribus,* a Latin term that means "other things equal" and is used to sort out the effect of individual influence. Correlation is the tendency for the values of two variables to move together in a predictable way. Economics can be used by individuals, business, and governments as a policy tool to help them make better decisions.

CHECKPOINT 1.1

■ **Define economics and explain the kinds of questions that economist try to answer.**

Quick Review

- *Self-interest* The choices that people make that they think are the best for them.
- *Social interest* The choices that are best for society as a whole.

Additional Practice Problems 1.1

1. Which of the following headlines deals with *what, how,* and *for whom* questions?:
   a. A new government program is designed to provide high-quality school lunches for children from poorer families.
   b. Intel researchers discover a new chip-making technology.
   c. Regis Hairstyling sets a record for hairstylings in month of July

2. Which of the following headlines concern social interest and self interest?
   a. A new government program is designed to provide high-quality school lunches for children from poorer families.
   b. Intel researchers discover a new chip-making technology.
   c. Regis Hairstyling sets a record for hairstylings in month of July.

Solutions to Additional Practice Problems 1.1

1a. "More lunches" is a *what* question and "for children from poorer families" is a *for whom* question.

1b. "New chip-making technology" is a *how* question because it deals with how computer chips will be manufactured.

1c. "Record for hairstylings" is a *what* question because it notes that a record number of hairstylings have taken place in July.

2a. The decision to implement a new government program is a decision that is most likely made in the social interest. The self-interest of the government bureaucrat who made the decision might also be involved, particularly if the bureaucrat also will help manage the program.

2b. Intel's decision to research new chip-making technology is made in Intel's self-interest.

2c. Regis's decision to offer hairstylings is made in its self-interest as are the decisions of the people who had their hair styled by Regis.

■ **Self Test 1.1**

Fill in the blanks

Economic questions arise because ____ (human wants; resources) exceed the ____ (human wants; resources) available to satisfy them. Faced with ____, people must make choices. Choices that are the best for the person who makes them are choices made in ____ (self-interest; social interest). Choices that are best for everyone as a whole are choices made in ____ (self-interest; social interest).

True or false

1. Faced with scarcity, we must make choices.
2. The question of *what* refers to what production method should a firm use?
3. The answers to the *what, how* and *for whom* questions depend on the interactions of the choices people, businesses, and governments make.
4. If Sam buys a pizza because she is hungry, her choice is made in the social interest.
5. Because everyone is a member of society, all choices made in self-interest are also in the social interest.

Multiple choice

1. The characteristic from which all economic problems arise is
   a. political decisions.
   b. providing a minimal standard of living for every person.
   c. how to make a profit.
   d. hunger.
   e. scarcity.

2. Scarcity results from the fact that
   a. people's wants exceed the resources available to satisfy them.
   b. not all goals are desirable.
   c. we cannot answer the major economic questions.
   d. choices made in self-interest are not always in the social interest.
   e. the population keeps growing.

3. To economists, scarcity means that
   a. limited wants cannot be satisfied by the unlimited resources.
   b. a person looking for work is not able to find work.
   c. the number of people without jobs rises when economic times are bad.
   d. there can never be answers to the *what, how* or *for whom* questions.
   e. unlimited wants cannot be satisfied by the limited resources.

4. The question "Should we produce video tapes or DVD discs?" is an example of a ____ question.
   a. what
   b. how
   c. for whom
   d. where
   e. why

5. The question "Should we produce houses using bricks or wood?" is an example of a ____ question.
   a. what
   b. how
   c. for whom
   d. where
   e. why

6. The question "Should economics majors or sociology majors earn more after they graduate?" is an example of a ____ question.
   a. what
   b. how
   c. for whom
   d. where
   e. why

7. If a decision is made and it is the best choice for society, the decision is said to be
   a. a valid economic choice.
   b. made in self-interest.
   c. made in social interest.
   d. consistent with scarcity.
   e. a want-maximizing choice.

Short answer and numeric questions

1. Will there ever come a time without scarcity?

2. If there was no scarcity, would there be a need for economics?

3. What are the three major questions answered by people's economic choices?

4. Why is the distinction between choices made in self-interest and choices made in social interest important?

CHECKPOINT 1.2

■ **Explain the core ideas that define the economic way of thinking.**

Quick Review

- *Opportunity cost* The opportunity cost of something is the best thing you must give up to get it.

- *Marginal cost* The opportunity cost that arises from a one-unit increase in an activity.

- *Marginal benefit* The benefit that arises from a one-unit increase in an activity.

- *Rational choice* A choice that uses the available resources to most effectively satisfy the wants of the person making the choice.

- *Positive statement* A positive statement tells what is currently understood about the way the world operates. We can test a positive statement.

- *Normative statement* A normative statement tells what ought to be. It depends on values. We cannot test a normative statement.

Practice Problems 1.2

1. What are the opportunity costs of using this *Study Guide*?

2. Kate usually plays tennis for two hours a week and her grade on each math test is usually 70 percent. Last week, after playing two hours of tennis, Kate thought long and hard about playing for another hour. She decided to play another hour of tennis and cut her study time by one additional hour. But the grade on last week's math test was 60 percent.

   a. What was Kate's opportunity cost of the third hour of tennis?
   b. Given that Kate made the decision to play the third hour of tennis, what can you conclude about the comparison of her marginal benefit and marginal cost of the second hour of tennis?
   c. Was Kate's decision to play the third hour of tennis rational?

3. Classify each of the following statements as positive or normative:

   a. There is too much poverty in the United States.
   b. An increase in the gas tax will cut pollution.
   c. Cuts to social security in the United States have been too deep.

Solutions to Additional Practice Problems 1.2

1. The opportunity cost is mainly the time spent using the *Study Guide* because that time could be devoted to other activities. The highest-valued activity forgone, be it studying for another class, or sleeping, or some other activity, which is forgone because of the time spent using the *Study Guide* is the opportunity cost. Once you have purchased this *Study Guide*, its price is *not* an opportunity cost of using the *Study Guide* because you have already paid the price. The price is, instead, a sunk cost.

2a. The opportunity cost of the third hour of tennis was the 10 percentage point drop on her math test grade because she cut her studying time by one hour to play an additional hour of tennis. If Kate had not played tennis for the third hour, she would have studied and her grade would not have dropped.

2b. Kate chose to play the third hour of tennis, so the marginal benefit of the third hour of tennis was greater than the marginal cost of the third hour. If the marginal benefit of the third hour of tennis was less than the marginal cost of the third hour, Kate would have chosen to study rather than play tennis.

2c. Even though her grade fell, Kate's choice used the available time to most effectively satisfy her wants because the marginal benefit of the third hour of playing tennis exceeded the marginal cost of the third hour. This was a choice made in her self-interest.

3a. A normative statement because it depends on the speaker's values and cannot be tested.

3b. A positive statement because it can be tested by increasing the gas tax and then measuring the change in pollution.

3c. A normative statement because it depends on the speaker's values (someone else might propose still deeper cuts) and cannot be tested.

■ Self Test 1.2

Fill in the blanks

A ____ choice uses the available resources to most effectively satisfy the wants of the person making the choice. The opportunity cost of an activity is ____ (all of the activities forgone; the highest-valued alternative forgone). The benefit of an activity is measured by what you ____ (are willing to; must) give up. We make a rational choice to do an activity if the marginal benefit of the activity ____ the marginal cost. (Macroeconomics; Microeconomics) ____ is the study of the choices of individuals and businesses, the interaction of these choices, and the influences that governments exert on these classes. A statement that tells "what is" is a ____ (positive; normative) statement. A statement that tells "what ought to be" is a ____ (positive; normative) statement. The term meaning "other things being equal" is ____ (*ceteris paribus*; sunk cost).

True or false

1. Instead of attending his microeconomics class for two hours, Jim can play a game of tennis or watch a movie. For Jim the opportunity cost of attending class is forgoing the game of tennis *and* watching the movie.

2. Marginal cost is what you gain when you get one more unit of something.

3. A rational choice involves comparing the marginal benefit of an action to its marginal cost.

4. A change in marginal benefit or a change in marginal cost brings a change in the incentives that we face and leads us to change our actions.

5. The subject of economics divides into two main parts, which are macroeconomics and microeconomics.

6. The statement, "When more people volunteer in their communities, crime rates decrease" is a positive statement.

Multiple choice

1. Jamie has enough money to buy either a Mountain Dew, or a Pepsi, or a bag of chips. He chooses to buy the Mountain Dew. The opportunity cost of the Mountain Dew is
   a. the Pepsi and the bag of chips.
   b. the Pepsi or the bag of chips, whichever the highest-valued alternative forgone.
   c. the Mountain Dew.
   d. the Pepsi because it is a drink, as is the Mountain Dew.
   e. zero because he enjoys the Mountain Dew.

2. The benefit of an activity is
   a. purely objective and measured in dollars.
   b. the gain or pleasure that it brings.
   c. the value of its sunk cost.
   d. measured by what must be given up to get one more unit of the activity.
   e. not measurable on the margin.

3. The cost of a one-unit increase in an activity
   a. is the total one-unit cost.
   b. is called the marginal cost.
   c. decreases as you do more of the activity.
   d. is called the marginal benefit/cost.
   e. is called the sunk cost.

4. The marginal benefit of an activity is
   i. the benefit from a one-unit increase in the activity.
   ii. the benefit of a small, unimportant activity.
   iii. measured by what the person is willing to give up to get one additional unit of the activity.
   a. i only.
   b. ii only.
   c. iii only.
   d. i and iii.
   e. ii and iii.

5. If the marginal benefit of the next slice of pizza exceeds the marginal cost, you will
   a. eat the slice of pizza.
   b. not eat the slice of pizza.
   c. be unable to choose between eating or not eating.
   d. eat half the slice.
   e. More information is needed about how much the marginal benefit exceeds the marginal cost to determine if you will or will not eat the slice.

6. When people make rational choices, they
   a. behave selfishly.
   b. do not consider their emotions.
   c. weigh the costs and benefits of their options and act to satisfy their wants.
   d. necessarily make a decision in the social interest.
   e. are necessarily making the best decision.

7. Which of the following is a microeconomic issue?
   a. Why has unemployment risen nation-wide?
   b. Why has economic growth been rapid in China?
   c. What is the impact on the quantity of Pepsi purchased if consumers' tastes change in favor of non-carbonated drinks?
   d. Why is the average income lower in Africa than in Latin America?
   e. Why did overall production within the United States increase last year?

8. A positive statement
   a. must always be right.
   b. cannot be tested.
   c. can be tested against the facts.
   d. depends on someone's value judgment.
   e. cannot be negative.

9. Which of the following is an example of a normative statement?
   a. If cars become more expensive, fewer people will buy them.
   b. Car prices should be affordable.
   c. If wages increase, firms will fire some workers.
   d. Fewer people die in larger cars than in smaller cars.
   e. Cars emit pollution.

10. The Latin term *ceteris paribus* means
    a. after this, therefore because of this.
    b. other things being equal.
    c. what is correct for the part is not correct for the whole.
    d. on the margin.
    e. when one variable increases, the other variable decreases.

Short answer and numeric questions

1. What is an opportunity cost?

2. You have $12 and can buy a pizza, a movie on a DVD, or a package of CD-Rs. You decide to buy the pizza and think that if you hadn't been so hungry, you would have purchased the DVD. What is the opportunity cost of your pizza?

3. What is a sunk cost?

4. What is benefit and how is it measured?

5. What is a marginal cost? A marginal benefit? How do they relate to rational choice?

6. Explain the difference between microeconomics and macroeconomics.

7. Becky is writing an essay about the law that requires all passengers in a car to use a seat belt and its effectiveness. What might be a positive statement and a normative statement that she will include in her essay?

SELF TEST ANSWERS

■ CHECKPOINT 1.1

Fill in the blanks

Economic questions arise because <u>human wants</u> exceed the <u>resources</u> available to satisfy them. Faced with <u>scarcity</u>, people must make choices. Choices that are the best for the person who makes them are choices made in <u>self-interest</u>. Choices that are best for everyone as a whole are choices made in <u>social interest</u>.

True or false

1. True; page 2
2. False; page 3
3. True; page 4
4. False; page 4
5. False; page 5

Multiple choice

1. e; page 2
2. a; page 2
3. e; page 2
4. a; page 3
5. b; page 3
6. c; page 4
7. d; page 4

Short answer and numeric questions

1. There will never be a time without scarcity because human wants are unlimited; page 2.

2. If there was no scarcity, then there likely would be no need for economics. Economics studies the choices that people make to cope with scarcity, so if there was no scarcity, then people's choices would not be limited by scarcity; page 3.

3. The questions are "*What* goods and services get produced and in what quantities?", "*How* are goods and services produced?", and "*For whom* are the goods and services produced?" page 3.

4. In general economists believe that people make choices according to their self-interest. These choices might or might not be in the social interest. Part of what economists study is when choices made in people's self-interest also further the social interest; page 5.

■ CHECKPOINT 1.2

Fill in the blanks

A <u>rational</u> choice uses the available resources to most effectively satisfy the wants of the person making the choice. The opportunity cost of an activity is <u>the highest-valued alternative forgone</u>. The benefit of an activity is measured by what you <u>are willing to</u> give up. We make a rational choice to do an activity if the marginal benefit of the activity <u>exceeds</u> the marginal cost. <u>Microeconomics</u> is the study of the choices of individuals and businesses, the interaction of these choices, and the influences that governments exert on these classes. A statement that tells "what is" is a <u>positive</u> statement. A statement that tells "what ought to be" is a <u>normative</u> statement. The term meaning "other things being equal" is <u>*ceteris paribus*</u>.

True or false

1. False; page 11
2. False; page 12
3. True; page 13
4. True; page 13
5. True; page 14
6. True; page 15

Multiple choice

1. b; page 11
2. b; page 11
3. b; page 12
4. d; page 12
5. a; page 13
6. c; page 13
7. c; page 14
8. c; page 15
9. b; page 15
10. b; page 15

Short answer and numeric questions

1. The opportunity cost of something is the highest-valued other thing that must be given up. The opportunity cost is only the single highest-valued alternative forgone, *not* all alternatives forgone; page 11.

2. The opportunity cost of the pizza is the highest-valued alternative forgone, which in this case is the DVD. The opportunity cost is *not* the DVD and the CD-Rs because you would not have been able to purchase both of them with your $12; page 11.

3. A sunk cost is a previously occurred and irreversible cost; page 11.

4. The benefit of something is the gain or pleasure that it brings. Economists measure the benefit of something by what a person is willing to give up to get it; pages 11, 12.

5. Marginal cost is the cost of a one-unit increase in an activity. Marginal benefit is the benefit of a one-unit increase in an activity. A rational choice is made by comparing the marginal cost and marginal benefit, so that if the marginal benefit of an activity exceeds or equals the marginal cost, the activity is undertaken; pages 12-13.

6. Microeconomics studies individual units within the economy, such as a consumer, a firm, a market, and so forth. Macroeconomics studies the overall, or aggregate, economy, such as the overall unemployment rate, or overall economic growth rate; page 14.

7. A positive statement is "People who wear seat belts are involved in fewer road deaths." This statement can be tested. A normative statement is "People should be free to choose whether to wear a seat belt or not." This statement cannot be tested; page 15.

Appendix: Making and Using Graphs

APPENDIX IN PERSPECTIVE

After you have completed the appendix, you will have thoroughly reviewed the graphs used in your economics course.

■ Making and using graphs.

Graphs represent quantities as distances. The vertical axis is the y-axis and the horizontal axis is the x-axis. A scatter diagram plots a graph of one variable against the value of another variable. A time-series graph measures time along the x-axis and the variable (or variables) of interest along the y-axis. A cross-section graph shows the values of an economic variable for different groups in the population at a point in time. Graphs can show the relationship between two variables in an economic model. Variables that move in the same direction have a positive, or direct, relationship. Variables that move in the opposite direction have a negative, or inverse, relationship. Some relationships have minimum or maximum points. The slope of a relationship is the change in the value of the variable measured on the y-axis divided by the change in the value of the variable measured on the x-axis. To graph a relationship among more than two variables, we use the *ceteris paribus* assumption and graph the relationship between two of the variables, holding the other variables constant.

CHECKPOINT 1

■ Making and using graphs.

Additional Practice Problems

1. You have data on the average monthly rainfall and the monthly expenditure on umbrellas in Seattle, Washington. What sort of graph would be the best to reveal if any relationship exists between these variables?

2. In Figure A1.1, draw a straight line showing a positive relationship and another straight line showing a negative relationship.

■ FIGURE A1.1

Year	Price (dollars per gallon)
1994	0.79
1995	0.79
1996	0.82
1997	0.80
1998	0.68
1999	0.73
2000	1.09
2001	1.02
2002	0.94
2003	1.13

3. The table has the average price of a gallon of gasoline, excluding taxes, for ten years. In Figure A1.2, label the axes and then plot these data. What type of graph are you creating? What is the general trend of gas prices during this decade?

■ **FIGURE A1.2**

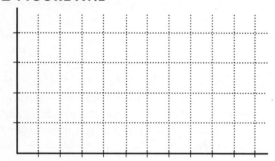

4. Figure A1.3 shows the relationship between the price of a paperback book and the quantity of paperback books a publisher is willing to sell. What is the slope of the line in Figure A1.3?

■ **FIGURE A1.3**

Price (dollars per paperback book)

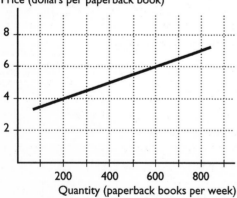

Quantity (paperback books per week)

Solution to Additional Practice Problems 1

1. A scatter diagram would be the best graph to use. A scatter diagram would plot the monthly value of, say, rainfall along the vertical axis (the y-axis) and the monthly value of umbrella expenditure along the horizontal axis (the x-axis).

■ **FIGURE A1.4**

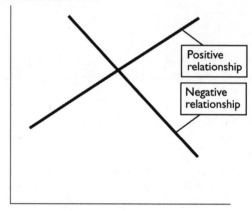

2. Figure A1.4 has two lines, one showing a positive relationship and the other showing a negative relationship. Your figure does not need to have identical lines. The key point your figure needs is that the line for the positive relationship slopes up as you move rightward along it and the line for the negative relationship slopes down as you move rightward along it.

■ **FIGURE A1.5**

Price (dollars per gallon)

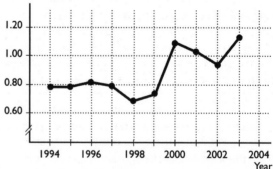

Year

3. Figure A1.5 labels the axes and plots the data in the table. The graph is a time-series graph. The trend is positive because gas prices generally increased during these years.

■ FIGURE A1.6

Price (dollars per paperback book)

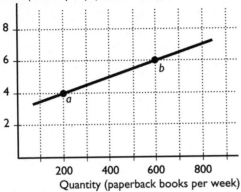

Quantity (paperback books per week)

4. The slope of a line is the change the variable measured on the *y*-axis divided by the change in the variable measured on the *x*-axis. To calculate the slope of the line in the figure, use points *a* and *b* in Figure A1.6. Between *a* and *b*, *y* rises by 2, from 4 to 6. And *x* increases by 400, from 200 to 600. The slope equals 2/400 = 0.005.

■ Self Test 1

Fill in the blanks

In a graph, the vertical line is called the _____ (*x*-axis; *y*-axis) and the horizontal line is called the _____ (*x*-axis; *y*-axis). A _____ (scatter diagram; time-series graph; cross-section graph) is a graph of the value of one variable against the value of another variable. A _____ (scatter diagram; time-series graph; cross-section graph) measures time along the *x*-axis and the variable along the *y*-axis. A _____ (scatter diagram; time-series graph; cross-section graph) shows the values of an economic variable for different groups in the population at a point in time. If the graph of a relationship between two variables slopes up to the right, the two variables have a _____ (positive; negative) relationship. If the graph between two variables is a vertical line, the two variables _____ (are; are not) related. The slope of a relationship is the change in the value of the variable measured along the _____ (*x*-axis; *y*-axis) divided by the change in the value of the variable measured along the _____ (*x*-axis; *y*-axis). By using the *ceteris paribus*

assumption, it _____ (is; is not) possible to graph a relationship that involves more than two variables.

True or false

1. A point that is above and to the right of another point will have a larger value of the *x*-axis variable and a larger value of the *y*-axis variable.

2. A scatter diagram shows the values of an economic variable for different groups in a population at a point in time.

3. A time-series graph compares values of a variable for different groups at a single point in time.

4. A trend is a measure of the closeness of the points on a graph.

5. A positive relationship is always a linear relationship.

6. A relationship that starts out sloping upward and then slopes downward has a maximum.

7. A graph that shows a horizontal line indicates variables that are unrelated.

8. The slope at a point on a curve can be found by calculating the slope of the line that touches the point and no other point on the curve.

Multiple choice

1. Demonstrating how an economic variable changes from one year to the next is best illustrated by a
   a. scatter diagram.
   b. time-series graph.
   c. linear graph.
   d. cross-section graph.
   e. trend-line

2. To show the values of an economic variable for different groups in a population at a point in time, it is best to use a
   a. scatter diagram.
   b. time-series graph.
   c. linear graph.
   d. cross-section graph.
   e. trend diagram.

3. If whenever one variable increases, another variable also increases, these variables are
   a. positively related.
   b. negatively related.
   c. inversely related.
   d. cross-sectionally related.
   e. not related.

4. A graph of the relationship between two variables is a line that slopes down to the right. These two variables are ____ related.
   a. positively
   b. directly
   c. negatively
   d. not
   e. trend-line

5. Two variables are unrelated if their graph is
   i.   a vertical line.
   ii. a 45 degree line.
   iii. a horizontal line.
   a. i only.
   b. ii only.
   c. iii only.
   d. i and iii.
   e. i, ii, and iii.

■ **FIGURE A1.7**

Price (dollars per pound of rutabagas)

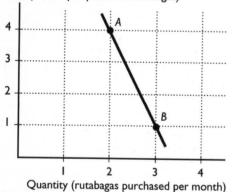

Quantity (rutabagas purchased per month)

6. In figure A1.7, between points A and B, what is the slope of the line?
   a. 4
   b. 1
   c. 3
   d. −3
   e. 0

■ **FIGURE A1.8**

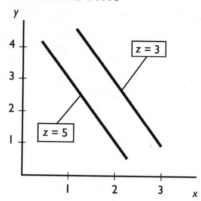

7. In Figure A1.8, an increase in z leads to a
   a. movement up along one of the lines showing the relationship between x and y.
   b. movement down along one of the lines showing the relationship between x and y.
   c. rightward shift of the line showing the relationship between x and y.
   d. leftward shift of the line showing the relationship between x and y.
   e. trend change in both x and y.

8. In Figure A1.8, *ceteris paribus*, an increase in x is associated with
   a. an increase in y.
   b. a decrease in y.
   c. an increase in z.
   d. a random change in z.
   e. no change in either y or z.

Complete the graph

Year	Workers (millions)
1990	6.5
1991	6.5
1992	6.6
1993	6.8
1994	7.1
1995	7.4
1996	7.5
1997	7.6
1998	7.8
1999	7.9

1. The table above gives the number of people working in restaurants and bars in the United States during the decade of the 1990s.

■ **FIGURE A1.9**

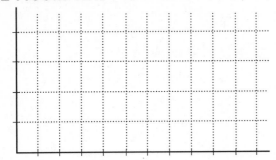

In Figure A1.9, measure time on the horizontal axis and the number of workers on the vertical axis, and then plot these data.

a. What type of graph are you creating?

b. Using your figure, what was the trend in the number of people working in restaurants and bars during the 1990s?

Year	Revenue (billions of dollars)	Workers (millions)
1990	190	6.5
1991	194	6.5
1992	200	6.6
1993	213	6.8
1994	222	7.1
1995	230	7.4
1996	239	7.5
1997	254	7.6
1998	267	7.8
1999	285	7.9

2. The table above gives the annual revenue for restaurants and bars and the number of people employed in restaurants and bars in the United States during the decade of the 1990s. In Figure A1.10, measure the revenue along the horizontal axis and the number of workers along the vertical axis and plot the data.

a. What type of graph are you creating?

b. What relationship do you see in your figure between the revenue and the number of workers?

■ **FIGURE A1.10**

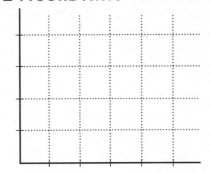

Price (dollars per sack of cat food)	Quantity (sacks of cat food per month)
1	10,000
2	8,000
3	7,000
4	4,000

3. The number of sacks of premium cat food that cat lovers will buy depends on the price of a sack of cat food. The relationship is given in the table above. In Figure A1.11, plot this relationship, putting the price on the vertical axis and the quantity on the horizontal axis.

■ **FIGURE A1.11**

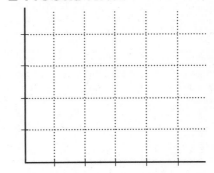

a. If the price of a sack of cat food is $2, how many sacks will be purchased?

b. If the price of a sack of cat food is $3, how many sacks will be purchased?

c. Is the relationship between the price and the quantity positive or negative?

4. In Figure A1.12, label the maximum and minimum points.

■ **FIGURE A1.12**

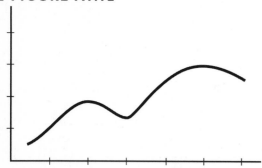

5. In Figure A1.13, draw a line through point *A* with a slope of 2. Label the line "1." Draw another line through point *A* with a slope of −2. Label this line "2."

■ **FIGURE A1.13**

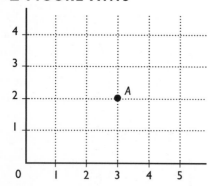

Price (dollars per compact disc)	Quantity of compact discs purchased, low income	Quantity of compact discs purchased, high income
11	4	5
12	3	4
13	1	3
14	0	2

6. Bobby says that he buys fewer compact discs when the price of a compact disc is higher. Bobby also says that he will buy more compact discs after he graduates and his income is higher. The table above shows the number of compact discs Bobby buys in a month at different prices when his income is low and when his income is high.

■ **FIGURE A1.14**

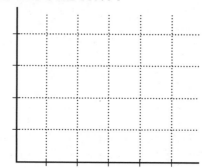

a. In Figure A1.14, put the price on the vertical axis and the quantity purchased on the horizontal axis. Show the relationship between the number of discs purchased and the price when Bobby's income is low.

b. On the same figure, draw the relationship between the number of discs purchased and the price when his income is high.

c. Does an increase in Bobby's income cause the relationship between the price of a compact disc and the number purchased to shift rightward or leftward?

Short answer and numeric questions

1. What are the three types of graphs?

2. If two variables are positively related, will the slope of a graph of the two variables be positive or negative? If two variables are negatively related, will the slope of a graph of the two variables be positive or negative?

3. If a line slopes upward to the right, is its slope positive or negative? If a line slopes downward to the right, is its slope positive or negative?

■ **FIGURE A1.15**

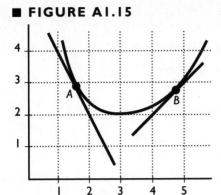

4. In Figure A1.15, what is the slope of the curved line at point *A*? At point *B*?

SELF TEST ANSWERS

■ CHECKPOINT 1

Fill in the blanks

In a graph, the vertical line is called the *y-axis* and the horizontal line is called the *x-axis*. A *scatter diagram* is a graph of the value of one variable against the value of another variable. A *time-series graph* measures time along the *x*-axis and the variable along the *y*-axis. A *cross-section graph* shows the values of an economic variable for different groups in the population at a point in time. If the graph of a relationship between two variables slopes up to the right, the two variables have a *positive* relationship. If the graph between two variables is a vertical line, the two variables *are not* related. The slope of a relationship is the change in the value of the variable measured along the *y-axis* divided by the change in the value of the variable measured along the *x-axis*. By using the *ceteris paribus* assumption, it *is* possible to graph a relationship that involves more than two variables.

True or false

1. True; page 23
2. False; page 24
3. False; page 24
4. False; page 24
5. False; page 26
6. True; page 28
7. True; page 28
8. True; page 29

Multiple choice

1. b; page 24
2. d; page 24
3. a; page 26
4. c; page 27
5. d; page 28
6. d; page 29
7. d; page 30
8. b; page 30

Complete the graph

■ FIGURE A1.16

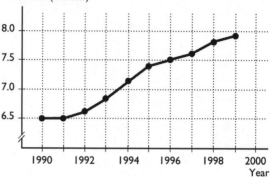

1. Figure A1.16 plots the data.
   a. This is a time-series graph; page 24.
   b. The trend is positive. During the 1990s there is an increase in the number of people working in restaurants and bars; page 24.

■ FIGURE A1.17

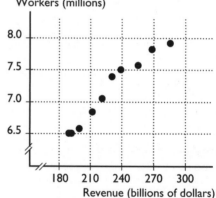

2. Figure A1.17 plots the data.
   a. The figure is a scatter diagram; page 24.
   b. The relationship between the revenue and the number of workers is positive; page 26.

■ **FIGURE A1.18**

Price (dollars per sack)

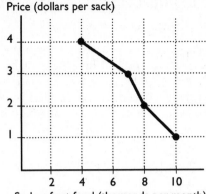

Sacks of cat food (thousands per month)

3. Figure A1.18 plots the relationship.
   a. If the price is $2 per sack, 8,000 sacks are purchased; page 23.
   b. If the price is $3 per sack, 7,000 sacks are purchased; page 23.
   c. The relationship between the price and quantity of sacks is negative; page 27.

■ **FIGURE A1.19**

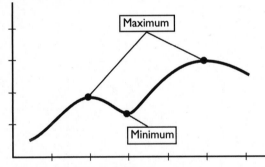

4. Figure A1.19 labels the two maximum points and one minimum point; page 28.

■ **FIGURE A1.20**

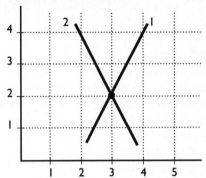

5. Figure A1.20 shows the two lines; page 29.

■ **FIGURE A1.21**

Price (dollars per compact disc)

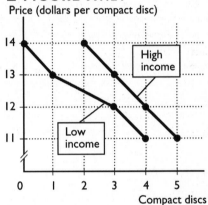

Compact discs

6. a. Figure A1.21 plots the relationship; page 30.
   b. Figure A1.21 plots the relationship; page 30.
   c. An increase in Bobby's income shifts the relationship rightward; page 30.

Short answer and numeric questions

1. The three types of graphs are scatter diagram, time-series graph, and cross-section graph; page 24.

2. If two variables are positively related, a graph of the relationship will have a positive slope. If two variables are negatively related, a graph of the relationship will have a negative slope; pages 26, 27, 29.

3. If a line slopes upward to the right, its slope is positive. If a line slopes downward to the right, its slope is negative; page 29.

4. The slope of a curved line at a point equals the slope of a straight line that touches that point and no other point on the curve. The slope of the curved line at point A is -2 and the slope of the curved line at point B is 1; page 29.

The U.S. and Global Economies

Chapter 2

Chapter 2 introduces fundamental concepts about how households, firms, markets, and government are linked together. A circular flow model is presented to show how goods and services and expenditures flow from and to households, firms, and the government.

■ **Describe what, how, and for whom goods and services are produced in the United States.**

The production of goods and services, the "what" question, is divided into four broad categories defined in terms of the ultimate buyer: individuals (consumption goods and services), businesses (capital goods), governments (government goods and services), and other countries (export goods and services). The "how" of production involves the factors of production: land, labor, capital, and entrepreneurship. Goods and services are sold to those who have income, so the personal distribution of income is one way of showing who ends up with our national output. The functional distribution of income shows how much is paid to the owners of each type of productive resource. The largest share of national income goes to labor, so workers get the largest share of our nation's goods and services.

■ **Use the circular flow model to provide a picture of how households, firms, and government interact.**

The circular flow model shows that households provide factors of production, and firms hire factors of production in factor markets. The circular flow also shows that households purchase goods and services, and firms sell goods and services in goods markets. The decisions made by households and firms (and the government) in these markets determine the answers to the "what," "how," and "for whom" questions. The federal government provides public goods and services, and makes social security and other benefit payments. In the circular flow, the government purchases goods and services in goods markets. It makes transfers to firms and households and also taxes them. The federal government's largest expenditure is Social Security benefits and its largest source of tax revenue is personal income taxes.

■ **Describe what, how, and for whom goods and services are produced in the global economy.**

Countries are divided into advanced economies, the richest 29 countries, and emerging market and developing economies. The advanced economies produce 44 percent of the world's total output, with 18 percent produced in the United States. Two third's of the world's oil reserves and two fifths of the natural gas reserves are in the Middle East. The share of agriculture in the advanced economies is much smaller than in the other countries but the advanced economies still produce one third of the world's food. The advanced economies have much more human capital and physical capital than the developing countries. Inequality of incomes across the entire world has decreased during the past twenty years, primarily because incomes in China and India have grown rapidly.

CHECKPOINT 2.1

■ **Describe what, how, and for whom goods and services are produced in the United States.**

Quick Review

- *Consumption goods and services* Goods and services that are bought by individuals and used to provide personal enjoyment and contribute to a person's standard of living.
- *Capital goods* Goods that are bought by businesses to increase their productive resources.
- *Government goods and services* Goods and services that are bought by governments.
- *Exports* Goods and services produced in the United States and sold in other countries.

Additional Practice Problems 2.1

1. Tell whether the following goods and services are consumption goods and services, capital goods, government goods and services, or exports.
   a. A taco at Taco Bell purchased for lunch by Shaniq.
   b. An HP printer manufactured in Idaho purchased by Maria in Peru.
   c. A new grill purchased by Taco Bell.
   d. A tour down the Colorado river from Rimrock Adventures purchased by the Miller family.
   e. CamelBak drinking packs purchased by the U.S. Marine Corp.
   f. CamelBak drinking packs purchased by Rimrock Adventures for use by their customers during tours.
   g. A CamelBak drinking pack purchased by Anne for use while mountain biking.
   h. A CamelBak drinking pack purchased by Sebastian, a German racing in the Tour de France.

2. How much labor is there in the United States? What determines the quantity of labor?

Solutions to Additional Practice Problems 2.1

1a. Shaniq's taco is a consumption good.
1b. Maria's printer is an export good.
1c. The new grill is a capital good.
1d. The tour is a consumption service.
1e. The drinking pack purchased by the Marines is a government good because it is purchased by the government.
1f. The drinking pack purchased by Rimrock Adventures is a capital good because it is purchased by a business.
1g. The drinking pack purchased by Anne is a consumption good.
1h. The drinking pack purchased by Sebastian is an export good.

2. In the United States, in 2005 about 149 million people had jobs or were available for work and they provided about 240 billion hours of labor a year. The quantity of labor depends on the size of the population, the percentage of the population that takes jobs, and on social relationships that influence things such as how many women take paid work. An increase in the proportion of women who have taken paid work has increased the quantity of labor in the United States over the past 50 years.

■ **Self Test 2.1**

Fill in the blanks

Goods and services that are bought by individuals and used to provide personal enjoyment and to contribute to a person's standard of living are ____ (consumption; capital; export) goods. Goods that are bought by businesses to increase their productive resources are ____ (consumption; capital; export) goods. Goods that are produced in the United States and sold in other countries are ____ (consumption; capital; export) goods. Of the four large groups of goods and services in the United States, ____ (consumption goods and services; capital goods; government goods and services; export goods and services) have the largest share of total production. Productive resources are called ____ and are grouped into four categories: ____,

____, ____, and ____. In 2005, ____ (labor; capital) received 64 percent of total income. The distribution of income among households is called the ____ (functional; personal) distribution of income.

True or false

1. Consumption goods and services include a slice of pizza purchased to eat at home.

2. A gold mine is included in the "land" category of productive resources.

3. Michael Dell, the person who founded and manages Dell computers, is an example of an entrepreneur.

4. In the United States, the factor of production that earns the most income is labor.

5. In the United States, the richest 20 percent of individuals earn approximately 30 percent of total income.

Multiple choice

1. When the total U.S. production of goods and services is divided into consumption goods and services, capital goods, government goods and services, and export goods and services, the largest component is
   a. consumption goods and services.
   b. capital goods.
   c. government goods and services.
   d. export goods and services.
   e. capital goods and government goods and services tie for the largest component.

2. An example of a capital good is
   a. a fiber optic cable TV system.
   b. an insurance policy.
   c. a hair cut.
   d. an iPod.
   e. a slice of pizza.

3. Goods and services produced in the United States and sold in other countries are called
   a. consumption goods and services.
   b. capital goods.
   c. government goods and services.
   d. export goods and services.
   e. import goods and services.

4. Which of the following correctly lists the categories of productive resources?
   a. machines, buildings, land, and money
   b. hardware, software, land, and money
   c. capital, money, and labor
   d. owners, workers, and consumers.
   e. land, labor, capital, and entrepreneurship

5. Human capital is
   a. solely the innate ability we are born with.
   b. the money humans have saved.
   c. the knowledge humans accumulate through education and experience.
   d. machinery that needs human supervision.
   e. any type of machinery.

6. Wages are paid to ____ and interest is paid to ____.
   a. entrepreneurs; capital
   b. labor; capital
   c. labor; land
   d. entrepreneurs; land
   e. labor; entrepreneurs

7. Dividing the nation's income among the factors of production, the largest percentage is paid to
   a. labor.
   b. land.
   c. capital.
   d. entrepreneurship.
   e. labor and capital, with each receiving about 41 percent of the total income.

8. The personal distribution of income shows
   a. that labor receives the largest percentage of total income.
   b. how profit accounts for the largest fraction of total income.
   c. that the richest 20 percent of people earn 23 percent of total income.
   d. that interest accounts for most of the income of the richest 20 percent of people.
   e. that the poorest 20 percent of people earn 4 percent of total income.

Short answer and numeric questions

1. Is an automobile a consumption good or a capital good?

2. Compare the incomes earned by the poorest and richest 20 percent of individuals.

CHECKPOINT 2.2

■ **Use the circular flow model to provide a picture of how households, firms, and governments interact.**

Quick Review

- *Circular flow model* A model of the economy, illustrated in Figure 2.1, that shows the circular flow of expenditures and incomes that result from firms', households', and governments' choices.

■ **FIGURE 2.1**

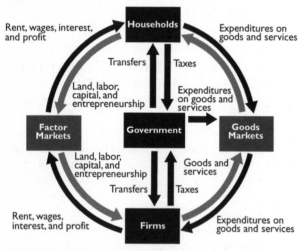

Additional Practice Problem 2.2

1. Describe where the following money flows fit in the circular flow.
   a. Shaniq pays for a taco at Taco Bell.
   b. Sam receives his monthly Social Security payment.
   c. Jennifer gets a $10,000 end of the year bonus from Bank of America, where she works.
   d. Exxon pays landowners in Texas $20,000 for the oil under their land.
   e. Bill pays property tax of $6,000.

2. In the circular flow, what is the relationship between the flow of expenditures into the goods markets (from households and the government) and the flow of revenues out of the goods markets to firms?

Solutions to Additional Practice Problems 2.2

1a. Shaniq's payment is an expenditure on a good that flows from households through the goods market to Taco Bell, a firm.

1b. Sam's check is a transfer payment from the government to households.

1c. Jennifer's payment is wages flowing from a firm, Bank of America, through the factor market to households.

1d. Exxon's payment is rent flowing from a firm, Exxon, through the factor market to households.

1e. Bill's payment is a tax flowing from households to government.

2. The flow of expenditures into the goods markets–the funds that households and the government spend on the goods and services they purchase–equals the flow of revenue out of the goods markets.

■ Self Test 2.2

Fill in the blanks

The ____ model shows the flows of expenditure and incomes. An arrangement that brings buyers and sellers together is a ____ (firm; household; market). A market in which goods and services are bought and sold is a ____ (goods; factor) market and a market in which factors of production are bought and sold is a ____ (goods; factor) market. In 2004, as a percentage of the total value of the goods and services produced in the United States, the federal government spent about ____ (20; 14) percent while state and local governments spent about ____ (20; 14) percent. A large part of what the federal government spends is ____ (social security payments; personal income taxes). The two components that account for most of the federal government's tax revenue are ____. The largest part of the expenditures of state and local governments is spending on ____ (education; highways).

True or false

1. Firms own the factors of production.

2. A market is any arrangement where buyers and sellers meet face-to-face.

3. Factors of production flow from households to firms through goods markets.

4. Rent, wages, interest, and profit are the payments made by firms to households through factor markets.

5. Social security payments are made by state and local governments.

6. The largest part of the expenditures of state and local government is on education.

Multiple choice

1. Within the circular flow model, economists define households as
   a. families with at least 2 children.
   b. families living in their own houses.
   c. individuals or groups living together.
   d. married or engaged couples.
   e. individuals or groups within the same legally defined family.

2. A market is defined as
   a. the physical place where goods are sold.
   b. the physical place where goods and services are sold.
   c. any arrangement that brings buyers and sellers together.
   d. a place where money is exchanged for goods.
   e. another name for a store such as a grocery store.

3. In the circular flow model,
   a. only firms sell in markets.
   b. only households buy from markets.
   c. some firms only sell and some firms only buy.
   d. the money used to buy goods and the goods themselves travel in the same direction.
   e. both firms and households buy or sell in different markets.

4. ____ choose the quantities of goods and services to produce, while ____ choose the quantities of goods and services to buy.
   a. Households; firms
   b. Firms; households and the government
   c. The government; firms
   d. Firms; only households
   e. Households; the government

5. A circular flow model shows the interrelationship between the ____ market and the ____ markets.
   a. household; goods
   b. household; factor
   c. business; household
   d. expenditure; income
   e. goods; factor

6. In the circular flow model, the expenditures on goods and services flow in the
   a. same direction as goods and services in all cases.
   b. same direction as goods and services *only if* they both flow through the goods market.
   c. same direction as goods and services *only if* they both flow through the factor market.
   d. opposite direction as goods and services.
   e. same direction as factor markets.

7. Of the following, the largest expenditure category of the federal government is
   a. the purchase of goods and services.
   b. interest on the national debt.
   c. grants to states and local governments.
   d. education.
   e. Social Security.

8. Of the following, the largest source of revenue for the federal government is
   a. personal income taxes.
   b. sales taxes.
   c. corporate income taxes.
   d. property taxes.
   e. lottery revenue.

Complete the graph

■ FIGURE 2.2

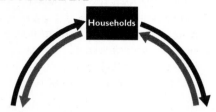

1. Figure 2.2 ignores the government and shows the flows into and out of households. Label the flows and identify who they come from and who they go to.

■ FIGURE 2.3

2. Figure 2.3 ignores the government and shows the flows into and out of firms. Label the flows and identify who they come from and who they go to.

■ FIGURE 2.4

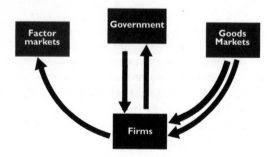

3. Figure 2.4 now includes the government and shows the money flows into and out of firms. Label the money flows.

Short answer and numeric questions

1. Ignoring taxes and transfer payments, what funds flow into firms and what funds flow out of them?

2. In the circular flow model, what are the sources of expenditures on goods and services?

3. Is it possible for something to affect households and not firms? To affect firms and not households? Explain your answers.

4. The circular flow reveals that which two groups interact to determine what will be the payments to the factors of production?

5. In 2004, which spent more, the federal government or state and local governments?

CHECKPOINT 2.3

■ **Describe what, how, and for whom goods and services are produced in the global economy.**

Quick Review

- *Advanced economies* The 29 countries (or areas) that have the highest living standards.

- *Emerging markets and Developing economies* Emerging markets are the 28 countries in Europe and Asia that were until the early 1990s part of the Soviet Union or its satellites and are changing the way they organize their economies. Developing economies are the 118 countries in Africa, the Middle East, Europe, and Central and South America that have not yet achieved a high standard of living for their people.

Additional Practice Problems 2.3

1. What percentage of the world's population live in developing economies? In places such as China, India, and Africa, what was the average income per day?

2. What percentage of the world's population live in advanced economies? In countries such as the United States, Canada, and Japan, what was the average income per day?

3. How does production within the advanced economies, the emerging market economies, and the developing economies compare?

4. How is it possible that income inequality within most countries has increased in recent years yet income inequality across the whole world has decreased in recent years?

Solutions to Additional Practice Problems 2.3

1. The world's population is about 6.5 billion. More than 5 billion of the people live in developing economies. So, approximately 80 percent of the world's population lives in developing economies. Average daily income in China is $14, in India is $8, and in Africa is $6. Because these are the average, many people live on less than these amounts.

2. About 1 billion people, or 15 percent of the world's population live in the 28 advanced economies. The average income per day in the United States was $108, in Canada was $90, and in Japan was $80.

3. Of the world's total production, the advanced economies produce 44 percent (18 percent is produced in the United States). The emerging market economies produce 16 percent of the world's production and the developing economies produce the remainder, 40 percent.

4. While income inequality within nations has been increasing, the difference in incomes among different nations has been decreasing. In particular, both China and India have seen rapid growth in income. The growth in income for these two poor but populous nations has decreased income inequality in the world as a whole.

■ **Self Test 2.3**

Fill in the blanks

Most of the world's population lives in the ____ (advanced economies; emerging market economies; developing economies). The lowest average income is in the ____ (advanced economies; emerging market economies; developing economies). Advanced economies produce about ____ (24; 44; 64) percent of the world's total production and the United States, alone, produces about ____ (6; 18; 33) percent of the world's total production. About ____ (33; 50; 67) percent of the world's proven oil reserves are located in ____ (North America; the Middle East). As a fraction of total output, agricultural is a ____ (larger; smaller) part of the economy in developing economies than in advanced economies. Factories in advanced economies are much ____ (less; more) capital intensive than in developing economies. During the past 20 years, the distribution of income in the world economy has become ____ (more; less) equal.

True or false

1. About 50 percent of the world's population lives in the advanced economies.

2. Mexico is an emerging market economy.

3. Taken as a group, the 118 developing economy nations produce a larger percentage of total world production than do the 29 advanced economy nations.

4. Most of the world's energy reserves are in North America.

5. Workers in the advanced economies have much more human capital than workers in the developing economies.

6. Income inequality within most nations has increased over the past years.

Multiple choice

1. The world population is approximately ____ people.
   a. 6.4 million
   b. 2 trillion
   c. 6.4 billion
   d. 1.4 trillion
   e. 640 million

2. The percentage of the world's population that lives in the advanced economies is
   a. more than 51 percent.
   b. between 41 percent and 50 percent.
   c. between 31 percent and 40 percent.
   d. between 20 percent and 30 percent.
   e. less than 20 percent.

3. Which of following groups of countries are *all* advanced economies?
   a. Australia, Brazil, and the United States
   b. Hong Kong, Japan, France, and the United Kingdom
   c. Italy, the United States, China, and Russia
   d. Singapore, Russia, France, and Chad
   e. Mexico, Canada, Germany, and Egypt

4. The emerging market economies are
   a. the largest grouping including the nations of China and India.
   b. in transition from state-owned production to free markets.
   c. most of the nations of Western Europe.
   d. the nations that are currently agricultural in nature.
   e. the nations with the highest standards of living.

5. As a percentage of total world production, production in the 29 advanced economies is about ____ percent of total world production and in the 118 developing economies is about ____ percent of total world production.
   a. 44; 40
   b. 23; 62
   c. 59; 12
   d. 30; 46
   e. 19; 73

6. Agricultural is about ____ percent of total production within advanced economies and the advanced economies produce about ____ percent of the world's food.
   a. 2; 33
   b. 12; 12
   c. 28; 63
   d. 4; 12
   e. 8; 20

7. Compared to the developing economies, the advanced economies have ____ human capital and ____ physical capital.
   a. more; more
   b. more; less
   c. the same; the same
   d. less; more
   e. less; less

8. Among the United States, Canada, Russia, India, and the United Kingdom, the country with the highest average income per person and the highest living standard is
   a. the United States.
   b. Russia.
   c. India.
   d. Canada.
   e. the United Kingdom.

Short answer and numeric questions

1. What are the groups the International Monetary Fund uses to classify countries? Describe each group. Which group has the largest number of countries? The largest number of people?

2. As a fraction of total production, how does agricultural production within the advanced economies compare to agricultural production within the developing economies? Why are the advanced economies able to produce about one third of the world's food?

3. How does the amount of human capital in the advanced economies compare to that in the developing economies?

4. How does the distribution of income within the United States compare to the distribution of income in the world economy?

SELF TEST ANSWERS

■ CHECKPOINT 2.1

Fill in the blanks

Goods and services that are bought by individuals and used to provide personal enjoyment and to contribute to a person's standard of living are <u>consumption</u> goods. Goods that are bought by businesses to increase their productive resources are <u>capital</u> goods. Goods that are produced in the United States and sold in other countries are <u>export</u> goods. Of the four large groups of goods and services in the United States, <u>consumption goods and services</u> have the largest share of total production. Productive resources are called <u>factors of production</u> and are grouped into four categories: <u>labor</u>, <u>land</u>, <u>capital</u>, and <u>entrepreneurship</u>. In 2005, <u>labor</u> received 64 percent of total income. The distribution of income among households is called the <u>personal</u> distribution of income.

True or false

1. True; page 34
2. True; page 36
3. True; page 39
4. True; page 40
5. False; page 40

Multiple choice

1. a; page 34
2. a; page 34
3. d; page 34
4. e; page 36
5. c; page 37
6. b; page 39
7. a; page 40
8. e; page 40

Short answer and numeric questions

1. An automobile might be either a consumption or a capital good. It is a consumption good if it is purchased by a household. It is a capital good if it is purchased by a business for use within the business; page 34.

2. The richest 20 percent of households earn about 50 percent of the total U.S. income. The poorest 20 percent of individuals have an average income of about $10,000 and r about 4 percent of the total U.S. income; page 40.

■ CHECKPOINT 2.2

Fill in the blanks

The <u>circular flow</u> model shows the flows of expenditures and incomes. An arrangement that brings buyers and sellers together is a <u>market</u>. A market in which goods and services are bought and sold is a <u>goods</u> market and a market in which factors of production are bought and sold is a <u>factor</u> market. In 2004, as a percentage of the total value of the goods and services produced in the United States, the federal government spent about <u>20</u> percent while state and local governments spent about <u>14</u> percent. A large part of what the federal government spends is <u>social security payments</u>. The two components that account for most of the federal government's tax revenue are <u>personal income taxes and Social Security taxes</u>. The largest part of the expenditures of state and local governments is spending on <u>education</u>.

True or false

1. False; page 42
2. False; pages 42-43
3. False; pages 42-43
4. True; pages 42-43
5. False; page 44
6. True; page 47

Multiple choice

1. c; page 42
2. c; page 42
3. e; pages 42-43
4. b; pages 42-43
5. e; pages 42-43
6. d; page 43
7. e; page 46
8. a; page 46

Complete the graph
■ FIGURE 2.5

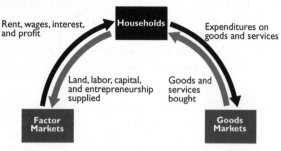

1. Figure 2.5 labels the flows. Rent, wages, interest, and profits (or losses) flow from the labor market while land, labor, capital, and entrepreneurship flow to the factor market. In addition, expenditures on goods and services flow to the goods market, and goods and services flow from the goods market; page 43.

■ FIGURE 2.6

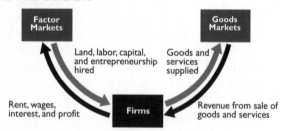

2. Figure 2.6 labels the flows. Revenue from the sale of goods and services, which are the expenditures on goods and services, flow to firms from the goods market and payments of rent, wages, interest, and profit (or loss) flow from firms into the factor market. Land, labor, capital, and entrepreneurship flow to firms from the factors markets, and goods and services flow from firms into the goods markets; page 43.

3. Figure 2.7 labels the money flows into and out of firms. The difference between this figure and Figure 2.6 is the addition of transfers and taxes; page 45.

■ FIGURE 2.7

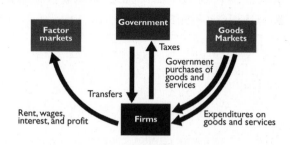

Short answer and numeric questions

1. Funds that flow into firms are households' expenditures and government purchases of goods and services. Funds that flow out of firms are payments for rent, wages, interest, and profit (or loss) to households in exchange for the factors of production; pages 43, 45.

2. The circular flow identifies two sources of expenditures on goods and services, expenditures by households and expenditures by the government; page 45.

3. The circular flow shows that at the macroeconomic level it is impossible for something to influence only firms or only households. An influence that changes households' buying behavior in goods markets affects firms because they sell to households in goods markets; page 43.

4. Payments to the factors of production are determined by the interaction of households, who own and provide the factors of production, and firms, who employ the factors; page 43.

5. In 2004, the federal government spent $2.4 trillion and state and local governments spent $1.7 trillion. The federal government spent significantly more than state and local governments; page 46.

■ CHECKPOINT 2.3

Fill in the blanks

Most of the world's population lives in the developing economies. The lowest average income is in the developing economies. Advanced economies produce about <u>44</u> percent of the world's total production and the United States, alone, produces about <u>18</u> percent of the world's total production. About <u>67</u> percent of the world's proven oil reserves are located in <u>the Middle East</u>. As a fraction of total output, agricultural is a <u>larger</u> part of the economy in developing economies than in advanced economies. Factories in advanced economies are much <u>more</u> capital intensive than in developing economies. During the past 20 years, the distribution of income in the world economy has become <u>more</u> equal.

True or false
1. False; page 49
2. False; page 49
3. False; page 50
4. False; page 51
5. True; page 53
6. True; page 55

Multiple choice
1. c; page 49
2. e; page 49
3. b; page 49
4. b; page 49
5. a; page 50
6. a; page 52
7. a; page 53
8. a; page 55

Short answer and numeric questions
1. The groups are the advanced economies and the emerging market and developing economies. Advanced economies have the highest standard of living. Emerging market and developing economies have yet to achieve a high standard of living. The emerging market economies are changing their economies from government management and state-ownership of capital to market-based economies similar to that in the United States. There are more nations, 118, and more people, almost 5 billion, in developing economies; page 49.

2. Agriculture accounts for about 1.8 percent of total production in advanced economies and about 14 percent of total production within developing economies. Even though advanced economies have a much smaller fraction of their total production devoted to food, because the farms within these nations are large, efficient, and well-equipped with capital and because farmers within these nations are paid by their governments to produce food, the advanced economies produce about one third of world's food; page 52.

3. The human capital possessed by workers in the advanced economies is *much* larger than that in the developing economies. People in the advanced economies have vastly more education, more on-the-job training and, in general, better health than in the developing economies; page 53.

4. The distribution of income within the United States is more equal than the distribution of income in the world economy. In the United States, the poorest 20 percent of households receive about 4 percent of the total income and the richest 20 percent of households receive about 50 percent of total income. In the world economy, the poorest 20 percent of households receive about 2 percent of total income and the richest 20 percent receive about 70 percent of total income; page 54.

Chapter

The Economic Problem

3

Chapter 3 develops an economic model, the production possibilities frontier or *PPF* model. The *PPF* shows how the opportunity cost of a good or service increases as more of the good or service is produced and how societies and individuals gain by specializing according to comparative advantage.

■ **Use the production possibilities frontier to illustrate the economic problem.**

The production possibilities frontier, *PPF*, is the boundary between the combinations of goods and services that can be produced and those that cannot be produced, given the available factors of production and technology. Production points outside the *PPF* are unattainable. Points on and inside the *PPF* are attainable. Production points on the *PPF* are production efficient. Moving along the *PPF* producing more of one good, less of another good is produced—a tradeoff. Moving from inside the *PPF* to a point on the *PPF*, more of some goods and services can be produced without producing less of others—a free lunch.

■ **Calculate opportunity cost.**

Along the *PPF* all choices involve a tradeoff. Along the *PPF*, the opportunity cost of the good on the *x*-axis is equal to the decrease in the good on the *y*-axis divided by the increase in the good on the *x*-axis. As more of a good is produced, its opportunity cost increases, so the *PPF* is bowed outward. The opportunity cost increases because resources are not equally productive in all activities. In the real world, most activities have increasing opportunity cost.

■ **Define efficiency and describe an efficient use of resources.**

Allocative efficiency occurs when we produce the quantities of goods and services that people value most highly. Allocative efficiency requires production efficiency and producing at the highest-valued point on the *PPF*. The marginal benefit curve is downward sloping and the marginal cost curve is upward sloping. Allocative efficiency requires producing where the curves intersect, that is, the quantity that makes the marginal benefit equal the marginal cost.

■ **Explain what makes production possibilities expand.**

Economic growth is the sustained expansion of production possibilities. If more capital is accumulated production possibilities increase and the *PPF* shifts outward. The (opportunity) cost of economic growth is that resources used to increase capital cannot be used to produce current consumption goods and services.

■ **Explain how people gain from specialization and trade.**

A person has a comparative advantage in an activity if he or she can perform the activity at lower opportunity cost than someone else. People can gain from specializing in production according to comparative advantage and then trading with others. An absolute advantage occurs when one person is more productive than another person in several or even all activities. A person can have an absolute advantage in all activities but cannot have a comparative advantage in all activities.

CHECKPOINT 3.1

■ **Use the production possibilities frontier to illustrate the economic problem.**

Quick Review

- *Production possibilities frontier* The boundary between combinations of goods and services that can be produced and combinations that cannot be produced, given the available factors of production and the state of technology.

- *Unattainable points* Production points outside the *PPF* are unattainable.

- *Tradeoff* A constraint or limit to what is possible that forces an exchange or a substitution of one thing for something else.

Additional Practice Problem 3.1

Possibility	Fish (pounds)		Fruit (pounds)
A	0.0	and	36.0
B	4.0	and	35.0
C	7.5	and	33.0
D	10.5	and	30.0
E	13.0	and	26.0
F	15.0	and	21.0
G	16.5	and	15.0
H	17.5	and	8.0
I	18.0	and	0.0

1. The table above shows Crusoe's *PPF*. Can Crusoe gather 21 pounds of fruit and catch 30 pounds of fish? Explain your answer. Suppose that Crusoe discovers another fishing pond with more fish, so that he can catch twice as many fish as before. Now can Crusoe gather 21 pounds of fruit and catch 30 pounds of fish? Explain your answer.

Solution to Additional Practice Problem 3.1

1. Initially, Crusoe cannot gather 21 pounds of fruit and catch 30 pounds of fish. This production point lies outside his *PPF* and so is unattainable. Once Crusoe discovers the new pond, however, he can gather 21 pounds of fruit and catch 30 pounds of fish. (In Row *F*, double the amount of Crusoe's fish.) The *PPF* depends on the available factors of production and when the factors of production increase, Crusoe's production possibilities change.

■ **Self Test 3.1**

Fill in the blanks

The ____ is the boundary between the combinations of goods and services that can and that cannot be produced given the available ____ (goods; factors of production) and ____ (number of services; state of technology). Production points outside the *PPF* ____ (are unattainable; are attainable; represent a free lunch). Production points ____ (on; beyond; within) the *PPF* are production efficient. Society has the possibility of a free lunch if production occurs ____ (inside; on; outside) the *PPF*. When resources are fully employed we face a ____ (free lunch; tradeoff).

True or false

1. A point outside the production possibilities frontier is unattainable.

2. If all the factors of production are fully employed, the economy will produce at a point on the production possibilities frontier.

3. Moving from one point on the *PPF* to another point on the *PPF* illustrates a free lunch.

4. All production points on the *PPF* are production efficient.

Multiple choice

1. The production possibilities frontier is a graph showing the
   a. exact point of greatest efficiency for producing goods and services.
   b. tradeoff between free lunches.
   c. maximum combinations of goods and services that can be produced.
   d. minimum combinations of goods and services that can be produced.
   e. resources available for the economy's use.

2. The production possibilities frontier is a boundary that separates
   a. the combinations of goods that can be produced from the combinations of services.
   b. attainable combinations of goods and services that can be produced from unattainable combinations.
   c. equitable combinations of goods that can be produced from inequitable combinations.
   d. reasonable combinations of goods that can be consumed from unreasonable combinations.
   e. affordable production points from unaffordable points.

3. Points inside the *PPF* are all
   a. unattainable and have fully employed resources.
   b. attainable and have fully employed resources.
   c. unattainable and have some unemployed resources.
   d. attainable and have some unemployed resources.
   e. unaffordable.

4. Points on the *PPF* are all
   a. unattainable and have fully employed resources.
   b. free lunches.
   c. inefficient.
   d. attainable and have some unemployed resources.
   e. production efficient.

5. During a time with high unemployment, a country can increase the production of one good or service
   a. without decreasing the production of something else.
   b. but must decrease the production of something else.
   c. and must increase the production of something else.
   d. by using resources in the production process twice.
   e. but the opportunity cost is infinite.

6. Moving along the production possibilities frontier itself illustrates
   a. the existence of tradeoffs.
   b. the existence of unemployment of productive resources.
   c. the benefits of free lunches.
   d. how free lunches can be exploited through trade.
   e. how tradeoffs need not occur if the economy is efficient.

Complete the graph

■ **FIGURE 3.1**

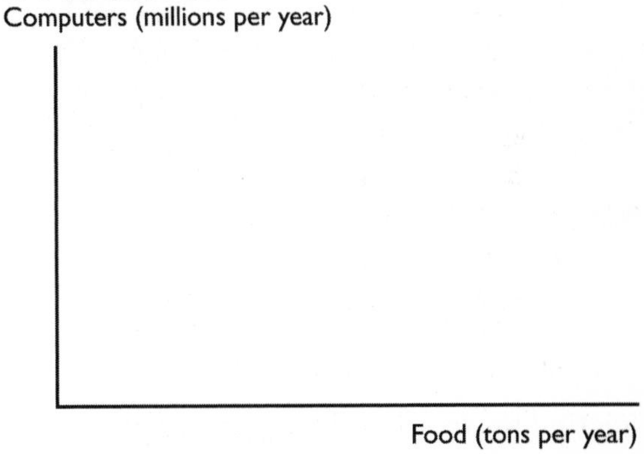

Computers (millions per year)

Food (tons per year)

1. In Figure 3.1, draw a production possibilities frontier showing combinations of computers and food. Label the points that are attainable and unattainable. Label the points that have full employment and the points that have unemployment.

Short answer and numeric questions

1. What factors limit the amount of our production?

2. What points are production efficient? Moving between these points, is there a tradeoff or a free lunch?

3. What is the relationship between unemployment and a free lunch? Between full employment and a tradeoff?

CHECKPOINT 3.2

■ Calculate opportunity cost.

Quick Review

- *Opportunity cost is a ratio* Along a *PPF*, the opportunity cost of one good equals the quantity of the other good forgone divided by the increase in the good.

Additional Practice Problem 3.2

Possibility	Fish (pounds)		Fruit (pounds)
A	0.0	and	36.0
B	4.0	and	35.0
C	7.5	and	33.0
D	10.5	and	30.0
E	13.0	and	26.0
F	15.0	and	21.0
G	16.5	and	15.0
H	17.5	and	8.0
I	18.0	and	0.0

1. The table above shows Robinson Crusoe's production possibilities. How does Crusoe's opportunity cost of a pound of fish change as he catches more fish?

Solution to Additional Practice Problem 3.2

Move from	Increase in fish (pounds)	Decrease in fruit (pounds)	Opportunity cost of fish (pounds of fruit)
A to B	4.0	1.0	0.25
B to C	3.5	2.0	0.57
C to D	3.0	3.0	1.00
D to E	2.5	4.0	1.60
E to F	2.0	5.0	2.50
F to G	1.5	6.0	4.00
G to H	1.0	7.0	7.00
H to I	0.5	8.0	16.00

1. The table above shows Crusoe's opportunity cost of a pound of fish. His opportunity cost of a pound of fish increases as he catches more fish. As he moves from point A to point B and catches his first fish, the opportunity cost is only 0.25 pounds of fruit per pound of fish. But as he moves from point H to point I and catches only fish, the opportunity cost has increased to 16.0 pounds of fruit per pound of fish.

■ Self Test 3.2

Fill in the blanks

Along a production possibilities frontier, the opportunity cost of obtaining one more unit of a good is the amount of another good that is ____ (gained; forgone). The opportunity cost is equal to the quantity of the good forgone ____ (plus; divided by) the increase in the quantity of the other good. As more of a good is produced, its opportunity cost ____.

True or false

1. Moving from one point on the *PPF* to another point on the *PPF* has no opportunity cost.

2. When moving along the *PPF*, the quantity of CDs increases by 2 and the quantity of DVDs decreases by 1, so the opportunity cost is 2 CDs minus 1 DVD.

3. Increasing opportunity costs are common.

Multiple choice

1. The opportunity cost of one more slice of pizza in terms of sodas is the
   a. number of pizza slices we have to give up to get one extra soda.
   b. number of sodas we have to give up to get one extra slice of pizza.
   c. total number of sodas that we have divided by the total number of pizza slices that we have.
   d. total number of pizza slices that we have divided by the total number of sodas that we have.
   e. price of pizza minus the price of the soda.

2. Moving between two points on a *PPF*, a country gains 6 automobiles and forgoes 3 trucks. The opportunity cost of 1 automobile is
   a. 3 trucks.
   b. 6 automobiles – 3 trucks.
   c. 2 trucks.
   d. 1/2 of a truck.
   e. 1 automobile.

3. Moving between two points on a *PPF*, a country gains 8 desktop computers and forgoes 4 laptop computers. The opportunity cost of 1 desktop computer is
   a. 4 laptops.
   b. 8 desktops.
   c. 1 desktop.
   d. 2 laptops.
   e. 1/2 of a laptop.

4. A country produces only cans of soup and pens. If the country produces on its *PPF* and increases the production of cans of soup, the opportunity cost of additional
   a. cans of soup is increasing.
   b. cans of soup is decreasing.
   c. cans of soup remain unchanged.
   d. ink pens is increasing.
   e. More information is needed to determine what happens to the opportunity cost.

5. Moving along a country's *PPF*, a reason opportunity costs increase is that
   a. unemployment decreases as a country produces more and more of one good.
   b. unemployment increases as a country produces more and more of one good.
   c. technology declines as a country produces more and more of one good.
   d. some resources are better suited for producing one good rather than the other.
   e. technology must advance in order to produce more and more of one good.

6. Increasing opportunity costs exist
   a. in the real world.
   b. as long as there is high unemployment.
   c. only in theory but not in real life.
   d. for a country but not for an individual.
   e. inside the *PPF* but not on the *PPF*.

Complete the graph

Production point	MP3 players (millions per year)		DVD players (millions per year)
A	4.0	and	0.0
B	3.0	and	3.0
C	2.0	and	4.0
D	1.0	and	4.7
E	0.0	and	5.0

1. The table shows the production possibilities for a nation.
   a. Placing MP3 players on the vertical axis, label the axes in Figure 3.2 and graph the production possibilities frontier.

■ **FIGURE 3.2**

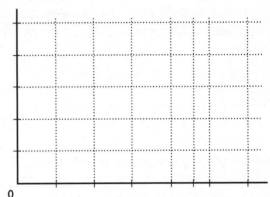

   b. What is the opportunity cost per DVD player of moving from point *A* to point *B*? *B* to *C*? *C* to *D*? *D* to *E*? How does the opportunity cost change as more DVD players are produced?

Short answer and numeric questions

Production point	Cans of soda (millions per year)		Candy bars (millions per year)
A	8.0	and	0.0
B	6.0	and	4.0
C	4.0	and	6.0
D	2.0	and	7.0
E	0.0	and	7.5

1. The table above shows the production possibilities for Sweetland.
   a. What is the opportunity cost per candy bar player of moving from point *A* to point *B*? *B* to *C*? *C* to *D*? *D* to *E*?

b. What is the opportunity cost per can of soda of moving from point *E* to point *D*? *D* to *C*? *C* to *B*? *B* to *A*?

c. How does the opportunity cost of a candy bar change as more candy bars are produced? How does the opportunity cost of a soda change as more sodas are produced?

2. What is the opportunity cost of increasing the production of a good while moving along a *PPF*? Why does this opportunity cost increase?

3. What does it mean for the opportunity cost to be a ratio?

CHECKPOINT 3.3

■ Define efficiency and describe an efficient use of resources.

Quick Review

- *Marginal benefit* The benefit that a person receives from consuming one more unit of a good or service.
- *Marginal cost* The opportunity cost of producing one more unit of a good or service.
- *Allocative efficiency* When we produce the combination of goods and services on the *PPF* that we value most highly.
- *Production efficiency* A situation in which we cannot produce more of one good without producing less of some other good—production is on the *PPF*.

Additional Practice Problem 3.3

1. Explain the relationship between production efficiency and allocative efficiency.

Solution to Additional Practice Problem 3.3

1. Production efficiency is a situation in it is impossible to produce more of one good or service without producing less of some other good or service—production is at a point on the *PPF*. Allocative efficiency is the most highly valued combination of goods and services on the *PPF*.

All the combinations of goods on the *PPF* achieve production efficiency. But only one combination is the most highly valued and this point is the allocative efficient production point. The combination that is most highly valued is the combination where the marginal benefit equals the marginal cost.

■ Self Test 3.3

Fill in the blanks

_____ (Production; Allocative) efficiency occurs at each combination of goods and services on the *PPF*. _____ (Production; Allocative) efficiency occurs when the economy produces the most highly valued combination of goods and services on the *PPF*. If a production point is on the *PPF* the point is definitely _____ (production; allocative) efficient. As more of a good is consumed, its marginal benefit _____ (increases; decreases), and as more of a good is produced, its marginal cost _____ (increases; decreases). Allocative efficiency occurs when the marginal benefit of a good is _____ (greater than; equal to; less than) the marginal cost of the good.

True or false

1. All combinations of goods and services on the production possibilities frontier are combinations of allocative efficiency.

2. The marginal benefit of a good increases as more of the good is consumed.

3. Marginal benefit is derived from the production possibilities frontier.

4. A production point can be allocative efficient but not production efficient.

Multiple choice

1. Allocative efficiency occurs when
   a. the most highly valued goods and services are produced.
   b. all citizens have equal access to goods and services.
   c. the environment is protected at all cost.
   d. goods and services are free.
   e. production takes place at any point on the *PPF*.

2. Production efficiency occurs
   a. anywhere inside or on the production possibilities frontier.
   b. when the total cost of production is minimized.
   c. at all points on the production possibilities frontier.
   d. at only one point on the production possibilities frontier.
   e. at all points inside the production possibilities frontier.

3. Marginal benefit equals the
   a. benefit that a person receives from consuming another unit of a good.
   b. additional efficiency from producing another unit of a good.
   c. increase in profit from producing another unit of a good.
   d. cost of producing another unit of a good.
   e. total benefit from consuming all the units of the good or service.

4. In general, the marginal cost curve
   a. has a positive slope.
   b. has a negative slope.
   c. is horizontal.
   d. is vertical.
   e. is U-shaped.

5. Allocative efficiency is achieved when the marginal benefit of a good
   a. exceeds marginal cost by as much as possible.
   b. exceeds marginal cost but not by as much as possible.
   c. is less than its marginal cost.
   d. equals the marginal cost.
   e. equals zero.

Complete the graph

1. In Figure 3.1 you indicated the points in a production possibilities frontier that are unattainable, attainable with full employment, and attainable with unemployment. In that figure, now indicate the points that are production efficient. Can you tell which point is allocatively efficient?

■ FIGURE 3.3
Marginal benefit and marginal cost (trucks per tractor)

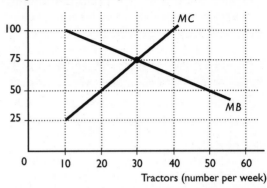

2. An economy produces only trucks and tractors and Figure 3.3 shows the marginal benefit and marginal cost of tractors. How many tractors are produced at the point of allocative efficiency?

Short answer and numeric questions

1. Along a production possibilities frontier, to produce the first skateboard, 1 pair of roller blades must be forgone. To produce the second skateboard, 2 more pairs of roller blades must be forgone. Is the marginal cost of the second skate board 2 or 3 pairs of roller blades?

Production point	Cans of soda (millions per year)		Candy bars (millions per year)
A	8.0	and	0.0
B	6.0	and	4.0
C	4.0	and	6.0
D	2.0	and	7.0
E	0.0	and	7.5

2. The table above shows the production possibilities for Sweetland.
   a. The table below shows the marginal benefit schedule for cans of soda. Complete the table by calculating the marginal cost.

Cans of soda (millions per year)	Marginal benefit (bars per can)	Marginal cost (bars per can)
6.0	1.50	___
4.0	2.50	___
2.0	3.50	___

   b. What is the allocative efficient quantity of cans of soda? Of candy bars?

3. Why does allocative efficiency require producing where marginal benefit equals marginal cost rather than where marginal benefit exceeds marginal cost?

CHECKPOINT 3.4

■ **Explain what makes production possibilities expand.**

Quick Review

- *Opportunity cost of growth* The opportunity cost of economic growth is the current consumption goods and services forgone.

Additional Practice Problem 3.4

1. Does economic growth eliminate scarcity?

Solution to Additional Practice Problem 3.4

1. Economic growth does not eliminate scarcity. Scarcity exists as long as people's wants exceed what can be produced. Economic growth increases the goods and services that can be produced but people's wants will continue to outstrip the ability to produce. While economic growth means that additional wants can be satisfied, people's wants are infinite and so scarcity will continue to be present even with economic growth.

■ **Self Test 3.4**

Fill in the blanks

A sustained expansion of production possibilities is called ____. Economic growth shifts the *PPF* ____ (inward; outward). The *PPF* shows that economic growth requires ____ (a decrease; an increase) in the current production of consumption goods.

True or false

1. Economic growth abolishes scarcity.
2. The opportunity cost of economic growth is less consumption goods in the future.
3. Production possibilities per person in the United States have remained constant during the last 30 years.

Multiple choice

1. To increase its economic growth, a nation should
   a. limit the number of people in college because they produce nothing.
   b. encourage spending on goods and services.
   c. encourage education because that increases the quality of labor.
   d. increase current consumption.
   e. eliminate expenditure on capital goods.

2. Other things being equal, if Mexico devotes more resources to train its population than Spain,
   a. Mexico will be able to eliminate opportunity cost faster than Spain.
   b. Mexico will be able to eliminate scarcity faster than Spain.
   c. Spain will grow faster than Mexico.
   d. Mexico will grow faster than Spain.
   e. Mexico will have more current consumption than Spain.

3. If a nation devotes a larger share of its current production to consumption goods, then
   a. its economic growth will slow down.
   b. the *PPF* will shift outward.
   c. the *PPF* will shift inward.
   d. some productive factors will become unemployed.
   e. it must produce at a point within its PPF.

4. Which of the following statements is (are) correct?
   i. As an economy grows, the opportunity costs of economic growth necessarily decrease.
   ii. Economic growth has no opportunity cost.
   iii. The opportunity cost of economic growth is current consumption forgone.
   a. i only.
   b. ii only.
   c. iii only.
   d. i and iii.
   e. i and ii.

5. When a country's production possibilities frontier shifts outward over time, the country is experiencing
   a. no opportunity cost.
   b. economic growth.
   c. higher unemployment of resources.
   d. a decrease in unemployment of resources.
   e. an end to opportunity cost.

6. The opportunity cost of economic growth is ____ and the benefit of economic growth is ____.
   a. increased current consumption; increased future consumption
   b. increased current consumption; decreased future consumption
   c. decreased current consumption; increased future consumption
   d. decreased current consumption; decreased future consumption.
   e. nothing; increased future consumption.

Complete the graph

■ FIGURE 3.4

Automobiles (millions per year)

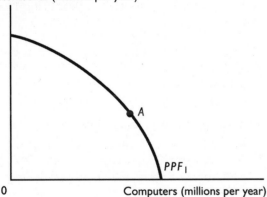

1. In the above figure, illustrate what happens if there is a technological breakthrough in the production of computers but not in the production of automobiles.
   a. Suppose the economy was initially producing at point *A*. After the breakthrough, is it possible for the economy to produce more computers *and* more automobiles?

Short answer and numeric questions

1. What is the opportunity cost of economic growth?

2. What is the benefit of economic growth?

CHECKPOINT 3.5

■ Explain how people gain from specialization and trade.

Quick Review

- *Comparative advantage* The ability of a person to perform an activity or produce a good or service at a lower opportunity cost than someone else.

Additional Practice Problem 3.5

1. Tony and Patty produce scooters and snowboards. The figure shows their production possibilities per day. With these production possibilities, the opportunity cost of a snowboard for

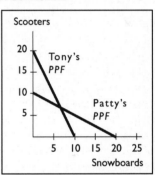

Patty is 1/2 a scooter and for Tony is 2 scooters. Patty has a lower opportunity cost and therefore she has the comparative advantage in snowboards. The opportunity cost of a scooter for Patty is 2 snowboards and for Tony is 1/2 of a snowboard. Tony has a lower opportunity cost and so he has the comparative advantage in scooters.

Suppose Patty acquires new equipment for scooter production that lets her produce a maximum of 60 rather than 10 scooters a day, should Patty and Tony specialize and trade?

Solution to Additional Practice Problem 3.5

1. Once Patty can produce 60 scooters a day, her opportunity costs change. Her opportunity cost of a scooter falls to 1/3 of a snowboard per scooter and her opportunity cost of a snowboard rises to 3 scooters per snowboard. With these opportunity costs, the comparative ad-

vantages have switched: Patty now has a comparative advantage in scooters and Tony in snowboards. Patty and Tony should still specialize and trade, only now Patty will specialize in scooters and Tony will specialize in snowboards. Comparative advantage can switch as the production possibilities frontier shifts outward.

■ Self Test 3.5

Fill in the blanks

A person has ____ (a comparative; an absolute) advantage in an activity if that person can perform the activity at a lower opportunity cost than someone else. If people specialize according to ____ (comparative; absolute) advantage and then trade, they can get ____ (outside; inside) their production possibilities frontiers. A person has ____ (a comparative; an absolute) advantage if they are more productive than someone else in all activities. It ____ (is; is not) possible for someone to have a comparative advantage in all activities. It ____ (is; is not) possible for someone to have an absolute advantage in all activities.

True or false

1. A person has an absolute advantage in an activity if the person can perform the activity at lower opportunity cost than someone else.

2. To achieve the gains from trade, a producer specializes in the product in which he or she has a comparative advantage and then trades with others.

3. Specialization and trade can make both producers better off even if one of them has an absolute advantage in producing all goods.

Multiple choice

1. "Comparative advantage" is defined as a situation in which one person can produce
   a. more of all goods than another person.
   b. more of a good than another person.
   c. a good for a lower dollar cost than another person.
   d. a good for a lower opportunity cost than another person.
   e. all goods for lower opportunity costs than another person.

For the next three questions, use the following information: Scott and Cindy both produce only pizza and tacos. In one hour, Scott can produce 20 pizzas or 40 tacos. In one hour, Cindy can produce 30 pizzas or 40 tacos.

2. Scott's opportunity cost of producing 1 taco is
   a. 1/2 of a pizza.
   b. 1 pizza.
   c. 2 pizzas.
   d. 20 pizzas.
   e. 2 tacos

3. Cindy's opportunity cost of producing 1 taco is
   a. 3/4 of a pizza.
   b. 1 pizza.
   c. 30 pizzas.
   d. 40 pizzas.
   e. 1 taco.

4. Based on the data given,
   a. Cindy has a comparative advantage in producing tacos.
   b. Scott has a comparative advantage in producing tacos.
   c. Cindy and Scott have the same comparative advantage when producing tacos.
   d. neither Cindy nor Scott has a comparative advantage when producing tacos.
   e. Cindy and Scott have the same comparative advantage when producing pizzas.

5. In one hour John can produce 20 loaves of bread or 8 cakes. In one hour Phyllis can produce 30 loaves of bread or 15 cakes. Which of the following statements is true?
   a. Phyllis has a comparative advantage when producing bread.
   b. John has a comparative advantage when producing cakes.
   c. Phyllis has an absolute advantage in both goods.
   d. John has an absolute advantage in both goods.
   e. Phyllis has a comparative advantage in producing both cakes and bread.

6. In one hour John can produce 20 loaves of bread or 16 cakes. In one hour Phyllis can produce 30 loaves of bread or 15 cakes. Which of the following statements is true?
   a. Phyllis has a comparative advantage when producing cakes.
   b. John has a comparative advantage when producing cakes.
   c. Phyllis has an absolute advantage in both goods.
   d. John has an absolute advantage in both goods.
   e. Phyllis has a comparative advantage in producing both cakes and bread.

Complete the graph

■ FIGURE 3.5

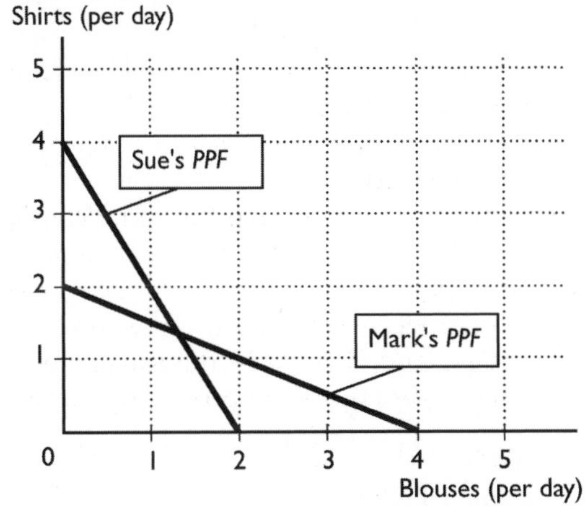

1. Figure 3.5 shows Mark and Sue's *PPFs*.

a. What is Sue's opportunity cost of producing a shirt? What is Mark's opportunity cost of producing a shirt?
b. Who has the comparative advantage in producing shirts?
c. What is Sue's opportunity cost of producing a blouse? What is Mark's opportunity cost of producing a blouse?
d. Who has the comparative advantage in producing blouses?
e. Who should specialize in producing blouses and who should specialize in producing shirts?
f. If Mark and Sue specialize according to their comparative advantage, indicate the total production of shirts and blouses by putting a point in Figure 3.4 showing the total production. Label the point *A*.
g. How does point *A* show the gains from trade?

Short answer and numeric questions

1. Why should people specialize according to their comparative advantage?
2. To achieve gains from trade, the opportunity costs of the trading partners must diverge. Why?
3. When it comes to trading one good for another, why is comparative advantage crucial and absolute advantage unimportant?

SELF TEST ANSWERS

■ CHECKPOINT 3.1

Fill in the blanks

The <u>production possibilities frontier or PPF</u> is the boundary between the combinations of goods and services that can and that cannot be produced given the available <u>factors of production</u> and <u>state of technology</u>. Production points outside the *PPF* <u>are unattainable</u>. Production points <u>on</u> the *PPF* are production efficient. Society has the possibility of a free lunch if production occurs <u>inside</u> the *PPF*. When resources are fully employed we face a <u>tradeoff</u>.

True or false

1. True; page 64
2. True; page 64
3. False; page 65
4. True; pages 64-65

Multiple choice

1. c; page 62
2. b; page 64
3. d; page 64
4. e; pages 64-65
5. a; page 65
6. a; page 65

Complete the graph

■ FIGURE 3.6
Computers (millions per year)

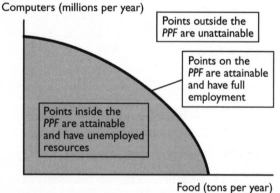

Points outside the *PPF* are unattainable

Points on the *PPF* are attainable and have full employment

Points inside the *PPF* are attainable and have unemployed resources

Food (tons per year)

1. Figure 3.6 shows a production possibilities frontier between computers and food; pages 63-64.

Short answer and numeric questions

1. The factors that limit the amount of our production are the available resources and the state of technology; page 62.

2. All points *on* the production possibilities are production efficient. Moving from one point to another incurs an opportunity cost so there is tradeoff; pages 64-66

3. When the nation is producing at a point with unemployment, there are free lunches available because the production of some goods and services can be increased without decreasing the production of anything else. When the nation is producing at full employment, it is on the *PPF* and so only trade-offs are available: If the production of one good or service is increased, the production of something else must be decreased; pages 65-66.

■ CHECKPOINT 3.2

Fill in the blanks

Along a production possibilities frontier, the opportunity cost of obtaining one more unit of a good is the amount of another good that is <u>forgone</u>. The opportunity cost is equal to the quantity of the good forgone <u>divided by</u> the increase in the quantity of the other good. As more of a good is produced, its opportunity cost <u>increases</u>.

True or false

1. False; page 68
2. False; page 69
3. True; page 70

Multiple choice

1. b; page 68
2. d; page 68
3. e; page 68
4. a; page 69
5. d; page 70
6. a; page 70

Complete the graph

■ FIGURE 3.7

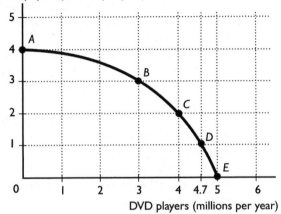

MP3 players (millions per year)

DVD players (millions per year)

1. a. Figure 3.7 illustrates the production possibilities frontier; page 68.

   b. The opportunity cost of moving from point *A* to point *B* to is 0.33 MP3 players per DVD player; from *B* to *C* is 1.00 MP3 player per DVD player; from *C* to *D* is 1.43 MP3 players per DVD player; and, from *D* to *E* is 3.33 MP3 players per DVD player. The opportunity cost increases; page 68

Short answer and numeric questions

1. a. The opportunity cost of moving from point *A* to point *B* to is 0.5 cans of soda per candy bar; from *B* to *C* is 1.0 can of soda per candy bar; from *C* to *D* is 2.0 cans of soda per candy bar; and, from *D* to *E* is 4.0 cans of soda per candy bar; page 68.

   b. The opportunity cost of moving from point *E* to point *D* to is 0.25 candy bars per can of soda; from *D* to *C* is 0.50 candy bars per can of soda; from *C* to *B* is 1.00 candy bar per can of soda; and, from *B* to *A* is 2.00 candy bars per can of soda; page 68.

   c. As more candy bars are produced, the opportunity cost increases. As more cans of soda are produced, the opportunity cost increases; page 69.

2. The opportunity cost of increasing production of one good is the production of some other good forgone. The opportunity cost increases, so that increasingly large amounts of the other good are forgone, because resources are not equally productive in all activities. When initially increasing the production of one good, resources that are well suited for its production are used. When still more of the good is produced, resources that are less well suited must be used. Because the resources are ill suited, more are necessary to increase the production of the first good, and the forgone amount of the other good increases; page 70.

3. The opportunity cost is the amount of a good forgone to gain an additional unit another good. We divide the quantity of the good forgone by the increase in the other good. So opportunity cost is a ratio—the change in the quantity of one good divided by the change in the quantity of another good; page 70.

■ CHECKPOINT 3.3

Fill in the blanks

<u>Production</u> efficiency occurs at each combination of goods and services on the *PPF*. <u>Allocative</u> efficiency occurs when the economy produces the most highly valued combination of goods and services on the *PPF*. If a production point is on the *PPF* the point is definitely <u>production</u> efficient. As more of a good is consumed, its marginal benefit <u>decreases</u>, and as more of a good is produced, its marginal cost <u>increases</u>. Allocative efficiency occurs when the marginal benefit of a good is <u>equal to</u> the marginal cost of the good.

True or false

1. False; page 73
2. False; pages 73-74
3. False; pages 73-74
4. False; page72

Multiple choice

1. a; page 72
2. c; page 72
3. a; page 73
4. a; page 75
5. d; page 76

Complete the graph

■ **FIGURE 3.8**

Computers (millions per year)

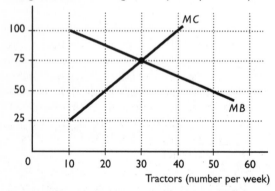

Points beyond the *PPF* are unattainable

Points on the *PPF* are attainable and have full employment

Points within the *PPF* are attainable and have unemployed resources

Points on the *PPF* are production efficient

Food (tons per year)

1. Figure 3.8 shows the production possibilities frontier with the production points that are production efficient labeled. Note that these are the points that are attainable with full employment. Although the allocative efficient point will be one on the *PPF*, it is not possible to determine which it is without additional information about the marginal benefits of the goods; pages 72-73.

■ **FIGURE 3.9**

Marginal benefit and marginal cost (trucks per tractor)

```
100 ┤            . . . .  MC . .
    │        .        .
 75 ┤ . . . . . . . . ×. . . . . . . . . .
    │     .        .       .
 50 ┤   .       .            .
    │ .      .                  . . . .
 25 ┤ .  .                       MB
    │.
  0 └──┬────┬────┬────┬────┬────┬──
      10   20   30   40   50   60
              Tractors (number per week)
```

2. Allocative efficiency is the most highly valued combination of goods and services on the *PPF*. It is the combination where marginal cost equals marginal benefit. In Figure 3.9, allocative efficiency is achieved when 30 tractors a week are produced; pages 76-77.

Short answer and numeric questions

1. The marginal cost of the second skate board is 2 pairs roller blades. Marginal cost is the opportunity cost of producing one more unit of a good or service. It is not the cost of all the units produced; page 75.

Cans of soda (millions per year)	Marginal benefit (bars per can)	Marginal cost (bars per can)
6.0	1.50	1.50
4.0	2.50	0.75
2.0	3.50	0.38

2. a. The completed table is above. The marginal cost from 2.0 million cans of soda to 4.0 million is 0.50 candy bars per soda and the marginal cost from 4.0 million cans of soda to 6.0 million cans of soda is 1.0 candy bars per soda. So the marginal cost at 4.0 million cans of soda is the average, 0.75 candy bars per can of soda; pages 68, 75.

   b. Marginal benefit equals marginal cost at 6.0 million cans of soda, so this is the allocatively efficient quantity of soda. The production possibilities table shows that with this quantity of soda, 4.0 million candy bars are produced, so 4.0 million candy bars is the allocatively efficient quantity of candy bars; pages 76-77.

3. As long as the marginal benefit from an additional good or service exceeds the marginal cost, the unit should be produced because its production benefits society more than it costs society to produce. Producing where marginal benefit equals marginal cost insures that *all* units that have a net benefit for society are produced, so this level of production is the point of allocative efficiency; page 76.

■ CHECKPOINT 3.4

Fill in the blanks

A sustained expansion of production possibilities is called economic growth. Economic growth shifts the *PPF* outward. The *PPF* shows that economic growth requires a decrease in the current production of consumption goods.

True or false

1. False; page 79
2. False; pages 79-80
3. False; page 80

Multiple choice

1. c; page 79
2. d; pages 79-80
3. a; page 79
4. d; page 79
5. b; page 79
6. c; pages 79-80

Complete the graph

■ FIGURE 3.10

Automobiles (millions per year)

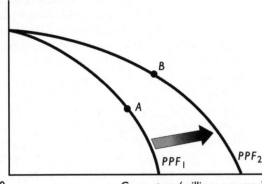

0   Computers (millions per year)

1. Figure 3.10 illustrates the new production possibilities frontier. Because the technological breakthrough did not affect automobile production, the maximum amount of automobiles that can be produced on the vertical axis does not change; pages 79-80.
1. a. Figure 3.10 shows that it is possible for the production of *both* automobiles and computers to increase, as a movement from the initial point *A* to a possible new point *B* illustrates; page 79.

Short answer and numeric questions

1. Economic growth requires either developing new technologies, accumulating more human capital, or accumulating more capital. All of these avenues require resources, so the opportunity cost of economic growth is the decrease in the current production of goods and services; page 79.
2. The benefit from economic growth is increased consumption per person in the future after the production possibilities frontier has expanded; page 79.

■ CHECKPOINT 3.5

Fill in the blanks

A person has <u>a comparative</u> advantage in an activity if that person can perform the activity at a lower opportunity cost than someone else. If people specialize according to <u>comparative</u> advantage and then trade, they can get <u>outside</u> their production possibilities frontiers. A person has <u>an absolute</u> advantage if they are more productive than someone else in all activities. It <u>is not</u> possible for someone to have a comparative advantage in all activities. It <u>is</u> possible for someone to have an absolute advantage in all activities.

True or false

1. False; pages 81-82
2. True; page 82
3. True; pages 82-83

Multiple choice

1. d; page 81
2. a; page 81
3. a; page 81
4. b; pages 81-82
5. c; page 82
6. b; page 82

Complete the graph

1. a. Sue's opportunity cost of a shirt is 1/2 of a blouse because, when moving along her *PPF* to produce 1 more shirt she forgoes 1/2 of a blouse. Mark's opportunity cost of a shirt is 2 blouses; page 81
   b. Sue has the comparative advantage in producing shirts because her opportunity cost is lower; page 81.
   c. Sue's opportunity cost of a blouse is 2 shirts because, when moving along her *PPF*, to produce 1 more blouse she forgoes 2 shirts. Mark's opportunity cost of a blouse is 1/2 of a shirt; page 81.
   d. Mark has the comparative advantage in producing blouses because his opportunity cost is lower; page 81.

e. Mark should specialize in producing blouses and Sue should specialize in producing shirts; page 82.

■ **FIGURE 3.11**

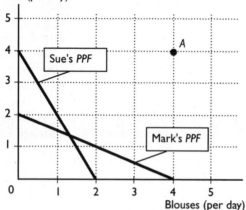

Shirts (per day)

f. Mark produces 4 blouses and Sue produces 4 shirts, so a total of 4 shirts and 4 blouses are produced. Figure 3.11 shows this production as point *A*; pages 82-83.

g. If the total production at point *A* is divided evenly, both Mark and Sue will receive 2 shirts and 2 blouses. When both were producing only for themselves, they could not produce 2 shirts and 2 blouses because this point is beyond both their *PPF*s. By specializing and trading, Mark and Sue get outside their *PPF*s; page 83.

Short answer and numeric questions

1. A person's comparative advantage is the good that the person can produce at a lower opportunity cost than other people. When this person specializes in the production of the good, it is produced at the lowest cost; page 82.

2. If the trading partners' opportunity costs are the same, there is no incentive for them to trade. For instance, if two people produce either gum or soda and both have the same opportunity cost of 5 gums for 1 soda, neither is willing to buy or sell to the other. Only when opportunity costs diverge will one person be willing to buy (the person with the higher opportunity cost) and the other willing to sell (the person with the lower opportunity cost); page 82.

3. People are willing to trade if they can obtain a good at lower opportunity cost than what it costs them to produce the good. Comparative advantage tells which person has a lower opportunity cost. Even if a person has an absolute advantage in all goods, he or she does not have a comparative advantage in all goods. So comparative advantage determines who produces a product and who buys it; page 82.

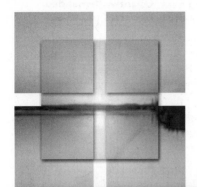

Demand and Supply

Chapter

4

The tools of demand and supply explain how competitive markets work. We use the demand and supply tools to determine the quantities and prices of the goods and services produced and consumed.

■ **Distinguish between quantity demanded and demand and explain what determines demand.**

The quantity demanded is the amount of any good, service, or resource that people are willing and able to buy during a specified period at a specified price. The law of demand states that other things remaining the same, if the price of a good rises (falls), the quantity demanded of that good decreases (increases). A demand curve is a graph of the relationship between the quantity demanded of a good and its price when all other influences on buying plans remain the same. The market demand is the sum of the demands of all the buyers in a market. A change in price leads to a *change in the quantity demanded* and a movement along the demand curve. Factors that *change demand* and shift the demand curve are: prices of related goods; income; expectations; number of buyers; and preferences.

■ **Distinguish between quantity supplied and supply and explain what determines supply.**

The quantity supplied is the amount of any good, service, or resource that people are willing and able to sell during a specified period at a specified price. The law of supply states that other things remaining the same, if the price of a good rises (falls), the quantity supplied of that good increases (decreases). A supply curve is a graph of the relationship between the quantity supplied of a good and its price when all other influences on selling plans remain the same. A change in price leads to a *change in the quantity supplied* and a movement along the supply curve. Factors that *change supply* and shift the supply curve are: prices of related goods; prices of resources and other inputs; expectations; number of sellers; and productivity. If supply increases (decreases), the supply curve shifts rightward (leftward).

■ **Explain how demand and supply determine price and quantity in a market, and explain the effects of changes in demand and supply.**

The equilibrium price and equilibrium quantity occur when the quantity demanded equals the quantity supplied. An increase in demand raises the price and increases the quantity. An increase in supply lowers the price and increases the quantity. An increase in both demand and supply increases the quantity and the price might rise, fall, or not change. An increase in demand and a decrease in supply raises the price and the quantity might increase, decrease, or not change.

■ **Explain how price floors, price ceilings, and sticky prices cause surpluses unemployment, and shortages.**

A price floor set above the equilibrium price creates a surplus. A price ceiling (or price cap) set below the equilibrium price creates a shortage. Sticky prices can create temporary shortages or surpluses.

CHECKPOINT 4.1

■ **Distinguish between quantity demanded and demand and explain what determines demand.**

Quick Review

- *Change in the quantity demanded* A change in the quantity of a good that people plan to buy that results from a change in the price of the good.
- *Law of demand* If the price of a good rises, the quantity demanded of that good decreases; and if the price of a good falls, the quantity demanded of that good decreases.
- *Change in demand* A change in the quantity that people plan to buy when any influence on buying plans, other than the price of the good, changes. These other influences include: prices of related goods, income, expectations, number of buyers, and preferences.

Additional Practice Problems 4.1

1. In the market for scooters, several events occur, one at a time. Explain the influence of each event on the quantity demanded of scooters and on the demand for scooters. Illustrate the effects of each event either by a movement along the demand curve or a shift in the demand curve for scooters and say which event (or events) illustrates the law of demand in action. These events are:
   a. The price of a scooter falls.
   b. The price of a bicycle falls.
   c. Citing rising injury rates, cities and towns ban scooters from sidewalks.
   d. Income increases.
   e. Scooters become unfashionable and the number of buyers decreases.

2. The information in the table shows the demand schedule for scooters in a town. Using this information, label the axes in Figure 4.1 and then graph the demand curve

Price (dollars per scooter)	Quantity demanded (scooters per week)
100	0
75	10
50	40
25	60

■ **FIGURE 4.1**

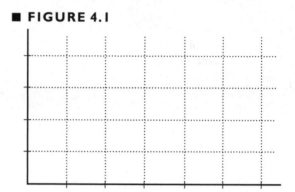

Solutions to Additional Practice Problems 4.1

1a. This problem emphasizes the distinction between a change in the quantity demanded and a change in demand. A fall in the price of a scooter brings an increase in the quantity demanded of scooters, which is illustrated by

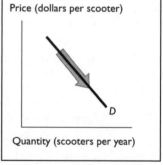

a movement down along the demand curve for scooters as shown in the figure. This event illustrates the law of demand in action.

1b. A bicycle is a substitute for a scooter because people can use neither for transportation.. With the lower price of a bicycle, some people who previously would have bought a scooter will now buy a bicycle instead. So a fall in the price of a bicycle decreases the demand for scooters. The demand curve for scooters shifts leftward as shown in the figure below.

1c. Rising injury rates and banning scooters from sidewalks changes preferences and makes scooters less desirable. The demand for scooters decreases and the demand curve for the scooters shifts leftward as shown in the figure by the shift from demand curve D_0 to demand curve D_1.

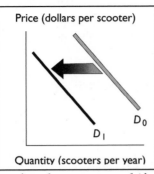

Price (dollars per scooter)

D_0

D_1

Quantity (scooters per year)

1d. A scooter is probably a normal good. So, people will buy more scooters when their income increases. The demand for scooters increases and the demand curve shifts rightward, as illustrated in the figure by the shift from demand curve D_1 to demand curve D_2.

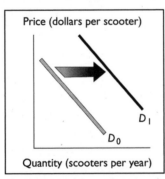

Price (dollars per scooter)

D_1

D_0

Quantity (scooters per year)

1e. A decrease in the number of buyers decreases the demand for scooters. The demand curve shifts leftward.

2. Figure 4.2 (at the top of the next column) labels the axes and plots the demand curve for scooters.

■ FIGURE 4.2

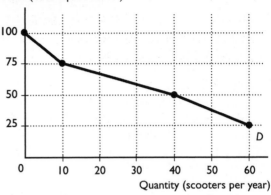

Price (dollars per scooter)

■ Self Test 4.1

Fill in the blanks

The ____ (demand schedule; law of demand) states that other things remaining the same, if the price of a good rises, the ____ (quantity demanded of; demand for) that good decreases. A ____ is a graph of the relationship between the quantity demanded of a good and its price. Demand curves are ____ (downward; upward) sloping. An increase in demand shifts the demand curve ____. Factors that change demand lead to a ____ (shift of; movement along) the demand curve. Factors that change demand are ____, ____, ____, ____, and ____.

True or false

1. The law of demand states that other things remaining the same, if the price of a good rises, the quantity demanded of that good increases.

2. If the quantity of ice cream demanded at each price increases, there is a movement along the demand curve for ice cream.

3. When Sue's income increases, her demand for movies increases. For Sue, movies are a normal good.

4. A rise in the price of a computer increases the demand for computers because a computer is a normal good.

5. If people's incomes fall, the demand for computers will decrease and there will be a movement along the demand curve.

Multiple choice

1. The "law of demand" indicates that if the University of Maine increases tuition, all other things remaining the same,
   a. the demand for classes will decrease at the University of Maine.
   b. the demand for classes will increase at the University of Maine.
   c. the quantity of classes demanded will increase at the University of Maine.
   d. the quantity of classes demanded will decrease at the University of Maine.
   e. both the demand for and the quantity of classes demanded will decrease at the University of Maine.

2. Other things remaining the same, the quantity of a good or service demanded will increase if the price of the good or service
   a. rises.
   b. falls.
   c. does not change.
   d. rises or does not change.
   e. rises or falls.

3. Teenagers demand more soda than other age groups. If the number of teenagers increases, everything else remaining the same,
   a. market demand for soda increases.
   b. market demand for soda decreases.
   c. market demand for soda does not change.
   d. there is a movement along the market demand curve for soda.
   e. None of the above answers is correct because the effect on the demand depends whether the supply curve shifts.

4. One reason the demand for laptop computers might increase is a
   a. fall in the price of a laptop computers.
   b. fall in the price of a desktop computer.
   c. a change in preferences as laptops have become more portable, with faster processors and larger hard drives.
   d. poor quality performance record for laptop computers.
   e. a decrease in income if laptops are a normal good.

5. The number of buyers of sport utility vehicles, SUVs, decreases sharply. So
   a. the demand curve for SUVs shifts leftward.
   b. the demand curve for SUVs shifts rightward.
   c. there is neither a shift nor a movement along the demand curve for SUVs.
   d. there is a movement down along the demand curve for SUVs.
   e. the supply curve for SUVs shifts rightward.

■ **FIGURE 4.3**

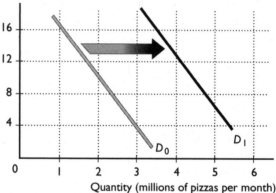

6. The shift of the demand curve for pizza illustrated in Figure 4.3 could be the result of
   a. a rise in income if pizza is a normal good.
   b. a fall in the price of fried chicken, a substitute for pizza.
   c. consumers coming to believe that pizza is unhealthy.
   d. the belief that pizza will fall in price next month.
   e. a fall in the price of a pizza.

7. The shift of the demand curve for pizza illustrated in Figure 4.3 could be the result of
   a. a rise in income if pizza is an inferior good.
   b. a fall in the price of soda, a complement for pizza.
   c. a decrease in the number of college students if college students eat more pizza than other age groups.
   d. a rise in the price of a pizza.
   e. a fall in the price of a pizza.

8. When moving along a demand curve, which of the following changes?
   a. the consumers' incomes
   b. the prices of other goods
   c. the number of buyers
   d. the price of the good
   e. the consumers' preferences

9. If the price of a CD falls,
   i. the demand curve for CDs shifts right-ward.
   ii. the demand curve for CDs will not shift.
   iii. there is a movement along the demand curve for CDs.
   a. i only.
   b. ii only.
   c. iii only.
   d. ii and iii.
   e. i and iii.

10. Pizza and tacos are substitutes and the price of a pizza increases. Which of the following correctly indicates what happens?
    a. The demand for pizzas decreases and the demand for tacos increases.
    b. The demand for both goods decreases.
    c. The quantity of tacos demanded increases and the quantity of pizza demanded decreases.
    d. The quantity of pizza demanded decreases and the demand for tacos increases.
    e. The demand for each decreases because both are normal goods.

Complete the graph

Price (dollars per bundle of cotton candy)	Quantity (bundles of cotton candy per month)
1	10,000
2	8,000
3	7,000
4	4,000

1. The demand schedule for cotton candy is given in the following table. In Figure 4.4, draw the demand curve. Label the axes.
   a. If the price of cotton candy is $2 a bundle, what is the quantity demanded?

■ **FIGURE 4.4**

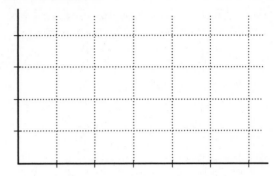

   b. If the price of cotton candy is $3 a bundle, what is the quantity demanded?
   c. Does the demand curve you drew slope upward or downward?

■ **FIGURE 4.5**

Price (dollars per pound of butter)

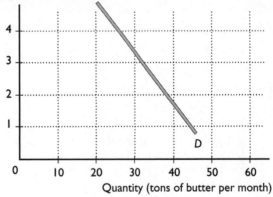

2. Butter is a normal good and margarine is substitute for butter. Figure 4.5 shows the demand curve for butter.
   a. In Figure 4.5, show how the demand curve shifts if incomes rise. Label this demand curve D_1.
   b. In Figure 4.5, show how the demand curve shifts if margarine falls in price. Label this demand curve D_2.
   c. If the price of butter falls from $4 a pound to $3 a pound, does the demand curve shift toward demand curve D_1, D_2, or neither? Explain your answer.

Short answer and numeric questions

Price (dollars per gallon)	Quantity demanded (gallons per week)
2.10	320
2.20	316
2.30	310
2.40	300
2.50	205

1. The table above gives the demand schedule for gasoline for a group of students. If the price of gasoline falls from $2.30 to $2.20 per gallon, how much gas will the students buy?

2. Explain the difference between a change in quantity demanded and a change in demand.

3. What is the difference between a movement along a demand curve and a shift in a demand curve?

CHECKPOINT 4.2

■ Distinguish between quantity supplied and supply and explain what determines supply.

Quick Review

- *Change in quantity supplied* A change in the quantity of a good that suppliers plan to sell that results from a change in the price of the good.
- *Change in supply* A change in the quantity that suppliers plan to sell when any influence on selling plans, other than the price of the good, changes. These other influences include: prices of related goods, prices of inputs, expectations, number of sellers, and productivity.

Additional Practice Problems 4.2

1. In the market for scooters, several events occur, one at a time. Explain the influence of each event on the quantity supplied of scooters and on the supply of scooters. Illustrate the effects of each event either by a movement along the supply curve or a shift in the supply curve for scooters and say which event (or events) illustrates the law of supply in action. These events are:
   a. The price of a scooter rises.
   b. The price of the steel used to make scooters rises.
   c. The number of firms making scooters decreases.
   d. Technological change increases the productivity of the factories making scooters.

Price (dollars per scooter)	Quantity (scooters per week)
100	60
75	50
50	30
25	10

■ FIGURE 4.6

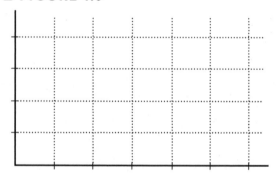

2. The information in the table shows the supply schedule for scooters in a town. Using this information, label the axes in Figure 4.4 and then graph the supply curve. Is the slope of the supply curve positive or negative? What does the slope of the supply curve demonstrate?

Solutions to Additional Practice Problems 4.2

1a. This problem emphasizes the distinction between a change in the quantity supplied and a change in supply. A rise in the price of a scooter brings an increase in the quantity

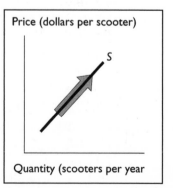

supplied of scooters, which is illustrated by a movement up along the supply curve for scooters as shown in the figure. There is no change in the supply and the supply curve does not shift. This event illustrates the law of supply in action.

1b. When the price of the steel used to make scooters rises, the cost to produce scooters increases. As a result, the supply of scooters decreases. The supply curve shifts leftward as illustrated in the figure.

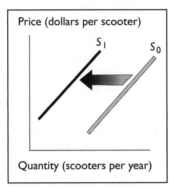

Price (dollars per scooter)

Quantity (scooters per year)

1c. A decrease in the number of firms producing scooters decreases the supply of scooters. The supply curve shifts leftward, as illustrated in the figure above.

1d. An increase in the productivity of the factories making scooters lowers the costs of producing scooters. The supply of scooters increases and the supply curve shifts rightward, as illustrated in the figure.

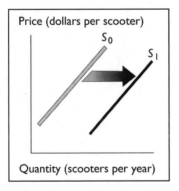

Price (dollars per scooter)

Quantity (scooters per year)

2. The axes are labeled and the supply curve is graphed in Figure 4.7. The slope of the supply curve is positive: An increase in the price of plywood increases the quantity demanded. The slope of the supply curve reflects the law of supply.

■ **FIGURE 4.7**

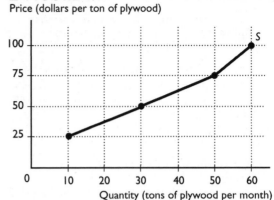

Price (dollars per ton of plywood)

Quantity (tons of plywood per month)

■ **Self Test 4.2**

Fill in the blanks

The ____ (quantity supplied; supply) of a good is the amount people are willing and able to sell during a specified period at a specified price. The law of supply states that other things remaining the same, if the price of a good rises, the quantity supplied ____. A supply curve is ____ (upward; downward) sloping. A change in the price of a good changes ____ (supply; the quantity supplied) and is illustrated by a ____ the supply curve. Factors that change supply are ____, ____, ____, ____, and ____.

True or false

1. The law of supply states that other things remaining the same, if the price of a good rises, the supply of the good increases.

2. When new technology for producing computers is used by manufacturers, the supply of computers increases.

3. If the wage rate paid to chefs rises and all other influences on selling plans remain the same, the supply of restaurant meals will increase.

4. If the price of coffee is expected to rise next month, the supply of coffee this month will decrease.

5. The supply of a good will increase and there will be a movement up along the supply curve of the good if the price of one of its substitutes in production falls.

Multiple choice

1. The quantity supplied of a good, service, or resource is ____ during a specified period and at a specified price.
   a. the amount that people are able to sell
   b. the amount that people are willing to sell
   c. the amount that people are able and willing to sell
   d. the amount that people are willing and able to buy
   e. the amount sold

2. One reason supply curves have an upward slope is because
   a. increased supply will require increased technology.
   b. people will pay a higher price when less is supplied.
   c. a higher price brings a greater profit, so firms want to sell more of that good.
   d. to have more of the good supplied requires more firms to open.
   e. None of the above answers is correct because supply curves have a downward slope.

3. Which of the following indicates that the law of supply applies to makers of soda?
   a. An increase in the price of a soda leads to an increase in the demand for soda.
   b. An increase in the price of a soda leads to an increase in the supply of soda.
   c. An increase in the price of a soda leads to an increase in the quantity of soda supplied.
   d. A decrease in the price of a soda leads to an increase in the quantity of soda demanded.
   e. A decrease in the price of a soda leads to an increase in the supply of soda.

4. If the costs to produce pizza increase, which will occur?
   a. The supply of pizza will decrease.
   b. The quantity of pizzas supplied will increase as sellers try to cover their costs.
   c. Pizza will cease to be produced and sold.
   d. The demand curve for pizza will shift leftward when the price of a pizza increases.
   e. The demand curve for pizza will shift rightward when the price of a pizza increases.

5. A rise in the price of a substitute in production for a good leads to
   a. an increase in the supply of that good.
   b. a decrease in the supply of that good.
   c. no change in the supply of that good.
   d. a decrease in the quantity of that good supplied.
   e. no change in either the supply or the quantity supplied of the good.

6. An increase in the productivity of producing jeans results in
   a. the quantity of jeans supplied increasing.
   b. the supply of jeans increasing.
   c. buyers demanding more jeans because they are now more efficiently produced.
   d. buyers demanding fewer jeans because their price will fall, which signals lower quality.
   e. some change but the impact on the supply of jeans is impossible to predict.

7. An increase in supply is shown by
   a. a rightward shift of the supply curve.
   b. a leftward shift of the supply curve.
   c. a movement up along the supply curve but no shift in the supply curve.
   d. a movement down along the supply curve but no shift in the supply curve.
   e. *both* a rightward shift of the supply curve *and* a movement up along the supply curve.

■ FIGURE 4.8

Price (dollars per pizza)

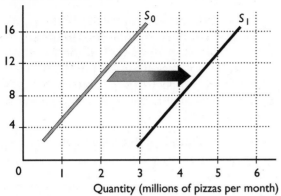

8. The shift of the supply curve of pizza illustrated in Figure 4.8 could be the result of
   a. a rise in the price of cheese used to produce pizza.
   b. a decrease in the number of firms producing pizza.
   c. an increase in the productivity of the firms producing pizza.
   d. a rise in the price of a substitute in production.
   e. a rise in the price of a pizza.

9. The shift of the supply curve of pizza illustrated in Figure 4.8 could be the result of
   a. a rise in income if pizza is a normal good.
   b. a fall in the price of soda, a consumer complement for pizza.
   c. an increase in the number of firms producing pizza.
   d. a rise in the price of a pizza.
   e. a rise in the wage paid the workers who make pizza.

10. Suppose the price of leather used to produce shoes increases. As a result, there is ____ in the supply of shoes and the supply curve of shoes ____.
    a. an increase; shifts rightward
    b. an increase; shifts leftward
    c. a decrease; shifts rightward
    d. a decrease; shifts leftward
    e. no change; does not shift

Complete the graph

Price (dollars per bundle of cotton candy)	Quantity (bundles of cotton candy per month)
1	4,000
2	8,000
3	10,000
4	12,000

1. The supply schedule for cotton candy is given in the table above. In Figure 4.4, you previously drew a demand curve for cotton candy. Now use the supply schedule to draw the supply curve in Figure 4.4.
   a. If the price of cotton candy is $2 a bundle, what is the quantity supplied?
   b. If the price of cotton candy is $3 a bundle, what is the quantity supplied?
   c. Does the supply curve you drew slope upward or downward?

■ FIGURE 4.9

Price (dollars per ton of rubber bands)

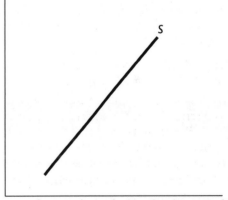

Quantity (tons of rubber bands per year)

2. Figure 4.9 shows a supply curve for rubber bands. Suppose the productivity of producing rubber bands increases. In Figure 4.9, illustrate the effect of this event.

■ **FIGURE 4.10**

Price (dollars per ton of copper)

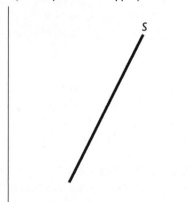

Quantity (tons of copper per year)

3. Figure 4.10 shows a supply curve for copper. The cost of the natural gas used to refine copper ore into copper rises. In Figure 4.10, show the effect of this event.

Short answer and numeric questions

1. What is the law of supply?

2. What influence(s) lead to a change in the quantity supplied?

3. What influences lead to a change in supply?

CHECKPOINT 4.3

■ **Explain how demand and supply determine the price and quantity in a market and explain the effects of changes in demand and supply.**

Quick Review

- *Market equilibrium* When the quantity demanded equals the quantity supplied.

Additional Practice Problems 4.3

1. Hot dogs are an inferior good and people's incomes rise. What happens to the equilibrium price and quantity of hot dogs?

2. Hot dog producers develop new technology that increases their productivity. What hap-

pens to the equilibrium price and quantity of hot dogs?

3. The price of a hot dog bun falls and, simultaneously, the number of hot dog producers increases. The effect of the fall in the price of a hot dog bun is less than the effect of the increase in the number of producers. What happens to the equilibrium price and quantity of hot dogs?

Solutions to Additional Practice Problems 4.3

1. When income increases, the demand for an inferior good decreases and the demand curve shifts leftward. The supply does not change and the sup-

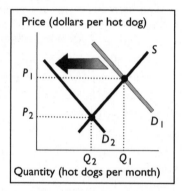

Price (dollars per hot dog)

ply curve does not shift. As a result, the equilibrium price of a hot dog falls and the equilibrium quantity decreases, as illustrated in the figure.

2. When the productivity of producing a good increases, the supply of the good increases and the supply curve shifts rightward. So the supply curve of hot dogs shifts rightward. The demand does

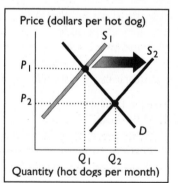

Price (dollars per hot dog)

not change and so the demand curve does not shift. The figure shows that the equilibrium price of a hot dog falls and the equilibrium quantity increases.

3. The fall in the price of a complement, hot dog buns, increases the demand for hot dogs and the demand curve for hot dogs shifts rightward.

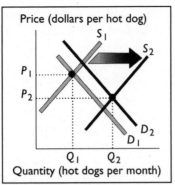

The increase in the number of producers increases the supply of hot dogs and the supply curve shifts rightward. Because the increase in supply exceeds the increase in demand, the price of a hot dog falls and the quantity increases, as shown in the figure.

■ Self Test 4.3

Fill in the blanks

The price at which the quantity demanded equals the quantity supplied is the ____. In a diagram, the ____ is determined where the supply and demand curves intersect. If the price exceeds the equilibrium price, the price ____ (rises; falls). An increase in demand ____ (raises; lowers) the equilibrium price and ____ (increases; decreases) the equilibrium quantity. An increase in supply ____ (raises; lowers) the equilibrium price and ____ (increases; decreases) the equilibrium quantity. If both the demand and supply increase, definitely the equilibrium ____ increases but the effect on the equilibrium ____ is ambiguous.

True or false

1. If the price of asparagus is below the equilibrium price, there is a shortage of asparagus and the price of asparagus will rise until the shortage disappears.

2. When the demand for skateboards decreases and the supply of skateboards remains unchanged, the quantity supplied of skateboards decreases as the price rises.

3. Automakers expect the price of an SUV to fall next year. If the demand for SUVs does not change, the equilibrium price of an SUV today will fall and the equilibrium quantity today will increase.

4. As summer comes to an end and winter sets in, the demand for and supply of hamburger buns decrease. The price of a hamburger bun definitely remains the same.

5. The number of buyers of grapefruit juice increases and at the same time severe frost decreases the supply of grapefruit juice. The price of grapefruit juice will rise.

Multiple choice

1. The equilibrium price of a good occurs if the
   a. quantity of the good demanded equals the quantity of the good supplied.
   b. quantity of the good demanded is greater than the quantity of the good supplied.
   c. quantity of the good demanded is less than the quantity of the good supplied.
   d. demand for the good is equal to the supply of the good.
   e. price of the good seems reasonable to most buyers.

2. Which of the following is correct?
   i. A surplus puts downward pressure on the price of a good.
   ii. A shortage puts upward pressure on the price of a good
   iii. There is no surplus or shortage at equilibrium.
   a. i and ii..
   b. i and iii.
   c. ii and iii.
   d. i, ii, and iii.
   e. only iii.

3. The number of buyers of ceiling fans increases, so there is an increase in the
   a. quantity of ceiling fans demanded and a surplus of ceiling fans.
   b. demand for ceiling fans and a rise in the price of a ceiling fan.
   c. demand for ceiling fans and a surplus of ceiling fans.
   d. supply of ceiling fans and no change in the price of a ceiling fan.
   e. demand for ceiling fans and in the supply of ceiling fans.

4. Which of the following is the best explanation for why the price of gasoline increases during the summer months?
   a. Oil producers have higher costs of production in the summer.
   b. Sellers have to earn profits during the summer to cover losses in the winter.
   c. There is increased driving by families going on vacation.
   d. There is less competition among oil refineries in the summer.
   e. The number of gas stations open 24 hours a day rises in the summer months and so the price must rise to cover the higher costs.

5. Suppose that the price of lettuce used to produce tacos increases. As a result, the equilibrium price of a taco ____ and the equilibrium quantity ____.
   a. rises; increases
   b. rises; decreases
   c. falls; increases
   d. falls; decreases
   e. does not change; decreases

6. The technology associated with manufacturing computers has advanced enormously. This change has led to the price of a computer ____ and the quantity ____.
   a. rising; increasing
   b. rising; decreasing
   c. falling; increasing
   d. falling; decreasing
   e. falling; not changing

7. Candy makers accurately anticipate the increase in demand for candy for Halloween so that the supply of candy and the demand for candy increase the same amount. As a result, the price of candy ____ and the quantity of candy ____.
   a. rises; does not change
   b. falls; increases
   c. does not change; increases
   d. does not change; does not change
   e. rises; rises

8. During 2005 the supply of petroleum decreased while at the same time the demand for petroleum increased. If the magnitude of the increase in demand was greater than the magnitude of the decrease in supply, then the equilibrium price of gasoline ____ and the equilibrium quantity ____.
   a. increased; increased
   b. increased; decreased
   c. increased; did not change
   d. decreased; did not change
   e. did not change; increased

Complete the graph

1. In Checkpoint 4.1 you drew a demand curve in Figure 4.4; in Checkpoint 4.2, you drew a supply curve in that figure. Return to Figure 4.4 and answer the following questions.
   a. If the price of cotton candy is $1, what is the situation in the market?
   b. If the price of cotton candy is $3, what is the situation in the market?
   c. What is the equilibrium price and equilibrium quantity of cotton candy?

■ **FIGURE 4.11**

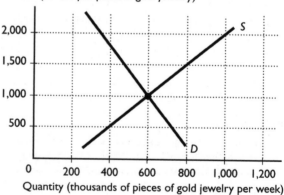

2. Figure 4.11 shows the supply and demand for gold jewelry. In the figure, show what happens to the price and quantity if gold jewelry is a normal good and people's incomes rise.

■ FIGURE 4.12

Price (dollars per piece of gold jewelry)

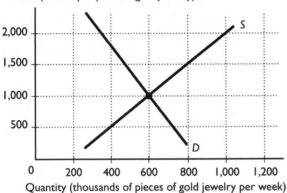

Quantity (thousands of pieces of gold jewelry per week)

3. Figure 4.12 shows the supply and demand for gold jewelry. Suppose that consumers think that silver jewelry is a substitute for gold jewelry. In Figure 4.12, show what happens to the price and quantity if the price of silver jewelry falls.

■ FIGURE 4.13

Price (dollars per piece of gold jewelry)

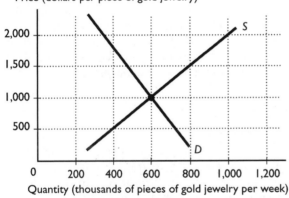

Quantity (thousands of pieces of gold jewelry per week)

4. Figure 4.13 shows the supply and demand for gold jewelry. Suppose the price of the gold that is used to produce gold jewelry rises. In the figure, show what happens to the price and quantity of gold jewelry.

Short answer and numeric questions

1. How is a shortage different from a surplus?

Price (dollars per sweatshirt)	Quantity demanded (sweatshirts per season)	Quantity supplied (sweatshirts per season)
35	13	32
30	15	25
25	19	19
20	27	12
15	37	8

2. The table gives the demand and supply schedules for sweatshirts. At what price will the quantity demanded be equal to the quantity supplied? What is the equilibrium quantity?

3. People read that drinking orange juice helps prevent heart disease. What is the effect on the equilibrium price and quantity of orange juice?

4. The cost of memory chips used in computers falls. What is the effect on the equilibrium price and quantity of computers?

5. New cars are a normal good and people's incomes increase. Simultaneously, auto manufacturers must pay more for their workers' health insurance. What is the effect on the price and quantity of new cars?

CHECKPOINT 4.4

■ **Explain how price floors, price ceilings, and sticky prices cause surpluses, unemployment, and shortages.**

Quick Review

- *Price floor* The lowest price at which it is legal to trade a good, service, or factor of production. The minimum wage is a price floor.

- *Price ceiling* or *price cap* The highest price at which it is legal to trade a good, service, or factor of production.

Additional Practice Problems 4.4

1. The figure shows the market for temp workers in the United States:

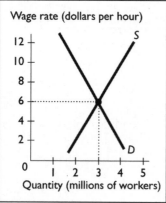

Wage rate (dollars per hour)

Quantity (millions of workers)

a. What is the equilibrium wage rate of temp workers and what is the equilibrium quantity of temp workers employed?

b. If the United States introduces a minimum wage for temp workers of $4 an hour, how many tempt workers are employed and how many are unemployed?

c. If the United States introduces a minimum wage for temp workers of $10 an hour, how many temp workers are employed and how many are unemployed?

2. What is a sticky price and how can a sticky price in the labor market create unemployment?

Solutions to Additional Practice Problems 4.4

1a. The quantity of labor supplied equals the quantity of labor demanded at a wage rate of $6 an hour, so $6 an hour is the equilibrium wage rate. The equilibrium quantity of temp workers employed is 3 million.

1b. The minimum wage of $4 an hour is less than the equilibrium wage, so the minimum wage has no effect. The wage rate remains equal to $6 an hour. Zero workers are unemployed and 3 million temp workers are employed.

1c. The minimum wage is above the equilibrium wage of $6 an hour, so the wage cannot adjust to its equilibrium. The figure shows that

at the minimum wage of $10 per hour, the quantity of temp workers demanded is 2 million, so 2 million will be employed. But at this wage rate 4 million people would like to work, so 2 million workers (4 million – 2 million) are unemployed.

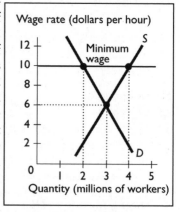

Wage rate (dollars per hour)

Minimum wage

Quantity (millions of workers)

2. A sticky price occurs when buyers and sellers agree on a price for a fixed period of time or a seller sets a price that changes infrequently. Many workers have contracts with their employers in which the wage rate to be paid for several years is specified. This wage rate can create unemployment when the demand for labor decreases. The wage rate cannot fall to its new equilibrium value. At the relatively high sticky wage, the quantity of labor demanded is less than the quantity of labor supplied. The surplus of workers are unemployed.

■ Self Test 4.4

Fill in the blanks

A price _____ (ceiling; floor) is the highest price at which it is legal to trade a particular good, service, or factor of production. In order to affect the market price and quantity, a price floor must be set _____ (above; below) the equilibrium price. A minimum wage is an example of a price _____ (ceiling; floor). A minimum wage creates unemployment when it is set _____ (above; below) the equilibrium wage rate. Sticky prices _____ (can; cannot) create unemployment.

True or false

1. A rent ceiling always lowers the rent paid.

2. A minimum wage is an example of a price ceiling.

3. Firms hire labor, so they determine how much labor to supply in a market.

4. When firms enter into long-term contracts with labor unions that fix wage rates for several years, the wage rate is sticky.

Multiple choice

1. Price caps
   a. prevent the market price from going above a certain value.
   b. prevent the market price from going below a certain value.
   c. keep the market prices higher than would otherwise be the case.
   d. match the quantity demanded with the quantity supplied of any given good or service.
   e. attempt to keep the price equal to or above the price set as the ceiling price.

2. When the government imposes a price cap on a product below the equilibrium price, the government creates
   a. a shortage.
   b. a surplus.
   c. equilibrium in the market.
   d. a shortage only if the quantity demanded is less than the quantity supplied.
   e. a surplus only if the quantity supplied is less than the quantity demanded.

3. To affect the market's price and quantity, a price floor must be set
   a. above the equilibrium price.
   b. below the equilibrium price.
   c. at the equilibrium price.
   d. equal to the market's price cap.
   e. so that it is not sticky.

4. The minimum wage is an example of
   a. an equilibrium price.
   b. a price floor.
   c. a price ceiling.
   d. a price cap.
   e. a fully flexible price.

5. A two-year labor contract is an example of a
   a. price ceiling.
   b. price floor.
   c. sticky price.
   d. price cap.
   e. shortage.

6. The result of sticky prices in a market is
   a. quicker adjustment of prices.
   b. no adjustment of prices.
   c. a slower adjustment of prices.
   d. to change the price but not the quantity bought and sold.
   e. the rapid elimination of any surpluses.

Complete the graph

1. In Checkpoint 4.1 you drew a demand curve in Figure 4.4; in Checkpoint 4.2, you drew a supply curve in that figure. Return to Figure 4.4 and answer the following questions.
   a. Suppose the government imposes a price cap for cotton candy of $1. What is the situation in the market?
   b. Suppose the government imposes a price floor for cotton candy of $3. What is the situation in the market?
   c. How do your answers to parts (a) and (b) compare with your answers to Checkpoint 4.3 Complete the Graph Question 1, parts (a) and (b)?

Short answer and numeric questions

Price (cents per kilowatt-hour)	Quantity demanded (kilowatt-hours)	Quantity supplied (kilowatt-hours)
17	2,700	2,700
15	2,900	2,600
13	3,100	2,500
11	3,300	2,400

1. The table gives the demand and supply schedules for electricity. At what price is the quantity demanded equal to the quantity supplied? Suppose the government sets a price cap of 11¢ per kilowatt. What is the impact of this price cap?

2. What is the effect of a minimum wage set below the equilibrium wage rate? Set above the equilibrium wage rate? Explain why your answers to the two questions differ.

SELF TEST ANSWERS

■ CHECKPOINT 4.1

Fill in the blanks

The <u>law of demand</u> states that other things remaining the same, if the price of a good rises, the <u>quantity demanded of</u> that good decreases. A <u>demand curve</u> is a graph of the relationship between the quantity demanded of a good and its price. Demand curves are <u>downward</u> sloping. An increase in demand shifts the demand curve <u>rightward</u>. Factors that change demand lead to a <u>shift of</u> the demand curve. Factors that change demand are <u>prices of related goods</u>, <u>income</u>, <u>expectations</u>, <u>number of buyers</u>, and <u>preferences</u>.

True or false

1. False; page 91
2. False; page 94
3. True; page 93
4. False; page 93
5. False; page 94

Multiple choice

1. d; page 91
2. b; page 91
3. a; page 94
4. c; page 94
5. a; page 94
6. a; pages 93-94
7. b; pages 93-94
8. d; page 94
9. d; page 94
10. d; page 94

Complete the graph

1. a. Figure 4.14 illustrates the demand curve, labeled *D* in the diagram. (The supply curve is from the first "Complete the Graph" question in Checkpoint 4.2.)
   a. 8,000 bundles per month
   b. 7,000 bundles per month
   c. The demand curve slopes downward; pages 92.

■ FIGURE 4.14

Price (dollars per bundle of cotton candy)

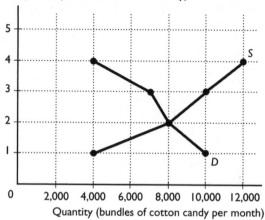

Quantity (bundles of cotton candy per month)

■ FIGURE 4.15

Price (dollars per pound of butter)

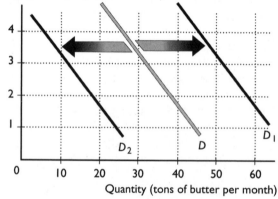

Quantity (tons of butter per month)

2. a. The demand increases and the demand curve shifts rightward, as shown in Figure 4.15 by the shift to D_1; page 94
   b. The demand decreases and the demand curve shifts leftward, as shown in Figure 4.15 by the shift to D_2; page 94
   c. The demand curve does not shift. The fall in the price of butter leads to an increase in the quantity demanded and a movement along the demand curve, not a shift of the demand curve; page 94.

Short answer and numeric questions

1. When the price falls from $2.30 a gallon to $2.20 a gallon, the quantity of gasoline de-

manded increases from 310 gallons to 316 gallons; page 92.

2. A change in the quantity demanded occurs when the price of the good changes. A change in demand occurs when any other influence on buying plans other than the price of the good changes; page 94.

3. A movement along a demand curve reflects a change in the quantity demanded and is the result of a change in the price of the product. A shift in a demand curve reflects a change in demand and is the result of a change in any factor, other than the price, that affects demand; page 94.

■ CHECKPOINT 4.2

Fill in the blanks

The <u>quantity supplied</u> of a good is the amount people are willing and able to sell during a specified period at a specified price. The law of supply states that other things remaining the same, if the price of a good rises, the quantity supplied <u>increases</u>. A supply curve is <u>upward</u> sloping. A change in the price of a good changes <u>the quantity supplied</u> and is illustrated by a <u>movement along</u> the supply curve. Factors that change supply are <u>prices of related goods</u>, <u>prices of resources and other inputs</u>, <u>expectations</u>, <u>number of sellers</u>, and <u>productivity</u>.

True or false

1. False; page 96
2. True; page 99
3. False; page 98
4. True; page 98
5. False; pages 98-99

Multiple choice

1. c; page 96
2. c; page 96
3. c; page 96
4. a; page 98
5. b; page 98
6. b; page 99

7. a; page 99
8. c; pages 98-99
9. c; page 99
10. d; pages 98-99

Complete the graph

1. The supply curve is illustrated in Figure 4.14, labeled S in the diagram.
   a. 8,000 bundles per month.
   b. 10,000 bundles per month.
   c. The supply curve slopes upward; page 97.

■ FIGURE 4.16

Price (dollars per box of rubber bands)

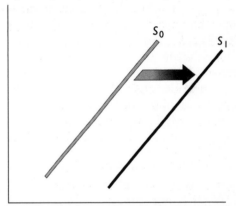

Quantity (boxes of rubber bands per year)

2. Figure 4.16 illustrates the shift; page 99.

■ FIGURE 4.17

Price (dollars per ton of copper)

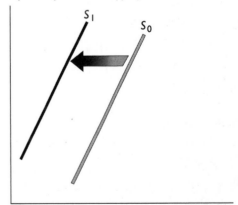

Quantity (tons of copper per year)

3. Figure 4.17 illustrates the shift; pages 98-99.

Short answer and numeric questions

1. If other things remain the same, when the price of a good or service falls (rises), sellers decrease (increase) the quantity they supply. page 96.

2. Change in the price of the product; page 99.

3. Changes in: prices of related goods; prices of resources and other inputs; expectations; number of sellers; and productivity; page 99.

■ CHECKPOINT 4.3

Fill in the blanks

The price at which the quantity demanded equals the quantity supplied is the equilibrium price. In a diagram, the equilibrium price is determined where the supply and demand curves intersect. If the price exceeds the equilibrium price, the price falls. An increase in demand raises the equilibrium price and increases the equilibrium quantity. An increase in supply lowers the equilibrium price and increases the equilibrium quantity. If both the demand and supply increase, definitely the equilibrium quantity increases but the effect on the equilibrium price is ambiguous.

True or false

1. True; pages 101-102
2. False; page 103
3. True; page 104
4. False; page 106
5. True; page 106

Multiple choice

1. a; page 101
2. d; pages 101-102
3. b; page 103
4. c; page 103
5. b; page 104
6. c; page 104
7. c; page 106
8. a; page 106

Complete the graph

1. a. A shortage of 6,000 bundles a month; pages 101-102.

   b. A surplus of 3,000 bundles a month; pages 101-102.

   c. The equilibrium price is $2 a bundle of cotton candy and the equilibrium quantity is 8,000 bundles a month; page 101.

■ **FIGURE 4.18**

Price (dollars per piece of gold jewelry)

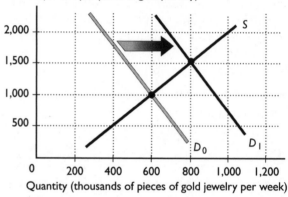

Quantity (thousands of pieces of gold jewelry per week)

2. Figure 4.18 shows the effect of the increase in income. The increase in income increases the demand for normal goods, such as gold jewelry. The demand curve shifts rightward and the supply curve does not shift. The price of gold jewelry rises, to $1,500 in the figure, and the quantity increases, to 800 pieces per week in the figure; page 103.

■ **FIGURE 4.19**

Price (dollars per piece of gold jewelry)

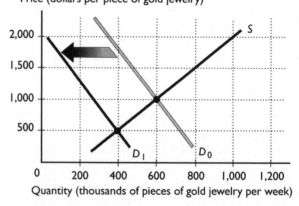

Quantity (thousands of pieces of gold jewelry per week)

3. Figure 4.19 shows the effect of the fall in

price of silver jewelry. A fall in the price of a substitute decreases the demand gold jewelry. The demand curve shifts leftward and the supply curve does not shift. The price of gold jewelry falls, to $500 in the figure, and the quantity decreases, to 400 pieces per week in the figure; page 104.

■ **FIGURE 4.20**

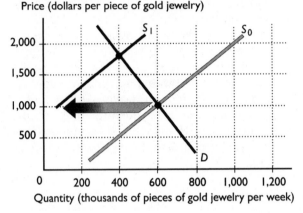

Price (dollars per piece of gold jewelry)

4. Figure 4.20 shows the effect of the fall in the price of gold. The price of gold is a cost to the producers of gold jewelry. A rise in the cost decreases the supply of the good. The supply curve shifts leftward and the demand curve does not shift. The price of gold jewelry rises, to $1,750 in the figure, and the quantity decreases, to 400 pieces per week in the figure; page 104.

Short answer and numeric questions

1. When a shortage exists, the price of the good is below the equilibrium price. The quantity demanded is greater than the quantity supplied. When a surplus exists, the price of the good is above the equilibrium price. The quantity demanded is less than the quantity supplied; page 101.

2. The quantity demanded equals the quantity supplied when the price is $25. The equilibrium quantity is 19 sweatshirts; page 101.

3. The increase in preferences increases the demand for orange juice and the demand curve shifts rightward. The price of orange

juice rises and the quantity increases; page 103.

4. The fall in cost increases the supply of computers. The supply curve of computers shifts rightward. The price falls and the quantity increases; page 104.

5. The increase in income increases the demand for normal goods and shifts the demand curve for new cars rightward. The increase in health insurance premiums decreases the supply of new cars and shifts the supply curve of new cars leftward. The price of a new car definitely rises. The effect on the quantity is ambiguous: it rises if the demand effect is larger, falls if the supply effect is larger, and does not change if the two effects are the same size; page 106.

■ **CHECKPOINT 4.4**

Fill in the blanks

A price ceiling is the highest price at which it is legal to trade a particular good, service, or factor of production. In order to affect the market price and quantity, a price floor must be set above the equilibrium price. A minimum wage is an example of a price floor. A minimum wage creates unemployment when it is set above the equilibrium wage rate. Sticky prices can create unemployment.

True or false

1. False; page 111
2. False; page 109
3. False; page 109
4. True; page 113

Multiple choice

1. a; page 111
2. a; pages 111-113
3. a; page 110
4. b; page 109
5. c; page 113
6. c; page 113

Complete the graph

1. a. With a price cap of $1, there is a shortage of 6,000 bundles; pages 111-113.
    b. With a price floor of $3, there is a surplus of 3,000 bundles; pages 109-110.
    c. The shortages and surpluses in the answers above are the same as the shortages and surpluses in the answers to questions in Checkpoint 4.3. Government-imposed price caps and floors create shortages and surpluses *exactly* the same way that non-equilibrium prices create shortages and surpluses, though government created shortages and surpluses persist as long as the policies persist; pages 109- 113.

Short answer and numeric questions

1. The quantity demanded equals quantity supplied at the equilibrium price of 17¢ per kilowatt-hour. A price ceiling of 11¢ per kilowatt is below the equilibrium price. At the price cap, the quantity demanded is 3,300 kilowatt-hours and the quantity supplied is 2,400 kilowatt-hours, so a shortage of 900 kilowatt-hours exists; pages 112-113.

2. A minimum wage set below the equilibrium wage rate has no effect. The minimum wage is the lowest legal wage. When set below the equilibrium wage rate, the equilibrium wage remains legal. Nothing is changed because the market wage remains equal to the equilibrium wage. When the minimum wage is set above the equilibrium wage, the equilibrium wage becomes illegal. The wage becomes the minimum wage. At the higher minimum wage, the quantity of labor demanded is less than the quantity of labor supplied and unemployment results; page 110.

GDP and the Standard of Living

Chapter 5

CHAPTER IN PERSPECTIVE

■ **Define GDP and explain why the value of production, income, and expenditure are the same for an economy.**

The standard of living is the level of the consumption of the goods and services that people enjoy, on the average. It is measured by the average income per person. Gross Domestic Product, GDP, is the market value of all the final goods and services produced within a country in a given time period. Only final goods and services are included in GDP; intermediate goods and services are not included. Expenditures are consumption expenditure (C), investment (I), government expenditures on goods and services (G), and net exports (NX). Total expenditure equals $C + I + G + NX$. Firms pay out everything they receive as incomes to the factors of production. We call total income Y. The circular flow shows that total expenditure equals total income so that $Y = C + I + G + NX$.

■ **Describe how economic statisticians measure GDP in the United States.**

GDP is measured using the expenditure approach and the income approach. The expenditure approach adds the four sources of expenditure: consumption expenditure, investment, government expenditures on goods and services, and net exports. Expenditures on used goods and financial assets are not in GDP. The income approach adds two categories of income (wages plus interest, rent, and profit). This sum is net domestic product at factor cost. To get to GDP from this, subsidies are subtracted, and indirect taxes and depreciation are added. A statistical discrepancy is added or subtracted so that GDP using the income approach equals GDP using the expenditure approach. Disposable person income is the income received by households minus the personal income taxes paid.

■ **Distinguish between nominal GDP and real GDP and define the GDP deflator.**

Real GDP is the value of final goods and services produced in a given year expressed in the prices of a base year; nominal GDP is the value of final goods and services produced in a given year using prices of that year. The chained-dollar method of calculating real GDP links the prices used to compute real GDP to the base year by calculating and then averaging annual growth rates of real GDP using current year prices and past year prices. The GDP deflator is an average of current prices expressed as a percentage of base-year prices. It equals (nominal GDP ÷ real GDP) × 100.

■ **Describe and explain the limitations of real GDP as a measure of the standard of living.**

Real GDP per person can be used to compare the standard of living over time or across nations. Real GDP fluctuates in a business cycle, going from an expansion to a peak to a recession to a trough. GDP is not a perfect measure of the standard of living because it does not measure household production, underground production, the value of leisure time, the environmental quality, health and life expectancy, or political freedom and justice.

CHECKPOINT 5.1

■ **Define GDP and explain why the value of production, income, and expenditure are the same for an economy.**

Quick Review

- *Total expenditure* Total expenditure is the total amount received by producers of final goods and services and equals $C + I + G + NX$.
- *Total income* Total income is the income paid to all factors of production and equals total expenditure.

Additional Practice Problems 5.1

1. Last year consumption expenditure was $70 billion, investment was $16 billion, government purchases of goods and services were $12 billion, exports were $4 billion, and imports were $3 billion.
   a. What did GDP last year equal?
   b. This year imports increased to $5 billion. If all the other types of expenditure stay the same, what does GDP this year equal?

2. Suppose that GDP equals $12 trillion, consumption expenditure equals $7 trillion, investment equals $3.5 trillion, and government expenditure on goods and services equals $2.5 trillion. What does net exports equal?

3. One of the four expenditure categories is net exports. How can net exports be negative?

Solutions to Additional Practice Problems 5.1

1a. To solve this problem use the equality between GDP and expenditure, GDP = $C + I + G + NX$. Last year's GDP = $70 billion + $16 billion + $12 billion + ($4 billion − $3 billion) = $99 billion.

1b. This year, imports increased from $3 billion to $5 billion, so replace the $3 billion in the calculation with $5 billion and GDP for this year is $97 billion. The $2 billion increase in imports results in a $2 billion decrease in GDP.

2. GDP = $C + I + G + NX$. So $NX = GDP − C − I − G$. In this case, NX = $12 trillion − $7 trillion − $3.5 trillion − $2.5 trillion, which equals −$1 trillion.

3. Net exports equals the value of exports of goods and services minus the value of imports of goods and services. If, as is the case in the United States, the value of imports exceeds the value of exports, net exports will be negative.

■ **Self Test 5.1**

Fill in the blanks

The market value of all the final goods and services produced within a country in a given time period is _____ (GDP; investment). _____ (Two; Three; Four) groups buy the final goods and services produced. Net exports equals the value of _____ (imports; exports) minus the value of _____ (imports; exports). $C + I + G + NX$ equals _____ and _____.

True or false

1. The computer chip that Dell Corp. buys from Intel Corp. is a final good.

2. Expenditure on a bulldozer is consumption expenditure.

3. The value of net exports of goods and services can be negative.

4. The value of production equals income, which equals expenditure.

Multiple choice

1. The abbreviation "GDP" stands for
   a. Gross Domestic Product.
   b. Gross Domestic Prices.
   c. General Domestic Prices.
   d. Great Domestic Prices.
   e. Government's Domestic Politics.

2. GDP is equal to the _____ value of all the final goods and services produced within a country in a given period of time.
   a. production
   b. market
   c. wholesale
   d. retail
   e. typical

3. The following are all *final* goods except
   a. flour used by the baker to make cup cakes.
   b. bread eaten by a family for lunch.
   c. pencils used by a 6th grader in class.
   d. Nike shoes used by a basketball player.
   e. a computer used by Intel to design new computer chips.

4. Investment is defined as
   a. the purchase of a stock or bond.
   b. financial capital.
   c. what consumers do with their savings.
   d. the purchase of new capital goods by firms.
   e. spending on capital goods by governments.

5. In one year, a firm increases its production by $9 million and increases sales by $8 million. All other things in the economy remaining the same, which of the following is true?
   a. GDP increases by $8 million and inventory investment decreases by $1 million.
   b. GDP increases by $9 million and inventory investment increases by $1 million.
   c. Inventory investment decreases by $1 million.
   d. GDP increases by $8 million and investment increases by $1 million.
   e. GDP increases by $17 million.

6. Total expenditure equals
   a. $C + I + G + NX$.
   b. $C + I + G - NX$.
   c. $C + I - G + NX$.
   d. $C - I + G + NX$.
   e. $C - I - G - NX$.

Short answer and numeric questions

1. Why aren't intermediate goods or services counted in GDP?

2. Classify each of the following into the components of U.S. GDP: consumption expenditure, investment, government purchases of goods and services, exports, or imports.
   a. The purchase of a Sony DVD player made in Japan.

   b. A family's purchase of a birthday cake at the local Safeway grocery store.
   c. Microsoft's purchase of 1,000 Dell computers.
   d. The purchase of a new pizza oven by Pizza Hut.
   e. The government's purchase of 15 stealth fighters.

3. Why does total expenditure equal total income?

CHECKPOINT 5.2

■ **Describe how economic statisticians measure GDP in the United States.**

Quick Review

- *Expenditure approach* GDP equals the sum of consumption expenditure, investment, government purchases, and net exports.
- *Income approach* GDP equals the sum of wages plus interest, rent, and profit minus subsidies plus indirect taxes and depreciation plus or minus any statistical discrepancy. The sum of the first two income categories is net domestic product at factor.

Additional Practice Problem 5.2

Item	Amount (billions of dollars)
Wages	5,875
Consumption expenditure	6,987
Indirect taxes less subsidies	630
Interest, rent, and profit	2,248
Depreciation	1,329
Investment	1,586
Statistical discrepancy	0
Net exports	−349

1. The table above gives some of the items in the U.S. National Income and Product Accounts in 2001.
   a. Calculate U.S. GDP in 2001.
   b. Did you use the expenditure approach or the income approach to make this calculation?

c. What was the government's expenditure on goods and services in 2001?

Solution to Additional Practice Problem 5.2

1a. This question focuses on calculating GDP. To solve problems such as this, you need to know how to use the expenditure approach and the income approach. The expenditure approach adds four categories of expenditure while the income approach adds the two income categories and then makes a few additional adjustments.

To calculate GDP using the expenditure approach the four categories of expenditure you need to know are: consumption, investment, government expenditure, and net exports. The table does not give the value of government expenditures on goods and services, so you cannot find GDP using the expenditure approach.

To calculate GDP using the income approach you need to know the values of wages and of interest, rent, and profit. Adding these two together yields net domestic income at factor cost. To adjust to GDP, you need also indirect taxes less subsidies, depreciation, and any statistical discrepancy. All these items are listed in the table, so GDP can be calculated using the income approach. In this case, GDP = $5,875 billion + $2,248 + $630 billion + $1,329 billion + $0, which is $10,082 billion.

1b The only way GDP can be calculated in part (a) is by the income approach, which is the approach used.

1c. GDP was calculated in part (a) using the income approach. The expenditure approach notes that GDP = $C + I + G + NX$. Subtract C, I, and NX from both sides of the equation to show that G = GDP − C − I − NX. Using the values of GDP, C, I, and NX yields G = $10,082 billion − $6,987 billion − $1,586 billion + $349 billion = $1,858 billion. (The net exports were negative, so −(−$349 billion) equals + $349 billion).

■ Self Test 5.2

Fill in the blanks

The ____ approach and the ____ approach are two methods used to calculate GDP. Expenditure on used goods ____ (is; is not) included in GDP. Wages is part of the ____ (expenditure; income) approach to calculating GDP. To calculate GDP, depreciation is ____ (added to; subtracted from) net domestic product at factor cost. GNP equals GDP ____ (plus; minus) net factor income from abroad. For the United States, the difference between GDP and GNP is ____ (large; small).

True or false

1. The expenditure approach measures GDP by using data on consumption expenditure, investment, government expenditures on goods and services, and net exports of goods and services.

2. In the United States, expenditure on used goods is becoming an increasingly large fraction of GDP.

3. The income approach uses data on consumption expenditure, investment, government purchases of goods and services, and net exports of goods and services to calculate GDP.

4. Disposable personal income is usually larger than GDP.

Multiple choice

1. In calculating GDP, economists
   a. measure total expenditure as the only true measure.
   b. can measure either total expenditure or total income.
   c. measure total income as the only true measure.
   d. measure total income minus total expenditure.
   e. measure total income plus total expenditure.

2. The expenditure approach to measuring GDP is based on summing
   a. wages, interest, rent, and profit.
   b. each industry's production.
   c. the total values of final goods, intermediate goods, used goods, and financial assets.
   d. consumption expenditure, investment, government expenditures on goods and services, and net exports of goods and services.
   e. consumption expenditure, investment, government expenditures on goods and services, and net exports of goods and services minus wages, interest, rent, and profit.

3. Suppose GDP is $10 billion, consumption expenditure is $7 billion, investment is $2 billion, and government expenditures on goods and services is $2 billion. Net exports of goods and services must be
   a. $1 billion.
   b. –$1 billion.
   c. $2 billion.
   d. –$2 billion.
   e. $10 billion.

4. According to the expenditure approach to measuring GDP, in the United States the largest component of GDP is
   a. consumption expenditure.
   b. investment.
   c. government expenditures on goods and services.
   d. net exports of goods and services.
   e. wages.

5. Which of the following is <u>NOT</u> one of the income categories used in the income approach to measuring GDP?
   a. wages
   b. rent
   c. interest
   d. taxes paid by persons
   e. profit

6. If the statistical discrepancy equals zero, then once income is totaled across the income categories of the income approach, to calculate GDP we must
   a. add the amount of income saved and spent.
   b. add indirect taxes and depreciation and subtract subsidies.
   c. subtract indirect taxes and subsidies and then add depreciation.
   d. do nothing because the income sum equals GDP.
   e. add subsidies and then subtract depreciation and indirect taxes.

Short answer and numeric questions

Item	Amount (dollars)
Wages	3,900
Consumption expenditure	4,000
Indirect taxes minus subsidies	400
Interest, rent, and profit	1,400
Government expenditures	1,000
Investment	1,100
Net exports	300
Statistical discrepancy	300

1. The table above gives data for a small nation:
   a. What is the nation's GDP? Did you use the expenditure or income approach to calculate GDP?
   b. What is the net domestic product at factor cost?
   c. What does depreciation equal?

2. What adjustments must be made to net domestic product at factor cost to convert it to GDP? Why must these adjustments be made?

3. What adjustments must be made to GDP to calculate GNP? To calculate disposable personal income?

CHECKPOINT 5.3

■ **Distinguish between nominal GDP and real GDP and define the GDP deflator.**

Quick Review

- *Real GDP* The value of the final goods and services produced in a given year valued at the prices of a base year.
- *Nominal GDP* The value of the final goods and services produced in a given year valued at the prices that prevailed in that year.

Additional Practice Problems 5.3

1. In a small, tropical nation suppose real GDP in 2004 was $5 billion and nominal GDP in 2004 was $10 billion. In 2005, nominal GDP was $12 billion. If GDP in 2005, measured using 2004 prices was $11.5 billion and GDP in 2004, measured using 2005 prices was $11 billion, what does real GDP in 2005 equal?
2. Nominal GDP = $10 trillion, real GDP = $9 trillion. What is the GDP deflator?
3. Real GDP = $8 trillion, GDP deflator = 120. What is nominal GDP?
4. Nominal GDP = $12 trillion, GDP deflator = 120. What is real GDP?

Solution to Practice Problem 5.3

1. This question gives you practice in how real GDP is calculated. Take each part step-by-step:

   First we need the growth rate of GDP from 2004 to 2005 measured using 2004 prices. Nominal GDP in 2004 (which is GDP in 2004 measured using 2004 prices) was $10 billion and GDP in 2005 measured using 2004 prices was $11.5 billion. So the growth in GDP using 2004 prices was [($11.5 billion − $10.0 billion) ÷ $10 billion] × 100, which is 11.5 percent.

   Next we need the growth rate of GDP from 2004 to 2005 measured using 2005 prices. GDP in 2004 measured with 2005 prices was $11 billion and nominal GDP in 2005 (which is GDP in 2005 measured using 2005 prices) was $12 billion. So the growth in GDP using 2005 prices was [($12 billion − $11 billion) ÷ $11 billion] × 100, which is 9.1 percent.

   Finally, we average the two growth rates to give a growth rate of 10.3 percent between 2004 and 2005. This percentage change is applied to real GDP in 2004, $5 billion, to give real GDP in 2005, so that real GDP in 2005 equals ($5 billion) × (1.103) which is $5.52 billion.

2. GDP deflator = (Nominal GDP ÷ Real GDP) × 100 = ($10 trillion ÷ $9 trillion) × 100 = 111.1.

3. Rearranging the formula used in problem 2 gives (GDP deflator × Real GDP) ÷ 100 = Nominal GDP, so (120 × $8 trillion) ÷ 100 = $9.6 trillion.

4. Once again rearranging the formula used in problem 2 gives (Nominal GDP ÷ GDP deflator) × 100 = Real GDP, so ($12 trillion ÷ 120) × 100 = $10 trillion.

■ **Self Test 5.3**

Fill in the blanks

_____ (Real; Nominal) GDP values production during the year using constant prices; _____ (real; nominal) GDP values production using prices that prevailed during the year. If the GDP deflator rises, nominal GDP rises more _____ (rapidly; slowly) than real GDP. The GDP deflator equals 100 times _____ (real nominal) GDP divided by _____ (real; nominal) GDP.

True or false

1. Nominal GDP increases only if the production of final goods and services increases.
2. Real GDP is just a more precise name for GDP.
3. Real GDP equals nominal GDP in the base year.
4. If real GDP is $600 billion and nominal GDP is $750 billion, then the GDP deflator is 125.

Multiple choice

1. Nominal GDP can change
   a. only if prices change.
   b. only if the quantities of goods and services change.
   c. only if prices increase.
   d. if either prices or the quantities of goods and services change.
   e. only if prices *and* the quantities of the goods and services change.

2. The difference between nominal GDP and real GDP is
   a. the indirect taxes used in their calculations.
   b. the prices used in their calculations.
   c. that nominal GDP includes the depreciation of capital and real GDP does not.
   d. that nominal GDP includes net exports of goods and services and real GDP includes net imports.
   e. that real GDP includes the depreciation of capital and nominal GDP does not.

3. Real GDP measures the value of goods and services produced in a given year valued using
   a. base year prices.
   b. prices of that same year.
   c. no prices.
   d. future prices.
   e. government approved prices.

4. If nominal GDP increases, then real GDP
   a. must decrease.
   b. must increase.
   c. must not change.
   d. could increase, decrease, or not change.
   e. could either increase or not change but cannot decrease.

5. The GDP deflator is a measure of
   a. taxes and subsidies.
   b. changes in quantities.
   c. prices.
   d. depreciation.
   e. changes in nominal GDP.

6. The GDP deflator is calculated as
   a. (nominal GDP ÷ real GDP) × 100.
   b. (real GDP ÷ nominal GDP) × 100.
   c. (nominal GDP + real GDP) ÷ 100.
   d. (nominal GDP − real GDP) ÷ 100.
   e. (real GDP − nominal GDP) ÷ 100.

7. Nominal GDP is $12.1 trillion and real GDP is $11.0 trillion. The GDP deflator is
   a. 90.1.
   b. 121.
   c. 110.
   d. 91.0.
   e. 110.

Short answer and numeric questions

Item	Data for 2005		Data for 2006	
	Quantity	Price	Quantity	Price
Pizza	100	$10.00	150	$20.00
Soda	50	$2.00	75	$4.00

1. An economy produces only pizza and soda. The table above gives the quantities produced and prices in 2005 and 2006. The base year is 2005.
   a. What is nominal GDP in 2005?
   b. What is real GDP in 2005?
   c. What is nominal GDP in 2006?
   d. What is real GDP in 2006?

2. If you want to measure the change in production, is it better to use nominal GDP or real GDP? Why?

3. How does the chained-dollar method of calculating real GDP link the current year's real GDP to the base year's real GDP?

4. Calculate the price level for each of the following combinations of nominal GDP and real GDP.
   a. Nominal GDP = $12 trillion, real GDP = $10 trillion.
   b. Nominal GDP = $12 trillion, real GDP $16 trillion.
   c. Nominal GDP = $8 trillion, real GDP = $4 trillion.

CHECKPOINT 5.4

■ **Describe and explain the limitations of real GDP as a measure of the standard of living.**

Quick Review

- *Standard of living* The standard of living among different nations or over a period of time can be compared using real GDP per person.

- *Goods and services omitted from GDP* Household production, underground production, leisure time, and environmental quality are omitted from GDP.

Additional Practice Problems 5.4

1. How has real GDP per person changed in the United States since 1964?

2. How do you think the standard of living in the United States today compares with the standard of living 150 years ago?

Solutions to Additional Practice Problems 5.4

1. Real GDP per person has increased substantially since 1964. In fact, real GDP per person has more than doubled since 1964. Historically, in the United States for the past 100 years real GDP per person has doubled about every 30 years.

2. The standard of living now is dramatically higher than it was 150 years ago. First, even though no totally accurate data on real GDP per person is available from 150 years ago, it is certain that real GDP per person is much higher today even after taking account of the fact that household production was more common 150 years ago. The underground economy is larger today, which boosts today's standard of living, and people today enjoy significantly more leisure time, which also boosts today's standard of living. Perhaps the edge on environment quality goes to the past. Considering health and life expectancy, and political freedom and social justice, people today are much better off than people 150 years ago. It is likely true that no country in history has ever enjoyed a standard of living as high as that in the United States today.

■ **Self Test 5.4**

Fill in the blanks

The value of household production ____ (is; is not) included in GDP. The value of people's leisure time ____ (is; is not) included in GDP. As it is calculated, GDP ____ (does; does not) subtract the value of environmental degradation resulting from production. Real GDP ____ (takes; does not take) into account the extent of a country's political freedom.

True or false

1. As currently measured, real GDP does not include the value of home production.

2. Production in the underground economy is part of the "investment" component of GDP.

3. The production of anti-pollution devices installed by electric utilities is not counted in GDP because the devices are designed only to eliminate pollution.

4. The measure of a country's real GDP does not take into account the extent of political freedom in the country.

Multiple choice

1. Which of the following is <u>NOT</u> part of the business cycle?
   a. recession
   b. peak
   c. inflation
   d. trough
   e. expansion

2. In the business cycle, what immediately precedes the time when real GDP is falling?
   a. recession
   b. peak
   c. depression
   d. trough
   e. expansion

3. The measurement of GDP handles household production by
   a. estimating a dollar value of the goods purchased to do housework.
   b. estimating a dollar value of the services provided.
   c. ignoring it.
   d. including it in exactly the same way that all other production is included.
   e. including it in real GDP but not in nominal GDP because there are no prices paid for the work.

4. You hire some of your friends to help you move to a new house and pay them a total of $200 and buy them dinner at Pizza Hut. Which of the following is true?
   a. The $200 should be counted as part of GDP but not the dinner at Pizza Hut.
   b. If your friends do not report the $200 on their tax forms, it becomes part of the underground economy.
   c. The dinner at Pizza Hut should be counted as part of GDP but not the $200.
   d. Hiring your friends is an illegal activity and should not be counted in GDP.
   e. Neither the $200 nor the dinner should be counted in GDP because both are household production.

5. The value of leisure time is
   a. directly included in GDP and, in recent years, has become an increasing large part of GDP.
   b. excluded from GDP.
   c. zero.
   d. directly included in GDP but, in recent years, has become a decreasing large part of GDP.
   e. directly included in GDP and, in recent years, has not changed much as a fraction of GDP.

6. A new technology is discovered that results in all new cars producing 50 percent less pollution. The technology costs nothing to produce and cars do not change in price. As a result of the technology, there is a reduction in the number of visits people make to the doctor to complain of breathing difficulties. Which of the following is true?
   a. real GDP decreases as a result of fewer doctor services being provided.
   b. real GDP is not affected.
   c. nominal GDP increases to reflect the improvement in the health of the population.
   d. real GDP will decrease to reflect the decrease in pollution.
   e. nominal GDP does not change and real GDP increases because people's health increases.

7. The calculation of GDP using the income approach EXCLUDES
   a. rent.
   b. interest.
   c. environmental quality.
   d. wages.
   e. profit.

8. Good health and life expectancy are
   a. included in GDP but not in our standard of living.
   b. included in both GDP and in our standard of living.
   c. included in our standard of living but not in GDP.
   d. not included in either our standard of living or in GDP.
   e. sometimes included in GDP if they are large enough changes but are never included in our standard of living.

Short answer and numeric questions

1. What are the parts of a business cycle? What is their order?

2. What general categories of goods and services are omitted from GDP? Why is each omitted?

3. If you cook a hamburger at home, what happens to GDP? If you go to Burger King and purchase a hamburger, what happens to GDP?

SELF TEST ANSWERS

■ CHECKPOINT 5.1

Fill in the blanks

The market value of all the final goods and services produced within a country in a given time period is <u>GDP</u>. <u>Four</u> groups buy the final goods and services produced. Net exports equals the value of <u>exports</u> minus the value of <u>imports</u>. $C + I + G + NX$ equals <u>total expenditure</u> and <u>total income</u>.

True or false

1. False; page 120
2. False; page 121
3. True; page 122
4. True; page 123

Multiple choice

1. a; page 120
2. b; page 120
3. a; page 120
4. d; page 121
5. b; page 121
6. a; page 122

Short answer and numeric questions

1. Intermediate goods or services are not counted in GDP because if they were, they would be double counted. A computer produced by Dell Corp. is included in GDP. But if the Intel chip that is part of the computer is also included in GDP, then the Intel chip is counted twice: once when it is produced by Intel, and again when it is included in the computer produced by Dell; page 120.

2. a. Import; page122.
   b. Consumption expenditure; page 121.
   c. Investment; page 121.
   d. Investment; page 121.
   e. Government expenditure on goods and services; 122.

3. Total expenditure is the amount received by producers of final goods and services from the sales of these goods and services Because firms pay out everything they receive as incomes to the factors of production, total expenditure equals total income. From the viewpoint of firms, the value of production is the cost of production, and the cost of production is equal to income. From the viewpoint of consumers of goods and services, the value of production is the cost of buying the production, which equals expenditure; page 123.

■ CHECKPOINT 5.2

Fill in the blanks

The <u>expenditure</u> approach and the <u>income</u> approach are two methods used to calculate GDP. Expenditure on used goods <u>is not</u> included in GDP. Wages is part of the <u>income</u> approach to calculating GDP. To calculate GDP, depreciation is <u>added to</u> net domestic product at factor cost. GNP equals GDP <u>plus</u> net factor income from abroad. For the United States, the difference between GDP and GNP is <u>small</u>.

True or false

1. True; page 125
2. False; page 126
3. False; page 127
4. False; page 129

Multiple choice

1. b; page 125
2. d; page 125
3. b; page 125
4. a; page 125
5. d; page 127
6. b; page 128

Short answer and numeric questions

1. a. GDP = $6,400, which is the sum of consumption expenditure, investment, government expenditures on goods and services, and net exports. The expenditure approach was used; page 125.

b. Net domestic product at factor cost equals $5,300, the sum of wages plus interest, rent, and profit; page 127.

c. The difference between GDP and net domestic product at factor cost, which is $1,100, equals indirect taxes minus subsidies plus depreciation plus any statistical discrepancy. The statistical discrepancy equals zero. Indirect taxes minus subsidies equals $400, so depreciation equals $700; page 128.

2. To change net domestic product at factor cost to GDP, three sets of adjustments must be made. First, net domestic product at factor cost is measured at firms' costs; to convert costs to equal the market prices paid, taxes must be added and subsidies subtracted. Second, net domestic product does not include depreciation but GDP does. So, depreciation must be added. Finally, any statistical discrepancy must be added or subtracted; page 128.

3. To calculate GNP, net factor income from abroad must be added (or subtracted, if it is negative) from GDP. Then, to calculate disposable personal income, from GNP depreciation and retained profits must be subtracted, transfer payments must be added, and then any statistical discrepancy must be either added or subtracted; page 128.

■ CHECKPOINT 5.3

Fill in the blanks

Real GDP values production during the year using constant prices; nominal GDP values production using prices that prevailed during the year. If the GDP deflator rises, nominal GDP rises more rapidly than real GDP. The GDP deflator equals 100 times nominal GDP divided by real GDP.

True or false

1. False; page131
2. False; page 131

3. True; page 131
4. True; page 132

Multiple choice

1. d; page 131
2. b; page 131
3. a; page 131
4. d; page 131
5. c; page 132
6. a; page 132
7. e; page 132

Short answer and numeric questions

1. a. Nominal GDP = $(100 \times \$10) + (50 \times \$2) =$ $1,100, the sum of expenditure on pizza and expenditure on soda; page 131.

   b. Because 2005 is the base year, real GDP = nominal GDP, so real GDP = $1,100; page 131.

   c. Nominal GDP = $(150 \times \$20) + (75 \times \$4) =$ $3,300, the sum of expenditure on pizza and expenditure on soda; page131.

   d. Using 2005 prices, GDP grew from $1,100 in 2005 to $1,650 in 2006, a percentage increase of 50 percent. Using 2006 prices, GDP grew 50 percent between 2005 and 2006. The average growth is 50 percent, so real GDP in 2006 is 50 percent higher than in 2005, so that real GDP in 2006 is $1,650; page 131.

2. To measure the change in production, it is necessary to use real GDP. Nominal GDP changes whenever production *or* prices change. Real GDP uses constant prices and changes only when production changes; page 131.

3. From one year to the next, real GDP is scaled by the percentage change from the first year to the next. For instance, real GDP in 2005 is linked to real GDP in 2004 by the percentage change from 2004, and real GDP in 2006 in turn is linked to real GDP in 2005 by the percentage change from 2005, and so on. These links are like the links in a chain. They link real GDP in the current year back to the base year and the base year prices; page 132.

4. a. GDP deflator = ($12 trillion ÷ $10 trillion) × 100 = 120; page 132.

   b. GDP deflator = ($12 trillion ÷ $16 trillion) × 100 = 75; page 132.

   c. GDP deflator = ($8 trillion ÷ $4 trillion) × 100 = 290; page 132.

■ CHECKPOINT 5.4

Fill in the blanks

The value of household production is not included in GDP. The value of people's leisure time is not included in GDP. As it is calculated, GDP does not subtract the value of environmental degradation resulting from production. Real GDP does not take into account the extent of a country's political freedom.

True or false

1. True; page 137
2. False; page 137
3. False; page 138
4. True; page 139

Multiple choice

1. c; page 135
2. b; page 136
3. c; page 137
4. b; page 137
5. b; page 137
6. a; page 138
7. c; page 138
8. c; page 139

Short answer and numeric questions

1. The business cycle is made up of the expansion phase, when real GDP is growing; the peak, when real GDP reaches its highest level; the recession phase, when real GDP is falling for at least 6 months; and the trough, when real GDP is at its lowest level. The order of the business cycle is from expansion to peak to recession to trough, and then back to expansion; pages 135-136.

2. Goods and services omitted from GDP are household production, underground production, leisure time, and environmental quality. GDP measures the value of goods and services that are bought in markets. Because household production, leisure time, and environmental quality are not purchased in markets, they are excluded from GDP. Even though underground production frequently is bought in markets, the activity is unreported and is not included in GDP; pages 137-138.

3. If you cook a hamburger at home, the meat you purchased is included in GDP but the production of the hamburger is not included in GDP because it is household production. If you buy a hamburger at Burger King, the production of the hamburger is included in GDP; page 137.

Jobs and Unemployment

Chapter 6

CHAPTER IN PERSPECTIVE

Chapter 6 explores one of the economy's important markets, the labor market, by defining indicators of its performance and explaining how these indicators have changed over time. Chapter 6 also discusses unemployment and its relationship to real GDP.

■ **Define the unemployment rate and other labor market indicators.**

The Current Population Survey is a monthly survey of 60,000 households across the country that is the basis for the nation's labor market statistics. The working-age population is non-institutionalized people aged 16 and over who are not in the U.S. Armed Forces. The labor force is the sum of the employed and unemployed. To be unemployed, a person must have no employment, be available for work, and either have made an effort to find a job during the previous four weeks or be waiting to be recalled to a job from which he or she was laid off. The unemployment rate is the percentage of people in the labor force who are unemployed. The labor force participation rate is the percentage of the working-age population who are members of the labor force. A discouraged worker is a person who is available and willing to work but has not made specific efforts to find a job within the previous four weeks. Full-time workers are those who usually work 35 hours or more a week. Part-time workers are those who usually work less than 35 hours per week. Involuntary part-time workers and part-time workers who are looking for full-time work. Aggregate hours are the total number of hours worked by all the people employed.

■ **Describe the trends and fluctuations in the indicators of labor market performance in the United States.**

From 1965 to 2005, the average unemployment rate was 5.9 percent. The lowest unemployment rates were achieved in the late 1960s and in the late 1990s. In the Great Depression of the 1930s, the U.S. unemployment rate reached 25 percent. From 1965 to 2005, the labor force participation rate had generally an upward trend and is a bit less than 67 percent. The labor force participation rate for men decreased and for women increased. About 17 percent of workers have part-time jobs. The involuntary part-time rate rises during recessions and falls during expansions. Aggregate hours have an upward trend. The average workweek has fallen from 38.5 hours in 1965 to just below 34 hours in 2005.

■ **Describe the sources and types of unemployment, define full employment, and explain the link between unemployment and real GDP.**

People who become unemployed are job losers, job leavers, entrants, or reentrants. People who leave unemployment are hires, recalls, or withdrawals. Unemployment is either frictional (normal labor turnover), structural (changes in necessary job skills or job locations), seasonal (changes in the seasons), or cyclical (changes in the business cycle). The duration of unemployment increases in recessions. Full employment occurs when there is no cyclical unemployment. At full employment, the unemployment rate is the natural unemployment rate. The unemployment rate rises in recessions.

CHECKPOINT 6.1

■ Define the unemployment rate and other labor market indicators.

Quick Review

- *Unemployment rate* The unemployment rate is the percentage of the people in the labor force who are unemployed. That is,

$$\text{Unemployment rate} = \frac{\text{(Unemployed people)}}{\text{(Labor force)}} \times 100$$

- *Labor force participation rate* The labor force participation rate is the percentage of the working-age population who are members of the labor force. It equals

$$\text{Participation rate} = \frac{\text{(Labor force)}}{\text{(Working-age people)}} \times 100$$

- *Aggregate hours* The aggregate hours are the total number of hours worked by all the people employed, both full time and part time, during a year.

Additional Practice Problems 6.1

1. Determine the labor market status of each of the following people:
   a. Don is 21 and a full-time college student.
   b. Shirley works for 20 hours a week as an administrative assistant and is looking for a full-time job.
   c. Clarence was laid off from his job selling keyboards to computer manufacturers and is actively seeking a new job.
   d. Pat quit her job as an account executive 6 months ago but, unable to find a new position, has stopped actively searching.

2. The Bureau of Labor Statistics reported that in June 2005, the labor force was 149.1 million, employment was 141.6 million, and the working-age population was 225.9 million. Average weekly hours for that month were 33.7. Calculate for that month the:
   a. Unemployment rate.
   b. Labor force participation rate.
   c. Aggregate hours worked in a week.

Solutions to Additional Practice Problems 6.1

1a. Don is neither working nor looking for work, so he is not in the labor force.

1b. Shirley is working for pay for more than 1 hour a week, so she is employed and part of the labor force. She is working less than 35 hours a week, so she is a part-time worker. Because she is looking for a full-time job, Shirley is an involuntary part-time worker.

1c. Clarence is actively seeking a new job, so he is unemployed. Clarence is part of the labor force.

1d. Pat is neither working nor actively looking for work, so she is not in the labor force. Pat is a discouraged worker.

2a. The labor force equals the sum of the number of people employed and the number of people unemployed. Subtracting the number employed from the labor force gives the number of unemployed. The labor force is 149.1 million and the number of employed is 141.6 million, so the number unemployed is 149.1 million − 141.6 million, which is 7.5 million. To calculate the unemployment rate, divide the number of unemployed by the labor force and multiply by 100. The unemployment rate equals (7.5 million ÷ 149.1 million) × 100, which is 5.0 percent.

2b. The labor force participation rate is the percentage of the working-age population who are members of the labor force. The labor force participation rate equals the labor force divided by the working-age population all multiplied by 100, which is (149.1 million ÷ 225.9 million) × 100 = 66.0 percent.

2c. In June, 2005, 141.6 million people worked an average of 33.7 hours a week, so the aggregate hours worked in a week is 141.6 million × 33.7 hours, which is 4,771.9 million hours.

■ Self Test 6.1

Fill in the blanks

The ____ (working-age population; labor force) is the total number of people aged 16 years and over and who are not in jail, hospital, or some other form of institutional care. The unemployment rate equals the ____ divided by the ____, all multiplied by 100. The labor force participation rate equals the ____ divided by the ____, all multiplied by 100. Involuntary part-time workers ____ (are; are not) counted as employed. The total number of hours worked in a year by all the people employed are ____.

True or false

1. When contacted by the Bureau of Labor Statistics, Bob states that he has been laid off by Ford Motor Corporation, but expects to be recalled within the next three weeks. Bob is considered part of the labor force.

2. People are counted as unemployed as long as they are working less than 40 hours per week.

3. The unemployment rate decreases when unemployed workers find jobs.

4. The labor force participation rate measures the percentage of the labor force that is employed.

5. If the number of discouraged workers increases, the unemployment rate will increase.

Multiple choice

1. Assume the U.S. population is 300 million. If the working age population is 240 million, 150 million are employed, and 6 million are unemployed, what is the size of the labor force?
   a. 300 million
   b. 240 million
   c. 156 million
   d. 150 million
   e. 144 million

2. To be counted as employed by the BLS, you must have worked for pay ____ in the week before the survey.
   a. at least 1 hour
   b. at least 5 hours
   c. more than 20 hours
   d. 40 hours
   e. None of the above are right because the BLS counts anyone who works volunteer hours at a non-profit institution or school as employed.

3. Which of the following statements about the United States is (are) correct?
   i. The size of the labor force is greater than the number of employed people.
   ii. The size of the labor force is greater than the number of unemployed people.
   iii. The number of unemployed people is greater than the number of employed people.
   a. ii only.
   b. iii only.
   c. ii and iii.
   d. i and ii.
   e. i, ii, and iii.

4. If you are available and willing to work but have not actively looked for work in the past month then you are ____ of the labor force and are ____.
   a. part; counted as unemployed
   b. part; not counted as unemployed
   c. not part; not counted as unemployed
   d. not part; counted as unemployed only if you have had a job within the last 12 months
   e. not part; counted as unemployed regardless of whether or not you have held a job within the last 12 months

5. The unemployment rate equals
   a. (number of people without a job) ÷ (population) × 100.
   b. (number of people unemployed) ÷ (labor force) × 100.
   c. (number of people without a job) ÷ (working-age population) × 100.
   d. (number of people unemployed) ÷ (population) × 100.
   e. (working-age population − number of people employed) ÷ (labor force) × 100.

6. If the working age population is 200 million, 150 million are employed, and 6 million are unemployed, the unemployment rate is ____.
   a. 3.0 percent
   b. 25.0 percent
   c. 4.0 percent
   d. 12.0 percent
   e. 3.8 percent

7. A discouraged worker is
   a. counted as employed by the BLS but is not part of the labor force.
   b. counted as employed by the BLS and is part of the labor force.
   c. counted as unemployed by the BLS and is part of the labor force.
   d. not part of the labor force.
   e. counted as unemployed by the BLS but is not part of the labor force.

8. While in school, Kiki spends 20 hours a week as a computer programmer for Microsoft and studies 30 hours a week.
   a. Kiki is classified as a full-time worker, working 50 hours a week.
   b. Kiki is classified as a part-time worker, working 30 hours a week.
   c. Kiki is classified as a part-time worker, working 20 hours a week.
   d. Because Kiki is a student, she is not classified as working.
   e. Because Kiki is a student, she is classified as a full-time worker, working 20 hours a week at a paid job.

9. Part-time workers for noneconomic reasons are people who
   a. work less than 35 hours a week but would like to work more than 35 hours a week.
   b. work more than 35 hours a week but would like to work less than 35 hours a week.
   c. have lost their jobs within the last four weeks and are seeking another job.
   d. do not want to work full time.
   e. are discouraged workers.

Short answer and numeric questions

Category	Number of people
Total population	2,600
Working-age population	2,000
Not in the labor force	500
Employed	1,300

1. The table above gives the status of the population of a (small!) nation.
   a. What is the size of the labor force?

   b. What is the number of unemployed workers?
   c. What is the unemployment rate?
   d. What is the labor force participation rate?

Category	Number of people
Working-age population	3,000
Unemployed	100
Employed	1,900

2. The table above gives the status of the population of another (small!) nation.
   a. What is the size of the labor force?
   b. What is the unemployment rate?
   c. What is the labor force participation rate?

3. What criteria must a person meet to be counted as unemployed?

4. What is a discouraged worker? Explain why a discouraged worker is not counted as part of the labor force.

5. Are involuntarily part-time workers counted as employed or unemployed?

CHECKPOINT 6.2

■ **Describe the trends and fluctuations in the indicators of labor market performance in the United States.**

Quick Review

- *Labor force participation rate* The percentage of the working-age population who are members of the labor force.

- *Aggregate hours* The total number of hours worked by all the people employed, both full time and part time, during a year.

Additional Practice Problem 6.2

1. How does the unemployment rate change in a recession? Since 1965, when was the unemployment rate the highest and what did it equal?

2. How do aggregate hours change in a recession?

3. Are involuntary part-time workers counted as unemployed when calculating the unemployment rate? If they are, how do they affect the unemployment rate; if they are not, how would their inclusion affect the unemployment rate?

Solutions to Additional Practice Problems 6.2

1. The unemployment rate rises during recessions. Since 1965, the unemployment rate reached its peak of almost 10 percent during the 1982 recession.

2. Aggregate hours fall during a recession.

3. Involuntary part-time workers are *not* counted as unemployed. Indeed, they are counted as employed when computing the unemployment rate. If they were counted as, say, "partially" unemployed, the unemployment rate would increase. And, as Figure 6.4 in the textbook shows, the increase would be larger during recessions when the number of involuntary part-time workers increases.

■ Self Test 6.2

Fill in the blanks

The unemployment rate in 2005 was slightly ____ (higher; lower) than the average between 1965 and 2005. Since 1965, the male labor force participation rate ____ and the female participation rate ____. Since 1975, the percentage of workers who have part-time jobs ____ (rose; fell; barely changed). Since 1965, the total number of labor hours ____ and the length of the average workweek ____.

True or false

1. The average unemployment rate in the United States during the 1970s and 1980s was above the average unemployment rate during the 1960s and 1990s.

2. In recent years the U.S. unemployment rate rose above its 40-year average because of layoffs brought about by the technology that has created the "new economy."

3. Although the female labor force participation rate increased over the last 40 years, it is still less than the male labor force participation rate.

4. The percentage of involuntary part-time workers rises during a recession.

5. Aggregate hours worked in the United States have not grown as quickly as the number of people employed.

Multiple choice

1. From 1965 to 2005, the average unemployment rate in the United States was approximately
   a. 3 percent.
   b. 6 percent.
   c. 12 percent.
   d. 24 percent.
   d. 9 percent.

2. From 1995 to 2005, the unemployment rate in the United States
   a. was always lower than the unemployment rate in Japan.
   b. almost always equaled the unemployment rate in Canada.
   c. generally rose while the unemployment rate in France, Germany, and Italy fell.
   d. was lower than the unemployment rate in France, Germany, and Italy.
   e. was usually higher than the unemployment rate in Canada.

3. Which of the following statements is correct for the United States? Between 1965 and 2005,
   a. both the male and female labor force participation rates increased.
   b. the male labor force participation rate decreased rapidly, the female labor force participation rate decreased slowly, and the two rates are now equal.
   c. the male labor force participation rate decreased and the female labor force participation rate increased.
   d. both the male and female labor force participation rates decreased slowly.
   e. the male labor force participation rate did not change and the female labor force participation rate increased.

4. The total U.S. labor force participation rate increased since 1965 because
   a. the female labor force participation rate increased.
   b. more men are retiring early.
   c. fewer women are attending college.
   d. many blue-collar jobs with rigid work hours have been created in the last decade.
   e. the male labor force participation rate increased.

5. The women's labor force participation rate is
   a. larger in Japan than in the United States.
   b. larger in the United States than in France.
   c. larger in Spain than in the United States.
   d. larger in Spain than in Sweden.
   e. larger in the United States than in Sweden, Canada, or the United Kingdom.

6. Part-time workers were about ____ of all workers in 1975 and were about ____ in 2005.
   a. 16 percent; 50 percent
   b. 16 percent; 16 percent
   c. 2 percent; 4 percent
   d. 10 percent; 40 percent
   e. 35 percent; 22 percent

7. In the United States in 2005, involuntary part-time workers
   a. account for more than 66 percent of all part-time workers.
   b. account for between 36 percent and 65 percent of all part-time workers.
   c. account for between 5 percent and 10 percent of all part-time workers.
   d. account for between 11 percent and 20 percent of all part-time workers.
   e. account for between 21 percent and 35 percent of all part-time workers.

8. In the United States since 1965, aggregate hours have ____ and average weekly hours per worker have ____.
   a. risen; risen
   b. risen; fallen
   c. fallen; risen
   d. fallen; fallen
   e. risen; not changed

Short answer and numeric questions

1. During a recession, what happens to:
   a. the unemployment rate?
   b. aggregate hours?
   c. average weekly hours?

2. Compare the U.S. unemployment rate between 1990 to 2005 to the unemployment rate in
   a. Japan.
   b. Canada.

3. How does the unemployment rate during the Great Depression compare with more recent unemployment rates?

CHECKPOINT 6.3

■ **Describe the sources and types of unemployment, define full employment, and explain the link between unemployment and real GDP.**

Quick Review

- *Frictional unemployment* Unemployment that arises from normal labor market turnover.
- *Structural unemployment* Unemployment that arises when changes in technology or international competition change the skills needed to perform jobs or change the location of jobs.
- *Seasonal unemployment* Unemployment that arises because of seasonal weather patterns.
- *Cyclical unemployment* Unemployment that fluctuates over the business cycle, rising during a recession and falling during an expansion.

Additional Practice Problem 6.3

1. Each of the following people is actively seeking work. Classify each as either frictionally, structurally, seasonally, or cyclically unemployed:
   a. Perry lost his job because his company went bankrupt when faced with increased foreign competition.

b. Sam did not like his boss and so he quit his job.

c. Sherry just graduated from college.

d. Hanna lost her job selling cotton candy on the boardwalk when winter arrived and the tourists left.

e. Jose was fired when his company downsized in response to a recession.

f. Pat was laid off from her job at the Gap because customers decided they liked the fashions at JCPenney better.

Solution to Additional Practice Problem 6.3

1a. Perry is structurally unemployed.

1b. Sam is frictionally unemployed.

1c. Sherry is frictionally unemployed.

1d. Hanna is seasonally unemployed.

1e. Jose is cyclically unemployed.

1f. Pat is frictionally unemployed.

■ Self Test 6.3

Fill in the blanks

People who become unemployed are ____, ____, or ____. Unemployed people who stop looking for jobs are ____ (recalls; job losers; withdrawals). The normal unemployment from labor market turnover is called ____ unemployment, and the unemployment that fluctuates over the business cycle is called ____ unemployment. When ____ (frictional; structural; cyclical) unemployment equals zero, the economy is experiencing ____ employment. When potential GDP exceeds real GDP, the unemployment rate ____ (is higher than; is lower than) the natural unemployment rate.

True or false

1. If Amazon.Com Inc. must lay off 20 percent of its workers, the laid-off workers would be considered job leavers.

2. The only way to end a spell of unemployment is by finding a job.

3. The unemployment that arises when technology changes is termed technological unemployment.

4. When the U.S. economy is at full employment, the unemployment rate is zero.

5. Potential GDP is the level of real GDP produced when the economy is at full employment.

Multiple choice

1. Generally, most unemployed workers are ____; the fewest number of unemployed workers are ____.
   a. job losers; job leavers
   b. job leavers; reentrants and entrants
   c. job losers; reentrants and entrants
   d. reentrants and entrants; job leavers
   e. job leavers; job losers

2. Reentrants are people who
   a. are laid off.
   b. leave the labor force voluntarily.
   c. recently left school.
   d. have returned to the labor force.
   e. voluntarily leave their job.

3. Tommy graduates from college and starts to look for a job. Tommy is
   a. frictionally unemployed.
   b. structurally unemployed.
   c. cyclically unemployed.
   d. seasonally unemployed.
   e. not unemployed because he is looking for work.

4. If an entire industry relocates to a foreign country, the relocation leads to a higher rate of ____ unemployment.
   a. frictional
   b. structural
   c. seasonal
   d. cyclical
   e. structural and cyclical

5. Of the following, who is cyclically unemployed?
   a. Casey, who lost his job because the technology changed so that he was no longer needed.
   b. Katrina, an assistant manager who quit her job to search for a better job closer to home.
   c. Kathy, a steelworker who was laid off but has stopped looking for a new job because she can't find a new job.
   d. David, a new car salesman who lost his job because the economy went into a recession.
   e. Samantha, who worked part-time in JCPenney to help with the Christmas rush but was laid off in January.

6. In the United States, the highest unemployment rates occur among
   a. white female teenagers.
   b. black male teenagers.
   c. white females aged 20 and over.
   d. black males aged 20 and over.
   e. white males aged 20 and over.

7. When the economy is at full employment,
   a. the natural unemployment rate equals zero.
   b. the amount of cyclical unemployment equals zero.
   c. the amount of structural unemployment equals zero.
   d. there is no unemployment.
   e. the amount of frictional unemployment equals zero.

8. When the unemployment rate is less than the natural unemployment rate, real GDP is ____ potential GDP.
   a. greater than
   b. less than
   c. unrelated to
   d. equal to
   e. not comparable to

Short answer and numeric questions
1. What are sources of unemployment? How does unemployment end?
2. What are the four types of unemployment?
3. How does the average duration of unemployment change during a recession?
4. What is the relationship between full employment, the natural unemployment rate, and potential GDP?
5. If the unemployment rate exceeds the natural unemployment rate, what is the relationship between real GDP and potential GDP?

SELF TEST ANSWERS

■ CHECKPOINT 6.1

Fill in the blanks

The <u>working-age population</u> is the total number of people aged 16 years and over and who are not in jail, hospital, or some other form of institutional care. The unemployment rate equals the <u>number of people unemployed</u> divided by the <u>labor force</u>, all multiplied by 100. The labor force participation rate equals the <u>labor force</u> divided by the <u>working-age population</u>, all multiplied by 100. Involuntary part-time workers <u>are</u> counted as employed. The total number of hours worked in a year by all the people employed are <u>aggregate hours</u>.

True or false

1. True; page 146
2. False; page 146
3. True; page 147
4. False; page 148
5. False; page 148

Multiple choice

1. c; page 146
2. a; page 146
3. c; page 146
4. c; page 146
5. b; page 147
6. e; page 147
7. d; page 148
8. c; page 148
9. d; page 148

Short answer and numeric questions

1. a. 1,500; page 146.
   b. 200; page 146.
   c. 13.3 percent; page 147.
   d. 75.0 percent; page 148.
2. a. 2,000; page 146.
   b. 5.0 percent; page 147.
   c. 66.7 percent; page 148.
3. The person must be without employment, available for work, and actively searching or waiting to be recalled to a job from which he or she was laid off; page 146.
4. A discouraged worker is an unemployed worker who is not actively looking for a job. A discouraged worker is not unemployed because the worker is not actively seeking a job; page 148.
5. Employed; page 148.

■ CHECKPOINT 6.2

Fill in the blanks

The unemployment rate in 2005 was slightly <u>lower</u> than the average between 1965 and 2005. Since 1965, the male labor force participation rate <u>fell</u> and the female participation rate <u>rose</u>. Since 1975, the percentage of workers who have part-time jobs <u>barely changed</u>. Since 1965, the total number of labor hours <u>rose</u> and the length of the average workweek <u>fell</u>.

True or false

1. True; page 151
2. False; page 151
3. True; pages 152-153
4. True; page 154
5. True; page 154

Multiple choice

1. b; page 151
2. d; page 153
3. c; pages 152-153
4. a; pages 152-153
5. b; page 155
6. b; page 154
7. d; page 154
8. b; pages 154-155

Short answer and numeric questions

1. a. The unemployment rate rises; page 151.
   b. Aggregate hours fall; page 155.
   c. Average weekly hours falls; page 155.
2. a. The Japanese unemployment rate between 1999 and 2001 was slightly greater than the U.S. unemployment rate. During the

other years, the Japanese unemployment rate was slightly lower; page 153.

b. The Canadian unemployment rate has mirrored changes in the U.S. unemployment rate but has been about 4 percentage points higher; page 153.

3. The unemployment rate during the Great Depression was *much* higher, reaching near 25 percent, than the recent unemployment rate, which reached its peak of approximately 10 percent in 1982; pages 152.

■ CHECKPOINT 6.3

Fill in the blanks

People who become unemployed are job losers, job leavers, or entrants and reentrants. Unemployed people who stop looking for jobs are withdrawals. The normal unemployment from labor market turnover is called frictional unemployment, and the unemployment that fluctuates over the business cycle is called cyclical unemployment. When cyclical unemployment equals zero, the economy is experiencing full employment. When potential GDP exceeds real GDP, the unemployment rate is higher than the natural unemployment rate.

True or false

1. False; page 157
2. False; page 158
3. False; page 159
4. False; page 161
5. True; pages 163

Multiple choice

1. a; pages 157-158
2. d; page 157
3. a; page 159
4. b; page 159
5. d; page 160
6. b; page 161
7. b; page 161
8. a; page 163

Short answer and numeric questions

1. Sources of unemployment are job losers, job leavers, entrants, and reentrants. People who end a period of unemployment rate are hires, recalls, or withdrawals; pages 157-158.

2. Unemployment is either frictional, structural, seasonal, or cyclical; pages 158-160.

3. The average duration of unemployment (the length of time a person is unemployed) rises in a recession; page 160.

4. When the economy is at full employment, the unemployment rate is the natural unemployment rate. When the economy is at full employment, the amount of GDP produced is potential GDP; pages 161-163.

5. If the unemployment rate exceeds the natural unemployment rate, real GDP is less than potential GDP; page 163.

The CPI and the Cost of Living

Chapter 7

Chapter 7 explores how the cost of living is measured. It discusses the Consumer Price Index, CPI, explains how it is constructed, and examines its biases. Chapter 7 demonstrates how to adjust money values for changes in the price level. In addition, Chapter 7 discusses the real wage rate and the real interest rate, and also shows how both are calculated.

■ **Explain what the Consumer Price Index (CPI) is and how it is calculated.**

The Consumer Price Index (CPI) measures the average of the prices paid by urban consumers for a fixed market basket of consumer goods and services. The CPI compares the cost of the fixed market basket of goods and services at one time with the cost of the fixed market basket in the reference base period, currently 1982–1984. The CPI in the base period is 100. If the CPI is now 150, it costs 50 percent more to buy the same goods and services than it cost in the base period. To construct the CPI market basket, households are surveyed on what they buy. Then, each month the Bureau of Labor Statistics checks the prices of the 80,000 goods and services in the basket. To calculate the CPI, the cost of the market basket using current prices is divided by the cost of the basket using base period prices and the result is multiplied by 100. The inflation rate is the percentage change in the price level from one year to the next and is equal to [(CPI in current year – CPI in previous year) ÷ (CPI in previous year)] × 100.

■ **Explain the limitations of the CPI as a measure of the cost of living.**

The CPI has four sources of bias that lead to an inaccurate measure of the cost of living. These biases are the new goods bias (new goods replace old goods), the quality change bias (goods and services increase in quality), the commodity substitution bias (changes in relative prices lead consumers to change the items they buy), and the outlet substitution bias (consumers switch to shopping more often in discount stores). The overall CPI bias has been estimated to overstate inflation by 1.1 percentage points per year. The CPI bias distorts private contracts and increases government outlays. The GDP deflator is constructed using, in part, the CPI, and so the GDP deflator inherits the same biases as the CPI. The GDP deflator is not a good measure of the cost of living because it includes prices of goods and services households never buy.

■ **Adjust money values for inflation and calculate real wage rates and real interest rates.**

Comparing values measured in dollars in different years is misleading if the value of money changes. To make the comparison, the nominal values must be converted to real values. The real wage rate measures the quantity of goods and services that an hour's work can buy and equals the nominal wage rate divided by the CPI and multiplied by 100. The real interest rate equals the nominal interest rate minus the inflation rate.

CHECKPOINT 7.1

■ **Explain what the Consumer Price Index (CPI) is and how it is calculated.**

Quick Review

- *CPI market basket* The goods and services in the CPI and the relative importance attached to each of them.
- *CPI formula* The CPI equals:

$$\frac{\text{Cost of CPI basket at current period prices}}{\text{Cost of CPI basket at base period prices}} \times 100.$$

- *Inflation rate* The inflation rate equals:

$$\frac{(\text{CPI in current year} - \text{CPI in previous year})}{\text{CPI in previous year}} \times 100.$$

Additional Practice Problem 7.1

Item	Quantity (2005)	Price (2005)	Quantity (2006)	Price (2006)
Limes	20	$1.00	15	$1.00
Biscuits	30	$1.00	45	$0.75
Rum	10	$10.00	8	$11.00

1. A Consumer Expenditure Survey in Scurvy shows that people consume only limes, biscuits, and rum. The Consumer Expenditure Survey for both 2005 and 2006 are in the table above. The reference base year is 2005.
   a. What and how much is in the CPI market basket?
   b. What did the CPI market basket cost in 2005? What was the CPI in 2005?
   c. What did the CPI market basket cost in 2006? What was the CPI in 2006?
   d. What was the inflation rate between 2005 and 2006?

Solution to Additional Practice Problem 7.1

1a. The market basket is 20 limes, 30 biscuits, and 10 rums, the quantities consumed in the base year of 2005.

1b. In 2005 the market basket cost 20 × $1.00 + 30 × $1.00 + 10 × $10.00 = $150. Because this is the reference base year, the CPI = 100.0.

1c. In 2006 the market basket cost 20 × $1.00 + 30 × $0.75 + 10 × $11.00 = $152.50. The CPI in 2006 is equal to ($152.50) ÷ ($150.00) × 100, which is 101.7.

1d. The inflation rate equals [(101.7 − 100.0) ÷ 100] × 100 = 1.7 percent.

■ **Self Test 7.1**

Fill in the blanks

The ____, also called the CPI, is a measure of the average of the prices paid by urban consumers for a fixed market basket of consumer goods and services. In the base reference period, the CPI equals ____. Each ____ (month; year) the Bureau of Labor Statistics checks the prices of the goods and services in the CPI basket. The CPI equals the cost of the CPI basket at current prices ____ (plus; minus; divided by) the cost of the CPI basket at base period prices, all multiplied by 100. To measure changes in the cost of living, the ____ (inflation rate; CPI in the base reference period) is used.

True or false

1. In the reference base period, the CPI equals 1.0.

2. The CPI market basket is changed from one month to the next.

3. If the cost of the CPI basket at current period prices equals $320, then the CPI equals 320.

4. If the cost of the CPI basket at current period prices exceeds the cost of the CPI basket at base period prices, the inflation rate between these two periods is positive.

5. If the CPI increases from 110 to 121, the inflation rate is 11 percent.

Multiple choice

1. The CPI is reported once every
   a. year.
   b. quarter.
   c. month.
   d. week.
   e. other year.

2. The Consumer Price Index (CPI) measures
   a. the prices of a few consumer goods and services.
   b. the prices of those consumer goods and services that increased in price.
   c. the average of the prices paid by urban consumers for a fixed market basket of goods and services.
   d. consumer confidence in the economy.
   e. the average of the costs paid by businesses to produce a fixed market basket of consumer goods and services.

3. If a country has a CPI of 105.0 last year and a CPI of 102.0 this year, then
   a. the average prices of goods and services increased between last year and this year.
   b. the average prices of goods and services decreased between last year and this year.
   c. the average quality of goods and services decreased between last year and this year.
   d. there was an error when calculating the CPI this year.
   e. the quantity of consumer goods and services produced decreased between last year and this year.

4. The period for which the Consumer Price Index is defined to equal 100 is called the
   a. reference base period.
   b. base year.
   c. starting point.
   d. zero period.
   e. beginning period.

5. The good or service given the most weight in the CPI basket when calculating the CPI is
   a. food and beverages.
   b. taxes.
   c. housing.
   d. medical care.
   e. recreation.

6. Suppose a basket of consumer goods and services costs $180 using the base period prices, and the same basket of goods and services costs $300 using the current period prices. The CPI for the current year period equals
   a. 166.7.
   b. 66.7.
   c. 160.0.
   d. 60.0.
   e. 300.0.

7. Suppose the CPI for 1980 was 82.3 and for 1981 was 90.9. Based on this information, we can calculate that the inflation rate in 1981 was
   a. 10.4 percent.
   b. 8.6 percent.
   c. 90.9 percent.
   d. 82.3 percent.
   e. 9.09 percent.

8. In the United States since 1975, on average the inflation rate in the last ten years was
   a. higher than between 1975 to 1980.
   b. higher than in the 1980s.
   c. lower than between 1975 to 1980.
   d. much higher than between 1985 to 1995.
   e. negative.

Short answer and numeric questions

Item	Quantity (2005)	Price (2005)	Quantity (2006)	Price (2006)
Pizza	10	$10.00	15	$10.00
Burritos	20	$1.00	25	$0.75
Rice	30	$0.50	20	$1.00

1. The table above gives the expenditures of households in the small nation of Studenvia. In Studenvia, 2005 is the reference base period.
   a. What is the cost of the CPI basket in 2005?
   b. What is the cost of the CPI basket in 2006?
   c. What is the CPI in 2005?
   d. What is the CPI in 2006?
   e. What is the inflation rate in 2006?

2. Suppose the CPI was 100.0 in 2002, 110.0 in 2003, 121.0 in 2004, and 133.1 in 2005. What is the inflation rate in 2003, 2004, and 2005?

3. If the price level rises slowly, is the inflation rate positive or negative? Why?

CHECKPOINT 7.2

■ **Explain the limitations of the CPI as a measure of the cost of living.**

Quick Review

- *Commodity substitution bias* People cut back on their purchases of items that become relatively more costly and increase their consumption of items that become relatively less costly.

Additional Practice Problems 7.2

1. Nowadays when households buy broccoli, they discard some of it because it is bruised. Suppose 20 percent is discarded. Now new, genetically engineered broccoli is developed that does not bruise so that all the broccoli that is purchased can be used. People prefer the new broccoli, so they switch to buying the new broccoli. If the price of the new broccoli is 10 percent higher than the old, what actually happens to the CPI and what should happen to the CPI?

2. When the price of textbook is $95 a book, Anthony buys his books at the bookstore closest to him. When textbooks rise in price to $125 a book at that store, Anthony drives several miles away to a store where the books are sold for only $110. How does Anthony's decision affect the CPI?

Solutions to Additional Practice Problems 7.2

1. With the introduction of the new broccoli, the CPI will rise because the new broccoli's price is higher (10 percent) than the old broccoli. But, the CPI should actually decrease because people pay only 10 percent more for 20 percent more (useable) broccoli. This problem illus-

trates how the quality change bias can bias the CPI upwards.

2. Anthony's decision reflects outlet substitution. When the price of a good rises, consumers, such as Anthony, switch the stores from which they buy goods and services to less expensive outlets. But the CPI, as constructed, does not take into account this point. The CPI will record that the price of textbooks rose by $30, from $95 to $125. For Anthony, however, the true increase in the cost was only $15, from $95 to $110 a book, plus the cost of his time and gasoline to get to the new store. The outlet substitution bias means that the CPI overstates the true rise in the cost of living.

■ **Self Test 7.2**

Fill in the blanks

The sources of bias in the CPI as a measure of the cost of living are the ____, ____, ____, and ____. The Boskin Commission concluded that the CPI ____ (overstates; understates) inflation by ____ (1.1; 2.2; 3.3) percentage points a year. The CPI bias leads to ____ (an increase; a decrease) in government outlays.

True or false

1. The CPI is a biased measure of the cost of living.

2. Commodity substitution bias refers to the ongoing replacement of old goods by new goods.

3. The bias in the CPI is estimated to overstate inflation by approximately 1.1 percentage points a year.

4. The CPI bias can distort private contracts.

5. Inflation measured using the GDP deflator is generally lower than inflation measured using the CPI.

Multiple choice

1. All of the following create bias in the CPI <u>EXCEPT</u> the
   a. new goods bias.
   b. outlet substitution bias.
   c. commodity substitution bias.
   d. GDP deflator bias.
   e. quality change bias.

2. An example of the new goods bias in the calculation of the CPI is a price increase in
   a. butter relative to margarine.
   b. an MP3 player relative to a Walkman.
   c. a 2006 Honda Civic LX relative to a 2001 Honda Civic LX.
   d. textbooks bought through the campus bookstore relative to textbooks bought through Amazon.com.
   e. a Caribbean cruise for a couple who has never been on a cruise before.

3. Over the last decade, the price of a dishwasher has remained relatively constant while the quality of dishwashers has improved. The CPI
   a. is adjusted monthly to reflect the improvement in quality.
   b. is increased monthly to reflect the increased quality of dishwashers.
   c. has an upward bias if it is not adjusted to take account of the higher quality.
   d. has an upward bias because it does not reflect the increased production of dishwashers.
   e. should not take account of any quality changes because it is a price index not a quality index.

4. Joe buys chicken and beef. If the price of beef rises and the price of chicken does not change, Joe will
   a. buy more beef and help create a new goods bias for the CPI.
   b. buy more chicken and help create a commodity substitution bias for the CPI.
   c. buy the same quantity of beef and chicken and help create a commodity substitution bias for the CPI.
   d. buy less chicken and beef and thus help create a quality change bias for the CPI.
   e. buy more chicken and help eliminate the commodity substitution bias for the CPI.

5. The CPI bias was estimated by the Congressional Advisory Commission on the Consumer Price Index as
   a. understating the actual inflation rate by about 5 percentage points a year.
   b. understating the actual inflation rate by more than 5 percentage points a year.
   c. overstating the actual inflation rate by about 1 percentage point a year.
   d. overstating the actual inflation rate by more than 5 percentage points a year.
   e. understating the actual inflation rate by about 1 percentage point a year.

6. A consequence of the CPI bias is that it
   a. decreases government outlays.
   b. increases international trade.
   c. reduces outlet substitution bias.
   d. distorts private contracts.
   e. means that it is impossible to measure the inflation rate.

7. The fact that the CPI is a biased measure of the inflation rate means government outlays will
   a. increase at a faster rate than the actual inflation rate.
   b. increase at the same rate as the actual inflation rate.
   c. increase at a slower rate than the actual inflation rate.
   d. sometimes increase faster and sometimes increase slower than the actual inflation rate depending on whether the actual inflation rate exceeds 1.1 percent per year or is less than 1.1 percent per year.
   e. None of the above because the bias in inflation measured using the CPI has nothing to do with government outlays.

8. If we compare the recent measurements of inflation as recorded by the CPI and the GDP deflator we find that the
   a. two measures fluctuate together.
   b. CPI has consistently been at least 5 percentage points above the GDP deflator.
   c. GDP deflator has consistently been at least 5 percentage points above the CPI.
   d. two measures give very different inflation rates for most years.
   e. the CPI inflation rate was always positive but the GPI deflator inflation rate was sometimes negative.

Short answer and numeric questions

1. What are the sources of bias in the CPI? Briefly explain each.

2. Once you graduate, you move to a new town and sign a long-term lease on a townhouse. You agree to pay $1,000 a month rent and to change the monthly rent annually by the percentage change in the CPI. For the next 4 years, the CPI increases 5 percent each year. What will you pay in monthly rent for the second, third, and fourth years of your lease? Suppose the CPI overstates the inflation rate by 1 percentage point a year. If the CPI bias was eliminated, what would you pay in rent for the second, third, and fourth years?

CHECKPOINT 7.3

■ **Adjust money values for inflation and calculate real wage rates and real interest rates.**

Quick Review

- *Real wage rate* The real wage rate equals the nominal wage rate divided by the CPI and multiplied by 100.
- *Real interest rate* The real interest rate equals the nominal interest rate minus the inflation rate.

Additional Practice Problems 7.3

Year	Minimum wage (dollars per hour)	CPI
1955	0.75	26.7
1965	1.25	31.6
1975	2.10	56.7
1985	3.35	107.5
1995	4.25	152.4
2005	5.15	194.1

1. The table above shows the minimum wage and the CPI for six different years. The reference base period is 1982–1984.
   a. Calculate the real minimum wage in each year in 1982–1984 dollars.
   b. In which year was the minimum wage the highest in real terms?
   c. In which year was the minimum wage the lowest in real terms?

2. Suppose Sally has saved $1,000 dollars. Sally wants a 3 percent real interest rate on her savings. What nominal interest rate would she need to receive if the inflation rate is 7 percent?

Solutions to Additional Practice Problems 7.3

1a. Using the CPI to adjust nominal values to real values is a key use of the CPI. Keep in mind that to convert a nominal price (such as the nominal wage rate) into a real price (such as the real wage rate), you divide by the CPI and multiply by 100, but to convert the nominal interest rate into the real interest rate, you subtract the inflation rate.

Year	Real minimum wage (1982-1984 dollars per hour)
1955	2.81
1965	3.96
1975	3.70
1985	3.12
1995	2.79
2005	2.65

To convert the nominal minimum wages in the table to real prices, divide the price by the CPI in that year and then multiply by 100. In 1955, the nominal minimum wage gas was $0.75 an hour and the CPI was 26.7, so the real minimum wage is ($0.75 ÷ 26.7) × 100 = $2.81. The rest of the real minimum wages in the table above are calculated similarly.

1b. In real terms, the minimum wage was highest in 1975 when it equaled $3.70.

1c. In real terms, the minimum wage was the lowest in 2005 when it equaled $2.65.

2. The real interest rate equals the nominal interest rate minus the inflation rate. Rearranging this formula shows that the nominal interest rate equals the real interest rate plus the inflation rate. To get a 3 percent real interest rate with a 7 percent inflation rate, Sally needs the nominal interest rate to be equal to 3 percent plus 7 percent, or 10 percent.

■ Self Test 7.3

Fill in the blanks

The nominal wage rate is the average hourly wage rate measured in ____ (current; reference base year) dollars. The real wage rate is the average hourly wage rate measured in dollars of the ____ (current; given base) year. The real wage rate equals the nominal wage rate (plus; times; divided by) the CPI multiplied by 100. The real interest rate equals the nominal interest rate ____ (plus; minus; divided by) the ____ (CPI; inflation rate).

True or false

1. The CPI was 171 in 2000 and 24.4 in 1950, so the price level in 2000 was 7 times higher than what it was in 1950.

2. Real GDP equals nominal GDP divided by the CPI, multiplied by 100.

3. A change in the real wage rate measures the change in the goods and services that an hour's work can buy.

4. The nominal interest rate is the percentage return on a loan expressed in dollars; the real interest rate is the percentage return on a loan expressed in purchasing power.

5. If the nominal interest rate is 8 percent a year and the inflation rate is 4 percent a year, then the real interest rate is 4 percent a year.

Multiple choice

1. In 2005, in New York, apples cost $1.49 a pound. Suppose the CPI was 120 in 2005 and 140 in 2006. If there is no change in the real value of an apple in the year 2006, how much would a pound of apples sell for in 2006?
   a. $2.74
   b. $1.69
   c. $1.66
   d. $1.74
   e. $1.28

2. In 1970, the CPI was 39 and in 2000 it was 172. A local phone call cost $0.10 in 1970. What is the price of this phone call in 2000 dollars?
   a. $1.42
   b. $0.39
   c. $1.72
   d. $0.44 —
   e. $0.23

3. The nominal wage rate is the
   a. minimum hourly wage that a company can legally pay a worker.
   b. average hourly wage rate measured in the dollars of a given reference base year.
   c. minimum hourly wage rate measured in the dollars of a given reference base year.
   d. average hourly wage rate measured in current dollars.
   e. wage rate after inflation has been adjusted out of it.

4. In 2001, the average starting salary for an economics major was $29,500. If the CPI was 147.5, the real salary was
   a. $200.00 an hour.
   b. $20,000.
   c. $35,000.
   d. $43,513.
   e. $14,750.

5. If we compare the nominal wage versus the real wage in the United States since 1975, we see that the
   a. real wage rate increased steadily.
   b. nominal wage rate increased and the real wage rate did not change by very much.
   c. real wage rate increased more than the nominal wage rate.
   d. nominal wage rate increased at an uneven pace whereas the increase in the real wage rate was steady and constant.
   e. nominal wage rate and real wage rate both decreased.

6. The real interest rate is equal to the
   a. nominal interest rate plus the inflation rate.
   b. nominal interest rate minus the inflation rate.
   c. nominal interest rate times the inflation rate.
   d. nominal interest rate divided by the inflation rate.
   e. inflation rate minus the nominal interest rate.

7. You borrow at a nominal interest rate of 10 percent. If the inflation rate is 4 percent, then the real interest rate is
   a. the $10 in interest you have to pay.
   b. 16 percent.
   c. 2.5 percent.
   d. 6 percent.
   e. 14 percent.

8. In the United States between 1965 and 2005, the
   a. nominal and real interest rates both decreased in almost every year.
   b. nominal and real interest rates were both constant in almost every year.
   c. real interest rate was constant in most years and the nominal interest rate fluctuated.
   d. nominal interest rate was greater than the real interest rate in all years.
   e. nominal interest rate was greater than the real interest rate in about one half of the years and the real interest rate was greater than the nominal interest rate in the other half of the years.

Short answer and numeric questions

Job	Salary (dollars per year)	CPI
Job A	20,000	105
Job B	25,000	120
Job C	34,000	170

1. Often the cost of living varies from state to state or from large city to small city. After you graduate, suppose you have job offers in 3 locales. The nominal salary and the CPI for each job is given in the table above.
   a. Which job offers the highest real salary?
   b. Which job offers the lowest real salary?
   c. In determining which job to accept, what is more important: the real salary or the nominal salary? Why?

Year	Real interest rate (percent per year)	Nominal interest rate (percent per year)	Inflation rate (percent per year)
1999	____	10	5
2000	____	6	1
2001	4	6	____
2002	5	____	3

2. The table above gives the real interest rate, nominal interest rate, and inflation rate for various years in a foreign country. Complete the table.

3. In 1980, the nominal interest rate was 12 percent. In 2005, the nominal interest rate was 7 percent. From this information, can you determine if you would rather have saved $1,000 in 1980 or 2005? Explain your answer.

SELF TEST ANSWERS

■ CHECKPOINT 7.1

Fill in the blanks

The <u>Consumer Price Index</u>, also called the CPI, is a measure of the average of the prices paid by urban consumers for a fixed market basket of consumer goods and services. In the base reference period, the CPI equals <u>100</u>. Each <u>month</u> the Bureau of Labor Statistics checks the prices of the goods and services in the CPI basket. The CPI equals the cost of the CPI basket at current prices <u>divided by</u> the cost of the CPI basket at base period prices, all multiplied by 100. To measure changes in the cost of living, the <u>inflation rate</u> is used.

True or false
1. False; page 170
2. False; page 170
3. False; page 173
4. True; page 173
5. False; page 173

Multiple choice
1. c; page 170
2. c; page 170
3. b; page 170
4. a; page 170
5. c; page 171
6. a; page 173
7. a; page 173
8. c; pages 174

Short answer and numeric questions
1. a. The cost is $135; page 172.
   b. The cost is $145. The quantities used to calculate this cost are the base period, 2005, quantities; page 172.
   c. The CPI is 100; page 173.
   d. The CPI is 107.4; page 173.
   e. The inflation rate is 7.4 percent; page 173.
2. The inflation rate for each year is 10 percent; page 173.

3. Whenever the price level rises, the inflation rate is positive. If the price level rises slowly, the inflation rate is small; if the price level rises rapidly, the inflation rate is large; page 174.

■ CHECKPOINT 7.2

Fill in the blanks

The sources of bias in the CPI as a measure of the cost of living are the <u>new goods bias</u>, <u>quality change bias</u>, <u>commodity substitution bias</u>, and <u>outlet substitution bias</u>. The Boskin Commission concluded that the CPI <u>overstates</u> inflation by <u>1.1</u> percentage points a year. The CPI bias leads to <u>an increase</u> in government outlays.

True or false
1. True; page 176
2. False; page 177
3. True; page 177
4. True; page 178
5. True; pages 179

Multiple choice
1. d; page 176
2. b; page 176
3. c; pages 176-177
4. b; page 177
5. c; page 177
6. d; pages 177-178
7. a; page 178
8. a; page 179

Short answer and numeric questions
1. There are four sources of bias in the CPI: the new goods bias, the quality change bias, the commodity substitution bias, and the outlet substitution bias. The new goods bias refers to the fact that new goods replace old goods. The quality change bias occurs because at times price increases in existing goods are the result of increased quality. The commodity substitution bias occurs because consumers

buy fewer goods and services when their prices rise compared to other, comparable products. The fixed market basket approach taken in the CPI's calculation cannot take account of this method by which households offset higher prices. Finally, the outlet substitution bias refers to the fact that when prices rise, people shop more frequently at discount stores to take advantage of the lower prices in these stores; pages 176-177.

2. The monthly rent increases by 5 percent each year. For the second year the monthly rent equals $1,000 × 1.05, which is $1,050. For the third year the monthly rent equals $1,050 × 1.05, which is $1,102.50. And for the fourth year the monthly rent equals $1,102.50 × 1.05, which is $1,157.63. If the CPI bias was eliminated, the monthly rent would increase by 4 percent each year. The monthly rent would be $1,040 for the second year, $1,081.60 for the third year, and $1,124.86 for the third year; page 178.

■ CHECKPOINT 7.3

Fill in the blanks

The nominal wage rate is the average hourly wage rate measured in <u>current</u> dollars. The real wage rate is the average wage rate measured in dollars of the <u>given base</u> year. The real wage rate equals the nominal wage rate <u>divided by</u> the CPI multiplied by 100. The real interest rate equals the nominal interest rate <u>minus</u> the <u>inflation rate</u>.

True or false

1. True; page 181
2. False; page 181
3. True; page 183
4. True; page 184
5. True; page 184

Multiple choice

1. d; page 181
2. d; page 181
3. d; page 182
4. b; page 182
5. b; page 183
6. b; page 184
7. d; page 184
8. d; page 185

Short answer and numeric questions

1. a. The real salary equals (nominal salary ÷ CPI) times 100. The real salary is $19,048 for Job A, $20,833 for Job B, and $20,000 for Job C. The real salary is highest for Job B; page182.

   b. The real salary is lowest for Job A; page 182.

   c. The real salary is more important than the nominal salary because the real salary measures the quantity of goods and services you will be able to buy; pages 182-183.

Year	Real interest rate (percent per year)	Nominal interest rate (percent per year)	Inflation rate (percent per year)
1999	<u>5</u>	10	5
2000	<u>5</u>	6	1
2001	4	6	<u>2</u>
2002	5	<u>8</u>	3

2. The completed table is above; page184.

3. You cannot determine when you would rather have been a saver. Savers are interested in the real interest rate because the real interest rate is the percentage return expressed in purchasing power. Without knowing the inflation rate, there is not enough data given to compute the real interest rate; page 184.

Potential GDP and the Natural Unemployment Rate

Chapter 8

Chapter 8 studies the forces that determine potential GDP and the influences on the natural unemployment rate. It begins by introducing different macroeconomic schools of thought. The two main schools of thought are classical macroeconomics and Keynesian macroeconomics. Classical macroeconomics asserts that markets work well and, while the economy will fluctuate, no government intervention is needed. But classical macroeconomics couldn't explain why the Great Depression lasted so long. Keynesian economics was borne during the Great Depression and asserted that depressions were the result of too little spending. Keynesian economics called for government intervention to assist the economy. But it focused exclusively on the short run. The new macroeconomics developed in the 1970s. This theory focuses on how macroeconomic outcomes are the result of microeconomic choices. Most economists now believe that maintaining economic growth is more important than eliminating business cycle fluctuations because the Lucas wedge (the cost of slower economic growth) is much larger than Okun gaps (the cost of business cycle recessions).

■ **Explain the forces that determine potential GDP and the real wage rate and employment at full employment.**

Potential GDP is the amount of GDP that would be produced if the economy were at full employment. The production function shows the maximum quantity of real GDP that can be produced as the quantity of labor employed changes and all other influences on production remain the same. Its shape reflects diminishing returns, so that each additional hour of labor employed produces a successively smaller addition of real GDP. The quantity of labor employed is determined in the labor market. The quantity of labor demanded increases (decreases) as the real wage rate falls (rises). The quantity of labor supplied increases (decreases) as the real wage rate rises (falls). Labor market equilibrium occurs at the intersection of the labor supply curve and the labor demand curve. When the labor market is in equilibrium, the economy is at full employment and real GDP, determined using the production function, equals potential GDP.

■ **Explain the forces that determine the natural unemployment rate.**

The natural unemployment rate is the unemployment rate at full employment and consists of frictional and structural unemployment. Two fundamental causes of unemployment are job search, which is the activity of looking for a job, and job rationing, which occurs when the real wage rate exceeds the equilibrium wage rate creating a surplus of labor. The amount of job search depends on demographic change, unemployment benefits, and structural change. Job rationing occurs when there is an efficiency wage, a minimum wage, or a union wage because all of these factors force the real wage above the equilibrium real wage.

CHECKPOINT 8.1

■ **Explain the forces that determine potential GDP and the real wage rate and employment at full employment.**

Quick Review

- *Production function* The production function shows the relationship between the maximum quantity of real GDP that can be produced as the quantity of labor employed changes when all other influences on production remain constant.
- *Equilibrium in a market* The equilibrium in a market occurs at the intersection of the demand and supply curves.

Additional Practice Problem 8.1

Quantity of labor demanded (billions of hours per year)	Real GDP (hundreds of billions of 2001 dollars)	Real wage rate (2001 dollars per hour)
0	0	50
10	5	40
20	9	30
30	12	20
40	14	10

1. The table above describes an economy's production function and its demand for labor. The table below describes the supply of labor in this economy.

Quantity of labor supplied (billions of hours per year)	Real wage rate (2001 dollars per hour)
0	10
10	20
20	30
30	40
40	50

a. Make graphs of the production function and the labor market.
b. Does the production function show diminishing returns?
c. What is the equilibrium employment, real wage rate, and potential GDP?

d. Suppose that the population grows so that the quantity of labor supplied increases by 20 billion hours at every real wage rate. What is the effect on the real wage rate and on potential GDP?

Solution to Additional Practice Problem 8.2

1a. The production function is a graph of the first two columns of the first table. The figure to the right shows the relationship between labor and real GDP.

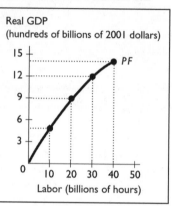

The second figure to the right shows the labor market. The labor demand curve is the first and third columns in the first table. It shows the relationship between the real wage rate and the quantity of labor demanded. The labor supply curve is from the second table and shows the relationship between the real wage rate and the quantity of labor supplied.

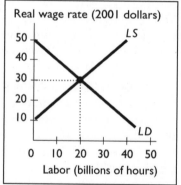

1b. The production function shows diminishing returns because every additional 10 billion hours of labor employed increases real GDP by less.

1c. Find the equilibrium in the labor market. Then use the production function to determine how much GDP this full-employment quantity of labor produces, which is the potential GDP. Equilibrium employment is where the labor demand curve and the labor supply curve intersect. The second figure in part (a) shows that the equilibrium real wage rate is $30 an hour and the equilibrium employment is 20 billion hours per year. The production function, in the first figure in part (a), shows that when 20 billion hours of labor are employed, GDP is $900 billion, so potential GDP equals $900 billion.

Quantity of labor supplied (billions of hours per year)	Real wage rate (2001 dollars per hour)
20	10
30	20
40	30
50	40
60	50

1d. The new labor supply schedule is given in the table above and shown in the figure. In the figure, the labor supply curve shifts rightward from LS1 to

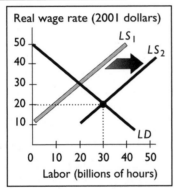

LS2. The equilibrium quantity of labor increases to 30 billion hours and the equilibrium real wage rate falls to $20. The production function in the first table in the practice problem shows that when employment is 30 billion hours, real GDP is $1,200 billion. So, the increase in the population increases potential GDP to $1,200 billion.

■ Self Test 8.1

Fill in the blanks

____ (Classical; Keynesian) macroeconomics asserts that government intervention is needed to achieve full employment. The new macroeconomics says that macro outcomes depend on ____ (macro; micro) choices. The relationship that shows the maximum quantity of real GDP

that can be produced as the quantity of labor employed changes is ____ (the production function; potential GDP). The quantity of labor demanded ____ (increases; decreases) as the real wage rate falls and the quantity of labor supplied ____ (increases; decreases) as the real wage rate falls. If the real wage rate exceeds the equilibrium real wage rate, there is a ____ (shortage; surplus) of labor. When the labor market is in equilibrium, there is ____ and real GDP equals ____.

True or false

1. Classical macroeconomics says that markets work well and government intervention cannot improve on the performance of markets.

2. New macroeconomists agree that the problem of business cycle fluctuations is much more important than the problem of sustaining economic growth.

3. Real GDP can exceed potential GDP permanently.

4. The production function shows how the quantity of labor hired depends on the real wage rate.

5. The nominal wage rate influences the quantity of labor demanded because what matters to firms is the number of dollars they pay for an hour of labor.

6. At the labor market equilibrium the real wage rate is such that the quantity of labor demanded equals the quantity of labor supplied.

7. When the labor market is in equilibrium, the economy is at full employment and real GDP equals potential GDP.

Multiple choice

1. ____ adopts the view that how the economy works depends on the micro choices people make.
   a. Classical macroeconomics
   b. Keynesian economics
   c. The new macroeconomics
   d. The Lucas wedge
   e. The Okun gap

2. Potential GDP
   a. is the quantity of GDP produced when the economy is at full employment.
   b. can never be exceeded.
   c. can never be attained.
   d. is another name for real GDP.
   e. is another name for nominal GDP.

3. With fixed quantities of capital, land, and entrepreneurship and fixed technology, the amount of real GDP produced increases when ____ increases.
   i.   the quantity of labor employed
   ii. the inflation rate
   iii. the price level
   a. i only.
   b. ii only.
   c. iii only.
   d. ii and iii.
   e. i, ii, and iii.

4. The production function graphs the relationship between
   a. nominal GDP and real GDP.
   b. real GDP and the quantity of labor employed.
   c. real GDP and capital.
   d. nominal GDP and the quantity of labor employed.
   e. real GDP and the supply of labor.

5. The quantity of labor demanded definitely increases if the
   a. real wage rate rises.
   b. real wage rate falls.
   c. nominal wage rate rises.
   d. nominal wage rate falls.
   e. supply of labor decreases.

6. The supply of labor curve has a ____ slope because as the real wage rate rises, ____.
   a. negative; firms hire fewer workers
   b. positive; the opportunity cost of leisure rises
   c. positive; the opportunity cost of leisure falls
   d. negative; households work more hours
   e. positive; firms offer more jobs

7. The real wage rate is $35 an hour. At this wage rate there are 100 billion labor hours supplied and 200 billion labor hours demanded. There is a
   a. shortage of 300 billion hours of labor.
   b. shortage of 100 billion hours of labor.
   c. surplus of 100 billion hours of labor.
   d. surplus of 300 billion hours of labor.
   e. shortage of 200 billion hours of labor.

■ **FIGURE 8.1**

Real wage rate (2000 dollars per hour)

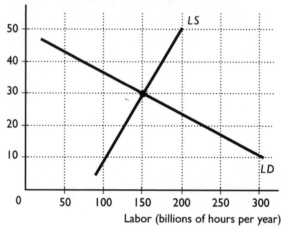

8. In Figure 8.1, the equilibrium real wage rate is ____ and equilibrium employment is ____ billions of hours per year.
   a. $50; 200
   b. $10; 100
   c. $30; more than 300
   d. $20; 125
   e. $30; 150

9. In Figure 8.1, full employment is reached when employment is ____ billions of hours a year.
   a. 150
   b. 200
   c. 250
   d. more than 300
   e. More information is needed about the nation's production function to answer the question.

10. When the labor market is in equilibrium, real GDP ____ potential GDP.
   a. is greater than
   b. is equal to
   c. is less than
   d. might be greater than, less than, or equal to
   e. is not comparable to

11. Compared to the U.S. production function, the European production function is
   a. higher.
   b. lower.
   c. the same.
   d. lower than the U.S. production function at low levels of employment and higher than the U.S. production function at high levels of employment.
   e. higher than the U.S. production function at low levels of employment and lower than the U.S. production function at high levels of employment.

Complete the graph

Quantity of labor (billions of hours per year)	Real GDP (billions of 2000 dollars)
0	0
10	400
20	725
30	900
40	960
50	1,000

1. The above table gives data for a nation's production function. In Figure 8.2, draw the production function. Label the axes. How are diminishing returns reflected?

2. Figure 8.3 illustrates the labor market for the nation with the production function given in the previous problem. In the figure, identify the equilibrium real wage rate and employment. Using the production function in Figure 8.2, what is the nation's potential GDP?

3. Suppose that both the labor supply and labor demand curves shift rightward by 10 billion labor hours and the production function does not change. What is the nation's potential GDP?

■ **FIGURE 8.2**

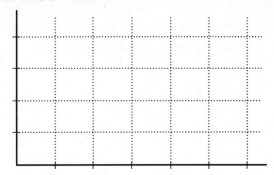

■ **FIGURE 8.3**

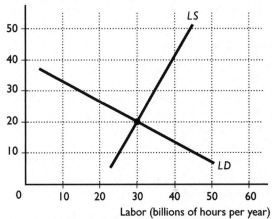

Real wage rate (2000 dollars per hour)

Labor (billions of hours per year)

Short answer and numeric questions

1. What are the differences between classical macroeconomics and Keynesian macroeconomics?

2. What is the relationship between equilibrium in the labor market and potential GDP? Be sure to explain the role played by the production function.

3. Suppose a nation's production function shifts upward. If the equilibrium quantity of labor does not change, what is the effect on the nation's potential GDP?

4. Suppose a nation's production function shifts upward and the equilibrium quantity of labor increases. What is the effect on the nation's potential GDP?

CHECKPOINT 8.2

■ **Explain the forces that determine the natural unemployment rate.**

Quick Review

• *Job search* Job search is the activity of looking for an acceptable vacant job. Job search is influenced by demographic changes, unemployment benefits, and structural change.

• *Job rationing* Job rationing is a situation that arises when the real wage rate is above the full-employment equilibrium level. An efficiency wage, a minimum wage, or a union wage can lead to job rationing.

Additional Practice Problems 8.2

1. Why do demographic changes affect the amount of job search?
2. What factors can keep the real wage rate above the full-employment level? How do these factors affect the amount of employment?
3. Since 1965, how has the real minimum wage generally changed in the United States? What effect would this trend have on the natural unemployment rate?

Solutions to Additional Practice Problems 8.2

1. Demographic changes affect the amount of job search because younger workers conduct more job search than do older workers. In particular, older workers generally have already settled into a career, whereas younger workers are often entering the labor market for the first time. As new entrants, younger workers must search for a job. In addition, younger workers often switch between jobs before settling upon their career and while they are switching, they are searching for a new job.

2. Job rationing, when the real wage rate is above the full-employment equilibrium level, is the result of efficiency wages, the minimum wage, and union wages. An efficiency wage is a real wage that a firm sets above the full-employment equilibrium level

in order to motivate its workers to work harder. A minimum wage is a government regulation that sets the lowest wage legal to pay. A union wage is a wage rate negotiated between a labor union and a firm. Because these wage rates are above the full-employment level, the quantity of labor employed is less than it otherwise would be.

3. Since 1965 there has been a general downward trend in the real minimum wage. The drop was most pronounced between 1967 and 1988, after which the real minimum wage has generally hovered near $5 an hour. The general downward trend in the real minimum wage reduces the amount of job rationing, thereby decreasing the natural unemployment rate.

■ **Self Test 8.2**

Fill in the blanks

The unemployment rate at full employment is the ____. The activity of looking for an acceptable vacant job is called ____ (job search; job rationing). An increase in unemployment benefits ____ (decreases; increases) job search. Job rationing occurs when the real wage rate is ____ (above; below) the equilibrium level. A minimum wage set above the equilibrium wage rate ____ (creates; does not create) unemployment. If the real wage rate is above the full-employment equilibrium level, the natural unemployment rate ____ (increases; decreases).

True or false

1. The amount of job search depends on a number of factors including demographic change.
2. An increase in unemployment benefits, other things remaining the same, will increase the amount of time spent on job search.
3. Job rationing has no effect on the natural unemployment rate.
4. Job rationing results in a shortage of labor.
5. Teenage labor is not affected by the minimum wage.

Multiple choice

1. In the United States since 1950, the average unemployment rate was highest during the decade of the
   a. 1950s.
   b. 1960s.
   c. 1970s.
   d. 1980s.
   e. 1990s.

2. The two fundamental causes of unemployment at full employment are
   a. seasonal jobs and technological change.
   b. foreign competition and financial bankruptcies.
   c. job search and job rationing.
   d. decreases in labor productivity and retirement benefits.
   e. demographic change and decreases in the demand for labor.

3. Job search is defined as
   a. the activity of looking for an acceptable, vacant job.
   b. saying you are looking when you are actually not looking.
   c. attending school to increase your employability.
   d. equivalent to job rationing.
   e. being paid an efficiency wage.

4. The higher unemployment benefits are, the
   a. higher the opportunity cost of job search.
   b. lower the opportunity cost of job search.
   c. shorter the time spent searching and accepting a suitable job.
   d. shorter the time spent searching for a suitable job and the higher the opportunity cost of being unemployed.
   e. lower the natural unemployment rate.

5. Job rationing occurs if
   a. the minimum wage is set below the equilibrium wage rate.
   b. an efficiency wage is set below the equilibrium wage rate.
   c. a union wage is set below the equilibrium wage rate.
   d. the real wage rate is pushed above the equilibrium wage rate.
   e. the Lucas wedge is positive.

6. The existence of union wages, efficiency wages, and the minimum wage
   a. raises the real wage rate above the equilibrium wage and creates a shortage of labor.
   b. lowers the real wage rate below the equilibrium wage and creates a shortage of labor.
   c. raises the real wage rate above the equilibrium wage and raises the natural unemployment rate.
   d. does not have an impact on the equilibrium wage rate or on the amount of unemployment.
   e. raises the real wage rate above the equilibrium wage and lowers the natural unemployment rate.

7. Intel wants to attract the most productive and knowledgeable workers. To achieve this goal it could pay ____ wage.
   a. an efficiency
   b. a minimum
   c. a nominal
   d. an equilibrium
   e. a Lucas wedge

8. Collective bargaining by unions can result in a union wage rate that is ____ the equilibrium real wage rate and creates a ____ of labor.
   a. above; surplus
   b. above; shortage
   c. below; surplus
   d. below; shortage
   e. equal to; surplus

■ **FIGURE 8.4**

Real wage rate (2000 dollars per hour)

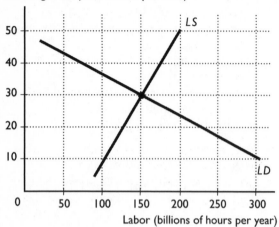

Labor (billions of hours per year)

9. In Figure 8.4, of the wages listed below, there is the most job rationing and unemployment if the real wage rate equals
   a. $10 per hour.
   b. $20 per hour.
   c. $30 per hour.
   d. $40 per hour.
   e. None of the above is correct because at any real wage rate there is never any job rationing.

10. In Figure 8.4, if there is any job rationing, the real wage rate must be ____ per hour and employment is ____ billion hours.
    a. less than $30; more than 150
    b. equal to $30; equal to 150
    c. less than $30; less than 150
    d. more than $30; less than 150
    e. less than $20; less than 150

Complete the graph

1. Figure 8.5 illustrates the labor market.
   a. What is the equilibrium wage rate? Equilibrium employment?
   b. What must a firm do to set an efficiency wage?
   c. Suppose the government imposes a minimum wage that creates a surplus of 60 billion hours of labor a year. What is the minimum wage?

■ **FIGURE 8.5**

Real wage rate (2000 dollars per hour)

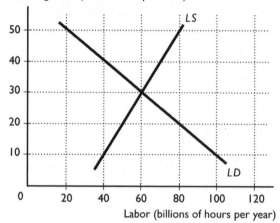

Labor (billions of hours per year)

   d. If a union negotiates on behalf of its members, what can you say about the range of wage rates the union will try to obtain?
   e. In your answers to (b), (c), and (d), is there any unemployment? Compare your answers to parts (b), (c), and (d). How does the employment that results in these situations compare with that in part (a)?

Short answer and numeric questions

Real wage rate (2001 dollars per hour)	Quantity of labor demanded (billions of hours per year)	Quantity of labor supplied (billions of hours per year)
10	180	150
20	160	160
30	140	170
40	120	180

1. The above table gives the labor demand and labor supply schedules for a nation.
   a. What is the equilibrium wage rate?
   b. Suppose firms set an efficiency wage of $30 an hour. What is the effect of this wage rate?
   c. Suppose the government sets a minimum wage of $30 an hour. What is the effect of the minimum wage?
   d. Suppose unions negotiate a wage of $30 an hour. What is the effect of the union wage?

e. How do your answers to parts (b), (c), and (d) compare?

2. The demographics of the United States are such that there will be an increase of young people entering the labor force between 2004 and 2012. What do you predict will be the effect on the U.S. unemployment rate?

3. Why do unemployment benefits affect the natural unemployment rate?

4. An efficiency wage is a wage that exceeds the equilibrium wage rate. Why would a firm pay an efficiency wage?

SELF TEST ANSWERS

■ CHECKPOINT 8.1

Fill in the blanks

<u>Keynesian</u> macroeconomics asserts that government intervention is needed to achieve full employment. The new macroeconomics says that macro outcomes depend on <u>micro</u> choices. The relationship that shows the maximum quantity of real GDP that can be produced as the quantity of labor employed changes is <u>the production function</u>. The quantity of labor demanded <u>increases</u> as the real wage rate falls and the quantity of labor supplied <u>decreases</u> as the real wage rate falls. If the real wage rate exceeds the equilibrium real wage rate, there is a <u>surplus</u> of labor. When the labor market is in equilibrium, there is <u>full employment of labor</u> and real GDP equals <u>potential GDP</u>.

True or false

1. True; page 192
2. False; page 193
3. False; page 195
4. False; page 196
5. False; page 197
6. True; page 200
7. True; page 201

Multiple choice

1. c; page 193
2. a; page 195
3. a; page 195
4. b; page 196
5. b; page 198
6. b; pages 199-200
7. b; page 201
8. e; pages 200-201
9. a; page 201
10. b; page 201
11. b; page 202

Complete the graph

1. Figure 8.6 illustrates the production function. In the table, diminishing returns are demonstrated by the fact that each additional 10 bil-

■ FIGURE 8.6

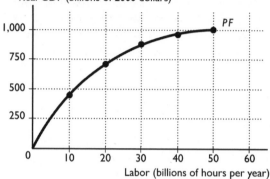
Real GDP (billions of 2000 dollars)

lion hours of labor increases real GDP by a smaller amount. In the figure, diminishing returns are illustrated by the slope of the production function, which becomes less steep as the quantity of labor increases; pages 196-197.

2. The equilibrium real wage rate is $20 an hour and the equilibrium employment is 30 billion hours. Potential GDP is $900 billion; page 201.

3. If both the labor demand and labor supply curves shift rightward by 10 billion labor hours, then equilibrium employment increases by 10 billion hours to 40 billion hours. Potential GDP increases to $960 billion; page 201.

Short answer and numeric questions

1. Classical macroeconomics believes that markets work well and government intervention cannot improve the economy. Keynesian economics believes that a market economy is unstable and needs government intervention to help it reach full employment and sustained economic growth; page 192.

2. The equilibrium quantity of labor is the amount of full employment. The production function shows how much GDP this full-employment quantity of labor produces and this quantity of GDP is potential GDP; page 201.

2. If the production function shifts upward, the amount of real GDP produced by every quantity of labor increases. The nation's potential GDP increases; pages 196, 201.

4. On both counts, the upward shift of the production function and the increase in employment, potential GDP increases; pages 196, 201.

■ CHECKPOINT 8.2

Fill in the blanks

The unemployment rate at full employment is the natural unemployment rate. The activity of looking for an acceptable, vacant job is called job search. An increase in unemployment benefits increases job search. Job rationing occurs when the real wage rate is above the equilibrium level. A minimum wage set above the equilibrium wage rate creates unemployment. If the real wage rate is above the full-employment equilibrium level, the natural unemployment rate increases.

True or false

1. True; page 205
2. True; page 205
3. False; page 206
4. False; pages 206-208
5. False; page 207

Multiple choice

1. d; page 204
2. c; page 205
3. a; page 205
4. b; page 205
5. d; pages 206-207
6. c; page 207
7. a; page 207
8. a; page 207
9. d; page 208
10. d; pages 207-208

Complete the graph

1. a. The equilibrium wage rate is $30 and employment is 60 billion hours; page 201.

b. An efficiency wage is set higher than the equilibrium wage rate, so the firm must set the wage rate above $30; page 207.

c. A minimum wage of $50 an hour creates a labor surplus of 60 billion hours a year; pages 207-208.

d. The union will strive to set a wage rate that is higher than the competitive wage, so the union will try to set a wage that is higher than $30; page 207.

e. In each of the answers to parts (a), (b), and (c), unemployment occurs. And in each of the answers, employment is less than 60 billion hours; page 208.

Short answer and numeric questions

1. a. The equilibrium wage rate is $20 an hour because that is the wage rate at which the quantity of labor demanded equals the quantity supplied. Employment is 60 billion hours; page 201.

b. If firms set an efficiency wage of $30 an hour, there is a labor surplus of 30 billion hours a year (170 billion hours supplied minus 140 billion hours demanded); pages 207-208.

c. If the government sets a minimum wage of $30 an hour, there is a labor surplus of 30 billion hour a year; pages 207-208.

d. If unions negotiate a wage of $30 an hour, there is a labor surplus of 30 billion hours a year; pages 207-208.

e. In each of the answers to parts (b), (c), and (d) there is a labor surplus of 30 billion hours a year. All three of the events raise the wage rate above its equilibrium and create unemployment. All three of the events lower employment; page 208.

2. The natural unemployment rate increases as more young people enter the labor force and search for jobs. The natural unemployment rate in the United States likely will increase between 2004 and 2012; page 205.

3. If unemployment benefits increase, the opportunity cost of job search decreases. Workers spend more time unemployed, searching

for jobs and so the natural unemployment rate increases; page 205.

4. A firm pays an efficiency wage rate to motivate its employees to work hard. The employees will work hard to avoid being let go because they know that if they have to take another job, they are likely to be paid the lower equilibrium wage; page 207.

and services. Net investment equals ____ (gross investment; depreciation) minus ____ (gross investment; depreciation). ____ (Saving; Wealth) is the value of all the things people own. A ____ (bond; stock) is a certificate of ownership and claim to the profit that a firm makes and a ____ (bond; stock) is a debt for the issuer.

True or false

1. Financial capital and physical capital are two different names for the same thing.

2. Net investment equals gross investment minus depreciation.

3. The nation's capital stock at the end of 2006 equals the capital stock at the beginning of 2006 plus gross investment during 2006.

4. Wealth and income are the same thing.

5. A bond issued by a firm is a certificate of ownership and claim to the profits that the firm makes.

Multiple choice

1. Which of the following is <u>NOT</u> an example of physical capital?
   a. a building
   b. a bond
   c. a dump truck
   d. a lawn mower
   e. a computer

2. The decrease in the value of capital that results from its use and obsolescence is
   a. appreciation.
   b. deconstruction.
   c. depreciation.
   d. gross investment.
   e. net investment.

3. Which of the following formulas is correct?
   a. Net investment = gross investment + depreciation
   b. Net investment = gross investment + capital
   c. Net investment = gross investment − depreciation
   d Net investment = gross investment − saving
   e. Net investment = gross investment − wealth

4. Intel's capital at the end of the year equals Intel's capital at the beginning of the year
   a. minus its stock dividends.
   b. plus net investment.
   c. minus depreciation.
   d. plus gross investment.
   e. plus depreciation.

5. U.S. capital at the end of 2006 equals U.S. capital at the beginning of 2006 plus
   a. nothing, because capital can't change in just one year.
   b. gross investment during 2006.
   c. gross investment during 2006 minus net investment in 2006.
   d. net investment during 2006.
   e. depreciation during 2006 minus gross investment during 2006.

Year	Gross investment (trillions of 2000 dollars)	Depreciation (trillions of 2000 dollars)
2006	1.9	0.8
2007	2.0	0.9

6. The table above gives a nation's investment and depreciation. If the capital stock equaled $25.0 trillion at the end of 2005, at the end of 2006 the capital stock equaled
   a. $25.0 trillion.
   b. $25.8 trillion.
   c. $24.2 trillion.
   d. $26.9 trillion.
   e. $26.1 trillion.

7. The table above gives a nation's investment and depreciation. If the capital stock equaled $23.0 trillion at the end of 2006, net investment in 2007 equaled
   a. $25.9 trillion.
   b. $25.0 trillion.
   c. $0.9 trillion.
   d. $2.0 trillion.
   e. $1.1 trillion.

8. The Ng's family's wealth at the end of the year equals their wealth at the beginning of the year
   a. minus personal income taxes.
   b. plus saving.
   c. minus consumption.
   d. plus income.
   e. plus consumption minus income.

9. Economists use the term "financial markets" to mean the markets in which
   a. firms purchase their physical capital.
   b. firms supply their goods and services.
   c. households supply their labor services.
   d. firms get the funds that they use to buy physical capital.
   e. the government borrows to fund any budget surplus.

10. A stockholder ____ an owner of the firm and a bondholder ____ an owner of the firm.
    a. is; is
    b. is; is not
    c. is not; is
    d. is not; is not
    e. might be; is not

Short answer and numeric questions
1. What is the relationship between physical capital and financial capital?

2. What is the difference between gross investment and capital?

3. In 2003, Regis Hair Salon purchased 10 hair dryers for $3,300 each. During the year, depreciation was $13,000. What was the amount of Regis' gross investment and net investment?

Year	Gross investment (trillions of 2000 dollars)	Depreciation (trillions of 2000 dollars)	Net investment (trillions of 2000 dollars)
2005	2.3	0.2	____
2006	2.5	0.3	____
2007	2.8	0.4	____

4. The table above gives gross investment and depreciation for three years.
   a. Complete the net investment column.

   b. If the capital was $22.3 trillion at the beginning of 2005, what was it at the beginning of 2006? 2007? 2008?

5. The Bouton family earns an income of $80,000 a year after taxes by directing local television shows. Their consumption expenditures during the year are $75,000.
   a. What is the amount of their saving over the year?
   b. If their wealth at the beginning of the year was $100,000, how much is their wealth at the end of the year?

CHECKPOINT 9.2

■ **Explain how investment and saving decisions are made and how these decisions interact in financial markets to determine the real interest rate and the amount of investment and saving.**

Quick Review
   b. *Investment demand* The relationship between the quantity of investment demanded and the real interest rate, other things remaining the same.
   c. *Saving supply* The relationship between the quantity of saving supplied and the real interest rate, other things remaining the same.

Additional Practice Problems 9.2
1. Suppose you buy a lottery ticket and the top prize is $10 million. Your current income is $30,000 a year and you save $1,500 a year. Glory be, you win the lottery and your income this year is $10,030,000! Do you think you will save more or less than $1,500 this year? In your answer, focus on the amount of your income this year and what you expect it to be in the future.

2. New Cell is a biotech company that is exploring ways to rejuvenate older cells so as to restore the cell's youth. New Cell's investment

demand curve is shown in the figure. Suppose that New Cell makes a break-through in its technology that increases the ex-pected rate of profit from invest-ment. In the figure, show the effect of this change on New Cell's investment demand curve.

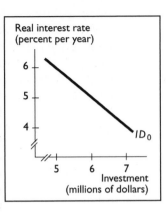

3. In 2005, the King family had a disposable in-come of $50,000, net assets of $100,000, and an expected future disposable income of $50,000 a year. At a real interest rate of 4 percent a year, the King family would save $10,000 a year; at a real interest rate of 6 percent a year, they would save $12,500 a year; and at a real interest rate of 8 percent a year, they would save $15,000 a year.

   a. In the figure, draw a graph of the King family's sav-ing supply curve.

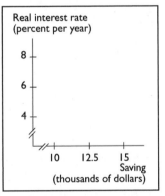

   b. In 2006, the King family expects its fu-ture dispos-able income to increase to $60,000 a year. If other things remain the same, explain how this change influences the King family's saving supply. Illustrate the effect of this change on the King fam-ily's saving supply curve.

   c. In 2007, the stock market booms and the King family's net assets increase in value. If the King family expects its future dis-posable income to be $50,000 and other things remain the same, explain how this change influences the King family's sav-

ing supply. What is the effect on the King family's saving supply curve?

4. Draw a graph illustrating the effect on the equilibrium real interest rate and equilibrium saving and investment when saving supply in-creases and investment demand increases by more.

Solutions to Additional Practice Problems 9.2

1. You will save more than $1,500 this year. First, your disposable income is much higher this year, and saving increases when disposable in-come increases. Second, your expected future income is much lower than your income this year because you cannot expect to win the lot-tery two years running! When expected future income is lower, saving increases. For both rea-sons you will save a *lot* more than $1,500.

2. An increase in the expected rate of profit increases investment demand and shifts the in-vestment demand curve rightward. In the figure, First Call's investment demand curve shifts rightward from ID_0 to ID_1.

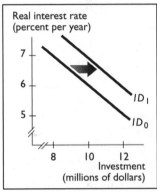

3a. The figure illus-trates the King family's saving supply curve. The saving supply curve, SS_0, slopes upward because an increase in the real interest rate increases the quantity the King family will save.

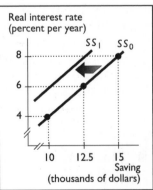

3b. An increase in expected future income decreases the amount of saving at each real interest rate. The King family's saving supply decreases and the saving supply curve shifts leftward. In the above figure, the saving supply curve shifts leftward from SS_0 to SS_1.

3c. An increase in the buying power of net assets decreases the amount people save at each real interest rate. The King family's saving supply decreases and the saving supply curve shifts leftward. In the above figure, the saving supply curve shifts leftward from SS_0 to SS_1.

4. The figure that shows the investment demand curve and the saving supply curve illustrates how the real interest rate is determined. Use this diagram the same way you use the supply and demand figures you studied in Chapter 4. Equilibrium occurs where the investment demand curve intersects the saving supply curve and a shift in either curve changes the equilibrium real interest rate and the equilibrium quantity of investment and saving.

In this case, the increase in saving supply shifts the saving supply curve rightward. The increase in investment demand shifts the investment demand curve rightward. The shift in the investment demand curve exceeds the shift in the saving supply curve, so, as illustrated in the figure, the real interest rate rises, from 5.5 percent to 6.0 percent, and the quantity of investment and saving increases, from $10 trillion to $11 trillion.

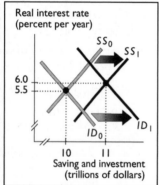

■ Self Test 9.2

Fill in the blanks

Other things remaining the same, the higher the real interest rate, the ____ (greater; smaller) the quantity of investment demanded. Population growth ____ (increases; decreases) investment demand. Other things remaining the same, the higher the real interest rate, the ____ (greater; smaller) the quantity of saving supplied. An increase in disposable income ____ (increases; decreases) saving. When saving supply increases, the saving supply curve shifts ____ (rightward; leftward). The financial market is in equilibrium when the quantity of saving supplied ____ the quantity of investment demanded.

True or false

1. Other things remaining the same, the higher the real interest rate, the smaller the quantity of investment demanded.

2. When the expected rate of profit changes, there is a movement along the investment demand curve.

3. The real interest rate is the opportunity cost of consumption expenditure.

4. An increase in the buying power of net assets leads to a decrease in saving.

5. If the real interest rate is greater than the equilibrium real interest rate, there is a shortage of saving in the financial market.

Multiple choice

1. If the real interest rate falls, other things being the same, the quantity of investment demanded ____ and the quantity of saving supplied ____.
   a. increases; decreases
   b. increases; increases
   c. decreases; does not change
   d. does not change; decreases
   e. decreases; decreases

2. Investment demand
   a. increases in a recession.
   b. decreases in an expansion.
   c. increases when firms are optimistic about their future prospects.
   d. increases when the buying power of net assets increases.
   e. decreases when the buying power of net assets increases.

■ FIGURE 9.1

Real interest rate (percent per year)

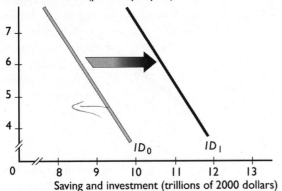

3. The shift of the investment demand curve in Figure 9.1 illustrates _____ investment demand and could be the result of _____.
   a. an increase; a rise in the buying power of net assets
   b. an increase; a fall in the buying power of net assets
   c. a decrease; businesses being less optimistic about the future
   d. a decrease; a rise in the expected rate of profit
   e. an increase; a rise in the expected rate of profit

4. Other things remaining the same, a _____ in the real interest rate _____ the quantity of saving supplied and _____ the quantity of financial capital supplied.
   a. fall; increases; increases
   b. rise; increases; increases
   c. fall; increases; decreases
   d. fall; decreases; increases
   e. rise; increases; decreases

5. An increase in the buying power of a household's net assets leads to
   a. an increase in savings.
   b. an increase in investment.
   c. a decrease in savings.
   d. a decrease in investment.
   e. no change in either saving or investment.

6. If the real interest rate falls, there is
   a. an upward movement along the saving supply curve.
   b. a downward movement along the saving supply curve.
   c. a rightward shift of the saving supply curve and no shift in the investment demand curve.
   d. a leftward shift of the saving supply curve and no shift in the investment demand curve.
   e. a leftward shift of the saving supply curve and a rightward shift in the investment demand curve.

7. If, at the current interest rate, the quantity of saving supplied is less than the quantity of investment demanded, then the
   a. saving supply curve will shift rightward and the interest rate will rise.
   b. saving supply curve will shift leftward and the interest rate will fall.
   c. interest rate will fall.
   d. interest rate will rise.
   e. saving supply curve will shift leftward and the interest rate will rise.

8. In the financial market, the real interest rate changes until
   a. saving supply is greater than investment demand.
   b. saving supply is smaller than investment demand.
   c. saving supply and investment demand are equal.
   d. the quantity of saving supplied equals the quantity of investment demanded.
   e. the investment demand curve and the saving supply curve have shifted so that they are in equilibrium.

9. If the economy enters a recession, the investment demand curve shifts _____ and the real interest rate _____.
   a. rightward; rises
   b. rightward; falls
   c. leftward; rises
   d. leftward; falls
   e. leftward; does not change

■ FIGURE 9.2

Real interest rate (percent per year)

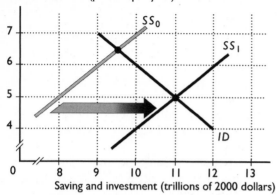

Saving and investment (trillions of 2000 dollars)

10. In Figure 9.2, _____ has increased and the equilibrium quantity of investment _____.
    a. the buying power of net assets; increases
    b. the expected rate of profit; increases
    c. the expected rate of profit; decreases
    d. expected future income; decreases
    e. disposable income; increases

Complete the graph

■ FIGURE 9.3

Real interest rate (percent per year)

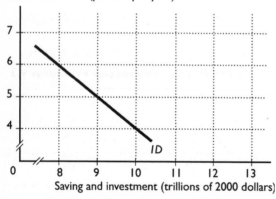

Saving and investment (trillions of 2000 dollars)

1. Figure 9.3 shows an investment demand curve.
   a. Because the economy enters an expansion, the expected rate of profit increases. Show the effect of this change on investment demand in Figure 9.3.

■ FIGURE 9.4

Real interest rate (percent per year)

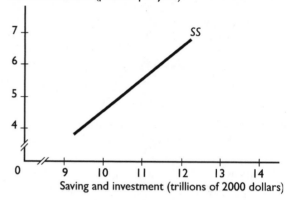

Saving and investment (trillions of 2000 dollars)

2. Figure 9.4 shows a saving supply curve.
   a. Suppose disposable income increases. Show the effect of this change on saving supply in Figure 9.4.
   b. Suppose the buying power of net assets increases. Show the effect of this change on saving supply in Figure 9.4.

Real interest rate (percent per year)	Investment (trillions of 2000 dollars)	Saving (trillions of 2000 dollars)
4	12	10
5	11	11
6	10	12
7	9	13

■ FIGURE 9.5

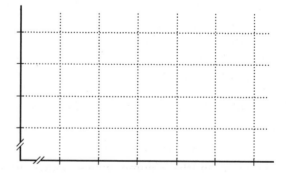

3. The table above gives a saving supply schedule and an investment demand schedule.
   a. Label the axes and then draw the saving supply curve and investment demand curve in Figure 9.5.

b. What is the equilibrium real interest rate? What is the equilibrium quantity of investment and saving?

c. Suppose that firms become more optimistic about the expected rate of profit. In Figure 9.5, show this change. What is the effect on the real interest rate and quantity of investment and saving?

Short answer and numeric questions

1. Why does an increase in the real interest rate decrease the quantity of investment demanded?

2. What factors shift the investment demand curve? The saving supply curve?

3. Why is the real interest rate the opportunity cost of consumption expenditure?

4. Suppose the real interest rate is less than its equilibrium value. What forces drive the real interest rate to its equilibrium?

CHECKPOINT 9.3

■ **Explain how government influences the real interest rate, investment, and saving.**

Quick Review

d. *Government saving* Government saving equals net taxes minus government purchases, or $NT - G$.

e. *Crowding-out effect* The tendency for a government budget deficit to decrease investment.

f. *Ricardo-Barro effect* A government deficit has no effect on the real interest rate or investment.

Additional Practice Problems 9.3

1. The table in the column above shows the investment demand schedule and the supply schedule of private saving.

   a. If the government's budget is balanced, what is the equilibrium real interest rate, the equilibrium the quantity of private saving and the equilibrium quantity of investment?

b. If the government budget surplus is $200 billion, and there is no Ricardo-Barro effect, what is the equilibrium real interest rate, the quantity of private saving, and the quantity of investment?

Real interest rate (percent per year)	Investment	Private saving
	(trillions of 2000 dollars per year)	
4	2.7	2.1
5	2.6	2.2
6	2.5	2.3
7	2.4	2.4
8	2.3	2.5
9	2.2	2.6
10	2.1	2.7

c. If the government budget deficit is $200 billion, and there is no Ricardo-Barro effect, what is the equilibrium real interest rate, the quantity of private saving, and the quantity of investment? Is there any crowding out?

d. If the Ricardo-Barro effect occurs, how do your answers to part (b) and part (c) change? How does the equilibrium real interest rate and quantity of investment in these two cases compare to your answer to part (a)?

2. With a Ricardo-Barro effect, what is the impact of a government budget deficit or surplus? Does the size of the deficit or surplus matter?

Solutions to Additional Practice Problems 9.3

1a. With no budget deficit or surplus, private saving is total saving. The equilibrium real interest rate is 7 percent a year. The equilibrium quantity of private saving is $2.4 trillion and the equilibrium quantity of investment is $2.4 trillion.

1b. When the government has a $100 billion budget surplus, it is adding that amount to private saving, so at an interest rate of 7 percent, there is a surplus of saving. The real interest rate falls. When the real interest rate falls to 6 percent, the quantity of private saving is $2.3 trillion and the total quantity of saving is $2.5 trillion. The quantity of investment demand is also $2.5 trillion. The total quantity of saving supplied equals the quantity of investment demanded. So the equilibrium real interest rate is 6 percent, the equilibrium quantity of private saving is $2.3 trillion, and the equilibrium quantity of investment is $2.5 trillion.

1c. If the government runs a $200 billion deficit, *total* saving at every real interest rate is $200 billion less than the private saving shown in the table. When the real interest rate is 8 percent, the quantity of total saving supplied is $2.3 trillion (the $2.5 trillion private saving "plus" the negative $200 billion government saving). The quantity of investment demanded is $2.3 trillion, so the real interest rate of 8 percent is the equilibrium rate. Private saving is $2.5 trillion and investment is $2.3 trillion. In comparison to the situation with no government deficit, $100 billion of investment has been crowded out.

1d. If the Ricardo-Barro effect occurs, then when the government has a $200 billion surplus in part (b), private saving decreases by $200 billion. In this case, the equilibrium real interest rate is 7 percent, the equilibrium quantity of private saving is $2.2 trillion, and the equilibrium quantity of investment is $2.4 trillion.

When the government has a deficit of $200 billion in part (c), private saving increases by $200 billion. The equilibrium real interest rate is 7 percent, the equilibrium quantity of private saving is $2.6 trillion, and the equilibrium quantity of investment is $2.4 trillion.

When there is a Barro-Ricardo effect, a government budget deficit or surplus did not change the real interest or quantity of investment.

2. The Ricardo-Barro effect says that government deficits and surpluses do not matter. They have no effect on the real interest rate or on investment. Whether a deficit or surplus is large or small is inconsequential; it still does not change the real interest rate. According to the Ricardo-Barro effect, concern about the government's budget is misplaced!

■ Self Test 9.3

Fill in the blanks

Total saving equals private saving ____ (plus;

minus) government saving. A government budget surplus ____ (increases; decreases) government saving. The crowding-out effect is the tendency for a government budget deficit to ____ (increase; decrease) private investment. The Ricardo-Barro effect says that an increase in the government deficit will lead to ____ (an increase; a decrease) in private saving supply.

True or false

1. Investment, I, is financed by private saving, S, and government saving, $G - NT$.

2. With no Barro-Ricardo effect, an increase in government saving leads to a fall in the real interest rate.

3. With no Barro-Ricardo effect an increase in government saving leads to an increase in the quantity of investment.

4. The crowding-out effect is the tendency of a government budget surplus to crowd out private saving.

5. The Ricardo-Barro effect holds that the government budget deficit has no effect on the real interest rate or investment.

Multiple choice

1. With no Ricardo-Barro effect, a government budget surplus
   a. increases total saving supply.
   b. increases investment demand.
   c. decreases total saving supply.
   d. decreases investment demand.
   e. has no effect on either saving supply or investment demand.

2. Suppose net taxes are greater than government purchases. Then
   a. private saving is equal to investment.
   b. private saving is greater than investment and government saving is positive.
   c. private saving is less than investment and government saving is positive.
   d. there is a budget deficit.
   e. private saving is greater than investment and government saving is negative.

3. *(NT – G)* is
   a. always positive.
   b. always negative.
   c. positive if the government runs a budget surplus.
   d. negative if the government runs a budget surplus.
   e. equal to *(S – I)*.

4. During 2006, the world has net taxes of $5 trillion, government purchases of $4 trillion, and private savings of $6 trillion. Investment equals
   a. $5 trillion.
   b. $7 trillion.
   c. $10 trillion.
   d. $15 trillion.
   e. $6 trillion.

5. If there is no Ricardo-Barro effect, a government surplus
   a. raises the real interest rate because the investment demand curve shifts rightward.
   b. lowers the real interest rate because the investment demand curve shifts leftward.
   c. raises the real interest rate because the saving supply curve shifts leftward.
   d. lowers the real interest rate because the saving supply curve shifts rightward.
   e. does not change the real interest rate.

6. The "crowding-out effect" refers to how a government budget deficit
   a. shifts only the saving supply curve leftward.
   b. shifts only the investment demand curve leftward.
   c. shifts both the investment demand curve and saving supply curve leftward.
   d. decreases the equilibrium quantity of investment.
   e. increases the equilibrium quantity of investment.

7. If there is no Ricardo-Barro effect, a government budget deficit will ____ the equilibrium real interest rate and ____ the equilibrium quantity of investment.
   a. raise; increase
   b. raise; decrease
   c. lower; increase
   d. lower; decrease
   e. not change; not change

8. The Ricardo-Barro effect says that government budget deficits lead to
   a. a higher real interest rate.
   b. a lower real interest rate.
   c. no change in the real interest rate.
   d. an increase in investment demand.
   e. an increase in the quantity of investment.

Complete the graph

Real interest rate (percent per year)	Investment (trillions of 2000 dollars)	Private saving (trillions of 2000 dollars)
4	12	10
5	11	11
6	10	12
7	9	13

■ **FIGURE 9.6**

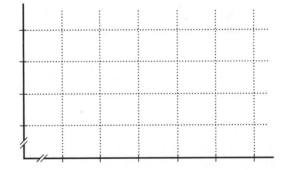

1. The above table has a private saving supply schedule and an investment demand schedule.
   a. Label the axes and then draw the private saving supply and investment demand curves in Figure 9.6.

b. If the government has no budget deficit or surplus, what is the equilibrium real interest rate and quantity of investment?

c. If the government has a $2 trillion deficit, and there is no Ricardo-Barro effect, draw the saving supply curve in Figure 9.6. What is the equilibrium real interest rate and quantity of investment?

d. If the government has a $2 trillion deficit, and there is a Ricardo-Barro effect, draw the saving supply curve in Figure 9.6. What is the equilibrium real interest rate and quantity of investment?

b. What was government saving in Row A? Row B? Row C? Row D?

c. In which rows did the government have a budget deficit? A budget surplus?

d. What is the relationship between your answers to parts (b) and (c)?

2. What is the crowding-out effect?

3. How does the Ricardo-Barro effect modify the conclusion of the crowding-out effect?

Short answer and numeric questions

Row	Investment	Private saving	Net taxes	Government purchases
	(trillions of 2000 dollars)			
A	12	13	5	___
B	12	11	5	___
C	___	10	6	4
D	11	___	7	6

1. The above table gives global data for investment, private saving, net taxes, and government purchases.

a. Complete the table.

SELF TEST ANSWERS

■ CHECKPOINT 9.1

Fill in the blanks

<u>Physical</u> capital consists of tools, instruments, machines, buildings, and other constructions that have been produced in the past and that are used to produce goods and services. Net investment equals <u>gross investment</u> minus <u>depreciation</u>. <u>Wealth</u> is the value of all the things people own. A <u>stock</u> is a certificate of ownership and claim to the profits that a firm makes and a <u>bond</u> is a debt for issuer.

True or false

1. False; page 216
2. True; page 216
3. False; page 216
4. False; page 218
5. False; page 219

Multiple choice

1. b; page 216
2. c; page 216
3. c; page 216
4. b; page 216
5. d; page 217
6. e; page 217
7. e; page 217
8. b; page 218
9. d; page 218
10. b; pages 218-219

Short answer and numeric questions

1. Physical capital is the tools, machines, buildings, and other constructions that have been produced in the past and are used to produce additional goods and services. Financial capital is the funds firms use to buy and operate physical capital. Hence a firm needs financial capital in order to buy a piece of physical capital; page 216.

2. Capital is the tools, machines, buildings, and other constructions that have been produced in the past and are used to produce additional goods and services. Investment is the purchase of new capital, so investment adds to the total amount of the nation's capital. Gross investment is the total amount of investment spent on new capital goods; page 216.

3. Regis' gross investment was $33,000, and net investment, which equals gross investment minus depreciation, was $20,000; page 216.

4. a. Net investment is gross investment minus depreciation, and is $2.1 trillion in 2005, $2.2 trillion in 2006, and $2.4 trillion in 2007; page 216.

   b. The capital changes by the amount of net investment. The capital stock at the beginning of 2006 is $24.4 trillion, at the beginning of 2007 is $26.6 trillion, and at the beginning of 2008 is $29.0 trillion; page 217.

5. a. Saving is the amount of income not paid as taxes or spent on consumption goods. So the Bouton family's saving during the year equals $80,000 − $75,000, which is $5,000; page 218.

   b. Saving adds to wealth, so the Bouton family's wealth increases by $5,000 to $105,000; page 218.

■ CHECKPOINT 9.2

Fill in the blanks

Other things remaining the same, the higher the real interest rate, the <u>smaller</u> the quantity of investment demanded. Population growth <u>increases</u> investment demand. Other things remaining the same, the higher the real interest rate, the <u>greater</u> the quantity of saving supplied. An increase in disposable income <u>increases</u> saving. When saving supply increases, the saving supply curve shifts <u>rightward</u>. The financial market is in equilibrium when the quantity of saving supplied <u>equals</u> the quantity of investment demanded.

True or false

1. True; page 221
2. False; pages 222-223

3. True; page 224
4. True; page 225
5. False; page 227

Multiple choice

1. a; pages 221, 224
2. c; page 223
3. e; pages 222-223
4. b; pages 221, 224
5. c; page 225
6. b; pages 224-225
7. d; page 227
8. d; page 227
9. d; pages 222, 228
10. e; pages 224, 226, 228

Complete the graph

■ FIGURE 9.7
Real interest rate (percent per year)

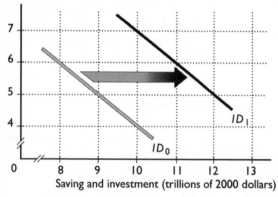

1. a. The decrease in the expected rate of profit decreases investment demand and the investment demand curve shifts leftward, from ID_0 to ID_1 in Figure 9.7; pages 222-223.

2. a. An increase in disposable income increases saving and the saving supply curve shifts rightward, from SS_0 to SS_1 in Figure 9.8 (at the top of the next column); pages 224-226.

   b. An increase in the buying power of net assets decreases saving and the saving supply curve shifts leftward, from SS_0 to SS_2; pages 225-226.

■ FIGURE 9.8
Real interest rate (percent per year)

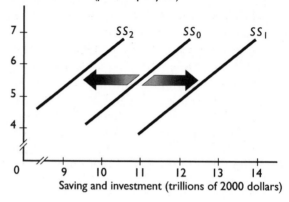

Saving and investment (trillions of 2000 dollars)

■ FIGURE 9.9
Real interest rate (percent per year)

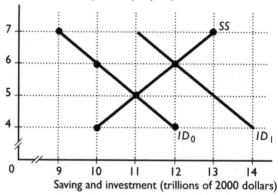

Saving and investment (trillions of 2000 dollars)

3. a. The axes are labeled and the curves are drawn in Figure 9.9. The saving supply curve is SS and the investment demand curve is ID_0; page 227.

   b. The equilibrium real interest rate is 5 percent a year. The equilibrium quantity of investment and saving is $11 trillion; page 227.

   c. The increase in optimism increases investment demand and shifts the investment demand curve rightward from ID_0 to ID_1. The real interest rate rises and the quantity of investment and saving increases; page 228.

Short answer and numeric questions

1. The real interest rate is the opportunity cost of the funds used to finance the purchase of

capital. The funds used to finance investment might be borrowed, or they might be the financial resources of the firm's owners. The opportunity cost of both sources of funds is the real interest rate. In the case of borrowed funds, the real interest rate is the opportunity cost because it is what is really paid to the lender. In the case of the owners' funds, the real interest rate is the opportunity cost because the funds could be loaned and earn the real interest rate. An increase in the real interest rate increases the opportunity cost of financing investment and so the quantity of investment demanded decreases; page 221.

2. The investment demand curve shifts when the expected rate of profit changes. Technological change, changes in the phase of the business cycle, population growth, subjective influences, and contagion effects all change the expected rate of profit and shift the investment demand curve. The saving supply curve shifts when disposable income, the buying power of net assets, and expected future disposable income change; pages 222-226.

3. If a dollar is spent on current consumption, it cannot be saved. If the dollar is saved, it would earn the real interest rate. Hence the real interest rate is what is forgone by spending a dollar on consumption and so the real interest rate is the opportunity cost of consumption; page 224.

4. If the real interest rate is less than the equilibrium real interest rate, the quantity of investment demanded exceeds the quantity of saving supplied. Borrowers can't find all the loans they want, but lenders are able to lend all the funds they have available. So the real interest rate rises and the quantity of investment demanded decreases, while the quantity of saving supplied increases. The equilibrium occurs when the interest rate is such that quantity of investment demanded equals the quantity of saving supplied; page 227.

■ CHECKPOINT 9.3

Fill in the blanks

Total saving equals private saving <u>plus</u> government saving. A government budget surplus <u>increases</u> government saving. The crowding-out effect is the tendency for a government budget deficit to <u>decrease</u> private investment. The Ricardo-Barro effect says that an increase in the government deficit will lead to <u>an increase</u> in private saving supply.

True or false

1. False; page 230
2. True; pages 230-231
3. True; page 231
4. False; pages 231-232
5. True; page 232

Multiple choice

1. a; page 230
2. c; page 230
3. c; page 230
4. b; page 230
5. d; pages 230-231
6. d; pages 231-232
7. b; page 231
8. c; page 232

Complete the graph

■ FIGURE 9.10

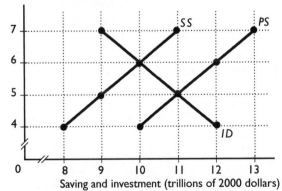

1. a. Figure 9.10 labels the axes and plots the curves. The private saving supply curve is

PS and the investment demand curve is *ID*; page 231.

b. If the government has no budget deficit or surplus, the private saving supply curve is the same as the total saving supply curve. The equilibrium real interest rate is 5 percent a year and the equilibrium quantity of investment is $11 trillion; page 232.

c. The total saving supply is labeled *SS* in Figure 9.10. At any interest rate, the quantity of total saving equals the quantity of private saving minus the government budget deficit of $2 trillion. The equilibrium real interest rate is 6 percent and the equilibrium quantity of investment is $10 trillion; pages 231-232.

d. With a Ricardo-Barro effect and a $2 trillion government deficit, private saving increases. At every interest rate, the quantity of private saving is $2 trillion more than the amount given in the table. Total saving, the sum of private saving plus the government deficit, is the same as the initial total saving curve, *PS*. The equilibrium real interest rate is 5 percent and the equilibrium quantity of investment is $11 trillion, the same as in part (a); page 232.

Short answer and numeric questions

Row	Investment	Private saving	Net taxes	Government purchases
		(trillions of 2000 dollars)		
A	12	13	5	<u>6</u>
B	12	11	5	<u>4</u>
C	<u>12</u>	10	6	4
D	11	<u>10</u>	7	6

1. a. The completed table is above; page 230.

   b. Government saving is –$1 trillion in Row A; $1 trillion in Row B; $2 trillion in Row C; and $1 trillion in Row D; page 230.

   c. The government has a budget deficit in Row A and budget surpluses in Rows B, C, and D; page 230.

   d. When government saving is negative, as in Row A, the government has a budget deficit. When government saving is positive, as in Rows B, C, and D, the government has a budget surplus; page 230.

2. The crowding-out effect is the tendency for a government budget deficit to decrease private investment; pages 231-232.

3. The Ricardo-Barro effect says that private savers increase their saving in response to a government budget deficit. The private saving supply curve shifts to offset any change in government saving. In this case, a government budget deficit has no effect on investment or the real interest rate; page 232.

Economic Growth

Chapter

10

Chapter 10 discusses the factors that determine economic growth, studies different theories that explain economic growth, and examines possible government polices to speed economic growth.

■ **Define and calculate the economic growth rate, and explain the implications of sustained growth.**

Economic growth is a sustained expansion of production possibilities measured as the increase in real GDP over a given time period. The economic growth rate is the annual percentage change of real GDP. The standard of living depends on real GDP per person, which equals real GDP divided by the population. The Rule of 70 is that the number of years it takes a variable to double approximately equals 70 divided by the annual growth rate of the variable.

■ **Identify the main sources of economic growth.**

Real GDP grows when the quantities of the factors of production grow or when technology advances. Labor productivity is the quantity of real GDP produced by one hour of labor. When labor productivity grows, real GDP per person grows. Growth of labor productivity depends on saving and investment in more physical capital, acquisition of more human capital, and discovery of better technologies.

■ **Review the theories of economic growth that explain why growth rates vary over time and across countries.**

The classical theory predicts that labor productivity growth is temporary. If real GDP rises above the subsistence level, a population explosion occurs so that labor productivity falls and real GDP per person returns to the subsistence level. The neoclassical theory asserts that real GDP per person will increase as long as technology keeps advancing. But technological change is assumed to be random. The new growth theory emphasizes that human capital growth and technological change is the result of choices. It also says that technological discoveries bring profit and competition destroys profit, thereby creating the incentive for more technological discoveries. When labor productivity increases because of technological change or an increase in capital, the production function shifts upward. The demand for labor increases so employment increases. The increase in employment and the shift of the production function both increase real GDP. The new growth theory predicts that our unlimited wants will lead us to ever greater productivity and perpetual economic growth.

■ **Describe policies that might speed economic growth.**

The preconditions for economic growth are economic freedom, property rights, and markets. Economic freedom occurs when people are able to make personal choices, their private property is protected, and they are free to buy and sell in markets. Governments can increase economic growth by creating incentives to save, invest, and innovate; by encouraging saving; by encouraging research and development; by encouraging international trade; and by improving the quality of education.

CHECKPOINT 10.1

■ **Define and calculate the economic growth rate, and explain the implications of sustained growth.**

Quick Review

- *Growth rate* The growth rate of real GDP equals

$$\frac{\left(\begin{array}{c}\text{Real GDP in}\\\text{current year}\end{array}\right) - \left(\begin{array}{c}\text{Real GDP in}\\\text{previous year}\end{array}\right)}{\left(\text{Real GDP in previous year}\right)} \times 100$$

- *Growth rate of real GDP per person* The growth rate of real GDP per person equals (growth rate of real GDP)–(growth rate of population).

- *Rule of 70* The number of years it takes for the level of any variable to double is approximately 70 divided by the annual percentage growth rate of the variable.

Additional Practice Problem 10.1

1. In the nation of Transylvania in 2007, real GDP was $3.0 million and the population was 1,000. In 2008, real GDP was $3.3 million and the population was 1,050.
   a. What is Transylvania's economic growth in 2008?
   b. What is the population growth rate?
   c. What is Transylvania's growth rate of real GDP per person?
   d. Did Transylvania's standard of living rise?
   e. Approximately how long will it take for real GDP per person to double?

Solution to Additional Practice Problem 10.1

1. This question uses three growth rate formulas. The first is the formula that calculates the economic growth rate; the second is the formula that calculates the growth rate of real GDP per person; the third is the Rule of 70.
1a. The economic growth rate is the growth rate of real GDP. Transylvania's economic growth rate equals [($3.3 million – $3.0 million) ÷ $3.0 million] × 100 = 10 percent.

1b. Transylvania's population growth rate equals [(1,050 – 1,000) ÷ 1,000] × 100 = 5 percent.

1c. Transylvania's real GDP per person growth rate equals the growth rate of real GDP minus the growth rate of the population, or 10 percent – 5 percent = 5 percent.

1d. Transylvania's real GDP per person rose, so Transylvania's standard of living increased.

1e. The number of years it takes for real GDP per person to double is given by the Rule of 70. Transylvania's real GDP per person is growing at 5 percent per year, so it will take approximately 70 ÷ 5 or 14 years for Transylvania's real GDP per person to double.

■ **Self Test 10.1**

Fill in the blanks

The growth rate of real GDP equals real GDP in the current year minus real GDP in the previous year divided by real GDP ____ in the (current; previous) year, all multiplied by 100. The growth rate of real GDP per person equals the growth rate of real GDP ____ (minus; plus) the growth rate of the population. The number of years it takes for the level of any variable to double is approximately ____ divided by the annual percentage growth rate of the variable.

True or false

1. If real GDP last year was $1.00 trillion and real GDP this year is $1.05 trillion, the growth rate of real GDP this year is 5 percent.

2. Real GDP per person equals real GDP divided by the population.

3. If a nation's population grows at 2 percent and its real GDP grows at 4 percent, then the growth rate of real GDP per person is 2 percent.

4. If real GDP is growing at 2 percent a year, it will take 70 years for real GDP to double.

Multiple choice

1. The economic growth rate is measured as the
   a. annual percentage change of real GDP.
   b. annual percentage change of employment.
   c. level of real GDP.
   d. annual percentage change of the population.
   e. amount of population.

2. Real GDP is $9 trillion in the current year and $8.6 trillion in the previous year. The economic growth rate between these years has been
   a. 10.31 percent.
   b. 4.65 percent.
   c. 5.67 percent.
   d. 7.67 percent.
   e. $0.4 trillion.

3. The standard of living is measured by
   a. real GDP.
   b. employment.
   c. employment per person.
   d. real GDP per person.
   e. the population.

4. If the growth rate of population is greater than a nation's growth rate of real GDP, then its real GDP per person
   a. falls.
   b. rises.
   c. does not change.
   d. might rise or fall.
   e. cannot be measured.

5. If real GDP increases by 6 percent and at the same time the population increases by 2 percent, then real GDP per person grows by
   a. 6 percent.
   b. 4 percent.
   c. 2 percent.
   d. 8 percent.
   e. 3 percent.

6. If a country experiences a real GDP growth rate of 4 percent a year, real GDP will double in
   a. 14 years.
   b. 17.5 years.
   c. 23.3 years.
   d. 35 years.
   e. 25 years.

Short answer and numeric questions

Year	Real GDP (billions of 2000 dollars)
2005	100.0
2006	110.0
2007	121.0
2008	133.1

1. The above table gives a nation's real GDP. What is the growth rate of real GDP in 2006? In 2007? In 2008?

Year	Real GDP growth rate (percent)	Population growth rate (percent)
2005	3	2
2006	4	2
2007	1	2
2008	4	4

2. The table above gives the growth rate of real GDP and the growth rate of population for a nation.
   a. What is the growth rate of real GDP per person for each year?
   b. In what years did the standard of living improve?

3. If a nation's real GDP grows at 3 percent a year, how long does it take for real GDP to double? If the growth rate is 4 percent, how long does it take for real GDP to double? If the growth rate is 5 percent, how long does it take real GDP to double?

CHECKPOINT 10.2

■ **Identify the main sources of economic growth.**

Quick Review

- *Labor productivity* Labor productivity equals real GDP divided by aggregate hours. When labor productivity grows, real GDP per person grows.

Additional Practice Problem 10.2

Item	2003	2004
Aggregate hours (billions)	232.2	234.5
Real GDP (trillions of 2000 dollars)	10.32	10.76

1. The table above provides some data on the U.S. economy in 2003 and 2004.

   a. Calculate the growth rate of real GDP in 2004.

   b. Calculate labor productivity in 2003 and 2004.

   c. Calculate the growth rate of labor productivity in 2004.

   d. How does the growth rate of labor productivity you calculated compare with the typical growth in the United States since 1960?

Solution to Additional Practice Problem 10.2

1a. The growth rate of real GDP in 2004 is [($10.76 trillion – $10.32 trillion) ÷ $10.32 trillion] × 100, which is 4.3 percent.

1b. Labor productivity is real GDP divided by aggregate hours. So labor productivity in 2003 is $10.32 trillion ÷ 232.2 billion hours, which is $44.44 per hour of labor. In 2004 labor productivity is $10.76 trillion ÷ 234.5 billion hours, which is $45.88 per hour of labor.

1c. The growth rate of labor productivity is labor productivity in 2004 minus the labor productivity in 2003, divided by labor productivity in 2003, all multiplied by 100. The growth rate of labor productivity equals [($45.88 per hour – $44.44 per hour) ÷ $44.44 per hour] × 100, which is 3.24 percent.

1d. The increase in labor productivity in 2004 was slower than in the early 1960s but was larger than has been the average since then.

■ **Self Test 10.2**

Fill in the blanks

All influences on real GDP growth can be divided into those that increase aggregate hours and ____ (labor productivity; population). Labor productivity equals real GDP ____ (multiplied by; divided by) aggregate hours. Saving and investment in physical capital ____ (increases; decreases) labor productivity. Education, training, and job experience increase ____ (investment in physical capital; human capital). To reap the benefits of technological change, capital must ____ (increase; decrease).

True or false

1. Real GDP increases if aggregate hours increase or labor productivity increases.

2. If labor productivity increases and aggregate hours do not change, then real GDP per person increases.

3. Higher wages are a source of growth in labor productivity.

4. The discovery and applications of new technology has increased labor productivity.

Multiple choice

1. The only source of growth in aggregate labor hours that is sustainable over long periods of time is

   a. an increase in the labor force participation rate.

   b. population growth.

   c. a decrease in labor productivity.

   d. a decrease in the unemployment rate.

   e. an increase in labor productivity.

2. Real GDP equals aggregate hours

   a. divided by labor productivity.

   b. minus labor productivity.

   c. plus labor productivity.

   d. multiplied by labor productivity.

   e. multiplied by human capital.

3. If real GDP is $1,200 billion, the population is 60 million, and aggregate hours are 80 billion, labor productivity is
   a. $5.00 an hour.
   b. $6.67 an hour.
   c. $15.00 an hour.
   d. $20,000.
   e. $150 an hour.

4. If aggregate hours are 100 billion hours and labor productivity is $40 an hour, than real GDP equals
   a. $100 billion.
   b. $40 billion.
   c. $100 trillion.
   d. $2.5 trillion.
   e. $4 trillion.

5. Which of the following lists gives factors that increase labor productivity?
   a. saving and investment in physical capital, and wage increases
   b. expansion of human capital, labor force increases, and discovery of new technologies
   c. expansion of human capital, population growth, and discovery of new technologies
   d. saving and investment in physical capital, expansion of human capital, and discovery of new technologies
   e. labor force increases and wage increases

6. Growth in physical capital depends most directly upon the amount of
   a. saving and investment.
   b. years the firm has been in existence.
   c. population growth.
   d. government expenditures.
   e. human capital.

7. Human capital is
   a. the same as labor productivity.
   b. a measure of the number of labor hours available.
   c. the accumulated skills and knowledge of workers.
   d. the average number of years of schooling of the labor force.
   e. is what people are born with and cannot be changed.

Short answer and numeric questions

Year	Real GDP (trillion of 2000 dollars)	Aggregate hours (billions)
1964	3.00	133.6
1974	4.32	158.7
1984	5.81	185.3
1994	7.84	211.5
2004	10.76	234.5

1. The table above has data from the United States. For each year, calculate labor productivity.

2. Real GDP is $9 trillion and aggregate hours are 200 billion. What is labor productivity?

3. Aggregate hours are 200 billion and labor productivity is $45 an hour. What is real GDP?

4. What three factors increase labor productivity?

CHECKPOINT 10.3

■ **Review the theories of economic growth that explain why growth rates vary over time and across countries.**

Quick Review

- *Classical growth theory* The clash between an exploding population and limited resources will eventually bring economic growth to an end. Income is driven to the subsistence level.
- *Neoclassical growth theory* Real GDP per person will increase as long as technology keeps advancing. No explanation is given for technological growth.
- *New growth theory* Unlimited wants will lead us to ever greater productivity and perpetual economic growth.

Additional Practice Problem 10.3

1. How do each of the growth theories reflect the period during which they were developed?

2. Some advisors urge less developed nations to restrict their birth rate. These advisors claim that a high birth rate impoverishes a nation.
   a. What growth theory are these advisors following?
   b. What would a new growth theory proponent say about this recommendation?

Solutions to Additional Practice Problems 10.3

1. The classical growth theory was developed during the industrial revolution. Observers such as Thomas Malthus, saw some technological advances and rapid population growth. They combined these two observations into the classical growth theory, which predicts a return to a subsistence level of real GDP per person.

   The neoclassical growth theory was developed in the 1950s, when rapid population growth was no longer a worry and when technological growth and the capital per hour of labor were starting to grow more rapidly. The neoclassical growth theory assigned a key role to these latter two factors and concluded that growth would persist as long as technology advanced.

   The new growth theory was developed in the 1980s, when technological growth exploded. The new growth theory assigns importance to technological growth. Based on the observation that technological growth has persisted during the past 200 years, the new growth theory concludes that technology, and so real GDP, will grow forever.

2a. These advisors are following the classical theory of economic growth. They believe that if real GDP per person rises in these nations, then the birth rate will increase and drive real GDP per person back to the subsistence level. They identify the low real GDP per person in these nations with a high birth rate and the resulting high population growth rate.

2b. A new growth theory proponent likely would disagree with the suggestion to limit the birth rate. According to this theory, the pace at which new discoveries are made and

at which technology advances depends on how many people are looking for a new technology and how intensively they are looking. In this case, limiting the population leads to a reduction in the discovery of new technologies and a decrease in the growth rate of real GDP per person.

■ Self Test 10.3

Fill in the blanks

The classical growth theory is the same as the ____ (Malthusian; new growth) theory. Classical growth theory says an increase in real GDP per person leads to more rapid growth in ____. Neoclassical growth theory asserts that economic growth continues as long as ____ (the population grows; technology advances). According to the neoclassical theory, technology advances occur as a result of ____ (people's choices; chance). New growth theory predicts that economic growth will persist ____ (temporarily; indefinitely). The description that growth is like a perpetual motion machine best fits the ____ (classical; neoclassical; new) growth theory.

True or false

1. The classical theory of growth concludes that eventually real GDP per person returns to the subsistence level.

2. According to the neoclassical theory, the rate of technological change does not influence the rate of economic growth.

3. The new growth theory predicts that economic growth can persist indefinitely.

4. An increase in labor productivity increases the demand for labor and shifts the production function downward.

Multiple choice

1. Classical growth theory predicts that increases in
   a. real GDP per person are permanent and sustainable.
   b. real GDP per person are temporary and not sustainable.
   c. resources permanently increase labor productivity.
   d. resources permanently increase real GDP per person.
   e. competition increase economic growth.

2. If real income is above the subsistence level then, according to classical growth theory,
   a. the population will increase.
   b. the population will decrease.
   c. the standard of living will continue to improve.
   d. labor productivity will increase.
   e. more technological advances occur.

3. Neoclassical growth theory predicts that economic growth is
   a. only temporary due to overpopulation.
   b. the result of technological advances.
   c. impossible due to extremes in weather.
   d. caused by women entering the work force.
   e. increased by decreasing labor productivity.

4. The new growth theory states that
   a. technological advances are the result of random chance.
   b. technological advances result from choices.
   c. technological advances are the responsibility of the government.
   d. the subsistence income level leads to technological advances.
   e. it is impossible to replicate production activities.

5. The theory that suggests that our unlimited wants will lead to perpetual economic growth is the
   a. classical growth theory.
   b. sustained growth theory.
   c. neoclassical growth theory.
   d. new growth theory.
   e. Keynesian growth theory.

6. An increase in labor productivity ____ and ____ the demand for labor.
   a. leads to a movement upward along the production function; increases
   b. leads to a movement upward along the production function; decreases
   c. shifts the production function upward; does not change
   d. shifts the production function downward; increases
   e. shifts the production function upward; increases

Short answer and numeric questions

1. What role do technological advances play in each of the three growth theories?

2. What role does population growth play in each of the three growth theories?

3. What role do diminishing returns play in the new growth theory?

4. Which growth theory is most pessimistic about the prospects for persistent economic growth? Which is most optimistic?

CHECKPOINT 10.4

■ Describe policies that might speed economic growth.

Quick Review

- *Preconditions for economic growth* The three preconditions are economic freedom, property rights, and markets.
- *Policies to achieve growth* Five policies are to create incentive mechanisms, encourage saving, encourage research and development, encourage international trade, and improve the quality of education.

Additional Practice Problem 10.4

1. In 1949 East and West Germany had about the same real GDP per person. By 1989 West Germany had a real GDP per person more than twice the level of East Germany's. Why did East Germany grow so much more slowly than West Germany over those 40 years?

Solution to Additional Practice Problem 10.4

1. In 1949, East Germany was formed with state ownership of capital and land, and virtually no economic freedom. West Germany was formed with private ownership of most capital and land, and significant economic freedom.

    West Germany had the preconditions for economic growth; East Germany did not. When East Germany collapsed in 1989, West Germany had more human capital, more capital per hour of labor, and better technology. The different incentives had given West German workers the incentive to acquire human capital, West German investors the incentive to acquire physical capital, and West German entrepreneurs the incentive to innovate new and better technology.

■ Self Test 10.4

Fill in the blanks

____, ____, and ____ are preconditions for economic growth. Policies the government can take to encourage faster economic growth are to ____ (create; discourage) incentive mechanisms; ____ (encourage; discourage) saving; ____ (encourage; discourage) research and development; ____ (encourage; discourage) international trade; and improve the quality of ____ (education; pollution control).

True or false

1. To achieve economic growth, economic freedom must be coupled with a democratic political system.

2. Markets slow specialization and hence slow economic growth.

3. Encouraging saving can increase the growth of capital and stimulate economic growth.

4. Limiting international trade will increase economic growth.

Multiple choice

1. Economic freedom means that
   a. firms are regulated by the government.
   b. some goods and services are free.
   c. people are able to make personal choices and their property is protected.
   d. the rule of law does not apply.
   e. the nation's government is a democracy.

2. Property rights protect
   a. only the rights to physical property.
   b. only the rights to financial property.
   c. all rights except rights to intellectual property.
   d. rights to physical property, financial property, and intellectual property.
   e. the government's right to impose taxes.

3. Which of the following statements is FALSE?
   a. Saving helps create economic growth.
   b. Improvements in the quality of education are important for economic growth.
   c. Free international trade helps create economic growth.
   d. Faster population growth is the key to growth in real GDP per person.
   e. Economic freedom requires property rights.

4. Saving
   a. slows growth because it decreases consumption.
   b. finances investment which brings capital accumulation.
   c. has no impact on economic growth.
   d. is very low in most East Asian nations.
   e. is important for a country to gain the benefits of international trade.

5. The fastest growing nations today are those with
   a. barriers that significantly limit international trade.
   b. the fastest growing exports and imports.
   c. government intervention in markets to ensure high prices.
   d. few funds spent on research and development.
   e. the least saving.

6. Economic growth is enhanced by
   a. free international trade.
   b. limiting international trade so that the domestic economy can prosper.
   c. discouraging saving, because increased saving means less spending.
   d. ignoring incentive systems.
   e. increasing welfare payments to the poor so they can afford to buy goods.

Short answer and numeric questions

1. Does persistent economic growth necessarily occur when a nation meets all the preconditions for growth?

2. What role do specialization and trade play in determining economic growth?

3. Is it possible for the government to create a large increase in the economic growth rate, say from 3 percent to 10 percent in a year?

SELF TEST ANSWERS

■ CHECKPOINT 10.1

Fill in the blanks

The growth rate of real GDP equals real GDP in the current year minus real GDP in the previous year divided by real GDP in the <u>previous</u> year, all multiplied by 100. The growth rate of real GDP per person equals the growth rate of real GDP <u>minus</u> the growth rate of the population. The number of years it takes for the level of any variable to double is approximately <u>70</u> divided by the annual percentage growth rate of the variable.

True or false

1. True; page 242
2. True; page 242
3. True; page 243
4. False; page 243

Multiple choice

1. a; page 242
2. b; page 242
3. d; page 242
4. a; page 243
5. b; page 243
6. b; page 243

Short answer and numeric questions

1. 10 percent; 10 percent; 10 percent; page 242.
2. a. 1 percent; 2 percent; –1 percent; 0 percent; page 243.
   b. 2005 and 2006; page 240.
3. Use the Rule of 70. So, 70 ÷ 3 = 23.3 years; 70 ÷ 4 = 17.5 years; 70 ÷ 5 = 14 years; page 243.

■ CHECKPOINT 10.2

Fill in the blanks

All influences on real GDP growth can be divided into those that increase aggregate hours and <u>labor productivity</u>. Labor productivity equals real GDP <u>divided by</u> aggregate hours.

Saving and investment in physical capital <u>increases</u> labor productivity. Education, training, and job experience increase <u>human capital</u>. To reap the benefits of technological change, capital must <u>increase</u>.

True or false

1. True; page 246
2. True; page 247
3. False; page 247
4. True; page 248

Multiple choice

1. b; page 246
2. d; page 246
3. c; page 246
4. e; page 246
5. d; page 247
6. a; page 247
7. c; page 247

Short answer and numeric questions

1. Labor productivity equals real GDP ÷ aggregate hours. So labor productivity in 1964 was $22.45 an hour; in 1974 was $27.22 an hour; in 1984 was $31.35 an hour; in 1994 was $37.07 an hour; and in 2004 was $45.88 an hour; page 246.
2. Labor productivity is $45 an hour; page 246.
3. Real GDP is $9 trillion; page 246.
4. Labor productivity is increased by three factors. First, increasing saving and investment in physical capital gives workers more capital with which to work. Second, increasing the amount of human capital makes workers more productive and increases labor productivity. Finally, discovering new technologies makes workers more productive and increases labor productivity; by pages 247-248.

■ CHECKPOINT 10.3

Fill in the blanks

The classical growth theory is the same as the Malthusian theory. Classical growth theory says an increase in real GDP per person leads to more rapid growth in population. Neoclassical growth theory asserts that economic growth continues as long as technology advances. According to the neoclassical theory, technology advances occur as a result of chance. New growth theory predicts that economic growth will persist indefinitely. The description that growth is like a perpetual motion machine best fits the new growth theory.

True or false

1. True; pages 252-253
2. False; page 254
3. True; pages 257-258
4. False; page 257

Multiple choice

1. b; pages 252-253
2. a; page 252
3. b; page 254
4. b; pages 255-256
5. d; page 257
6. e; page 257

Short answer and numeric questions

1. In the classical growth theory, advances in technology start a temporary period of economic growth; in the neoclassical growth theory, economic growth continues as long as technology advances; and in the new growth theory, economic growth continues indefinitely, in part because technology grows indefinitely; pages 252, 254, 255-257.

2. Population growth plays a crucial role only in the classical growth theory because in that theory population growth leads the economy back to a subsistence real income; pages 252-253.

3. The new growth theory assumes that the economy is not subject to diminishing returns. So as capital accumulates, labor productivity grows indefinitely; page 256.

4. The most optimistic theory is the new growth theory, which concludes that economic growth can continue forever. The most pessimistic theory is the classical theory, which concludes that the economy will return to a subsistence level of real income; pages 252-253, 256-258.

■ CHECKPOINT 10.4

Fill in the blanks

Economic freedom, property rights, and markets are preconditions for economic growth. Policies the government can take to encourage faster economic growth are to create incentive mechanisms; encourage saving; encourage research and development; encourage international trade; and improve the quality of education.

True or false

1. False; page 261
2. False; pages 261-262
3. True; page 262
4. False; page 263

Multiple choice

1. c; page 261
2. d; page 261
3. d; page 261-262
4. b; page 262
5. b; page 263
6. a; page 263

Short answer and numeric questions

1. No. The preconditions for growth are necessary for growth to occur. But for growth to be persistent, people must face incentives that encourage saving and investment, expansion of human capital, and the discovery and application of new technologies; pages 261-262.

2. Growth begins when people can specialize in the activities in which they have a comparative advantage and trade with each other. As an economy reaps the benefits from specialization and trade, production and consumption grow, real GDP per person increases, and the standard of living rises; page 262.

3. No, the government cannot create a huge increase in the economic growth rate. The government can pursue policies that will nudge the growth rate upward. And, over time, policies that create even small increases in the economic growth rate will have large benefits; page 263.

Money and the Monetary System

Chapter 11

Chapter 11 defines money, describes the U.S. monetary system, and describes the functions of the Federal Reserve System.

■ **Define money and describe its functions.**

Money is any commodity or token that is generally accepted as a means of payment. Money serves three functions. It is a medium of exchange (an object that is generally accepted in return for goods and services), a unit of account (an agreed-upon measure for stating the prices of goods and services), and a store of value (any commodity or token that can be held and exchanged later for goods and services). Money consists of currency (dollar bills and coins) and deposits at banks and other financial institutions. Currency in a bank is not money. Deposits are money but checks are not money. Credit cards, debit cards, and electronic checks are not money. M1 and M2 are two official measures of money. M1 is currency held by individuals and businesses and traveler's checks plus checkable deposits owned by individuals and businesses. M2 is M1 plus savings and time deposits, and money market funds and other deposits. Some items in M2 are not technically money because they are not a means of payment.

■ **Describe the monetary system and explain the functions of banks and other monetary institutions.**

The monetary system consists of the Federal Reserve and the banks and other institutions that accept deposits and provide the services that enable people and businesses to make and receive payments. Three types of financial institutions are commercial banks, thrift institutions, and money market funds. Banks make loans at a higher interest rate than the interest rate paid on deposits. A bank has four types of assets: cash assets, interbank loans, securities, and loans. A bank's cash assets consist of its reserves and funds that are due from other banks as payments for checks that are being cleared. Monetary institutions create liquidity, lower the costs of lending and borrowing, pool risks, and make payments.

■ **Describe the functions of the Federal Reserve System.**

The Federal Reserve System is the central bank of the United States. The Fed conducts the nation's monetary policy. The Board of Governors has seven members. There are 12 regional Federal Reserve banks. The Federal Open Market Committee is the Fed's main policy-making committee and consists of the Board of Governors, the president of the Federal Reserve Bank of New York, and four presidents of other regional Federal Reserve banks. The Fed uses three tools to control the quantity of money: required reserve ratios (the minimum percentage of deposits banks must hold as reserves), discount rate (the interest rate at which the Fed stands ready to lend reserves to commercial banks), and open market operations (purchase or sale of government securities by the Fed in the open market). The monetary base is the sum of coins, Federal Reserve notes, and banks' reserves held at the Fed. To decrease the quantity of money, the Fed can increase the required reserve ratio, raise the discount rate, or sell securities in the open market.

CHECKPOINT 11.1

■ **Define money and describe its functions.**

Quick Review

- *M1* M1 consists of currency held by individuals and businesses, and traveler's checks plus checkable deposits owned by individuals and businesses. Currency inside banks is not counted.

- *M2* M2 consists of M1 plus savings deposits and small time deposits, money market funds, and other deposits.

Additional Practice Problems 11.1

1. You go to the bank and withdraw $200 from your checking account. You keep $100 in cash and deposit the other $100 in your savings account. What is the change in M1? What is the change in M2?

2. Janice goes to her bank's website and transfers $300 from her checking account to her savings account. What is the change in M1? What is the change in M2

3. In January 2001, currency held by individuals and businesses was $534.9 billion; traveler's checks were $8.1 billion; checkable deposits owned by individuals and businesses were $559.3 billion; savings deposits were $1,889.7 billion; small time deposits were $1,052.6 billion; and money market funds and other deposits were $952 billion.
   a. What was M1 in January 2001?
   b. What was M2 in January 2001?

Solutions to Additional Practice Problems 11.1

1. Your checking account decreased by $200, your currency increased by $100, and your savings account increased by $100. M1, which includes your currency and your checkable deposit, is changed by the decrease in the checking account and the increase in currency. The net effect on M1 is –$200 + $100 = –$100, that is, M1 decreases by $100. M2, which includes your currency, your checkable deposits, and your savings account, does not change. The change

in your checkable deposits, –$200, is balanced by the change in your currency, +$100, and the change in your savings account, +100. There was no change in M2.

2. M1 decreases by $300. While the funds were in Janice's checking account, they were part of M1. But once they are transferred to her savings account, they are no longer part of M1. M2 does not change. The $300 was part of M2 when it was in Janice's checking account because funds in checking accounts are part of M1 and all of M1 is in M2. And, funds in savings accounts are also part of M2. So switching funds from a checking account to a savings account does not change M2.

3a. M1 is the sum of currency, traveler's checks, and checkable deposits owned by individuals and businesses. So, M1 equals $534.9 billion + $8.1 billion + $559.3 billion, which is $1,102.3 billion.

3b. M2 equals M1 plus savings deposits, small time deposits, and money market funds and other deposits. So M2 equals $1,102.3 billion + $1,889.7 billion + $1,052.6 billion + $952 billion, which is $4,996.6 billion.

■ **Self Test 11.1**

Fill in the blanks

Any commodity or token that is generally accepted as a means of payment is ____. A ____ (unit of account; store of value; medium of exchange) is an object that is generally accepted in return for goods and services. A ____ (unit of account; store of value; medium of exchange) is an agreed-upon measure for stating prices of goods and services. A ____ (unit of account; store of value; medium of exchange) is any commodity or token that can be held and exchanged later for goods and services. Currency inside the banks ____ (is; is not) money and currency outside the banks ____ (is; is not) money. A credit card ____ (is; is not) money. M1 is ____ (more; less) than M2. Checkable deposits ____ (are; are not) part of M1 and savings deposits ____ (are; are not) part of M1.

True or false

1. Using money as a medium of exchange is called barter.

2. Prices in terms of money reflect money's role as a unit of account.

3. Currency is money but checkable deposits at banks are not money.

4. A debit card is not money.

5. M1 and M2 are official measures of money.

Multiple choice

1. Which of the following best defines what money is now and what it has been in the past?
   a. currency
   b. currency plus checking deposits
   c. currency plus credit cards
   d. anything accepted as a means of payment
   d. anything used as a store of value

2. For something to be a "means of payment" means that the asset
   a. is valuable and backed by gold.
   b. is valuable and backed by the government.
   c. can be used to settle a debt.
   d. requires a double coincidence of wants.
   e. must be used when bartering.

3. Which of the following is not a function of money?
   i.   unit of account
   ii. store of value
   iii. unit of debt
      a. i only.
      b. ii only.
      c. iii only.
      d. Both ii and iii.
      e. Both i and ii.

4. Barter is
   a. the exchange of goods and services for money.
   b. the pricing of goods and services with one agreed upon standard.
   c. the exchange of goods and services directly for other goods and services.
   d. a generally accepted means of payment.
   e. storing money for use at a later date.

5. If someone buries money in a tin can beneath a tree, the money is functioning as a
   a. medium of exchange.
   b. unit of account.
   c. means of payment.
   d. store of value.
   e. bartering tool.

6. Credit cards, debit cards, and e-checks are
   a. always counted as money.
   b. not money.
   c. sometimes counted as money, depending on how they are used.
   d. sometimes counted as money, depending on what is purchased.
   e. sometimes counted as money, depending on what measure of money is being used.

7. Which of the following counts as part of M1?
   a. $5,000 worth of gold
   b. $5,000 worth of government bonds
   c. $5,000 in a checking account
   d. $5,000 credit line on a credit card
   e. $5,000 of real estate

8. M2 equals
   a. M1 and is just another name for currency outside of banks.
   b. M1 plus savings deposits, small time deposits, and money market fund deposits.
   c. M1 minus traveler's checks because they are not really money.
   d. currency plus savings deposits, all time deposits, and money market funds and other deposits.
   e. M1 plus savings deposits and small time deposits minus money market fund deposits.

9. If currency held by individuals and businesses is $800 billion; traveler's checks are $10 billion; checkable deposits owned by individuals and businesses are $700 billion; savings deposits are $4,000 billion; small time deposits are $1,000 billion; and money market funds and other deposits are $800 billion, then M1 equals ____ billion.
   a. $7,310
   b. $5,800
   c. $2,510
   d. $1,510
   e. $710

10. If currency held by individuals and businesses is $800 billion; traveler's checks are $10 billion; checkable deposits owned by individuals and businesses are $700 billion; savings deposits are $4,000 billion; small time deposits are $1,000 billion; and money market funds and other deposits are $800 billion, then M2 equals ____ billion.
    a. $7,310
    b. $5,800
    c. $2,510
    d. $1,510
    e. $710

Short answer and numeric questions

1. Why was it possible at one time to use whale's teeth as money?
2. What are the functions of money?
3. Why is currency money?
4. Why are e-checks not money?
5. In January 2005, currency held by individuals and businesses was $699.6 billion; traveler's checks were $7.5 billion; checkable deposits owned by individuals and businesses were $649.2 billion; savings deposits were $3,544.7 billion; small time deposits were $824.5 billion; and money market funds and other deposits were $711.4 billion.
   a. What was M1 in January 2005?
   b. What was M2 in January 2005?
6. Some parts of M2 are not money. Why are these parts included in M2?

CHECKPOINT 11.2

■ **Describe the monetary system and explain the functions of banks and other monetary institutions.**

Quick Review

- *Reserves* A bank's reserves consist of the currency in its vault plus the balance on its reserve account at a Federal Reserve Bank.

Additional Practice Problems 11.2

1. The Acme Bank just sold $100 in securities in exchange for a $100 bill. It made a $50 loan, and the borrower left with the cash. It also accepted a $60 cash deposit.
   a. How have the bank's reserves changed as a result of all these actions?
   b. How have its deposits changed?

2. A bank has the following deposits and assets: $300 in checkable deposits, $800 in savings deposits, $900 in small time deposits, $1,000 in loans to businesses, $950 in government securities, $20 in currency, and $30 in its reserve account at the Fed. Calculate the bank's:
   a. Total deposits
   b. Deposits that are part of M1
   c. Deposits that are part of M2
   d. Reserves
   e. What is the ratio of the bank's reserves to its deposits?

Solutions to Additional Practice Problems 11.2

1a. The $100 sale of securities adds $100 to reserves. The $50 loan which the borrower then withdrew as cash removes $50 from the bank and out of its reserves, and the $60 deposit adds to reserves. The net result is +$100 − $50 + $60, which is +$110. Acme has $110 more in reserves.

1b. The $60 deposit is the only transaction that affects its deposits, so deposits rise by $60.

2a. Total deposits are the sum of checkable deposits, $300, savings deposits, $800, and small time deposits, $900, which equals a total of $2,000.

2b. The only deposits that are part of M1 are checkable deposits, $300.

2c. All of the bank's deposits are part of M2, so deposits that are part of M2 are $2,000.

2d. Reserves are the currency in the bank's vault plus the balance on its reserve account at a Federal Reserve Bank. Reserves are $20 + $30, which equals $50.

2e. The ratio of reserves to deposits is $50 ÷ $2,000, which equals 2.5 percent.

■ Self Test 11.2

Fill in the blanks

The currency in a bank's vault is part of the bank's ____ (reserves; loans). Banks can borrow or lend reserves in the ____ (reserves; federal funds) market. At commercial banks in the United States, the majority of deposits ____ (are; are not) checkable deposits. An asset that can easily and with certainty be converted into money is called a ____ asset. Banks ____ (lower; raise) the costs of lending and borrowing.

True or false

1. A commercial bank accepts checkable deposits, savings deposits, and time deposits.

2. A commercial bank maximizes its stockholders' long-term wealth by refusing to make any risky loans.

3. When a credit union has excess reserves, it makes loans to its members at an interest rate called the federal funds rate.

4. Thrift institutions provide most of the nation's bank deposits.

5. By lending to a large number of businesses and individuals, a bank lowers the average risk it faces.

Multiple choice

1. A commercial bank's main goal is to
   a. provide loans to its customers.
   b. maximize the long-term wealth of its stockholders.
   c. help the government when it needs money.
   d. lend money to the Federal Reserve banks.
   e. open checking accounts.

2. A bank divides its assets into four parts:
   a. cash assets, interbank loans, securities, and loans.
   b. reserves, securities, bonds, and loans.
   c. reserves, bonds, cash securities, and interbank loans.
   d. securities, reserves, debts, and interbank cash.
   e. reserves, checkable deposits, securities, and loans.

3. A commercial bank's reserves are
   a. bonds issued by the U.S. government that are very safe.
   b. the provision of funds to businesses and individuals.
   c. currency in its vault plus the balance on its reserve account at a Federal Reserve Bank.
   d. savings and time deposits.
   e. its loans.

4. A bank has $400 in checking deposits, $800 in savings deposits, $700 in time deposits, $900 in loans to businesses, $300 in outstanding credit card balances, $500 in government securities, $10 in currency in its vault, and $20 in deposits at the Fed. The bank's deposits that are part of M1 are equal to
   a. $1,900.
   b. $400.
   c. $1,210.
   d. $530.
   e. $410.

5. Which of the following accepts deposits from or sell shares to the general public?
    i.   money market funds.
    ii. thrift institutions.
    iii. commercial banks.
    a. i only.
    b. ii only.
    c. iii only.
    d. ii and iii.
    e. i, ii, and iii.

6. Which of the following is a thrift institution?
    a. a savings and loan association
    b. a money market fund
    c. a commercial bank
    d. a loan institution
    e. the Federal Reserve

7. Banks and other monetary institutions perform which of the following functions?
    i.   create liquidity
    ii. pool the risks of lending
    iii. make loans to the Federal Reserve
    a. i only.
    b. ii only.
    c. iii only.
    d. i and ii.
    e. i, ii, and iii.

8. We define a liquid asset as
    a. any deposit held at a commercial bank.
    b. bank loans made to low-risk borrowers.
    c. any asset than can be converted into money easily and with certainty.
    d. any deposit held with the Federal Reserve.
    e. any liability of a commercial bank.

Short answer and numeric questions

1. What are a bank's reserves? How does a bank use its account at the Federal Reserve Bank?

2. Which is a larger percentage of M1: commercial bank deposits or thrift institution deposits?

3. What economic functions are performed by the nation's monetary institutions?

4. What does it mean for banks to "pool risk"?

CHECKPOINT 11.3

■ **Describe the functions of the Federal Reserve System.**

Quick Review

*   *Federal Reserve System* The Federal Reserve System is the central bank of the United States. It conducts the nation's monetary policy.

Additional Practice Problems 11.3

1. What are required reserve ratios?
2. What is the discount rate?
3. In August, 2005 Federal Reserve notes and coins were $785 billion, and banks' reserves at the Fed are $9 billion, the gold stock was $11 billion, and the Fed owned $742 billion of government securities. What did the monetary base equal?

Solutions to Additional Practice Problems 11.3

1. Banks are required by law to hold a certain fraction of their deposits as reserves. The Federal Reserve determines what fraction banks must hold as reserves. These fractions are called the banks' required reserve ratios.

2. Banks can borrow reserves from the Federal Reserve. The interest rate they pay on these loans is the discount rate.

3. The monetary base is the sum of the coins and Federal Reserve notes plus banks' reserves at the Fed. In this case the monetary base equals $785 billion + $9 billion, which is $794 billion.

■ **Self Test 11.3**

Fill in the blanks

The Fed conducts the nation's ____ policy. There are ____ (2; 6; 12) Federal Reserve Banks. The Fed's main policy-making committee is the ____ (Board of Governors; Federal Open Market Committee). The Fed sets the minimum percentage of deposits that must be held as reserves, which is called the ____ (discount rate; required reserve ratio). The interest rate at which the Fed stands ready to lend reserves to commercial banks is the ____ (discount; open market operation) rate. The purchase or sale of government securities by the Federal Reserve is an ____.

True or false
1. The Federal Reserve System is the central bank of the United States.
2. In practice, the power in the Fed resides with the Board of Governors.
3. An open market operation is the purchase or sale of government securities by the Federal Reserve from the U.S. government.
4. If banks use $1 million of reserves to buy $1 million worth of newly printed bank notes from the Fed, the monetary base does not change.
5. Federal Reserve notes are an asset of the Fed.

Multiple choice
1. Regulating the amount of money in the United States is one of the most important responsibilities of the
   a. State Department.
   b. state governments.
   c. Treasury Department.
   d. Federal Reserve.
   e. U.S. Mint.

2. The Board of Governors of the Federal Reserve System has
   a. 12 members appointed by the president of the United States.
   b. 12 members elected by the public.
   c. seven members appointed by the president of the United States.
   d. seven members elected by the public.
   e. seven members appointed to life terms.

3. The Fed's monetary policy is determined by the
   a. Federal Open Market Committee.
   b. Executive Council to the Governor.
   c. Regional Federal Reserve Banks.
   d. Board of Governors.
   e. Federal Monetary Policy Committee.

4. The most influential position in the Federal Reserve System is the
   a. president of the Federal Reserve Bank of New York.
   b. chairman of the Board of Governors.
   c. chairman of the Federal Reserve Bank presidents.
   d. president of the Federal Reserve Bank of Chicago.
   e. most senior member of the Board of Governors.

5. The Fed's policy tools include
   a. required reserve ratios, the discount rate, and open market operations.
   b. holding deposits for the U.S. government, reserve requirements, and the discount rate.
   c. setting regulations for lending standards and approving or rejecting loans banks make to large corporations.
   d. supervision of the banking system and buying and selling commercial banks.
   e. required reserve ratios, income tax rates, and open market operations.

6. The minimum percent of deposits that banks must hold is determined by the
   a. interest rate.
   b. discount rate.
   c. required reserve ratio.
   d. federal funds rate.
   e. ratio of M2 to M1.

7. The discount rate is the interest rate that
   a. commercial banks charge their customers.
   b. commercial banks charge each other for the loan of reserves.
   c. the Fed charges the government.
   d. the Fed charges commercial banks for the loan of reserves.
   e. the Fed pays commercial banks on their reserves held at the Fed.

8. The monetary base is the
   a. minimum reserves banks must hold to cover any losses from unpaid loans.
   b. sum of coins, Federal Reserve notes, and banks' reserves at the Fed.
   c. sum of gold and foreign exchange held by the Fed.
   d. sum of government securities and loans to banks held by the Fed.
   e. sum of coins, required reserves, and bank loans.

9. If Federal Reserve notes and coins are $765 billion, and banks' reserves at the Fed are $8 billion, the gold stock is $11 billion, and the Fed owns $725 billion of government securities, what does the monetary base equal?
   a. $765 billion.
   b. $773 billion.
   c. $776 billion.
   d. $744 billion.
   e. $1,509 billion.

10. If the Federal Reserve _____ the required reserve ratio, the quantity of money _____.
   a. lowers; increases
   b. lowers; decreases
   c. raises; does not change
   d. raises; increases
   e. Not enough information is given because the effect depends also on the size of the monetary base.

Short answer and numeric questions

1. How many people are on the Board of Governors of the Federal Reserve System? How are they selected?

2. What is the FOMC and who are its members?

3. Suppose that banks' deposits are $600 billion and that the required reserve ratio is 10 percent.
   a. What is the minimum amount of reserves banks must hold?
   b. Suppose the Federal Reserve lowers the required reserve ratio to 8 percent. Now what is the minimum amount of reserves banks must hold?
   c. Suppose the Federal Reserve raises the required reserve ratio to 12 percent. Now what is the minimum amount of reserves banks must hold?

4. What is the monetary base?

5. Are U.S. government securities an asset or a liability of the Federal Reserve? Are Federal Reserve notes an asset or a liability of the Federal Reserve?

SELF TEST ANSWERS

■ CHECKPOINT 11.1

Fill in the blanks

Any commodity or token that is generally accepted as a means of payment is <u>money</u>. A <u>medium of exchange</u> is an object that is generally accepted in return for goods and services. A <u>unit of account</u> is an agreed-upon measure for stating prices of goods and services. A <u>store of value</u> is any commodity or token that can be held and exchanged later for goods and services. Currency inside the banks <u>is not</u> money and currency outside the banks <u>is</u> money. A credit card <u>is not</u> money. M1 is <u>less</u> than M2. Checkable deposits <u>are</u> part of M1 and savings deposits <u>are not</u> part of M1.

True or false

1. False; page 271
2. True; page 271
3. False; page 272
4. True; page 274
5. True; page 275

Multiple choice

1. d; page 270
2. c; page 270
3. c; pages 270-271
4. c; page 271
5. d; page 271
6. b; pages 273-274
7. c; page 275
8. b; page 275
9. d; page 275
10. a; page 275

Short answer and numeric questions

1. It was possible to use whale's teeth as money because whale's teeth were generally accepted as a means of payment. At one time, most people were willing to trade goods and services in exchange for whale's teeth; page 270.

2. Money has three functions. It is a medium of exchange, an object that is generally accepted in return for goods and services. It is a unit of account, an agreed-upon measure for stating the prices of goods and services. And it is a store of value, a commodity or token that can be held and exchanged at a later date for goods and services; pages 270-271.

3. Currency is money because it is generally accepted as a means of payment. It is generally accepted because the government has declared that currency is money, so that currency is fiat money; page 272.

4. E-checks are not money because they are instructions to transfer money from one person's deposit account to another person's deposit account; page 274.

5. a. M1 is the sum of currency, traveler's checks, and checkable deposits owned by individuals and businesses. So, M1 equals $699.6 billion + $7.5 billion + $649.2 billion, which is $1,356.3 billion; page 275.

   b. M2 equals M1 plus savings deposits, small time deposits, and money market funds and other deposits. So M2 equals $1,356.3 billion + $3,544.7 billion + $824.5 billion + $711.4 billion, which is $6,436.9 billion; page 275.

6. Time deposits, money market funds, and some of the savings deposits included in M2 are not money. They are not money because they are not a means of payment. They are included in M2 because they are very easily converted into money; page 275.

■ CHECKPOINT 11.2

Fill in the blanks

The currency in a bank's vault is part of the bank's <u>reserves</u>. Banks can borrow or lend reserves in the <u>federal funds</u> market. At commercial banks in the United States, the majority of deposits <u>are not</u> checkable deposits. An asset that can easily and with certainty be converted into money is called a <u>liquid</u> asset. Banks <u>lower</u> the costs of lending and borrowing.

True or false

1. True; page 278
2. False; page 279
3. False; pages 279-280
4. False; page 281
5. True; page 282

Multiple choice

1. b; page 279
2. a; page 279
3. c; page 279
4. b; page 279
5. e; pages 278, 280
6. a; page 280
7. d; page 282
8. c; page 282

Short answer and numeric questions

1. A bank's reserves are the currency in its vault plus the balance on its reserve account at a Federal Reserve bank. A bank uses its account at the Fed to receive and make payments to other banks and to obtain currency; page 279.

2. Commercial bank deposits are a larger percentage of M1 than thrift institution deposits. Commercial bank deposits are about 38 percent of M1, while thrift institution deposits are about 10 percent; page 281.

3. The nation's monetary institutions perform four economic functions: They create liquidity, they lower the cost of lending and borrowing, they pool risks, and they make payments; pages 282-283.

4. "Pooling risk" refers to the point that making loans is risky because the borrower might not repay the loan. If a lender has loaned to only one borrower who does not repay the loan, the lender suffers a large loss. Banks make loans to many different borrowers and "pool" (or gather together) the risk of the loans. Although some loans will not be repaid, the majority will be repaid and so the average risk from failure to be repaid is lower; page 282.

■ **CHECKPOINT 11.3**

Fill in the blanks

The Fed conducts the nation's <u>monetary</u> policy. There are <u>12</u> Federal Reserve Banks. The Fed's main policy-making committee is the <u>Federal Open Market Committee</u>. The Fed sets the minimum percentage of deposits that must be held as reserves, which is called the <u>required reserve ratio</u>. The interest rate at which the Fed stands ready to lend reserves to commercial banks is the <u>discount</u> rate. The purchase or sale of government securities by the Federal Reserve is an <u>open market operation</u>.

True or false

1. True; page 285
2. False; page 286
3. False; page 288
4. True; page 288
5. False; page 288

Multiple choice

1. d; page 285
2. c; page 286
3. a; page 286
4. b; page 286
5. a; pages 287-288
6. c; page 287
7. d; page 287
8. b; page 288
9. b; page 288
10. a; page 289

Short answer and numeric questions

1. There are seven members on the Board of Governors of the Federal Reserve System. They are appointed by the president of the United States and confirmed by the U.S. Senate; page 286.

2. The FOMC is the Federal Open Market Committee and it is the main policy-making committee of the Federal Reserve. The members are the seven members of the Board of Governors, the president of the Federal Reserve Bank of New York, and, on an annual

rotating basis, four presidents of the other regional Federal Reserve banks; page 286.

3. a. If the required reserve ratio is 10 percent, banks must keep ($600 billion) × (0.10) = $60 billion as reserves; page 287.

   b. If the required reserve ratio is lowered to 8 percent, banks must keep ($600 billion) × (0.08) = $48 billion as reserves. A decrease in the required reserve ratio decreases the total amount of reserves banks must keep; page 287.

   c. If the required reserve ratio is raised to 12 percent, banks must keep ($600 billion) × (0.12) = $72 billion as reserves. An increase in the required reserve ratio increases the total amount of reserves banks must keep page 287.

4. The monetary base is the sum of coins, Federal Reserve notes, and banks' reserves at the Federal Reserve; page 288.

5. U.S. government securities are the Federal Reserve's largest asset. Federal Reserve notes (currency) are the largest liability of the Fed; page 288.

Money Creation and Control

Chapter 12

Chapter 12 explains how banks create money and how the money supply is controlled by the Fed.

■ **Explain how banks create money by making loans.**

Banks accept deposits. They hold some deposits as reserves and use the rest to buy government securities and make loans. Deposits are a liability of the bank; reserves, government securities, and loans are assets of the bank. When a check is written, the recipient deposits it in another bank. Deposits and reserves in the first bank decrease and in the second bank increase. The total amount of deposits, however, does not change. The required reserve ratio is the ratio of reserves to deposits that banks are required by regulation to hold. Excess reserves are actual reserves minus required reserves. Banks use excess reserves to buy government securities or make loans. When a bank makes a loan, it deposits the amount loaned in the checkable deposit of the borrower. The bank has now created money. To spend the loan, the borrower writes a check. The bank loses deposits and reserves when the check clears. The bank in which the check is deposited gains the reserves and deposits. This bank now has excess reserves, which it lends. When this loan is spent, a third bank gains reserves and deposits. The process is limited and eventually concludes because at each round the change in excess reserves shrinks. An initial increase in a bank's excess reserves leads to a larger increase in deposits because the initial increase is spread throughout different banks as the funds are repeatedly loaned and deposited throughout the banking system. The amount of the increase depends on the required reserve ratio; the larger the required reserve ratio, the smaller the increase.

■ **Explain how the Fed controls the quantity of money.**

Open market operations are the major policy tool the Fed uses to change the quantity of money. If the Fed buys government securities, banks' reserves increase and excess reserves increase. Banks lend the excess reserves, new deposits are created, and the quantity of money increases. If the Fed sells government securities, banks' reserves decrease and excess reserves decrease. Banks decrease their lending, deposits are destroyed, and the quantity of money decreases. Whether the Fed transacts with banks or the nonbank public does not change the effect of an open market operation. The monetary base changes by the amount of the open market purchase or sale but the quantity of money changes by more than the amount of the open market purchase or sale. The money multiplier is the number by which a change in the monetary base is multiplied to find the resulting change in the quantity of money. The money multiplier equals $(1 + C) \div (R + C)$ where C, the currency drain, is the ratio of currency to deposits and R is the required reserve ratio. A currency drain is currency held outside of the banks. The larger the currency drain and the larger the required reserve ratio, the smaller is the money multiplier because banks receive fewer deposits in each round of the multiplier lending and depositing process.

CHECKPOINT 12.1

■ **Explain how banks create money by making loans.**

Quick Review

- *Excess reserves* Excess reserves equal actual reserves minus required reserves.

Additional Practice Problem 12.1

1. The required reserve ratio is 0.05 and banks have no excess reserves. Katie deposits $500 in currency in her bank. Calculate:
   a. The change in the bank's reserves as soon as Katie makes the deposit.
   b. The bank's excess reserves as soon as Katie makes the deposit.
   c. The maximum amount that Katie's bank can loan.
   d. The maximum amount of new money that the banking system can create.
   e. The maximum amount of loans that the banking system can make.

Solution to Additional Practice Problem 12.1

1a. The new deposit of $500 increases the bank's actual reserves by $500.

1b. The bank is required to keep 5 percent of deposits as reserves. So required reserves increase by 5 percent of the deposit, or ($500) × (0.05), which is $25. As a result, excess reserves, which are actual reserves minus required reserves, increase by $500 − $25, which is $475.

1c. The crucial point to keep in mind is that banks can loan their excess reserves in order to boost their revenue and profit. So Katie's bank can loan a maximum of $475.

1d. The banking system creates money by creating deposits. When a bank in the banking system makes a loan, it does so by creating a deposit. Katie's bank loans 0.95 of the initial deposit. When that $475 loan is deposited in another bank that bank will have $475 × 0.95, or $451.25 in excess reserves that it will loan. At each round in the process, the new loan and deposit is 0.95 of the previous loan and deposit. The ultimate increase in deposits

equals $(1 \div [1 − L])$ × the initial increase in reserves, or $(1 \div [1 − 0.95])$ × $500 = $10,000.

1e. As a result of the banking system, there are $10,000 of new deposits created. Of this $10,000, the initial $500 is the result of Katie's deposit in her bank. The remaining deposits are created by the banking systems' loans, which, when spent, are deposited into a bank. So the maximum amount of loans the banking system can create equals the total increase in deposits minus the initial deposit, which is $10,000 − $500 = $9,500.

■ **Self Test 12.1**

Fill in the blanks

Assets on a bank's balance sheet include ____ (cash; checkable deposits) and ____ (loans; owner's equity). A liability on a bank's balance sheet is ____ (reserves; checkable deposits). Banks ____ (create; do not create) money when they make loans. Any individual bank ____ (can; cannot) create unlimited amounts of money. The deposit multiplier shows that an increase in ____ (money; reserves) can be used to create additional ____ (money; reserves).

True or false

1. The first step in creating a bank is to accept deposits.
2. Checkable deposits are an asset on the bank's balance sheet.
3. A commercial bank's cash and its reserves at a Federal Reserve bank are assets on its balance sheet.
4. Excess reserves increase when the required reserve ratio increases, all other things remaining the same.
5. When banks clear checks, they create money.
6. When a bank increases its loans, it creates money.
7. The required reserve ratio has no effect on the amount of money banks can create.
8. An immigrant enters the United States and deposits $190,000 into a bank. The required reserve ratio is 5 percent. When the entire sequence of loans and deposits is completed, deposits increase by a maximum of $3.8 million.

Multiple choice

1. Which of the following actions is NOT carried out by a bank?
   a. buy government securities
   b. clear checks
   c. make loans
   d. print money
   e. accept deposits

2. A bank's balance sheet is a statement that summarizes
   a. only the bank's loans.
   b. only the bank's reserves.
   c. the bank's assets and liabilities.
   d. the number of banks in a community.
   e. the bank's profit and loss.

3. Cash in a bank is part of the bank's
   a. owners' equity.
   b. liabilities.
   c. assets.
   d. government securities.
   e. deposits.

4. Which of the following is a bank liability?
   a. checkable deposits
   b. government securities
   c. equipment
   d. loans
   e. reserves

5. If the required reserve ratio is 20 percent, then for every dollar that is deposited in the bank, the bank must
   a. keep 20 cents as reserves.
   b. keep 80 cents as reserves.
   c. loan 80 cents.
   d. loan 20 cents.
   e. keep 20 cents as reserves and loan 20 cents.

6. A bank has checkable deposits of $500,000, loans of $300,000, and government securities of $200,000. If the required reserve ratio is 10 percent, the amount of required reserves is
   a. $20,000.
   b. $30,000.
   c. $50,000.
   d. $500,000.
   e. $80,000.

7. Excess reserves are the
   a. same as the required reserves.
   b. amount of reserves the Fed requires banks to hold.
   c. amount of reserves held above what is required.
   d. amount of reserves a bank holds at the Fed.
   e. amount of reserves banks keep in their vaults.

8. Keisha writes a $500 check to Larry drawn on Community Bank. Larry deposits the $500 check in his checking account at Neighbors Bank. When the check clears both banks, _____ by $500.
   a. Community Bank's assets decrease
   b. Community Bank's assets increase
   c. Community Bank's liabilities increase
   d. Neighbors Bank's assets decrease
   e. Neighbors Bank's liabilities decrease

9. Banks can make loans up to an amount equal to their
   a. total deposits.
   b. total reserves.
   c. required reserves.
   d. excess reserves.
   e. total government securities.

10. The banking system can create more money than an initial increase in excess reserves because
   a. banks are sneaky.
   b. the Fed lends it money.
   c. excess reserves are loaned and then wind up as deposits in another bank.
   d. banks charge more interest than they pay out.
   e. banks' total reserves increase when their excess reserves increase.

11. The ____ the required reserve ratio, the ____ the ____ in deposits from an initial new deposit of $100,000 in currency.
   a. larger; larger; decrease
   b. larger; larger; increase
   c. larger; smaller; decrease
   d. smaller; larger; decrease
   e. smaller; larger; increase

12. If the required reserve ratio is 15 percent and banks loan all of their excess reserves, a new deposit of $20,000 leads to a total increase in deposits of
   a. $3,000.
   b. $20,000.
   c. $133,333.
   d. $200,000.
   e. $300,000.

Short answer and numeric questions

Assets	Liabilities

1. The Bank of Townsville has reserves at the Fed of $100, owner's equity of $200, loans of $800, checkable deposits of $1,000, cash of $200, and government securities of $100. Arrange these entries in the balance sheet above.

2. The Bank of Utah has deposits of $500 million and reserves of $60 million. If the required reserve ratio is 10 percent, calculate the bank's excess reserves. How much can the bank loan? If the required reserve ratio is changed to 8 percent, calculate the bank's excess reserves. How much can the bank loan?

3. How does making a loan create a deposit?

Round	Increase in deposits (dollars)	Increase in reserves (dollars)	Increase in excess reserves (dollars)	Loan (dollars)
A	___	___	___	___
B	___	___	___	___
C	___	___	___	___
D	___	___	___	___

4. Meg tutors 10 students during finals week and is paid $500 in cash. She deposits the $500 in her bank. The required reserve ratio is 10 percent and banks always loan the maximum possible.
   a. Starting with Meg's $500 deposit, complete the above table.
   b. After the first four rounds, what is the total increase in deposits?
   c. What will be the total increase in deposits?

5. Shaniq deposits $100 in cash in her checking account.
   a. If the required reserve ratio is 10 percent, what will be the total increase in deposits created by the banking system?
   b. If the required reserve ratio is 5 percent, percent, what will be the total increase in deposits created by the banking system?
   c. What is the relationship between the required reserve ratio and the total increase in deposits creates by the banking system?

CHECKPOINT 12.2

■ **Explain how the Fed controls the quantity of money.**

Quick Review
- *Open market operation* The purchase or sale of government securities by the Fed in the open market.
- *Money multiplier* The number by which a change in the monetary base is multiplied to find the resulting change in the quantity of money.

Additional Practice Problems 12.2

1. If the Fed makes an open market sale of $1 million of government securities to Bank of America, what initial changes occur on the Fed's balance sheet and on Bank of America's balance sheet? Be sure to tell if each change affects an asset or a liability.

2. If the required reserve ratio is 10 percent and the currency drain is 30 percent, what is the size of the money multiplier? By how much will a $10 billion increase in the monetary base change the quantity of money?

3. If the required reserve ratio is 20 percent and the currency drain is 30 percent, what is the size of the money multiplier? By how much will a $10 billion increase in the monetary base change the quantity of money?

4. Using problems 2 and 3, what is the effect of a rise in the required reserve ratio on the increase in the quantity of money?

Solutions to Additional Practice Problems 12.2

1. When the Fed sells $1 million of government securities, the Fed's holding of government securities decreases by $1 million. The Fed decreases Bank of America's reserves at the Fed by $1 million. One of the Fed's assets, government securities, and one of its liabilities, reserve deposits, decrease by $1 million. For Bank of America, its holdings of government securities increase by $1 million and its reserves at the Fed decrease by $1 million. For Bank of America, one of its assets, government securities, increases by $1 million, and another of its assets, reserves at the Fed, decrease by $1 million.

2. The money multiplier equals $(1 + C) \div (R + C)$ where C is the currency drain and R is the required reserve ratio, both expressed as decimals. So the money multiplier equals $(1 + 0.3) \div (0.1 + 0.3)$, which is 3.25. So a $10 billion increase in the monetary base increases the quantity of money by 3.25 × $10 billion, or $32.5 billion.

3. The money multiplier equals $(1 + C) \div (R + C)$ where C is the currency drain and R is the required reserve ratio, both expressed as decimals. So the money multiplier equals $(1 + 0.3) \div (0.2 + 0.3)$, which is 2.6. So a $10 billion increase in the monetary base increases the quantity of money by 2.6 × $10 billion, or $26 billion.

4. An increase in the required reserve ratio shrinks the amount by which the quantity of money increases.

■ Self Test 12.2

Fill in the blanks

When the Fed purchases government securities, it ____ (decreases; increases) the quantity of money. An open market sale of government securities by the Fed ____ (decreases; increases) the monetary base and ____ (decreases; increases) banks' excess reserves. An increase in currency held outside the banks is called ____ (an excess currency removal; a currency drain; a multiplier reserve). If the money multiplier is 2.0, a $4 million increase in the monetary base will create an increase of ____ ($2; $8) million in the quantity of money. The larger the required reserve ratio, the ____ (larger; smaller) is the ____ (currency drain; money multiplier).

True or false

1. When the Fed buys securities in an open market operation, it pays for them with newly created bank reserves and money.

2. The Fed buys securities only from commercial banks.

3. When the Fed buys securities from a commercial bank, the banks' reserves and deposits at the Fed both increase.

4. When the Fed sells government securities, it decreases the quantity of banks' reserves.

5. When the Fed buys government securities, the effect on the money supply depends on whether the Fed buys the securities from a bank or the general public.

6. If the Fed increases the monetary base by $1 billion, the ultimate increase in the quantity of money will be less than $1 billion.

7. The larger the currency drain, the larger the money multiplier.

8. If the currency drain is 0.2 and the required reserve ratio is 0.1, the money multiplier is 1.675.

Multiple choice

1. When the Fed buys or sells securities, it is conducting _____ operation.
   a. a closed door
   b. an open market
   c. a multiplier
   d. a deposit
   e. a currency

2. When the Fed sells securities in an open market operation
   a. the monetary base increases and the money supply increases.
   b. the monetary base does not change.
   c. only commercial banks can be buyers.
   d. the federal funds rate does not change.
   e. buyers pay for the securities with money and bank reserves.

3. If the Fed buys securities from a commercial bank, the effect on the quantity of money
   a. is larger than when the Fed buys securities from the non-bank public.
   b. is less than when the Fed buys securities from the non-bank public.
   c. is the same as when the Fed buys securities from the non-bank public.
   d. depends on whether the bank was borrowing reserves from another bank.
   e. depends if the monetary base changes.

4. If the Fed buys government securities, then
   a. the quantity of money is not changed, just its composition.
   b. new bank reserves are created.
   c. the quantity of money decreases.
   d. bank reserves are destroyed.
   e. banks' excess reserves decrease.

5. The Citizens First Bank sells $100,000 of government securities to the Fed. This sale immediately
   a. decreases the quantity of money.
   b. decreases the bank's checkable deposits.
   c. increases the bank's reserves.
   d. decreases the bank's assets.
   e. increases the bank's required reserves..

6. The Fed buys $100 million U.S. government securities from Bank of America. Bank of America's balance sheet shows this transaction as _____ in total assets and _____ in reserves.
   a. no change; a $100 million decrease
   b. no change; a $100 million increase
   c. a $100 million increase; no change
   d. a $100 million increase; a $100 million increase
   e. a $100 million decrease; a $100 million decrease

7. When the Fed conducts an open market purchase, the first round changes in the money multiplier process are that excess reserves _____, bank deposits _____, and the quantity of money _____.
   a. decreases; decreases; decrease
   b. increases; do not change; increase
   c. decreases; increases; does not change
   d. do not change; increases; increase
   e. increase; increase; increases

8. A currency drain is cash
   a. lost in the drain.
   b. draining into the banks.
   c. held outside the banks.
   d. held at the Fed.
   e. held as reserves.

9. If the currency drain increases,
   a. the monetary base increases.
   b. banks' reserves decrease.
   c. the quantity of money increases.
   d. banks' reserves increase.
   e. the money multiplier increases.

10. The money multiplier is used to determine how much the
    a. monetary base increases when the Fed purchases government securities.
    b. quantity of money increases when the monetary base increases.
    c. monetary base increases when the quantity of money increases.
    d. quantity of money increases when the required reserve ratio increases.
    e. monetary base increases when the Fed sells government securities.

11. If the monetary base does not change and Fed increases the required reserve ratio, the money multiplier ____ and the quantity of money ____.
    a. increases; increases
    b. increases; decreases
    c. decreases; increases
    d. decreases; decreases
    e. decreases; does not change

12. The Fed makes an open market operation purchase of $200,000. The currency drain is 0.33 and the required reserve ratio is 0.10. By how much does the quantity of money increase?
    a. $800,000
    b. $333,333
    c. $2,000,000
    d. $618,604
    e. $465,116

Short answer and numeric questions

Round	Increase in deposits (dollars)	Increase in currency (dollars)	Increase in reserves (dollars)	Increase in excess reserves (dollars)
A			1,000	1,000
B	____	____	____	____
C	____	____	____	____
D	____	____	____	____

1. Suppose the Fed buys $1,000 of government securities from Hayward National Bank. The required reserve ratio is 0.10 and the currency drain is 0.25. Suppose that all banks loan all of their excess reserves. Complete the above table. Calculate the total increase in deposits and currency following the first four rounds of the multiplier process.

Round	Increase in deposits (dollars)	Increase in currency (dollars)	Increase in reserves (dollars)	Increase in excess reserves (dollars)
A			1,000	1,000
B	____	____	____	____
C	____	____	____	____
D	____	____	____	____

2. Suppose the Fed buys $1,000 of government securities from Fremont National Bank. The required reserve ratio is 0.10 and the currency drain is 1.00. Suppose that all banks loan all of their excess reserves. Complete the above table. Calculate the total increase in deposits and currency following the first four rounds of the multiplier process.

3. In which question, 1 or 2, was the increase in the quantity of money largest after four rounds?

4. Calculate the money multiplier when the required reserve ratio is 0.10 and the currency drain is 0.20. Calculate the money multiplier when the required reserve ratio is 0.10 and the currency drain is 0.60. As the currency drain increases, what happens to the magnitude of the money multiplier?

5. Calculate the money multiplier when the required reserve ratio is 0.10 and the currency drain is 0.20. Calculate the money multiplier when the required reserve ratio is 0.20 and the currency drain is 0.20. As the required reserve ratio increases, what happens to the magnitude of the money multiplier?

6. Why does an increase in the required reserve ratio or in the currency drain decrease the magnitude of the money multiplier?

SELF TEST ANSWERS

■ CHECKPOINT 12.1

Fill in the blanks

Assets on a bank's balance sheet include <u>cash</u> and <u>loans</u>. A liability on a bank's balance sheet is <u>checkable deposits</u>. Banks <u>create</u> money when they make loans. Any individual bank <u>cannot</u> create unlimited amounts of money. The deposit multiplier shows that an increase in <u>reserves</u> can be used to create additional <u>money</u>.

True or false

1. False; page 296
2. False; page 298
3. True; page 298
4. False; page 299
5. False; pages 299-300
6. True; pages 301-302
7. False; pages 302-304
8. True; page 304

Multiple choice

1. d; page 296
2. c; page 296
3. c; page 296
4. a; page 298
5. a; page 298
6. c; page 298
7. c; page 299
8. a; pages 299-300
9. d; page 301
10. c; pages 302-304
11. b; page 304
12. c; page 304

Short answer and numeric questions

Assets		Liabilities	
Cash	200	Deposits	1,000
Reserves at the Fed	100		
Loans	800		
Government securities	100	Owner's equity	200

1. The completed balance sheet is above; page 301.

2. The Bank of Utah's required reserves are $(0.10) \times (\$500 \text{ million}) = \$50$ million, so it has excess reserves of $10 million. It can loan the amount of its excess reserves, $10 million. If the required reserve ratio is 8 percent, the bank's required reserves are $40 million and so the bank has $20 million of excess reserves. When the required reserve ratio decreases, the amount the bank can loan increases; pages 298-299.

3. When a bank makes a loan, the bank deposits the loan in the borrower's checkable deposit. For instance, when Emma borrows $30,000 to buy machines for her business, the bank places the $30,000 in Emma's checkable deposit. As a result, when a loan is made, an equal sized deposit is created; page 301.

Round	Increase in deposits (dollars)	Increase in reserves (dollars)	Increase in excess reserves (dollars)	Loan (dollars)
A	500.00	500.00	450.00	450.00
B	450.00	450.00	405.00	405.00
C	405.00	405.00	364.50	364.50
D	364.50	364.50	328.05	328.05

4. a. The completed table is above; page 303.

   b. The total increase in deposits after the first four rounds is $1,719.50.

   c. The total increase in deposits is $(1 \div [1 - L])$ × the increase in reserves. L is the proportion of a round of loans and deposits to the previous round of loans and deposits. In this case, L is 0.90, so the total increase in deposits is $(1 \div [1 - 0.90]) \times \$500$, or 10.0 × $500.00, which equals $5,000; page 304.

5. a. The total increase in deposits is $(1 \div [1 - L])$ × the increase in reserves. L is the proportion of a round of loans and deposits to the previous round of loans and deposits. In this case, L is 0.90, so the total increase in deposits is $(1 \div [1 - 0.90]) \times \$100$, or 10.0 × $100.00, which equals $1,000; page 304.

5. b. When the required reserve ratio is 5 percent, L is 0.95. So the total increase in de-

posits is $(1 \div [1 - 0.95]) \times \$100$, or $20.0 \times \$100.00$, which equals $2,000; page 304.

5.c. When the required reserve ratio is smaller, the total increase in deposits is larger; page 304.

■ CHECKPOINT 12.2

Fill in the blanks

When the Fed purchases government securities, it <u>increases</u> the quantity of money. An open market sale of government securities by the Fed <u>decreases</u> the monetary base and <u>decreases</u> banks' excess reserves. An increase in currency held outside the banks is called <u>a currency drain</u>. If the money multiplier is 2.0, a $4 million increase in the monetary base will create an increase of <u>$8</u> million in the quantity of money. The larger the required reserve ratio, the <u>smaller</u> is the <u>money multiplier</u>.

True or false

1. True; page 306
2. False; page 306
3. True; page 307
4. True; page 309
5. False; pages 306-309
6. False; pages 309-310
7. False; page 311-312
8. False; page 312

Multiple choice

1. b; page 306
2. e; page 306
3. c; pages 306-309
4. b; page 307
5. c; page 307
6. b; page 307
7. e; page 309
8. c; page 309
9. b; page 309
10. b; page 311
11. d; page 312
12. d; page 312

Short answer and numeric questions

Round	Increase in deposits (dollars)	Increase in currency (dollars)	Increase in reserves (dollars)	Increase in excess reserves (dollars)
A			1,000.00	1,000.00
B	800.00	200.00	800.00	720.00
C	576.00	144.00	576.00	518.40
D	414.72	103.68	414.72	373.25

1. The completed table is above. After four rounds, currency increases by $447.68, deposits increase by $1,790.72, and the quantity of money increases by the sum of the increase in currency and the increase in deposits, which is $2,238.40; page 311.

Round	Increase in deposits (dollars)	Increase in currency (dollars)	Increase in reserves (dollars)	Increase in excess reserves (dollars)
A			1,000	1,000
B	500.00	500.00	500.00	450.00
C	225.00	225.00	225.00	202.50
D	101.25	101.25	101.25	91.13

2. The completed table is above. After four rounds, currency increases by $826.25, deposits increase by $826.25, and the quantity of money increases by the sum of the increase in currency and the increase in deposits, which is $1,652.50; page 311.

3. The increase in the quantity of money is greater when the currency drain is smaller, in question 1; page 311.

4. The money multiplier equals $(1 + C) \div (C + R)$ where C is the currency drain and R is the required reserve ratio. The money multiplier for the first part of the question equals $(1 + 0.20) \div (0.20 + 0.10)$, or $(1.20) \div (0.30)$ which is 4.00. The money multiplier for the second part of the question is $(1 + 0.60) \div (0.60 + 0.10)$, or $(1.60) \div (0.70)$, which is 2.29. As the currency drain increases, the magnitude of the money multiplier decreases; pages 311-312.

5. The money multiplier equals $(1 + C) \div (C + R)$ where C is the currency drain and R is the required reserve ratio. The money multiplier for the first part of the question equals

$(1 + 0.20) \div (0.20 + 0.10)$, or $(1.20) \div (0.30)$ which is 4.00. The money multiplier for the second part of the question is $(1 + 0.20) \div (0.20 + 0.20)$, or $(1.20) \div (0.40)$, which is 3.00. As the required reserve ratio increases, the magnitude of the money multiplier decreases; pages 311-312.

6. The money multiplier exists because of the repeating process of loaning, depositing the proceeds in another bank, and then making another loan. The more each bank loans, the greater the final increase in the quantity of money and the larger the money multiplier.

If the required reserve ratio increases in size, banks will be able to loan less of any additional deposit they receive. And if the currency drain increases, less is deposited in a bank and the bank will be able to loan less. Because an increase in the required reserve ratio and an increase in the currency drain decrease the amount that can be loaned, both decrease the size of the money multiplier; pages 311-312.

Money, Interest, and Inflation

Chapter 13

CHAPTER IN PERSPECTIVE

Chapter 13 discusses how the quantity of money determines the nominal interest rate and studies the relationship between money and the price level. It starts by pointing out that real factors, independent of the price level, determine potential GDP and other real variables. The effects of money on the economy differ in the short run and the long run. This chapter looks at the short run and long run but not at how the long run is reached—examining these ripple effects is the task of the next two chapters.

■ **Explain what determines the demand for money and how the demand for money and the supply of money determine the *nominal* interest rate.**

The inventory of money that households and firms choose to hold is the quantity of money demanded. The nominal interest rate is the opportunity cost of holding money. The demand for money curve shows the quantity of money demanded at each nominal interest rate. An increase in the price level or real GDP increases the demand for money and the demand for money curve shifts rightward. The supply of money is a fixed quantity. Equilibrium in the money market determines the nominal interest rate. In the short run, when the Fed increases the quantity of money, the nominal interest rate falls

■ **Explain how in the long run, the quantity of money determines the price level and money growth brings inflation.**

A one-time increase in the quantity of money lowers the nominal interest rate in the short run. In the long run, a one-time increase in the quantity of money brings an equal percentage increase in the price level and the nominal interest rate returns to its initial value. The quantity theory of money is the proposition when real GDP equals potential GDP, an increase in the quantity of money brings an equal percentage increase in the price level. The equation of exchange states that the quantity of money multiplied by the velocity of circulation equals nominal GDP. An increase in the quantity of money, with no change in potential GDP or velocity, leads to the same percentage increase in the price level. In rates of change, money growth plus velocity growth equals inflation plus real GDP growth. An increase in the growth of the quantity of money, with no change in the growth of velocity or real GDP, leads to an equal increase in the inflation rate. A hyperinflation is inflation at a rate that exceeds 50 percent a month.

■ **Identify the costs of inflation and the benefits of a stable value of money.**

The four costs of inflation are tax costs, shoe-leather costs, confusion costs, and uncertainty costs. Inflation is a tax. With inflation, households and business lose purchasing power, which is the tax on holding money. Inflation interacts with the income tax to lower saving and investment. Shoe-leather costs are costs that arise from an increase in the amount of running around that people do to try to avoid losses from the falling value of money. Confusion costs are costs of making errors because of rapidly changing prices. Uncertainty costs arise because long-term planning is difficult, so people have a shorter-term focus. Investment falls and the growth rate slows.

CHECKPOINT 13.1

■ **Explain what determines the demand for money and how the demand for money and the supply of money determine the *nominal* interest rate.**

Quick Review

- *Shifts in the demand for money curve* When real GDP, the price level, or financial technology change, the demand for money curve shifts.
- *Equilibrium nominal interest rate* The equilibrium nominal interest rate occurs where the demand for money curve intersects the supply curve because at this interest rate the quantity of money demanded equals the quantity supplied.

Additional Practice Problems 13.1

1. The figure shows the money market.
   a. What is the equilibrium nominal interest rate and quantity of money?
   b. Use the figure to show what happens to the interest rate if the Fed increases the quantity of money from $4.0 trillion to $4.1 trillion.

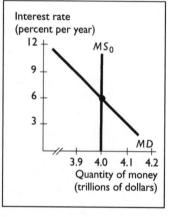

2. Tomorrow all stores will install retinal scanner identification machines, which allow people to make a purchase without having to carry a credit card. What effect will this technological advance have on the demand for money and on the nominal interest rate?

Solutions to Additional Practice Problems 13.1

1a. This problem shows how the nominal interest rate is determined in the money market.

You are using the supply and demand model introduced in Chapter 4. As the figure below shows, the equilibrium interest rate is 6 percent because this is the interest rate at which the quantity of money demanded equals the quantity of money supplied. The equilibrium quantity of money is $4.0 trillion.

1b. The Fed's increase in the quantity of money shifts the supply of money curve rightward, from MS_0 to MS_1. As a result, the equilibrium nominal interest rate falls from 6 percent to 3 percent.

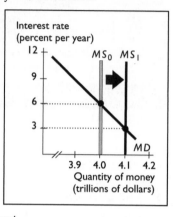

2. This change in technology makes credit purchases more attractive for consumers and merchants. There is an increase in credit purchases and a decrease in the purchases made with money. The demand for money decreases. People want to hold less money than they are actually holding. They buy bonds. The price of a bond rises and the nominal interest rate falls.

■ **Self Test 13.1**

Fill in the blanks

The nominal interest rate equals the real interest rate _____ (plus; minus; divided by) the inflation rate. The opportunity cost of holding money is the _____ (price level; nominal interest rate). An increase in real GDP _____ (increases; decreases) the demand for money and shifts the demand for money curve _____ (rightward; leftward). An increase in the price level _____ (increases; decreases) the demand for money and shifts the demand for money curve _____ (rightward; leftward). If the nominal interest rate is above the equilibrium level, people _____ (buy; sell) bonds, the price of a bond _____ (rises; falls), and the interest rate ____ (rises; falls). If the Fed decreases the quantity of money, the nominal interest rate ____ (rises; falls).

True or false

1. The real interest rate is the opportunity cost of holding money.

2. An increase in real GDP shifts the demand for money curve leftward.

3. If the price of a government bond rises, the interest rate on the bond rises.

4. When the interest rate is above its equilibrium level, people buy bonds and the interest rate falls.

5. An increase in the quantity of money lowers the interest rate.

Multiple choice

1. The quantity of money demanded
   a. is infinite.
   b. has no opportunity cost.
   c. is the quantity that balances the benefit of holding an additional dollar of money against the opportunity cost of doing so.
   d. is directly controlled by the Fed.
   e. changes very infrequently.

2. Which of the following statements is correct?
   a. Nominal interest rate = Real interest rate – Inflation rate
   b. Nominal interest rate = Real interest rate + Inflation rate
   c. Nominal interest rate = Inflation rate – Real interest rate
   d. Nominal interest rate = Inflation rate + Price index
   e. Nominal interest rate = Inflation rate ÷ Real interest rate

3. The opportunity cost of holding money is the
   a. real interest rate.
   b. nominal interest rate.
   c. inflation rate.
   d. time it takes to go to the ATM or bank.
   e. growth rate of real GDP.

4. The demand for money curve shows the relationship between the quantity of money demanded and
   a. the nominal interest rate.
   b. the real interest rate.
   c. the inflation rate.
   d. real GDP.
   e. nominal GDP.

5. The demand for money ____ when the ____.
   a. increases; price level increases
   b. decreases; price level increases
   c. remains constant; price level increases
   d. increases; interest rate increases
   e. increases; supply of money decreases

6. Every day ____ adjusts to make the quantity of money demanded equal the quantity of money supplied.
   a. the inflation rate
   b. the nominal interest rate
   c. the quantity of money
   d. potential GDP
   e. real GDP

7. If the nominal interest rate is above its equilibrium level, then
   a. people sell financial assets and the interest rate falls.
   b. people buy financial assets and the interest rate falls.
   c. the demand for money curve shifts rightward and the interest rate rises.
   d. the supply of money curve shifts leftward and the interest rate rises.
   e. the demand curve for money shifts leftward and the interest rate falls.

8. When the Fed increases the quantity of money, the
   a. equilibrium interest rate falls.
   b. equilibrium interest rate rises.
   c. demand for money curve shifts rightward.
   d. supply of money curve shifts leftward.
   e. demand for money curve shifts leftward.

Nominal interest rate (percent per year)	Quantity of money, (trillions dollars)
5	3.1
6	3.0
7	2.9
8	2.8
9	2.7
10	2.6

9. The table above gives the demand for money schedule. When the Fed increases the quantity of money from $2.7 trillion to $2.9 trillion, the interest rate ____ from ____.
   a. falls; 9 percent to 5 percent
   b. falls; 7 percent to 6 percent
   c. rises; 5 percent to 8 percent
   d. rises; 6 percent to 8 percent
   e. falls; 9 percent to 7 percent

■ **FIGURE 13.1**

Nominal interest rate (percent per year)

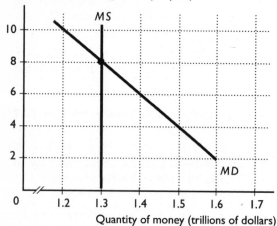

10. The figure above shows the money market. If the Fed increases the quantity of money from $1.3 trillion to $1.4 trillion, the interest rate ____ from ____.
    a. falls; 9 percent to 7 percent
    b. falls; 8 percent to 6 percent
    c. rises; 5 percent to 8 percent
    d. rises; 6 percent to 8 percent
    e. falls; 12 percent to 7 percent

Complete the graph

Nominal interest rate (percent per year)	Quantity of money, (trillions dollars)
5	1.2
6	1.0
7	0.8
8	0.6
9	0.4
10	0.2

1. The table above has data on the nominal interest rate and the quantity of money demanded.

■ **FIGURE 13.2**

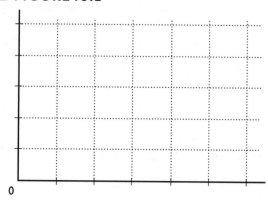

   a. Using the data, label the axes and plot the demand for money curve in Figure 13.2.
   b. Suppose the Fed sets the quantity of money at $0.6 trillion. Plot this quantity in Figure 13.1. What is the equilibrium nominal interest rate?
   c. Suppose the Fed wants to change the nominal interest rate so that it equals 6 percent a year. What action must the Fed take?

2. Figure 13.3 (on the next page) shows a demand for money curve and a supply of money curve.
   a. What is the equilibrium interest rate?
   b. Suppose the price level rises so that the demand for money changes by $0.2 trillion at every interest rate. Which direction does the demand for money curve shift? Draw the new demand for money curve in the figure. What is the equilibrium interest rate?

■ FIGURE 13.3

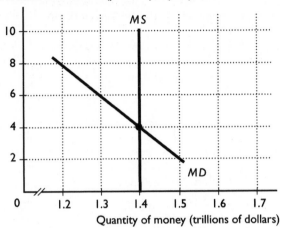

Nominal interest rate (percent per year)

Quantity of money (trillions of dollars)

Short answer and numeric questions

1. What are the benefits from holding money?

2. What is the opportunity cost of holding money and why is this the opportunity cost?

3. What effect will an increase in real GDP have on the demand for money curve?

4. Suppose a government bond pays $100 in interest each year. If you buy the bond for $1,000, what is the interest rate? If you buy the bond for $2,000 dollars, what is the interest rate? As the price of the bond increases, what happens to the interest rate?

5. How can the Fed lower the nominal interest rate?

CHECKPOINT 13.2

■ **Explain how in the long run, the quantity of money determines the price level and money growth brings inflation.**

Quick Review

- *Inflation rate in the long run* In the long run and other things remaining the same, a given percentage change in the quantity of money brings an equal percentage change in the price level.

- *Quantity theory of money* The proposition that when real GDP equals potential GDP, an increase in the quantity of money brings an equal percentage increase in the price level.

- *Equation of exchange* An equation that states that the quantity of money multiplied by the velocity of circulation equals the price level multiplied by real GDP, that is $M \times V = P \times Y$.

Additional Practice Problems 13.2

1. In the short run, how does an increase in the quantity of money affect the price level? The nominal interest rate?

2. In the long run, how does an increase in the quantity of money affect the price level? The nominal interest rate?

3. In the long run, according to the quantity theory of money, how does an increase in the growth rate of the quantity of money affect the inflation rate? The nominal interest rate?

4. The quantity of money is $90 billion, real GDP is $900 billion, and the price level is 110. What is the velocity of circulation?

Solutions to Additional Practice Problems 13.2

1. In the immediate short run, the price level does not change immediately but then starts to rise. In the short run, an increase in the quantity of money lowers the nominal interest rate.

2. In the long run, the price level rises. In the long run, the nominal interest rate does not change.

3. In the long run, an increase in the growth rate of the quantity of money raises the inflation rate by the same percentage. For instance, if the growth rate of the quantity of money increases by 3 percentage points, in the long run the inflation rate increases by 3 percentage points. In the long run, the nominal interest rate rises.

4. The velocity of circulation is the number of times in a year that the average dollar of money gets used to buy final goods and services. The velocity of circulation is calculated using the formula $V = (P \times Y) \div M$. Nominal GDP, which equals $P \times Y$, is $990 billion. So velocity equals ($990 billion) ÷ $90 billion = 11.

■ Self Test 13.2

Fill in the blanks

Other things remaining the same, a given percentage increase in the quantity of money brings an equal percentage ____ (increase; decrease) in the price level in the long run. An increase in the quantity of money ____ (lowers; raises; does not change) the nominal interest rate in the short run and ____ (lowers; raises; does not change) the nominal interest rate in the long run. The proposition that when real GDP equals potential GDP, an increase in the quantity of money brings an equal percentage increase in the price level is the ____ (quality; inflation; quantity) theory of money. If the velocity of circulation does not change, the inflation rate equals the growth rate of the ____ (quantity of money; nominal interest rate) ____ (minus; divided by) the growth rate of real GDP.

True or false

1. If the inflation rate is 2 percent a year and the real interest rate is 4 percent a year, the nominal interest rate is 6 percent a year.

2. In the long run, an increase in the quantity of money raises the price level and leaves the nominal interest rate unchanged.

3. $M \times P = V \times Y$ is the equation of exchange.

4. According to the quantity theory of money, in the long run with other things remaining the same, a 5 percent increase in the quantity of money brings a 5 percent increase in the price level.

5. According to the quantity theory of money, if the quantity of money grows 2 percent a year faster, the inflation rate falls by 2 percent a year.

Multiple choice

1. In the long run, the price level adjusts
   a. so that the real interest rate equals the nominal interest rate.
   b. so that the inflation rate equals zero.
   c. to achieve money market equilibrium at the long-run equilibrium interest rate.
   d. so that the inflation rate equals the growth rate of real GDP.
   e. so that the inflation rate is moderate.

2. If the equilibrium real interest rate is 4 percent a year and the inflation rate is 4 percent a year, then the nominal interest rate is ____ percent a year.
   a. 4
   b. 8
   c. 0
   d. 6
   e. 2

3. Other things remaining the same, if the quantity of money increases by a given percentage, then in the long run the ____ by the same percentage.
   a. price level rises
   b. price level falls
   c. real interest rate rises
   d. real interest rate falls
   e. nominal interest rate falls

4. In the long run, an increase in the quantity of money ____ the price level and ____ the nominal interest rate.
   a. raises; raises
   b. raises; does not change
   c. raises; lowers
   d. does not change; raises
   e. does not change; does not change

5. Suppose that $P \times Y$ is $5,000 million a year and the quantity of money is $500 million. Then the velocity of circulation is
   a. 50.
   b. 500.
   c. 10.
   d. 20.
   e. 2,500,000.

6. The quantity theory of money is a proposition about the
   a. Fed's methods it uses to change the quantity of money.
   b. relationship between nominal and real interest rate.
   c. relationship between a change in the quantity of money and the price level.
   d. relationship between financial assets and currency demanded.
   e. relationship between the nominal interest rate and the quantity of money demanded.

7. If the quantity of money grows at 3 percent a year, velocity does not grow, and real GDP grows at 2 percent a year, then the inflation rate equals
   a. 6 percent.
   b. 5 percent.
   c. 1 percent.
   d. –1 percent.
   e. 12 percent.

8. If the quantity of money grows at 4 percent a year, velocity grows at 2 percent, and real GDP grows at 2 percent a year, then the inflation rate equals
   a. 6 percent.
   b. 2 percent.
   c. 0 percent.
   d. 8 percent.
   e. 4 percent.

9. Hyperinflation is
   a. inflation caused by negative growth in the quantity of money.
   b. inflation at a rate that exceeds 50 percent a month.
   c. inflation caused by excessive growth in the demand for money.
   d. inflation at a rate that exceeds 5 percent a month.
   e. only theoretical and has never occurred in the real world.

Short answer and numeric questions

1. In the long run, what is the effect of a 5 percent increase in the quantity of money, other things remaining the same?

Year	Quantity of money (billions of dollars)	Velocity of circulation	Price level (2000 = 100)	Real GDP (billions of 2000 dollars)
2005	100	11	____	1,000
2006	110	11	____	1,000
2007	121	11	____	1,000

2. The table above gives data for the nation of Quantoland, a small nation to the south. In 2005, 2006, and 2007, real GDP equals potential GDP.
   a. Complete the table.
   b. Calculate the percentage change in the quantity of money in 2005 and 2006. Then calculate the percentage change in the price level in 2005 and 2006.
   c. What key proposition is illustrated in your answer to part (b)?

Year	Growth in quantity of money (percent)	Growth in velocity of circulation (percent)	Inflation rate (percent)	Growth in Real GDP (percent)
2005	4	2	____	3
2006	7	2	____	3
2007	____	1	4	3

3. The table above gives data for the nation of Velocoland, a small nation to the north. In 2005, 2006, and 2007, real GDP equals potential GDP.
   a. Complete the table.
   b. Between 2005 and 2006, by how much does the growth rate of the quantity of money change? By how much does the inflation rate change?

4. In the long run, if real GDP grows at 3 percent a year, velocity does not change, and the quantity of money grows at 5 percent a year, what is the inflation rate?

5. What is a hyperinflation? What leads to hyperinflation?

CHECKPOINT 13.3

■ **Identify the costs of inflation and the benefits of a stable value of money.**

Quick Review

• *The inflation rate and income tax* Inflation increases the nominal interest rate, and because income taxes are paid on nominal interest income, the true income tax rate rises with inflation.

Additional Practice Problem 13.3

1. In the island of Atlantis where you live, the inflation rate has been varying between 3 percent a year and 10 percent a year in recent years. You are willing to lend money if you are guaranteed a real interest rate of at least 2 percent a year. There are potential borrowers, but they will borrow only if they are guaranteed a real interest rate of not more than 5 percent a year.

    a. Can you successfully make a loan if everyone can accurately predict the inflation rate?

    b. Can you successfully make a loan if neither you nor the borrowers can accurately predict the inflation rate?

    c. What bearing does your answer to part b have on the cost of inflation?

Solution to Additional Practice Problem 13.3

1a. If you and the potential borrowers can accurately predict the inflation rate, it is possible to make a loan. If everyone knows the inflation rate is 10 percent a year, you are willing to lend as long as you receive a nominal interest rate of at least 12 percent a year. Borrowers are willing to pay a real interest rate of no more than 5 percent a year, so borrowers are willing to agree to a loan as long as the nominal rate is no more than 15 percent a year. Because they are willing to pay up to 15 percent a year and you are willing to take as little as 12 percent a year, you can make a loan and charge a nominal interest rate between 12 percent a year and 15 percent a year. Similarly, if everyone knows the infla-

tion rate is 3 percent a year, a loan can be made with a nominal interest rate between 5 percent a year and 8 percent a year.

1b. To receive a real interest rate of at least 2 percent a year you must receive a nominal interest rate of at least 12 percent a year in case inflation is 10 percent a year. If borrowers pay a nominal interest rate of 12 percent a year and inflation is 3 percent a year, they are paying a real interest rate of 9 percent a year, well above their maximum real interest rate of 5 percent a year. Because of the uncertainty about the inflation rate, you don't make the loan.

1c. The fact that inflation is uncertain means that the loan did not get made. Presumably the loan would benefit both the lender and the borrower. The fact that it cannot be made means that both are worse off, which reflects the uncertainty cost of inflation.

■ **Self Test 13.3**

Fill in the blanks

Inflation ____ (is; is not) a tax. The higher the inflation rate, the ____ (lower; higher) the true income tax rate on income from capital. During an inflation, the costs that arise from an increase in the velocity of circulation of money and an increase in the amount of running around to avoid incurring losses from the falling value of money are ____ (shoe-leather; confusion) costs. Increased uncertainty about inflation leads to a ____ (rise; fall) in investment.

True or false

1. Inflation is a tax.

2. The "shoe-leather costs" of inflation are the result of the increase in the velocity of circulation when inflation increases.

3. One of the benefits of inflation is that it makes the value of money change, which benefits both borrowers and lenders.

4. When there is a high inflation rate, the growth rate slows.

5. No country in the world has experienced hyperinflation since the end of the 1950s.

Multiple choice

1. All of the following are costs of inflation EX-CEPT
   a. tax costs.
   b. confusion costs.
   c. uncertainty costs.
   d. government spending costs.
   e. shoe-leather costs.

2. Becky holds $30,000 as money. After a year during which inflation was 5 percent a year, the inflation tax over that year is
   a. $500.
   b. $1,000.
   c. $1,500.
   d. $3,000.
   e. $5.

3. Suppose a country has a real interest rate of 4 percent and an inflation rate of 3 percent. If the income tax rate is 20 percent, then the after-tax real interest rate is
   a. 2.6 percent a year.
   b. 4.0 percent a year.
   c. 5.6 percent a year.
   d. 7.0 percent a year.
   e. 1.4 percent a year.

4. Shoe-leather costs arise from inflation because the velocity of circulation of money ____ as the inflation rate ____.
   a. increases; falls
   b. decreases; rises
   c. increases; rises
   d. does not change; rises
   e. does not change; falls

5. A consequence of hyperinflation is that people
   a. who make fixed-payment loans to others receive higher payments as inflation increases.
   b. spend time trying to keep their money holdings near zero.
   c. receive higher nominal wage hikes, which increases their purchasing power for goods and services.
   d. want to lend funds because interest rates are so high.
   e. increase the quantity of money demanded.

6. The uncertainty costs of inflation cause people to
   a. increase long-run investment.
   b. increase investment causing growth to decrease.
   c. focus on the short run, which decreases investment and slows growth.
   d. focus on the long run, which increases investment and speeds growth.
   e. incur more shoe leather costs.

7. The costs of inflation ____ when inflation is more rapid and ____ when inflation is more unpredictable.
   a. increase; increase
   b. increase; decrease
   c. decrease; increase
   d. increase; do not change
   e. do not change; increase

8. It is estimated that if the inflation rate is lowered from 3 percent a year to 0 percent a year, the growth rate of real GDP will rise by ____ percentage points a year.
   a. 0.06 to 0.09
   b. 1 to 3
   c. 2.3
   d. 3.2
   e. 0

Short answer and numeric questions

1. Jose holds $600 of money. If the inflation rate is 5 percent a year, what is Joe's inflation tax?

2. The real interest rate is 2 percent a year and the inflation rate is zero percent a year. If the income tax rate is 25 percent, what is the real after-tax interest rate? If the inflation rate rises to 6 percent a year, what is the real after-tax interest rate? If the inflation rate rises to 10 percent a year, what is the real after-tax interest rate?

3. Why does the velocity of circulation increase in a hyperinflation?

4. On what factors does the cost of inflation depend?

SELF TEST ANSWERS

■ CHECKPOINT 13.1

Fill in the blanks

The nominal interest rate equals the real interest rate <u>plus</u> the inflation rate. The opportunity cost of holding money is the <u>nominal interest rate</u>. An increase in real GDP <u>increases</u> the demand for money and shifts the demand for money curve <u>rightward</u>. An increase in the price level <u>increases</u> the demand for money and shifts the demand for money curve <u>rightward</u>. If the nominal interest rate is above the equilibrium level, people <u>buy</u> bonds, the price of a bond <u>rises</u>, and the interest rate <u>falls</u>. If the Fed decreases the quantity of money, the nominal interest rate <u>rises</u>.

True or false

1. False; page 322
2. False; page 323
3. False; page 325
4. True; page 325
5. True; pages 326-327

Multiple choice

1. c; page 321
2. b; page 322
3. b; page 322
4. a; pages 322-323
5. a; page 323
6. b; page 324
7. b; page 325
8. a; pages 326-327
9. e; pages 326-327
10. b; pages 326-627

Complete the graph

1. a. Figure 13.4 plots the demand for money curve; page 323.
   b. Figure 13.4 shows the supply of money curve when the Fed sets the quantity of money at $0.6 trillion. The equilibrium nominal interest rate is 8 percent a year at the intersection of the *MD* and *MS* curves; page 325.

■ FIGURE 13.4

Nominal interest rate (percent per year)

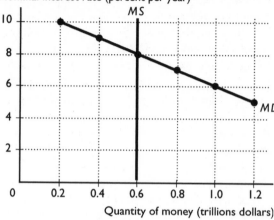

Quantity of money (trillions dollars)

c. If the Fed wants to lower the interest rate to 6 percent a year, it increases the quantity of money to $1.0 trillion; page 327.

■ FIGURE 13.5

Nominal interest rate (percent per year)

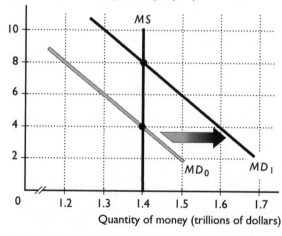

Quantity of money (trillions of dollars)

2. a. The equilibrium interest rate is 4 percent; page 325.
   b. The demand for money increases and the demand for money curve shifts rightward. Figure 13.5 shows the new equilibrium interest rate is 6 percent; pages 323, 326-327.

Short answer and numeric questions

1. The sources of benefit from holding money are that you can make payments and do transactions; page 321.

2. The opportunity cost of holding money is the nominal interest rate. By holding money rather than a financial asset, the nominal interest rate is forgone. For instance, if Seemi can earn 5 percent a year on a bond, then holding $1,000 in money costs her $50 a year; page 322.

3. An increase in real GDP increases the demand for money and shifts the demand for money curve rightward; page 323.

4. When the price of the bond is $1,000, the interest rate equals ($100 ÷ $1,000) × 100, which is 10 percent. When the price of the bond is $2,000, the interest rate equals ($100 ÷ $2,000) × 100, which is 5 percent. When the price of the bond increases, the interest rate falls; page 325.

5. If the Fed wants to lower the interest rate, it increases the quantity of money; pages 326-327.

■ CHECKPOINT 13.2

Fill in the blanks

Other things remaining the same, a given percentage increase in the quantity of money brings an equal percentage <u>increase</u> in the price level in the long run. An increase in the quantity of money <u>lowers</u> the nominal interest rate in the short run and <u>does not change</u> the nominal interest rate in the long run. The proposition that when real GDP equals potential GDP, an increase in the quantity of money brings an equal percentage increase in the price level is the <u>quantity</u> theory of money. If the velocity of circulation does not change, the inflation rate equals the growth rate of the <u>quantity of money minus</u> the growth rate of real GDP.

True or false

1. True; page 330
2. True; page 332
3. False; page 333
4. True; page 334
5. False; page 335

Multiple choice

1. c; page 330
2. b; page 330
3. a; pages 332, 334
4. b; page 332
5. c; page 333
6. c; page 333
7. c; page 335
8. e; page 335
9. b; page 337

Short answer and numeric questions

1. Other things remaining the same, in the long run a 5 percent increase in the quantity of money leads to a 5 percent increase in the price level; pages 332, 334.

Year	Quantity of money (billions of dollars)	Velocity of circulation	Price level (2000 = 100)	Real GDP (billions of 2000 dollars)
2005	100	11	<u>110.0</u>	1,000
2006	110	11	<u>121.0</u>	1,000
2007	121	11	<u>133.1</u>	1,000

2. a. The completed table is above. Use the equation of exchange to solve for the price level; pages 334.

b. In 2006, the percentage change in the quantity of money is [($110 billion − $100 billion) ÷ $100 billion] × 100, which is 10 percent.

In 2007, the percentage change in the quantity of money is [($121 billion − $110 billion) ÷ $110 billion] × 100, which also is 10 percent.

In 2006, the percentage change in the price level is [(121.0 − 110.0) ÷ 110.0] × 100, which is 10 percent.

In 2007, the percentage change in the price level is [(133.1 − 121.0) ÷ 121.0] × 100, which also is 10 percent.

c. The answer to part (b) illustrates the quantity theory of money, the proposition that, when real GDP equals potential GDP, an increase in the quantity of money brings an equal percentage increase in the price level; page 334.

Year	Growth in quantity of money (percent)	Growth in velocity of circulation (percent)	Inflation rate (percent)	Growth in Real GDP (percent)
2005	4	2	<u>3</u>	3
2006	7	2	<u>6</u>	3
2007	<u>6</u>	1	4	3

3. a. The completed table is above. Use the equation of exchange in growth rates to solve for the unknowns; page 335.

   b. Between 2005 and 2006, the growth rate of the quantity of money increased by 3 percentage points. Between these two years the inflation rate also increased by 3 percentage points; page 335.

4. The inflation rate equals money growth plus velocity growth minus real GDP growth. Velocity does not grow, so the inflation rate equals 5 percent a year minus 3 percent a year, which is 2 percent a year; page 335.

5. A hyperinflation is inflation at a rate that exceeds 50 percent a month. A hyperinflation is the result of extraordinarily rapid growth in the quantity of money; page 337.

■ CHECKPOINT 13.3

Fill in the blanks

Inflation <u>is</u> a tax. The higher the inflation rate, the <u>higher</u> the true income tax rate on income from capital. During an inflation, the costs that arise from an increase in the velocity of circulation of money and an increase in the amount of running around to avoid incurring losses from the falling value of money are <u>shoe-leather</u> costs. Increased uncertainty about inflation leads to a <u>fall</u> in investment.

True or false

1. True; page 339
2. True; page 340
3. False; pages 340-341
4. True; page 342

5. False; page 342

Multiple choice

1. d; page 339
2. c; page 339
3. a; pages 339-340
4. c; page 340
5. b; page 340
6. c; page 341
7. a; page 342
8. a; page 342

Short answer and numeric questions

1. With an inflation of 5 percent a year, Jose losses ($600 × 0.05) = $30 in purchasing power. His money will buy only $570 worth of goods and services. Jose is paying an inflation tax of $30; page 339.

2. The real after-tax interest rate equals the nominal after-tax interest rate minus the inflation rate. When inflation is zero percent a year, the nominal interest rate equals the real interest, which is 2 percent a year. With a 25 percent income tax, the nominal after-tax interest rate equals 1.5 percent a year, so the real after-tax interest rate is 1.5 percent a year. When the inflation rate is 6 percent a year, the nominal interest rate equals the real interest rate, 2 percent a year, plus the inflation rate, 6 percent, which is 8 percent a year. The nominal after-tax interest rate is 6 percent a year, so the real after-tax interest rate equals 6 percent a year minus the inflation rate, 6 percent a year, which is zero percent a year. When the inflation rate equals 10 percent a year, the nominal interest rate is 12 percent a year so the nominal after-tax interest rate is 9 percent a year. As a result, the real after-tax interest rate is 9 percent a year − 10 percent a year, which is −1 percent a year. In this case, the real after-tax interest rate is negative; pages 339-340.

3. The velocity of circulation increases because people try to spend their money as rapidly as possible to avoid incurring losses from the falling value of money. When people spend their money more rapidly, the velocity of cir-

culation increases, thereby creating more shoe-leather costs; page 340.

4. The costs of an inflation depend on its rate and its predictability. The higher the rate, the greater is the cost and the more unpredictable the rate, the greater is the cost; page 342.

AS-AD and the Business Cycle

Chapter

14

CHAPTER IN PERSPECTIVE

■ **Provide a technical definition of recession and describe the history of the U.S. business cycle and the global business cycle.**

A business cycle has two phases, expansion and recession, and two turning points, a peak and a trough. A standard definition of recession is a decrease in real GDP that lasts for at least two quarters. The United States has experienced 33 complete business cycles since 1854. The average length of an expansion is 35 months and the average length of a recession is 18 months. Since World War II, the average recession has been 11 months and the average expansion has been 59 months.

■ **Explain the influences on aggregate supply.**

Aggregate supply is the output from all firms. Other things remaining the same, a rise in the price level increases the quantity of real GDP supplied. Moving along the aggregate supply curve, the only influence on production plans that changes is the price level. All other influences on production plans, such as the money wage rate and the money price of other resources, remain constant. Along the potential GDP line, when the price level changes, the money wage rate and the money prices of other resources change by the same percentage as the change in the price level. Aggregate supply changes when potential GDP changes, the money wage rate changes, or the money prices of other resources change.

■ **Explain the influences on aggregate demand.**

The quantity of real GDP demanded is the total amount of final goods and services produced in the United States that people, businesses, governments, and foreigners plan to buy. A change in the price level brings changes in the buying power of money, the real interest rate, and the real prices of exports and imports, which influence the quantity of real GDP demanded. An increase in the price level decreases the quantity of real GDP demanded and brings a movement along the aggregate demand curve. Factors that change aggregate demand are expectations about the future, fiscal policy and monetary policy, and the state of the world economy. The aggregate demand multiplier is an effect that magnifies changes in expenditure plans and brings potentially large fluctuations in aggregate demand.

■ **Explain how fluctuations in aggregate demand and aggregate supply create the business cycle.**

Macroeconomic equilibrium occurs at the intersection of the aggregate supply and aggregate demand curves. The macroeconomic equilibrium can be a full-employment equilibrium, real GDP equals potential GDP, an above full-employment equilibrium, or a below full-employment equilibrium. Fluctuations in aggregate demand and aggregate supply lead to changes in real GDP and the price level. If real GDP exceeds potential GDP, an inflationary gap exists, which is eliminated by a decrease in aggregate supply and a rise in the price level. If real GDP is less than potential GDP, a recessionary gap exists, which is eliminated by an increase in aggregate supply and a fall in the price level.

CHECKPOINT 14.1

■ **Provide a technical definition of recession and describe the history of the U.S. business cycle and the global business cycle.**

Quick Review

- *Business cycle* The business cycle is the fluctuation in economic activity from an expansion to a peak to a recession to a trough and then to another expansion.
- *Recession* The conventional definition of a recession is a decrease in real GDP that lasts for at least six months.

Additional Practice Problems 14.1

Billions of 2000 dollars				
	Quarter			
Year	1	2	3	4
1973	4305	4355	4332	4373
1974	4335	4348	4306	4289
1975	4238	4269	4341	4398
1976	4497	4530	4552	4584
1977	4640	4731	4816	4817

1 The table shows real GDP in the Untied States from the first quarter of 1973 to the fourth quarter of 1977.

    a. Did the United States experience a recession during these years? If so, during which quarters?

    b. In which quarter was the United States at a business-cycle peak?

    c. In which quarter was the United States at a business-cycle trough?

    d. In what periods did the United States experience an expansion?

2. A country's real GDP grows at 5 percent a year for three quarters, slows to 0.5 percent a year for three quarters, and then increases back to 5 percent. Has the country experienced a recession?

Solutions to Additional Practice Problems 14.1

1a. Although GDP fell in the 3rd quarter of 1973 and the first quarter of 1974, it rebounded in each of the following quarters, so these do not qualify as recessions. The United States first experienced a recession from the 3rd quarter of 1974 until the 1st quarter of 1975, when real GDP decreased for three consecutive quarters.

1b. The United States was at a business cycle peak in the 2nd quarter of 1974. In the following quarters, real GDP decreased as the economy went into a recession.

1c. The United States was at a business cycle trough in the first quarter of 1975. In the quarters prior to this quarter, real GDP was decreasing. In the quarters following it, real GDP increased.

1d. The United States experienced an expansion from the 1st quarter of 1973 to the 2nd quarter of 1974 and then from the 2nd quarter of 1975 to the fourth quarter of 1977.

2. The standard definition of a recession is a decrease in real GDP that lasts for at least two quarters. The country has not experienced a decrease in real GDP so by the standard definition, a recession has not occurred.

■ Self Test 14.1

Fill in the blanks

A business cycle moves from an expansion to a ____ (peak; trough; recession), then to a ____ (peak; trough; recession), and then to a ____ (peak; trough; recession). A decrease in real GDP that lasts for at least two quarters is a ____. In the United States since 1854, the average length of an expansion is ____ (6; 35; 120) months and the average length of a recession is ____ (2; 18; 61) months. During the years since World War II the average expansion has ____ (shortened; lengthened) and the average recession has ____ (shortened; lengthened).

True or false

1. A recession begins at a trough and ends at a peak.

2. An expansion is a period during which real GDP decreases.

3. In the United States since 1854, there have been ten complete business cycles.

4. Potential GDP is not always equal to real GDP.

Multiple choice

1. The business cycle is
   a. a regular up and down movement in production and jobs.
   b. an irregular up and down movement in production and jobs.
   c. a regular movement in price changes.
   d. an irregular movement in price changes.
   e. an irregular up and down movement in the interest rate.

2. The turning point that reflects the end of an expansion is a
   a. peak.
   b. recession.
   c. trough.
   d. trend.
   e. stoppage.

3. A standard definition of recession is a decrease in real GDP that lasts for at least two
   a. years.
   b. quarters.
   c. months.
   d. weeks.
   e. reference periods.

4. Which organization or agency identifies and dates business-cycle phases and turning points in the United States?
   a. Bureau of Economic Analysis
   b. Department of Commerce
   c. National Bureau of Economic Research
   d. Federal Reserve System
   e. Bureau of the Treasury

5. Since 1854, the NBER has identified
   a. 82 complete business cycles.
   b. 33 expansions and 25 recessions.
   c. 33 complete business cycles.
   d. 25 expansions and 33 recessions.
   e. 17 complete business cycles.

6. During the twentieth century, recessions
   a. have shortened and expansions have lengthened.
   b. were as long as expansions.
   c. have lengthened and expansions have shortened.
   d. and expansions have shortened.
   e. and expansions have not changed in length.

Complete the graph

■ FIGURE 14.1

Real GDP (trillions of 2000 dollars)

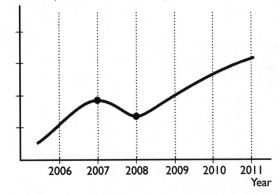

1. Figure 14.1 shows how GDP changes over time. In it, identify the different parts of the business cycle.

■ FIGURE 14.2

Real GDP (trillions of 2000 dollars)

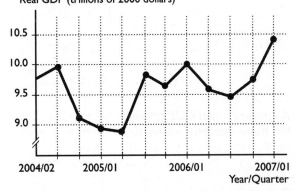

2. Identify when the economy in Figure 14.2 is experiencing recession.

Short answer and numeric questions

1. What is the standard definition of a recession?

2. Since World War II, how have the length of the average expansion and the average recession changed?

CHECKPOINT 14.2

■ **Explain the influences on aggregate supply.**

Quick Review

- *Aggregate supply* The relationship between the quantity of real GDP supplied and the price level when all other influences on production plans remain the same.

- *Factors that change aggregate supply* Aggregate supply decreases and the aggregate supply curve shifts leftward when potential GDP decreases, when the money wage rate rises, or when the money price of other resources rises.

Additional Practice Problem 14.2

1. The table shows the aggregate supply schedule for the United Kingdom.

Price level (GDP deflator)	Real GDP supplied (billions of 1995 pounds)
90	650
100	700
110	750
120	800
130	850

a. Plot the aggregate supply curve in the figure.

b. If the money wage rate in the United Kingdom increases, show the effect on the aggregate supply curve.

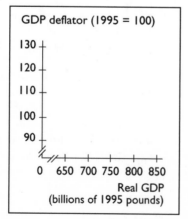

Is there a movement along the aggregate supply curve or a shift of the aggregate supply curve?

Solution to Additional Practice Problem 14.2

1a. The aggregate supply curve is plotted in the figure as AS_0. The aggregate supply curve has a positive slope, so as the price level rises, the quantity of real GDP supplied increases.

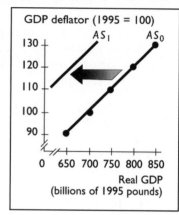

1b. To answer this Practice Problem remember that changes in the price level lead to changes in the aggregate quantity supplied and movements along the aggregate supply curve. Aggregate supply changes when any influence on production plans other than the price level changes. An increase in the money wage rate decreases aggregate supply and shifts the aggregate supply curve leftward, as illustrated by the shift to AS_1. A change in the money wage rate shifts the aggregate supply curve.

■ Self Test 14.2

Fill in the blanks

Moving along the aggregate supply curve, as the price level rises, the quantity of real GDP supplied _____ (decreases; does not change; increases) because the real wage rate _____ (falls; rises). Moving along the potential GDP line, the money wage rate _____ (changes; does not change) when the price level changes. When potential GDP increases, a _____ (movement along; shift of) the AS curve occurs. When the money wage rate changes, a _____ (movement along; shift of) the AS curve occurs.

True or false

1. Along the aggregate supply curve, a rise in the price level decreases the quantity of real GDP supplied.

2. A rise in the price level decreases potential GDP.

3. Anything that changes potential GDP shifts the aggregate supply curve.

4. An increase in potential GDP shifts the aggregate supply curve rightward.

Multiple choice

1. Moving along the potential GDP line, the money wage rate changes by the same percentage as the change in the price level so that the real wage rate
   a. increases.
   b. decreases.
   c. stays at the full-employment equilibrium level.
   d. might either increase or decrease.
   e. stays the same, though not necessarily at the full-employment equilibrium level.

2. The aggregate supply curve is
   a. upward sloping.
   b. downward sloping.
   c. a vertical line.
   d. a horizontal line.
   e. U-shaped.

3. When the price level falls,
   a. the AS curve shifts rightward but the potential GDP line does not shift.
   b. there is a movement upward along the AS curve.
   c. the AS curve shifts leftward but the potential GDP line does not shift.
   d. there is a movement downward along the AS curve.
   e. both the potential GDP line and the AS curve shift leftward.

4. As the price level rises relative to costs and the real wage rate falls, profits _____ and the number of firms in business _____.
   a. increase; increases
   b. increase; decreases
   c. decrease; increases
   d. decrease; decreases
   e. do not change; do not change

■ **FIGURE 14.3**

Price level (GDP deflator, 2000 = 100)

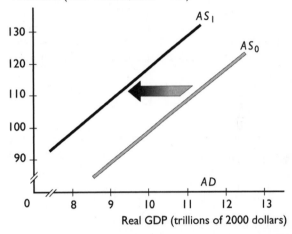

5. In Figure 14.3, which of the following might be the reason for a shift of the aggregate supply curve from AS_0 to AS_1?
   a. a fall in the money wage rate
   b. an increase in potential GDP
   c. an increase in investment
   d. a fall in the price of oil
   e. a rise in the money wage rate

6. When potential GDP increases,
   a. the AS curve shifts rightward.
   b. there is a movement up along the AS curve.
   c. the AS curve shifts leftward.
   d. there is a movement down along the AS curve.
   e. there is neither a movement along or a shift in the AS curve.

7. If the money wage rate rises,
   a. the *AS* curve shifts rightward.
   b. there is a movement up along the *AS* curve.
   c. the *AS* curve shifts leftward.
   d. there is a movement down along the *AS* curve.
   e. there is neither a movement along nor a shift in the *AS* curve.

Complete the graph

Price level (GDP deflator 2000 = 100)	Quantity of real GDP supplied (trillions of 2000 dollars)	Potential GDP (trillions of 2000 dollars)
140	17	13
130	15	13
120	13	13
110	11	13
100	9	13

■ **FIGURE 14.4**

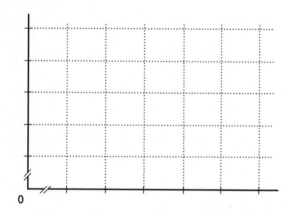

1. The table above gives the aggregate supply schedule and potential GDP schedule for a nation.
   a. Label the axes and then plot the *AS* curve and potential GDP line in Figure 14.4.
   b. Suppose the money wage rate falls. Show the effect of this change on aggregate supply and potential GDP in Figure 14.4.
   c. Use the data in the table to again plot the *AS* curve and potential GDP line in Figure 14.5. Be sure to label the axes.

■ **FIGURE 14.5**

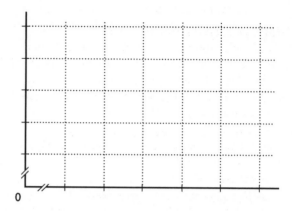

   d. Potential GDP increases by $2 trillion. Show the effect of this change on aggregate supply and potential GDP in Figure 14.5.

Short answer and numeric questions

1. Why does the *AS* curve slope upward?

2. Why does the aggregate supply curve shift when the money wage rate rises? Why doesn't the potential GDP line also shift?

3. What is the effect on aggregate supply if the money price of oil rises?

CHECKPOINT 14.3

■ **Explain the influences on aggregate demand.**

Quick Review

- *Aggregate demand* The relationship between the quantity of real GDP demanded and the price level when all other influences on expenditure plans remain the same.

- *Factors that change aggregate demand* Aggregate demand changes and the aggregate demand curve shifts if expected future income, inflation, or profit change; if the government or the Federal Reserve take steps that change expenditure plans, such as changes in taxes or in the quantity of money; or the state of the world economy changes.

Additional Practice Problem 14.3

1. Draw aggregate demand curves and illustrate the effects of each event listed below either by a movement along the aggregate demand curve or a shift in the aggregate demand curve. These events are:
   a. The price level falls.
   b. Firms increase their investment because the expected future rate of profit increases.
   c. The government cuts its taxes.

Solution to Additional Practice Problem 14.3

1a. To answer this Practice Problem, remember that a change in any factor that influences expenditure plans other than the price level brings a change in aggregate demand and a shift in the *AD* curve. In this part, it *is* the price level that changes, so there is a change in the quantity of real GDP demanded and a movement along the aggregate demand curve. Because the price level falls, there is a downward movement

along the aggregate demand curve, as illustrated.

1b. An increase in firms' investment increases aggregate demand. The aggregate demand curve shifts rightward, as shown in the figure by the shift from *AD*₀ to *AD*₁.

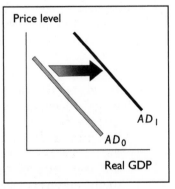

1c. When the government cuts its taxes, households' incomes rise and so they increase their consumption expenditure. Aggregate demand increases and the aggregate demand curve shifts rightward, as illustrated in the previous answer.

■ Self Test 14.3

Fill in the blanks

An increase in the price level ____ (decreases; increases) the quantity of real GDP demanded and a ____ (movement along; shift of) the aggregate demand curve occurs. An increase in expected future income shifts the *AD* curve ____ (leftward; rightward). A tax cut shifts the *AD* curve ____ (leftward; rightward). A decrease in foreign income shifts the *AD* curve ____ (leftward; rightward).

True or false

1. As the price level falls, other things remaining the same, the quantity of real GDP demanded increases.
2. An increase in expected future income will not increase aggregate demand until the income actually increases.
3. A decrease in government purchases shifts the aggregate demand curve rightward.
4. An increase in income in Mexico decreases aggregate demand in the United States because Mexicans will buy more Mexican-produced goods.

Multiple choice

1. When the price level rises there is a ____ the aggregate demand curve.
   a. rightward shift of
   b. movement down along
   c. leftward shift of
   d. movement up along
   e. rotation of

2. A rise in the price level
   a. raises the buying power of money.
   b. decreases the prices of exports.
   c. lowers the buying power of money.
   d. increases aggregate demand.
   e. makes the aggregate demand curve steeper.

3. When the price level rises, the real interest rate ____ and the quantity of real GDP demanded ____.
   a. rises; increases
   b. rises; decreases
   c. falls; increases
   d. falls; decreases
   e. does not change; does not change

■ **FIGURE 14.6**
Price level (GDP deflator, 2000 = 100)

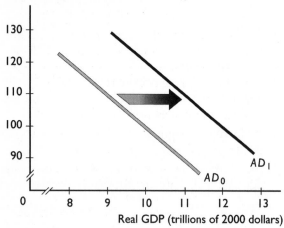

4. In Figure 14.6, the shift in the aggregate demand curve could be the result of
   a. an increase in the quantity of money
   b. a decrease in foreign incomes.
   c. a tax hike.
   d. a fall in the price level.
   e. a decrease in the expected future rate of profit.

5. A change in any of the following factors EXCEPT ____ shifts the aggregate demand curve.
   a. expectations about the future
   b. the money wage rate
   c. monetary and fiscal policy
   d. foreign income
   e. the foreign exchange rate

6. Which of the following shifts the aggregate demand curve leftward?
   a. a decrease in government expenditures on goods and services
   b. an increase in the price level
   c. a tax cut
   d. an increase in foreign income
   e. a decrease in the price level

7. When investment increases, the ____ in aggregate demand is ____ the change in investment.
   a. increase; greater than
   b. increase; smaller than
   c. increase; the same as
   d. decrease; the same as
   e. decrease; greater than

Complete the graph

■ **FIGURE 14.7**
Price level (GDP deflator, 2000 = 100)

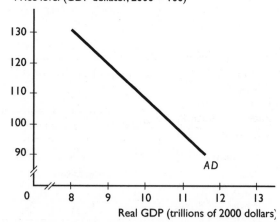

1. Figure 14.7 shows an aggregate demand curve.
   a. Suppose that government expenditures on goods and services increase. In Figure

14.7, illustrate the effect of this fiscal policy.

b. Suppose the Federal Reserve decreases the quantity of money. In Figure 14.7, illustrate the effect of this monetary policy.

Short answer and numeric questions

1. Why does an increase in the price level decrease the quantity of real GDP demanded?

2. Expected future profit increases. Explain the effect on aggregate demand.

3. The government increases its taxes. What is the effect on aggregate demand?

4. What is the aggregate demand multiplier?

CHECKPOINT 14.4

■ **Explain how fluctuations in aggregate demand and aggregate supply create the business cycle.**

Quick Review

- *Effect of decrease in aggregate demand* A decrease in aggregate demand, everything else remaining the same, lowers the price level and decreases real GDP.

- *Effect of decrease in aggregate supply* A decrease in aggregate supply, everything else remaining the same, raises the price level and decreases real GDP.

Additional Practice Problem 14.4

1. The table shows aggregate demand and aggregate supply schedules for the United Kingdom.

Price level (GDP deflator)	Real GDP demanded	Real GDP supplied
	(billions of 1995 pounds)	
90	800	650
100	775	700
110	750	750
120	725	800
130	700	850

a. Plot the aggregate demand curve.

b. Plot the aggregate supply curve.

c. What is the macroeconomic equilibrium?

d. If potential GDP in the United Kingdom is £800 billion, what is the type of macroeconomic equilibrium?

e. If the government increases its expenditures on goods and services, what is the effect on the British economy?

Solution to Additional Practice Problem 14.4

1a. The aggregate demand curve is plotted in the figure to the right. The aggregate demand curve has a negative slope, so as the price level falls, the quantity of real GDP demanded increases.

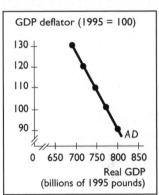

1b. The aggregate supply curve is plotted in the figure. The aggregate supply curve has a positive slope, so as the price level rises, the quantity of real GDP supplied increases.

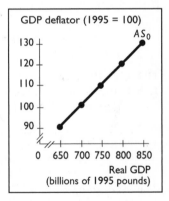

1c. The macroeconomic equilibrium is at a price level of 110 and real GDP of £750 billion. The macroeconomic equilibrium is at the intersection of the aggregate

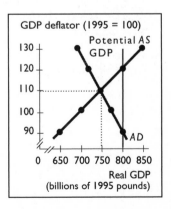

supply curve and the aggregate demand curve.

1d. Because potential GDP is £800 billion and the macroeconomic equilibrium is £750 billion, the economy is in a below full-employment equilibrium. Real GDP is less than potential GDP.

1e. If the government increases its expenditures on goods and services, the aggregate demand curve shifts rightward. As a result, the price level rises and real GDP increases, moving the nation closer to a full-employment equilibrium.

■ Self Test 14.4

Fill in the blanks

An increase in aggregate demand ____ (decreases; increases) real GDP. An increase in aggregate supply ____ (lowers; raises) the price level. Stagflation is a combination of ____ (expansion; recession) and a ____ (falling; rising) price level. When real GDP exceeds potential GDP, ____ (an inflationary; a recessionary) gap exists. When potential GDP exceeds real GDP, ____ (an inflationary; a recessionary) gap exists.

True or false

1. Starting from full employment, an increase in aggregate demand increases real GDP above potential GDP.

2. Starting from full employment, a decrease in aggregate demand shifts the aggregate demand curve leftward and creates an inflationary gap.

3. Starting from full employment, an increase in aggregate demand shifts the aggregate demand curve rightward and creates an inflationary gap.

4. A recessionary gap brings a rising price level to eliminate the gap.

Multiple choice

1. If the quantity of real GDP supplied equals the quantity of real GDP demanded, then
   a. nominal GDP must equal real GDP.
   b. real GDP must equal potential GDP.
   c. real GDP must be greater than potential GDP.
   d. real GDP might be greater than, equal to, or less than potential GDP.
   e. real GDP must be less than potential GDP.

■ FIGURE 14.8

Price level (GDP deflator, 2000 = 100)

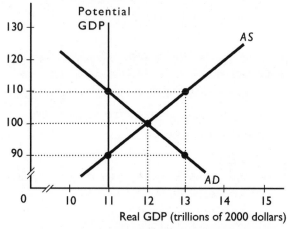

2. In Figure 14.8, the equilibrium price level is ____ and the equilibrium real GDP is ____ trillion.
   a. 110; $11
   b. 110; $13
   c. 100; $12
   d. 90; $11
   e. 90; $13

3. Figure 14.8 shows
   a. a full-employment equilibrium.
   b. an above full-employment equilibrium with an inflationary gap.
   c. an above full-employment equilibrium with a recessionary gap.
   d. a below full-employment equilibrium with an inflationary gap.
   e. a below full-employment equilibrium with a recessionary gap.

4. An increase in investment ____ aggregate demand, the aggregate demand curve shifts ____ and the economy is in the ____ phase of the business cycle.
   a. decreases; rightward; expansion
   b. increases; rightward; expansion
   c. decreases; leftward; recession
   d. increases; rightward; recession
   e. increases; leftward; recession

5. If the price of oil rises, the
   a. *AD* curve shifts rightward, real GDP increases, and the price level rises.
   b. *AS* curve shifts leftward, the price level rises, and real GDP decreases.
   c. *AD* curve and the *AS* curve shift leftward, real GDP decreases, and the price level rises.
   d. *AD* curve and the *AS* curve shift rightward, the price level rises, and real GDP decreases.
   e. *AS* curve shifts leftward, the price level rises, and real GDP increases.

6. Stagflation is a combination of ____ real GDP and a ____ price level.
   a. increasing; rising
   b. increasing; falling
   c. decreasing; rising
   d. decreasing; falling
   e. no change in; rising

7. An inflationary gap is created when
   a. real GDP is greater than potential GDP.
   b. real GDP equal to potential GDP.
   c. the inflation rate is less than potential inflation.
   d. the price level exceeds the equilibrium price level.
   e. potential GDP is greater than real GDP.

8. An economy is at full employment. If aggregate demand increases,
   a. an inflationary gap is created and the *AS* curve shifts leftward as the money wage rate rises.
   b. an inflationary gap is created and the *AD* curve shifts leftward.
   c. an inflationary gap is created and potential GDP increases to close the gap.
   d. a recessionary gap is created and the *AS* curve shifts leftward as the money wage rate falls.
   e. a recessionary gap is created and the *AS* curve shifts leftward as the money wage rate rises.

Complete the graph

■ **FIGURE 14.9**

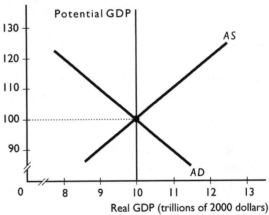

1. Figure 14.9 shows an economy. Suppose people expect an increase in the future expected rate of profit.
   a. In Figure 14.9, show the effect of the change in expectations on the price level and real GDP.
   b. In Figure 14.9, show how the economy returns to potential GDP.

■ FIGURE 14.10

Price level (GDP deflator, 2000 = 100)

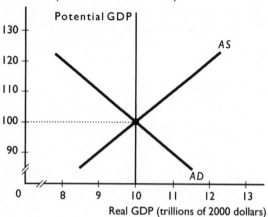

2. Figure 14.10 shows an economy. Show the effect a rise in the price of oil has on the price level and real GDP.

Short answer and numeric questions

1. What is stagflation? What can create stagflation?

2. What is an inflationary gap and how is it eliminated?

SELF TEST ANSWERS

■ CHECKPOINT 14.1

Fill in the blanks

A business cycle moves from an expansion to a peak, then to a recession, and then to a trough. A decrease in real GDP that lasts for at least two quarters is a recession. In the United States since 1854, the average length of an expansion is 35 months and the average length of a recession is 18 months. During the years since World War II the average expansion has lengthened and the average recession has shortened.

True or false

1. False; page 348
2. False; page 348
3. False; page 348
4. True; pages 350-351

Multiple choice

1. b; page 348
2. a; page 348
3. b; page 348
4. c; page 348
5. c; page 348
6. a; page 349

Complete the graph

■ FIGURE 14.11

Real GDP (trillions of 2000 dollars)

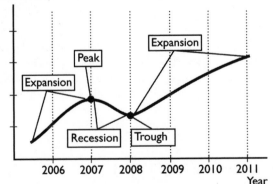

1. Figure 14.11 divides the data into the two phases and the two turning points of the business cycle; page 348.

2. A recession runs from the third quarter of 2004 to the second quarter of 2005 and from the first quarter of 2006 to the third quarter of 2006; page 348.

Short answer and numeric questions

1. The standard definition of a recession is a decrease in real GDP that lasts for at least two quarters (six months); page 348.
2. Since World War II, the average expansion has lengthened and the average recession has shortened; page 349.

■ CHECKPOINT 14.2

Fill in the blanks

Moving along the aggregate supply curve, as the price level rises, the quantity of real GDP supplied increases because the real wage rate falls. Moving along the potential GDP line, the money wage rate does not change when the price level changes. When potential GDP increases, a shift of the AS curve occurs. When the money wage rate changes, a shift of the AS curve occurs.

True or false

1. False; page 354
2. False; page 354
3. True; page 357
4. True; page 357

Multiple choice

1. c; page 354
2. a; page 355
3. d; page 354
4. a; page 356
5. e; page 358
6 a; page 357
7. c; page 358

Complete the graph

■ FIGURE 14.12

Price level (GDP deflator, 2000 = 100)

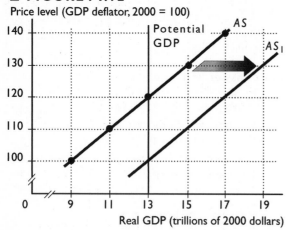

1. a. Figure 14.12 labels the axes. The aggregate supply curve is labeled *AS*; page 355.

   b. The fall in the money wage rate has no effect on potential GDP, so the potential GDP line does not change. Aggregate supply, however, increases so the *AS* curve shifts rightward, to an *AS* curve such as *AS*1; page 358.

■ FIGURE 14.13

Price level (GDP deflator, 2000 = 100)

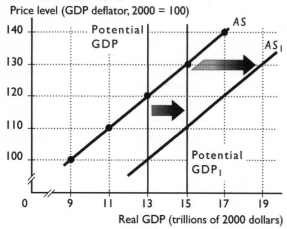

   c. Figure 14.13 labels the axes. The aggregate supply curve is labeled *AS*; page 355.

   d. The potential GDP line shifts rightward by $2 trillion, as indicated by the shift to Potential GDP1. The aggregate supply curve also shifts rightward by $2 trillion, as shown by the shift to *AS*1; page 357.

Short answer and numeric questions

1. The movement along the *AS* curve brings a change in the real wage rate (and changes in the real cost of other resources whose money prices are fixed). If the price level rises, the real wage rate falls.

   A fall in the real wage rate boosts a firm's profit. The number of firms in business increases.

   If the price level rises relative to costs, fewer firms will want to shut down, so more firms operate.

   If the price level rises and the money wage rate does not change, an extra hour of labor that was previously unprofitable becomes profitable. So, the quantity of labor demanded increases and production increases.

   For the economy as a whole, as the price level rises, the quantity of real GDP supplied increases; pages 355-357.

2. An increase in the money wage rate increases firms' costs. The higher are firms' costs, the smaller is the quantity that firms are willing to supply at each price level. Aggregate supply decreases and the *AS* curve shifts leftward. A change in the money wage rate does not change potential GDP. Potential GDP depends only on the economy's real ability to produce and on the full-employment quantity of labor, which occurs at the equilibrium real wage rate. The equilibrium real wage rate can occur at any money wage rate; page 358.

3. If the money price of oil rises, firm's costs increase. The higher are firms' costs, the smaller is the quantity that firms are willing to supply at each price level. Aggregate supply decreases and the aggregate supply curve shifts leftward; page 358.

■ CHECKPOINT 14.3

Fill in the blanks

An increase in the price level <u>decreases</u> the quantity of real GDP demanded and a <u>movement along</u> the aggregate demand curve occurs.

An increase in expected future income shifts the AD curve <u>rightward</u>. A tax cut shifts the AD curve <u>rightward</u>. A decrease in foreign income shifts the AD curve <u>leftward</u>.

True or false

1. True; page 360
2. False; page 362
3. False; page 363
4. False; page 364

Multiple choice

1. d; page 361
2. c; pages 360-361
3. b; page 361
4. a; page 363
5. b; paged 362-364
6. a; pages 362-364
7. a; page 364

Complete the graph

■ **FIGURE 14.14**

Price level (GDP deflator, 2000 = 100)

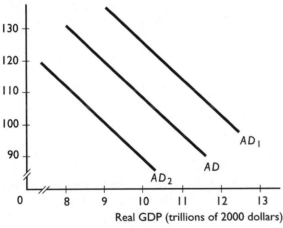

Real GDP (trillions of 2000 dollars)

1. a. In Figure 14.14, an increase in government purchases increases aggregate demand and shifts the AD curve rightward, from AD to AD₁; page 363.
   b. In Figure 14.14, a decrease in the quantity of money decreases aggregate demand and shifts the AD curve leftward, from AD to AD₂; page 363.

Short answer and numeric questions

1. An increase in the price level decreases the quantity of real GDP demanded because an increase in the price level lowers the buying power of money, raises the real interest rate, raises the real prices of exports, and lowers the real price of imports; pages 360-362.
2. An increase in expected future profit increases the investment that firms plan to undertake and increases aggregate demand; page 362.
3. The government can influence aggregate demand by changing taxes. When the government increases taxes, aggregate demand decreases; page 363.
4. The aggregate demand multiplier is an effect that magnifies changes in expenditure and increases fluctuations in aggregate demand. For example, an increase in investment increases aggregate demand and increases income. The increase in income induces an increase in consumption expenditure so aggregate demand increases by more than the initial increase in investment; page 364.

■ CHECKPOINT 14.4

Fill in the blanks

An increase in aggregate demand <u>increases</u> real GDP. An increase in aggregate supply <u>lowers</u> the price level. Stagflation is a combination of <u>recession</u> and a <u>rising</u> price level. When real GDP exceeds potential GDP, <u>an inflationary</u> gap exists. When potential GDP exceeds real GDP, <u>a recessionary</u> gap exists.

True or false

1. True; pages 366-367
2. False; pages 366-367, 370
3. True; pages 366-367, 370
4. False; page 370

Multiple choice

1. d; page 366
2. c; page 366
3. b; pages 366-367, 370

4. b; pages 366-367
5. b; page 368-369
6. c; page 368
7. a; page 370
8. a; page 370

Complete the graph

■ **FIGURE 14.15**

Price level (GDP deflator, 2000 = 100)

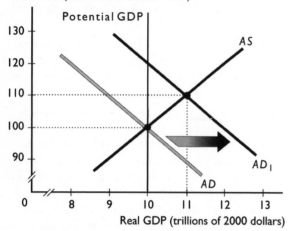

1. a. An increase in expected rate of profit increases firms' investment which increases aggregate demand. The aggregate demand curve shifts rightward from *AD* to *AD1* in Figure 14.15. The equilibrium price level rises to 110 and equilibrium real GDP increases to $11 trillion; pages 366-367.

   b. An inflationary gap now exists. The money wage rate rises and aggregate supply decreases. In Figure 14.16 (at the top of the next column), the *AS* curve shifts leftward. Eventually the *AS* curve moves to *AS1*. Real GDP returns to potential GDP, $10 trillion, and the price level rises to 120; page 370.

■ **FIGURE 14.16**

Price level (GDP deflator, 2000 = 100)

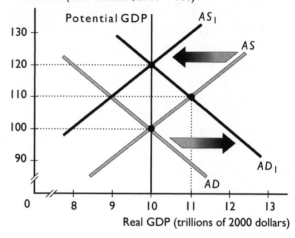

■ **FIGURE 14.17**

Price level (GDP deflator, 2000 = 100)

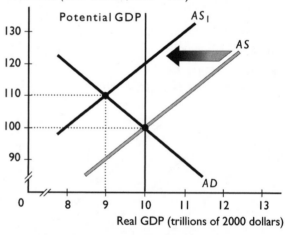

2. Figure 14.17 shows the effect of a rise in the price of oil. Aggregate supply decreases and the *AS* curve shifts leftward from *AS* to *AS1*. Real GDP decreases to $9 trillion and the price level rises to 110; page 368.

Short answer and numeric questions

1. Stagflation is a combination of recession (falling real GDP) and inflation (rising price level). Stagflation can be created by a decrease in aggregate supply; page 368.

2. An inflationary gap is a gap that exists when real GDP exceeds potential GDP. An inflationary gap brings a rising price level. Workers have experienced a fall in the buying power of their wages, and firms' profits have increased. Employment exceeds full employment. Workers demand higher wages. As the money wage rate rises, aggregate supply decreases and the aggregate supply curve shifts leftward. Eventually, real GDP will return to potential GDP and the inflationary gap is eliminated; page 370.

Aggregate Expenditure

Chapter 15

■ **Distinguish between autonomous expenditure and induced expenditure and explain how real GDP influences expenditure plans.**

Aggregate *planned* expenditure is planned consumption expenditure plus planned investment plus planned government expenditures plus planned net exports. Aggregate *planned* expenditure does not always equal real GDP. Induced expenditure are the components of aggregate expenditure that change when real GDP changes; autonomous expenditure are the components of aggregate expenditure that do not change when real GDP changes. The consumption function is the relationship between consumption expenditure and disposable income. The marginal propensity to consume, MPC, is the fraction of a change in disposable income that is spent on consumption. When real GDP increases, imports increase. The marginal propensity to import is the fraction of an increase in real GDP spent on imports.

■ **Explain how real GDP adjusts to achieve equilibrium expenditure.**

Equilibrium expenditure occurs when aggregate *planned* expenditure equals real GDP. It occurs at the point where the AE curve intersects the 45° line. If aggregate planned expenditure is less than real GDP, an unplanned increase in inventories occurs. Firms decrease production and real GDP decreases until real GDP equals aggregate planned expenditure and the economy is at equilibrium expenditure. If aggregate planned expenditure exceeds real GDP, an unplanned decrease in inventories occurs. Firms increase production and real GDP increases. The economy moves to its equilibrium expenditure.

■ **Describe and explain the expenditure multiplier.**

The expenditure multiplier is the amount by which a change in any component of autonomous expenditure is multiplied to determine the change that it creates in equilibrium expenditure and real GDP. The multiplier is greater than 1 because an increase in autonomous expenditure induces further changes in aggregate expenditure. If we ignore income taxes and imports, the multiplier equals $1 \div (1 - MPC)$. The multiplier is larger if the MPC is larger. Imports and income taxes reduce the size of the multiplier. In general, the multiplier equals $1 \div (1 - $ slope of AE curve$)$. An expansion is triggered by an increase in autonomous expenditure that increases aggregate planned expenditure and real GDP.

■ **Derive the AD curve from equilibrium expenditure.**

The AE curve is the relationship between aggregate planned expenditure and real GDP, when all other influences on expenditure plans remain the same. The AD curve is the relationship between the quantity of real GDP demanded and the price level. When the price level rises, aggregate planned expenditure decreases, the AE curve shifts downward, and equilibrium expenditure decreases. When the price level rises, aggregate planned expenditure increases, the AE curve shifts upward, and equilibrium expenditure increases. Each point of equilibrium expenditure corresponds to a point on the AD curve.

CHECKPOINT 15.1

■ **Distinguish between autonomous expenditure and induced expenditure and explain how real GDP influences expenditure plans.**

Quick Review

- *Autonomous expenditure* The components of aggregate expenditure that do not change when real GDP changes.
- *Consumption function* The relationship between consumption expenditure and disposable income, other things remaining the same.
- *Marginal propensity to consume, MPC* The fraction of a change in disposable income that is spent on consumption, which equals the change in consumption expenditure divided by the change in disposable income that brought it about.

Additional Practice Problems 15.1

1. Suppose disposable income increases by $1.5 trillion.

    a. If the marginal propensity to consume (*MPC*) is 0.8, what is the change in consumption expenditure?

    b. If the *MPC* equals 0.6, what is the change in consumption expenditure?

    c. What is the relationship between the *MPC* and the change in consumption expenditure for a given change in disposable income?

2. The figure shows the consumption function for a small nation. Calculate the marginal propensity to consume and autonomous consumption in the nation.

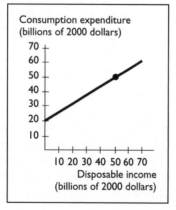

Consumption expenditure
(billions of 2000 dollars)

Disposable income
(billions of 2000 dollars)

Solutions to Additional Practice Problems 15.1

1a. The change in consumption expenditure equals the *MPC* multiplied by the change in disposable income. When the *MPC* is 0.8, the change in consumption expenditure equals ($1.5 trillion) × (0.8), which is $1.2 trillion.

1b. When the *MPC* is 0.6, the change in consumption expenditure is ($1.5 trillion) × (0.6), which is $0.9 trillion.

1c. The larger the *MPC*, the greater the change in consumption expenditure for a given change in disposable income.

2. The *MPC* is the slope of the consumption function and equals the change in consumption expenditure divided by the change in disposable income that brought it about. The figure shows that when disposable income increases from $0 to $50 billion, consumption expenditure increases from $20 billion to $50 billion. The *MPC* equals ($30 billion) ÷ ($50 billion), which is 0.60. Autonomous consumption is the amount of consumption when income equals zero and equals the *y*-axis intercept, $20 billion.

■ **Self Test 15.1**

Fill in the blanks

Aggregate planned expenditure ____ (does not always equal; always equals) real GDP. The components of aggregate expenditure that change when real GDP changes are ____ (induced; autonomous) expenditure. The components of aggregate expenditure that do not change when real GDP changes are ____ (induced; autonomous) expenditure. The ____ is the relationship between consumption expenditure and disposable income. The marginal propensity to consume equals the change in consumption expenditure ____ (plus; multiplied by; divided by) the change in disposable income that brought it about. The slope of the consumption function equals the ____. A change in disposable income is shown by a ____ (shift in; movement along) the consumption function, and a change in the buying power of money is shown by a ____ (shift in; movement along) the consumption function. Imports ____ (are; are not) a component of induced expenditure.

True or false

1. Induced expenditure increases as real GDP increases.
2. The slope of the consumption function is less than the slope of the 45° line.
3. The marginal propensity to consume equals consumption expenditure divided by disposable income.
4. The consumption function shifts when the buying power of net assets changes.

Multiple choice

1. The components of aggregate expenditure are consumption expenditure,
   a. interest, gross spending, and net spending.
   b. investment, government expenditures on goods and services, and net income.
   c. interest, government expenditures on goods and services, and net exports.
   d. investment, government expenditures on goods and services, and net exports.
   e. investment, government expenditures on goods and services, and net taxes.

2. Which of the following is true?
   a. Actual aggregate expenditure does not always equal real GDP.
   b. Aggregate planned expenditure always equals real GDP.
   c. Actual aggregate expenditure always equals real GDP.
   d. Aggregate planned expenditure and actual aggregate expenditures both are always equal to GDP.
   e. Actual aggregate expenditure cannot be measured.

3. Autonomous expenditure is the component of
   a. aggregate expenditure that changes when real GDP changes.
   b. induced expenditure that changes when real GDP changes.
   c. aggregate planned expenditure that changes only when government expenditures on goods and services change.
   d. aggregate expenditure that does not change when real GDP changes.
   e. aggregate expenditure that does not change when the interest rate changes.

4. The components of aggregate expenditure that change when real GDP changes are
   a. unplanned expenditure.
   b. induced expenditure.
   c. planned expenditure.
   d. autonomous expenditure.
   e. changeable expenditure.

5. The consumption function is the relationship between ____, other things remaining the same.
   a. consumption expenditure and saving
   b. real GDP and net taxes
   c. consumption expenditure and disposable income
   d. net taxes and disposable income
   e. consumption expenditure and net taxes

6. When disposable income increases from $9 trillion to $10 trillion, consumption expenditure increases from $6 trillion to $6.8 trillion. The *MPC* is
   a. 1.00.
   b. 0.80.
   c. 0.60.
   d. 0.68.
   e. $6.8 trillion.

■ FIGURE 15.1

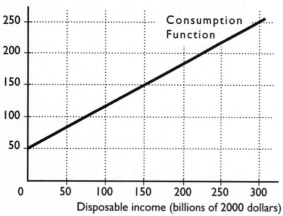

Consumption expenditure (billions of 2000 dollars)

Complete the graph

Disposable income (trillions of 2000 dollars)	Consumption expenditure, (trillions of 2000 dollars)
0.0	0.4
1.0	1.2
2.0	2.0
3.0	2.8
4.0	3.6
5.0	4.4

■ FIGURE 15.2

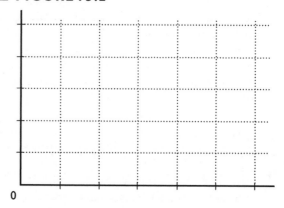

7. Figure 15.1 shows a consumption function. What is the amount of autonomous consumption?
   a. $0
   b. $50 billion
   c. $100 billion
   d. $150 billion
   e. $200 billion

8. Figure 15.1 shows a consumption function. What is the amount of induced consumption when disposable income equals $150 billion?
   a. $0
   b. $50 billion
   c. $100 billion
   d. $150 billion
   e. $200 billion

9. Figure 15.1 shows a consumption function. What does the MPC equal?
   a. 1.00
   b. 0.80
   c. 0.67
   d. 0.60
   e. 0.50

1. The table above has data on consumption expenditure and disposable income.
   a. Using the data, label the axes and plot the consumption function in Figure 15.2.
   b. Indicate the amount of autonomous consumption expenditure in Figure 15.2.
   c. What is the amount of saving if disposable income equals $1.0 trillion? $4.0 trillion?
   d. Calculate the marginal propensity to consume.
   e. Suppose the real interest rate falls and consumers increase their consumption by $0.6 trillion at every level of disposable income. Draw the new consumption function in Figure 15.2. What is the amount of autonomous consumption now?

Short answer and numeric questions

1. What is the relationship between actual aggregate expenditure and real GDP? Between aggregate planned expenditure and real GDP?

2. What is the difference between autonomous expenditure and induced expenditure?

3. In a graph with a consumption function, what does the *MPC* equal? What does autonomous consumption equal?

Change in disposable income (trillions of 2000 dollars)	Change in consumption expenditure (trillions of 2000 dollars)	Marginal propensity to consume, MPC
2	1.8	___
1	0.9	___
4	3.0	___

4. The table above shows the change in consumption expenditure when a change in disposable income occurs. Complete the table by calculating the marginal propensities to consume.

CHECKPOINT 15.2

■ **Explain how real GDP adjusts to achieve equilibrium expenditure.**

Quick Review

- *Equilibrium expenditure* The level of aggregate expenditure that occurs when aggregate planned expenditure equals real GDP.

Additional Practice Problem 15.2

GDP	C	I	G	X	M
50	50	20	25	25	10
100	85	20	25	25	15
150	120	20	25	25	20
200	155	20	25	25	25
250	190	20	25	25	30
300	225	20	25	25	35

1. The table gives the components of real GDP in billions of dollars.
   a. Draw the aggregate expenditure curve.
   b. What is equilibrium expenditure?
   c. At what levels of GDP does aggregate planned expenditure exceed real GDP? At what levels does real GDP exceed aggregate planned expenditure?

d. At what levels of GDP is unplanned inventory change negative? At what levels is unplanned inventory change positive?

e. What is the relationship between your answers to parts (c) and (d)?

f. By what process is the equilibrium expenditure reached?

Solution to Additional Practice Problem 15.2

1a. Aggregate planned expenditure equals $C + I + G + X - M$. To construct the *AE* curve add the components of aggregate planned expenditure together for each level of real GDP. The *AE* curve is illustrated in the figure, along with a 45° line.

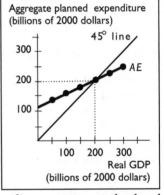

1b. Equilibrium expenditure occurs at the level of real GDP where the *AE* curve intersects the 45° line. The equilibrium expenditure is $200 billion.

1c. For all GDP less than $200 billion, aggregate planned expenditure exceeds real GDP. For all GDP greater than $200 billion, aggregate planned expenditure exceeds real GDP.

1d. For all GDP less than $200 billion, unplanned inventory change is negative. For all GDP greater than $200 billion, unplanned inventory change is positive.

1e. For all levels of GDP for which aggregate planned expenditure exceeds real GDP, unplanned inventory change is negative. And for all levels of GDP for which real GDP exceeds aggregate planned expenditure, unplanned inventory change is positive.

1f. If aggregate planned expenditure exceeds real GDP, unplanned inventory change is negative so firms increase production and real GDP increases. Eventually real GDP increases enough so that it equals aggregate planned expenditure and equilibrium is reached. If aggregate planned expenditure is less than real GDP, unplanned inventory change is positive and so firms decrease production and real GDP decreases. Eventually real GDP decreases by enough so that it equals aggregate planned expenditure and equilibrium is reached. When real GDP reaches $200 billion, aggregate planned expenditure equals real GDP. The economy is at equilibrium expenditure. The unplanned inventory change is zero and firms have no reason to change production.

■ Self Test 15.2

Fill in the blanks

Aggregate planned expenditure equals ____ plus ____ plus ____ plus ____ minus ____. As real GDP increases, aggregate planned expenditure ____ (increases; does not change; decreases). Equilibrium expenditure occurs when aggregate planned expenditure is the level of aggregate expenditure that equals ____. When aggregate planned expenditure exceeds real GDP, an unplanned ____ (increase; decrease) in inventories occurs and firms ____ (increase; decrease) production.

True or false

1. Equilibrium expenditure occurs at the intersection of the aggregate expenditure curve and the 45° line.

2. If planned expenditure is less than real GDP, unplanned inventories increase.

3. If aggregate planned expenditure exceeds real GDP, inventories decrease and firms decrease production.

4. If unplanned investment occurs, then the aggregate expenditure is not at its equilibrium level.

Multiple choice

1. The *AE* curve illustrates the relationship between
   a. aggregate planned expenditure and real GDP.
   b. real GDP and actual expenditure.
   c. real GDP and the interest rate.
   d. the interest rate and aggregate planned expenditure.
   e. the quantity of real GDP demanded and the price level.

2. Equilibrium expenditure occurs when
   a. aggregate planned expenditure equals real GDP.
   b. disposable income equals real GDP.
   c. disposable income equals consumption expenditures plus imports.
   d. real GDP plus net taxes equals disposable income.
   e. real GDP minus net taxes equals disposable income.

■ FIGURE 15.3

Aggregate planned expenditure (trillions of 2000 dollars)

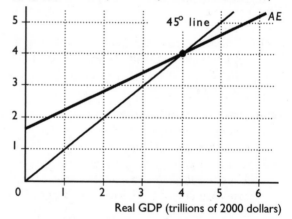

3. In Figure 15.3, equilibrium expenditure equals ____ trillion.
   a. $1
   b. $2
   c. $3
   d. $4
   e. $5

4. In Figure 15.3, if real GDP is $5 trillion, then
   a. the economy is at its equilibrium.
   b. inventories are above their target.
   c. inventories are below their target
   d. the price level will rise to restore equilibrium.
   e. the price level will fall to restore equilibrium.

5. When aggregate planned expenditure exceeds real GDP, there is
   a. a planned decrease in inventories.
   b. a planned increase in inventories.
   c. an unplanned decrease in inventories.
   d. an unplanned increase in inventory.
   e. an unplanned decrease in the price level.

6. If aggregate planned expenditure is greater than real GDP,
   a. an unplanned decrease in inventories leads to an increase in production.
   b. an unplanned increase in inventories leads to a decrease in production.
   c. a planned decrease in inventories leads to an decrease in production.
   d. a planned increase in inventories leads to an increase in production.
   e. an unplanned decrease in inventories leads to an increase in the price level.

7. If real GDP equals aggregate planned expenditure, then inventories
   a. rise above their target levels.
   b. fall below their target levels.
   c. equal their target levels.
   d. are either above or below their target levels depending on whether planned inventories are above or below their target levels.
   e. None of the above answers is necessarily correct because there is no relationship between inventories and aggregate planned expenditure.

8. Equilibrium expenditure is the level of expenditure at which
   a. firms' inventories are zero.
   b. firms' inventories are at the desired level.
   c. firms produce more output than they sell.
   d. aggregate planned expenditure minus planned changes in inventories equals real GDP.
   e. aggregate planned expenditure plus planned changes in inventories equals real GDP.

Complete the graph

GDP	C	I	G	X	M	AE
0.0	0.6	0.4	0.2	0.2	0.2	__
1.0	1.2	0.4	0.2	0.2	0.4	__
2.0	1.8	0.4	0.2	0.2	0.6	__
3.0	2.4	0.4	0.2	0.2	0.8	__
4.0	3.0	0.4	0.2	0.2	1.0	__
5.0	3.6	0.4	0.2	0.2	1.2	__

■ **FIGURE 15.4**

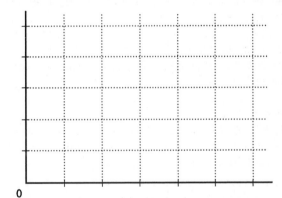

1. The table above gives the components of aggregate planned expenditure in trillions of 2000 dollars.
   a. Complete the table.
   b. Label the axes in Figure 15.4 and then plot the *AE* curve.
   c. In Figure 15.4, show the equilibrium expenditure.
   d. Over what range of GDP is there an unplanned increase in inventories? Over

what range of GDP is there an unplanned decrease in inventories?

e. What is the amount of planned and actual investment when GDP equals $3.0 trillion?

Short answer and numeric questions

1. What is the relationship between aggregate planned expenditure and real GDP? Explain the relationship.

2. In a diagram with an *AE* curve, what does the 45° line represent? Why is equilibrium expenditure determined by the intersection of the aggregate expenditure curve and the 45° line?

3. If aggregate planned expenditure is less than real GDP, what forces drive the economy to equilibrium expenditure?

CHECKPOINT 15.3

■ **Describe and explain the expenditure multiplier.**

Quick Review

- *Multiplier* The expenditure multiplier is the amount by which a change in any component of autonomous expenditure is magnified or multiplied to determine the change that it generates in equilibrium expenditure and real GDP.

- *Basic multiplier formula* The defining multiplier formula is:

$$\text{Multiplier} = \frac{\text{Change in equilibrium expenditure}}{\text{Change in autonomous expenditure}}.$$

- *Multiplier and the MPC* With no imports or income taxes, the multiplier is:

$$\text{Multiplier} = \frac{1}{(1 - MPC)}.$$

- *Multiplier, imports and income taxes* With imports and income taxes, the multiplier is:

$$\text{Multiplier} = \frac{1}{(1 - \text{slope of the } AE \text{ curve})}.$$

Additional Practice Problems 15.3

1. An economy has no imports or taxes, the *MPC* is 0.90, and real GDP is $12 trillion. If businesses increase investment by $0.1 trillion:
   a. Calculate the multiplier.
   b. Calculate the change in real GDP.
   c. Calculate the new level of real GDP.

2. An increase in autonomous expenditure of $2 trillion increases equilibrium expenditure by $4 trillion:
   a. Calculate the multiplier.
   b. Calculate the slope of the *AE* curve.

3. Suppose there are no income taxes or imports. How would the following events affect equilibrium expenditure and real GDP?
   a. Investment increases by $40 billion and the *MPC* equals 0.6.
   b. The president and Congress agree to increase military spending by $100 billion and the *MPC* is 0.8.

Solutions to Additional Practice Problems 15.3

1a. With no taxes or imports, the multiplier equals $1 \div (1 - MPC)$. The *MPC* is 0.9, so the multiplier equals $1 \div (1 - 0.9)$, which equals 10.0.

1b. The change in real GDP is equal to the multiplier times the change in investment, which is $10 \times \$0.1$ trillion = $1 trillion.

1c. Real GDP increases by $1 trillion from $12 trillion to $13 trillion.

2a. The multiplier equals the change in equilibrium expenditure divided by the change in autonomous expenditure. The multiplier equals $4 trillion ÷ $2 trillion, which is 2.

2b. The expenditure multiplier equals $1/(1 - \text{slope}$ of the *AE* curve). The multiplier is 2, so 2 = $1/(1 - \text{slope of the } AE \text{ curve})$. Multiply both sides by $(1 - \text{slope of the } AE \text{ curve})$ to get 2 × $(1 - \text{slope of the } AE \text{ curve}) = 1$. Solve for the slope of the *AE* curve, which is that the slope of the *AE* curve is 0.50.

3a. The increase in investment is an increase in autonomous expenditure. The change in equilibrium expenditure and real GDP equals the multiplier times the change in autonomous expenditure. The multiplier equals $1 \div (1 - MPC) = 1 \div (1 - 0.6) = 2.5$. The change in equilibrium expenditure and real GDP equals $(2.5) \times (\$40$ billion$)$, which is $100 billion. Equilibrium expenditure and real GDP increase by $100 billion.

3b. The increase in military spending is an increase in government purchases and is an increase in autonomous expenditure. The change in equilibrium expenditure and real GDP equals the multiplier times the change in autonomous expenditure. The multiplier equals $1 \div (1 - MPC)$. Because the MPC equals 0.8, the multiplier is 5.0. The change in equilibrium expenditure and real GDP equals $(5.0) \times (\$100$ billion$)$, which is $500 billion.

■ Self Test 15.3

Fill in the blanks

The multiplier equals the change in equilibrium expenditure ____ (minus; divided by; multiplied by) the change in autonomous expenditure. The multiplier is ____ (less than; greater than) 1. If there are no taxes or imports, the multiplier equals 1 divided by 1 minus the ____. Imports and income taxes make the multiplier ____ (larger; smaller). A recession is started by ____ (an increase; a decrease) in autonomous expenditure.

True or false

1. The multiplier is greater than 1.

2. If the multiplier equals 4, then a $0.25 trillion increase in investment increases real GDP by $1.0 trillion.

3. The smaller the marginal propensity to consume, the larger is the multiplier.

4. A country that has a high marginal tax rate has a larger multiplier than a country with a low marginal tax rate, other things being the same.

Multiple choice

1. The multiplier is equal to the change in ____ divided by the change in ____.
   a. autonomous expenditure; equilibrium expenditure
   b. dependent expenditure; autonomous expenditure
   c. real GDP; equilibrium expenditure
   d. equilibrium expenditure; autonomous expenditure
   e. the price level; real GDP

2. The multiplier is larger than one because
   a. an increase in autonomous expenditure induces further increases in aggregate expenditure.
   b. additional expenditure induces lower incomes.
   c. an increase in autonomous expenditure brings about a reduction in the real interest rate.
   d. an increase in autonomous expenditure induces further decreases in aggregate expenditure.
   e. the price level rises, thereby reinforcing the initial effect.

3. The multiplier equals 5 and there is a $3 million increase in investment. Equilibrium expenditure
   a. decreases by $15 million.
   b. increases by $3 million.
   c. increases by $5 million.
   d. increases by $15 million.
   e. increases by $0.60 million.

4. In an economy with no income taxes or imports, the marginal propensity to consume is 0.80. The multiplier is
   a. 0.20.
   b. 0.80.
   c. 1.25.
   d. 5.00.
   e. 10.00.

5. An increase in the marginal tax rate
   a. increases the multiplier.
   b. decreases the multiplier but cannot make it negative.
   c. has no effect on the multiplier.
   d. can either increase or decrease the multiplier.
   e. decreases the multiplier and can make it negative.

6. Which of the following increases the magnitude of the multiplier?
   a. a decrease in the marginal propensity to consume
   b. an increase in autonomous spending
   c. an increase in the marginal income tax rate
   d. a decrease in the marginal propensity to import
   e. an increase in investment

■ **FIGURE 15.5**
Aggregate planned expenditure (trillions of 2000 dollars)

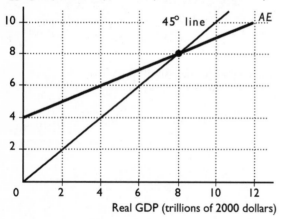

7. In Figure 15.5, the slope of the *AE* curve is ____ and the multiplier equals ____.
   a. 0.8; 5.0
   b. 0.4; 2.5
   c. 0.90; 10.0
   d. 0.50; 0.5
   e. 0.50; 2.0

8. If the slope of the *AE* curve is 0.5, then the multiplier equals
   a. 5.
   b. 4.
   c. 3.
   d. 2.
   e. 0.5.

9. At the beginning of a recession, the multiplier
   a. offsets the initial cut in autonomous expenditure and slows the recession.
   b. reinforces the initial cut in autonomous expenditure and adds force to the recession.
   c. offsets the initial cut in autonomous expenditure and reverses the recession.
   d. reinforces the initial cut in autonomous expenditure and reverses the recession.
   e. has no effect on the recession.

Complete the graph

■ **FIGURE 15.6**
Aggregate planned expenditure (trillions of 2000 dollars)

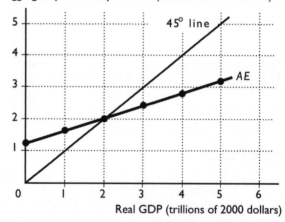

1. Figure 15.6 has the aggregate planned expenditure curve for a nation. (This is the same curve you plotted in the "Complete the Graph" problem in Checkpoint 15.2). Now suppose that government purchases increase by $1.2 trillion at every level of real GDP.
   a. In Figure 15.6 plot the new aggregate expenditure curve.

b. What is the new equilibrium expenditure? By how much did equilibrium expenditure change?

c. What is the slope of the *AE* curve?

d. What is the multiplier? Use the multiplier to find the change in equilibrium expenditure.

Short answer and numeric questions

Marginal propensity to consume, MPC	Multiplier
0.9	___
0.8	___
0.7	___
0.6	___
0.5	___
0.4	___

1. The table gives various values for the marginal propensity to consume. Suppose there are no income taxes or imports. Complete the table by calculating the values of the multiplier. What is the relationship between the *MPC* and the multiplier?

2. Why is the multiplier greater than 1?

3. How does the multiplier affect business cycle turning points?

CHECKPOINT 15.4

■ **Derive the *AD* curve from equilibrium expenditure.**

Quick Review

- *Equilibrium expenditure* The level of aggregate expenditure that occurs when aggregate planned expenditure equals real GDP.

- *Aggregate demand* The real GDP at equilibrium expenditure and the associated price level are the aggregate demand schedule.

Additional Practice Problem 15.4

1. Figure 15.7 shows the *AE* curve, *AE₀*, when the price level is 100.

 a. In the figure, show what occurs when the price level rises to 110 and aggregate

■ **FIGURE 15.7**

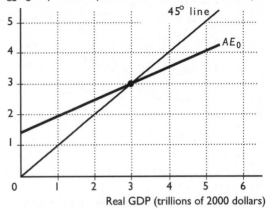

Aggregate planned expenditure (trillions of 2000 dollars)

planned expenditure decreases by $1 trillion at every level of real GDP. What is the new equilibrium expenditure?

b. In the figure, show what occurs when the price level falls to 90 and aggregate planned expenditure increases by $1 trillion at every level of real GDP. What is the new equilibrium expenditure?

c. Use the results from parts (a) and (b) to draw an aggregate demand curve in Figure 15.8.

■ **FIGURE 15.8**

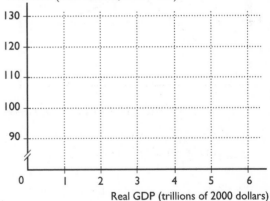

Price level (GDP deflator, 2000 = 100)

Solution to Additional Practice Problem 15.4

1a. Figure 15.9 (on the next page) shows the new aggregate expenditure curve, labeled *AE₁*. The new equilibrium expenditure is $1 trillion, where the *AE₁* curve intersects the 45° line.

■ FIGURE 15.9

Aggregate planned expenditure (trillions of 2000 dollars)

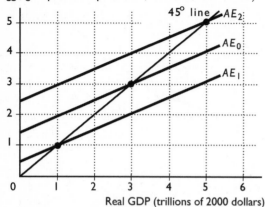

1b. Figure 15.9 shows the new aggregate expenditure curve, labeled AE_2. The new equilibrium expenditure is $5 trillion.

■ FIGURE 15.10

Price level (GDP deflator, 2000 = 100)

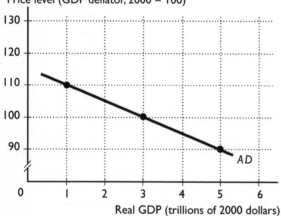

1c. Points on the aggregate demand schedule are the points of equilibrium expenditure. So each point of equilibrium expenditure corresponds to a point on the AD curve. When the price level is 110, real GDP is $1 trillion. When the price level is 100, real GDP is $3 trillion. And when the price level is 90, real GDP is $5 trillion. These points and the aggregate demand curve are shown Figure 15.10. The aggregate demand curve has been derived from the equilibrium expenditure model.

■ Self Test 15.4

Fill in the blanks

The _____ (AE; AD) curve is derived from the _____ (AE; AD) curve. The _____ (AE; AD) curve is the relationship between aggregate planned expenditure and real GDP. The _____ (AE; AD) curve is the relationship between the quantity of real GDP demanded and the price level. The _____ (AE; AD) curve is upward sloping and the _____ (AE; AD) curve is downward sloping. The _____ (AE; AD) curve shifts when the price level changes. There is a movement along the _____ (AE; AD) curve when the price level changes.

True or false

1. There is no relationship between equilibrium expenditure and the AD curve.

2. A change in the price level results in a movement along the AD curve.

3. A change in the price level results in a movement along the AE curve.

4. Each point of equilibrium expenditure on the AE curve corresponds to a point on the AD curve.

Multiple choice

1. A movement along the AE curve arises from a change in _____ and a movement along the AD curve arises from a change in _____.
   a. real GDP; the price level
   b. real GDP; investment
   c. the price level; the price level
   d. the price level; investment
   e. investment; the price level

2. The level of equilibrium expenditure at each price level determines
   a. the points on the AD curve.
   b. aggregate planned production.
   c. the price level.
   d. full employment.
   e. the points on the AE curve.

3. A change in the price level
   a. shifts the *AE* curve and creates a movement along the *AD* curve.
   b. creates a movement along the *AE* curve and shifts the *AD* curve.
   c. shifts the *AE* curve and the *AD* curve in the same direction.
   d. shifts the *AE* curve and the *AD* curve in opposite directions.
   e. creates a movement along both the *AE* curve and the *AD* curve.

4. The *AD* curve is the relationship between
   a. aggregate planned expenditure and the price level.
   b. aggregate planned expenditure and the quantity of real GDP demanded.
   c. the quantity of real GDP demanded and the price level.
   d. the quantity of real GDP demanded and the unemployment rate.
   e. aggregate planned expenditure and real GDP when the price level is fixed.

Complete the graph

■ **FIGURE 15.11**

Aggregate planned expenditure (trillions of 2000 dollars)

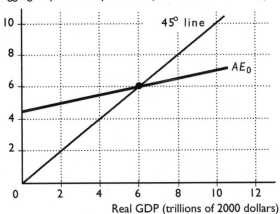

1. Figure 15.11 has the aggregate planned expenditure curve for a nation when the price level is 100. Autonomous expenditure equals $4.25 trillion.
   a. Suppose the price level rises to 120 and aggregate planned expenditure decreases

by $0.75 trillion at every level of real GDP. In the figure, show the new aggregate expenditure line. What does equilibrium expenditure now equal?

   b. Suppose that the price level falls to 100 and, compared to the situation when the price level equaled 110, aggregate planned expenditure increases by $0.75 trillion at every level of real GDP. In the figure, show the new aggregate expenditure line. What does equilibrium expenditure now equal?

■ **FIGURE 15.12**

Price level (GDP deflator, 2000 = 100)

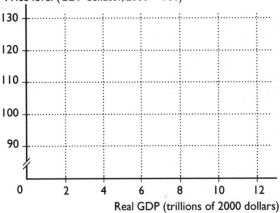

   c. Use the results from parts (a) and (b) to draw an aggregate demand curve in Figure 15.12.

Short answer and numeric questions

1. What is the relationship between the *AE* curve and the *AD* curve?

2. What is the effect on the *AE* curve when the price level rises? What is the effect on the *AD* curve when the price level rises?

SELF TEST ANSWERS

■ CHECKPOINT 15.1

Fill in the blanks

Aggregate planned expenditure <u>does not always equal</u> real GDP. The components of aggregate expenditure that change when real GDP changes are <u>induced</u> expenditure. The components of aggregate expenditure that do not change when real GDP changes are <u>autonomous</u> expenditure. The <u>consumption function</u> is the relationship between consumption expenditure and disposable income. The marginal propensity to consume equals the change in consumption expenditure <u>divided by</u> the change in disposable income that brought it about. The slope of the consumption function equals the <u>marginal propensity to consume</u>. A change in disposable income is shown by a <u>movement along</u> the consumption function, and a change in the buying power of money is shown by a <u>shift in</u> the consumption function. Imports <u>are</u> a component of induced expenditure.

True or false

1. True; page 380
2. True; page 381
3. False; page 382
4. True; page 383

Multiple choice

1. d; page 379
2. c; page 379
3. d; page 380
4. b; page 380
5. c; page 380
6. b; page 382
7. b; page 380
8. c; page 380
9. c; page 382

Complete the graph

1. a. Figure 15.13 plots the consumption function, labeled CF_0; page 381.
   b. Autonomous consumption is $0.4 trillion, the y-intercept of curve CF_0 in Figure 15.8; page 380.

■ FIGURE 15.13

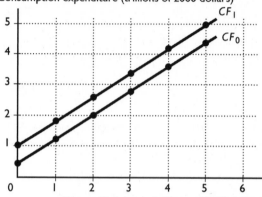

Consumption expenditure (trillions of 2000 dollars)

Disposable income (trillions of 2000 dollars)

c. If disposable income is $1.0 trillion, consumption expenditure is $1.2 trillion, so saving is –$0.2 trillion. If disposable income is $4.0 trillion consumption expenditure is $3.6 trillion, so saving is $0.4 trillion; page 381.

d. The marginal propensity to consume is 0.80; page 382.

e. The new consumption function is labeled CF_1 in Figure 15.4. Autonomous consumption is $1 trillion; page 380.

Short answer and numeric questions

1. Actual aggregate expenditure always equals real GDP. Aggregate planned expenditure does not necessarily equal real GDP. Actual expenditure equals planned expenditure plus the unplanned change in firms' inventories. If aggregate planned expenditures exceeds real GDP, the change in firms' inventories is smaller than planned, and if aggregate planned expenditure is less than real GDP, the change in firms' inventories is larger than planned; page 379.

2. Autonomous expenditures are the components of aggregate expenditure that do not change when real GDP changes. Induced expenditures are the components of aggregate expenditure that change when real GDP changes; page 380.

3. The *MPC* equals the slope of the consumption function. Autonomous consumption equals the *y*-axis intercept; pages 380, 382.

Change in disposable income (trillions of 2000 dollars)	Change in consumption expenditure (trillions of 2000 dollars)	Marginal propensity to consume, MPC
2	1.8	0.90
1	0.9	0.90
4	3.0	0.75

4. The completed table is above. The marginal propensity to consume is the change in consumption expenditure divided by the change in disposable income that brought it about; page 382.

■ CHECKPOINT 15.2

Fill in the blanks

Aggregate planned expenditure equals <u>consumption expenditure</u> plus <u>investment</u> plus <u>government purchases of goods and services</u> plus <u>exports</u> minus <u>imports</u>. As real GDP increases, aggregate planned expenditure <u>increases</u>. Equilibrium expenditure is the level of aggregate expenditure that occurs when aggregate planned expenditure equals <u>real GDP</u>. When aggregate planned expenditure exceeds real GDP, an unplanned <u>decrease</u> in inventories occurs and firms <u>increase</u> production.

True or false

1. True; page 388
2. True; page 389
3. False; page 389
4. True; page 389

Multiple choice

1. a; page 386
2. a; page 388
3. d; page 388
4. b; page 389
5. c; page 389
6. a; page 389
7. c; page 389

8. b; page 767

Complete the graph

GDP	C	I	G	X	M	AE
0.0	0.6	0.4	0.2	0.2	0.2	<u>1.2</u>
1.0	1.2	0.4	0.2	0.2	0.4	<u>1.6</u>
2.0	1.8	0.4	0.2	0.2	0.6	<u>2.0</u>
3.0	2.4	0.4	0.2	0.2	0.8	<u>2.4</u>
4.0	3.0	0.4	0.2	0.2	1.0	<u>2.8</u>
5.0	3.6	0.4	0.2	0.2	1.2	<u>3.2</u>

1. a. Aggregate planned expenditure equals *C* + *I* + *G* + *X* − *M*. The completed table is above; page 387.

■ FIGURE 15.14

Aggregate planned expenditure (trillions of 2000 dollars)

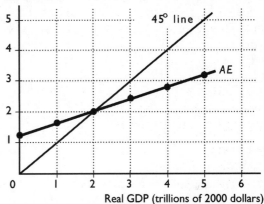

b. Figure 15.14 shows the aggregate planned expenditure curve; page 387.

c. A 45° line has been added to Figure 15.14. Equilibrium expenditure is where the 45° line intersects the aggregate expenditure curve, so equilibrium expenditure is $2 trillion; page 388.

d. An unplanned increase in inventories occurs when real GDP exceeds aggregate planned expenditure. In Figure 15.14, real GDP exceeds planned expenditure when real GDP is greater than $2 trillion; pages 388-389.

An unplanned decrease in inventories occurs when real GDP is less than aggregate planned expenditure. In Figure 15.14, real GDP is less than planned expenditure when real GDP is less than $2 trillion; pages 388-389.

e. When GDP is $3 trillion, planned investment is $0.4 trillion. When GDP is $3 trillion, aggregate planned expenditure is $2.4 trillion, so there is an unplanned increase in inventories of $0.6 trillion. The actual investment is $1 trillion, the sum of planned investment plus the unplanned change in inventories; page 389.

Short answer and numeric questions

1. As real GDP increases, aggregate planned expenditure increases, so there is a positive relationship between real GDP and aggregate planned expenditure. Aggregate planned expenditure increases when real GDP increases because, as real GDP increases, induced expenditure increases; pages 386-387.

2. Along the 45° line real GDP equals aggregate planned expenditure. Equilibrium expenditure occurs when aggregate planned expenditure equals real GDP, which is the point where the *AE* curve intersects the 45° line; page 388.

3. If aggregate planned expenditure is less than real GDP, people are spending less than firms are producing. There is an unplanned increase in inventories. Firms decrease production, and real GDP decreases. Firms continue to decrease production until the unplanned inventory change is zero. When this occurs, real GDP and aggregate expenditure are in equilibrium; page 389.

■ CHECKPOINT 15.3

Fill in the blanks

The multiplier equals the change in equilibrium expenditure <u>divided by</u> the change in autonomous expenditure. The multiplier is <u>greater than</u> 1. If there are no taxes or imports, the multiplier equals 1 divided by 1 minus the <u>marginal propensity to consume</u>. Imports and income taxes make the multiplier <u>smaller</u>. A recession is started by <u>a decrease</u> in autonomous expenditure.

True or false

1. True; pages 392-393
2. True; page 393
3. False; page 394
4. False; page 395

Multiple choice

1. d; page 393
2. a; pages 393-394
3. d; pages 392-393
4. d; page 394
5. b; page 395
6. d; pages 394-395
7. e; page 395
8. d; page 395
9. b; page 396

Complete the graph

■ FIGURE 15.15

Aggregate planned expenditure (trillions of 2000 dollars)

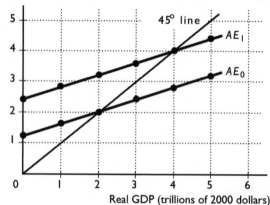

1. a. Figure 15.15 has the new *AE* curve, labeled *AE*₁ and the initial curve labeled *AE*₀; page 393.

b. Equilibrium expenditure increases by $2 trillion to $4 trillion; page 393.

c. The slope of the *AE* curve equals ($0.4 trillion) ÷ ($1.0 trillion), which is 0.40; page 393.

d. The formula for the multiplier is equal to $\dfrac{1}{(1-\text{slope of the } AE \text{ curve})}$. Thus the multiplier is $\dfrac{1}{(1-0.4)}$ = 1.67. The change is equal to the multiplier multiplied by the change in autonomous expenditure, which is (1.67) × ($1.2 trillion). The change in equilibrium expenditure is $2.0 trillion; pages 392, 395.

Short answer and numeric questions

Marginal propensity to consume, MPC	Multiplier
0.9	10.0
0.8	5.0
0.7	3.3
0.6	2.5
0.5	2.0
0.4	1.7

1. The multiplier equals 1 ÷ (1 − *MPC*). The completed table is above. As the *MPC* increases in size, the multiplier increases in size; pages 394.

2. The multiplier exceeds 1 because an initial change in autonomous expenditure leads to changes in induced expenditure. As a result, the change in aggregate expenditure exceeds the initial change in autonomous expenditure; pages 393-394.

3. The forces that bring business-cycle turning points are the swings in autonomous expenditure such as investment and exports. The multiplier gives momentum to the economy's new direction; page 396.

■ CHECKPOINT 15.4

Fill in the blanks

The *AD* curve is derived from the *AE* curve. The *AE* curve is the relationship between aggregate planned expenditure and real GDP. The *AD* curve is the relationship between the quantity of real GDP demanded and the price level. The *AE* curve is upward sloping and the *AD* curve is downward sloping. The *AE* curve shifts when the price level changes. There is a movement along the *AD* curve when the price level changes.

True or false

1. False; pages 398-399
2. True; pages 398-399
3. False; pages 398-399
4. True; pages 398-399

Multiple choice

1. a; page 398
2. a; pages 398-399
3. a; pages 398-399
4. c; page 398

Complete the graph

■ FIGURE 15.16

Aggregate planned expenditure (trillions of 2000 dollars)

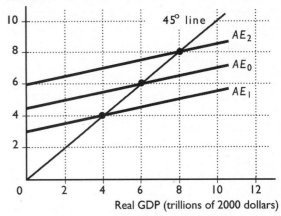

1. a. Figure 15.16 has the new *AE* curve, labeled *AE*₁ and the initial curve labeled *AE*₀ Equilibrium expenditure decreases by $2 trillion to $4 trillion; pages 398-399.

   b. Figure 15.16 has the new *AE* curve, labeled *AE*₂ Equilibrium expenditure increases by $2 trillion to $8 trillion; pages 398-399.

   c. Figure 3.17 (on the next page) shows the aggregate demand curve. The three points identified have been derived from Figure 15.16 and equilibrium expenditure. When the price level is 120, equilibrium expenditure and real GDP is $4 trillion. When the price level is 110, equilibrium expenditure and real GDP is $6 trillion. And when the price level is 100, equilibrium expenditure and real GDP is $8 trillion; page 398.

■ **FIGURE 15.17**

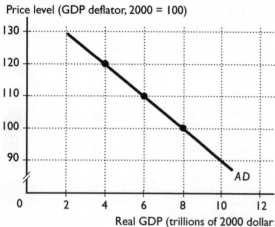

Price level (GDP deflator, 2000 = 100)

Short answer and numeric questions

1. The *AE* curve is used to derive the *AD* curve. Each point of equilibrium expenditure on the *AE* curve corresponds to a point on the *AD* curve; page 398.

2. When the price level rises, the *AE* curve shifts downward and there is a movement up along the *AD* curve. When the price level falls, the *AE* curve shifts upward and there is a movement down along the *AD* curve; pages 398-399.

Fiscal and Monetary Policy Effects

Chapter 16

Chapter 16 provides a description of both fiscal and monetary processes and policies. On the fiscal side, first the federal budget process is outlined. Then fiscal policies are identified and illustrated using the *AD-AS* model. On the monetary side, the basics of how monetary policy affects the economy are discussed, and then the *AD-AS* model is used to illustrate monetary policy. The limits to both fiscal and monetary policy are examined.

■ **Describe the federal budget process and explain the effects of fiscal policy.**

The federal budget is an annual statement of the expenditures, tax receipts, and surplus or deficit of the United States. If tax receipts exceed expenditures, the government has a budget surplus and if expenditures exceed tax receipts, the government has a budget deficit. Fiscal policy can be discretionary, which is policy initiated by an act of Congress, or automatic, which is policy that is triggered by the state of the economy. The government expenditure multiplier and the tax multiplier show that aggregate demand changes by more than an initiating change in government expenditures or taxes. If real GDP is less than potential GDP, expansionary fiscal policy, which is an increase in government expenditures or a tax cut, can move the economy to potential GDP. If real GDP is greater than potential GDP, contractionary fiscal policy, which is a decrease in government expenditures or a tax hike, can move the economy to potential GDP. A cut in taxes or an increase in government purchases of productive services also have supply-side effects that increase potential GDP and aggregate supply. The use of discretionary fiscal policy is hampered by law-making time lags, by estimating potential GDP, and by economic forecasting. Automatic stabilizers are features of fiscal policy, such as induced taxes and needs-tested spending, that stabilize real GDP without explicit action by the government.

■ **Describe the Federal Reserve's monetary policy process and explain the effects of monetary policy.**

Monetary policy is determined by the Federal Open Market Committee (FOMC). The Fed's purchase or sale of government securities affects the nominal interest rate and, in the short run, also the real interest rate. Changes in the interest rate impact decisions regarding investment, consumption, and net exports. When the Fed increases (decreases) the quantity of money, the interest rate falls (rises) and aggregate demand increases (decreases). To fight inflation, the Fed conducts an open market sale. The interest rate rises and expenditure decreases. The multiplier decreases aggregate demand. The *AD* curve shifts leftward and real GDP and the price level both decrease. If the Fed is worried about recession, it conducts an open market purchase, which lowers the interest rate. Aggregate demand increases so that real GDP and the price level increase. Monetary policy has no law-making lag, but estimating potential GDP is hard and economic forecasting is error prone. Monetary policy also has the drawback that it depends on how private decision makers respond to a change in the interest rate.

CHECKPOINT 16.1

■ **Describe the federal budget process and explain the effects of fiscal policy.**

Quick Review

- *Discretionary fiscal policy* Fiscal policy action that is initiated by an act of Congress.

- *Automatic fiscal policy* Fiscal policy that is triggered by the state of the economy.

- *Government expenditure multiplier* The magnification effect of a change in government expenditures on aggregate demand.

- *Tax multiplier* The magnification effect of a change in taxes on aggregate demand.

Additional Practice Problems 16.1

1. The figure shows the U.S. economy in 2009.

   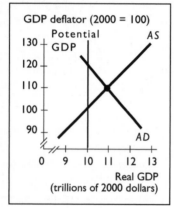

   a. What is the equilibrium price level and real GDP?

   b. Is there an inflationary gap or a recessionary gap?

   c. Should the government use an expansionary or contractionary fiscal policy to move the economy to potential GDP? What sorts of fiscal policies might be used?

   d. In the figure, show the effect of these policies after real GDP equals potential GDP. What is the new equilibrium price level and real GDP? (Ignore any supply-side effects from the policy.)

2. What is the balanced budget multiplier and why is it greater than zero?

Solutions to Additional Practice Problems 16.1

1a. The equilibrium price level and real GDP are determined by the intersection of the aggre-

gate demand, *AD*, curve and the aggregate supply, *AS*, curve. The figure shows that the equilibrium price is 110 and the equilibrium quantity of real GDP is $11 trillion.

1b. Real GDP of $11 trillion exceeds potential GDP of $10 trillion, so there is an inflationary gap.

1c. In order to close the inflationary gap, the government must use contractionary fiscal policy. A contractionary fiscal policy will "contract" real GDP so that it equals potential GDP. Contractionary fiscal policy includes an increase in taxes and/or a decrease in government expenditures.

1d. The figure shows the effect of the contractionary fiscal policy. Both an increase in taxes or a decrease in government expenditure decrease aggregate demand. The aggregate demand curve

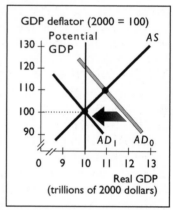

shifts leftward, from AD_0 to AD_1 in the figure. As a result, the price level falls from 110 to 100 and real GDP decreases from $11 trillion back to potential GDP of $10 trillion. The inflationary gap is eliminated.

2. The balanced budget multiplier is the magnification effect on aggregate demand of *simultaneous* changes in government expenditures and taxes that leave the budget balance unchanged. The balanced budget multiplier is not zero—it is positive—because the size of the government expenditure multiplier is larger than the size of the tax multiplier. That is, a $1 increase in government expenditures increases aggregate demand by more than a $1 increase in taxes decreases aggregate demand. So when both government expenditures and taxes increase by $1, aggregate demand still increases.

■ Self Test 16.1

Fill in the blanks

The national debt is ____ (tax receipts minus expenditures; the amount of debt outstanding that arises from past budget deficits). ____ (Automatic; Discretionary) fiscal policy is a fiscal policy action that is initiated by an act of Congress; ____ (automatic; discretionary) fiscal policy is a fiscal policy action triggered by the state of the economy. The government expenditures multiplier is the magnification of a change in government expenditures on aggregate ____ (demand; supply). A tax cut ____ (increases; decreases) aggregate supply and shifts the *AS* curve ____ (rightward; leftward). One limitation of discretionary fiscal policy is the ____ (needs-tested lag; law-making time lag).

True or false

1. Other things the same, a tax cut decreases the national debt.

2. The 2002 Bush tax cut package approved by Congress in 2002 is an example of discretionary fiscal policy.

3. The government expenditure multiplier is the magnification effect that a change in aggregate demand has on government expenditures on goods and services.

4. The magnitude of the tax multiplier is smaller than the government expenditure multiplier.

5. If government expenditures and taxes increase by the same amount, aggregate demand does not change.

6. To eliminate an inflationary gap, the government could decrease its expenditures on goods and services.

7. A tax cut increases aggregate supply but does not increase aggregate demand, so it increases real GDP and lowers the price level.

8. Automatic stabilizers are features of fiscal policy that work to stabilize real GDP without explicit action by the government.

Multiple choice

1. The annual statement of the expenditures, tax receipts, and surplus or deficit of the government of the United States is the federal
   a. surplus record.
   b. deficit record.
   c. budget.
   d. spending.
   e. debt to the public.

2. When government expenditures are less than tax receipts, the government has
   a. a budget with a positive balance.
   b. a budget deficit.
   c. a budget surplus.
   d. a budget with a negative debt.
   e. an illegal budget because expenditures must exceed tax receipts.

3. National debt decreases in a given year when a country has
   a. a budget deficit.
   b. a balanced budget.
   c. a budget supplement.
   d. a budget surplus.
   e. no discretionary fiscal policy.

4. Discretionary fiscal policy is a fiscal policy action, such as
   a. an interest rate cut, initiated by an act of Congress.
   b. an increase in payments to the unemployed, initiated by the state of the economy.
   c. a tax cut, initiated by an act of Congress.
   d. a decrease in tax receipts, initiated by the state of the economy.
   e. an increase in the quantity of money.

5. An example of automatic fiscal policy is
   a. an interest rate cut, initiated by an act of Congress.
   b. an increase in the quantity of money.
   c. a tax cut, initiated by an act of Congress.
   d. a decrease in tax receipts, triggered by the state of the economy.
   e. any change in the interest rate, regardless of its cause.

6. The government expenditure multiplier is the magnification effect of a change in government expenditures on
   a. aggregate demand.
   b. the budget deficit.
   c. tax receipts.
   d. aggregate supply.
   e. potential GDP.

7. The magnitude of the tax multiplier is ____ the magnitude of the government expenditure multiplier.
   a. equal to
   b. greater than
   c. smaller than
   d. the inverse of
   e. exactly one half

8. An example of expansionary fiscal policy is
   a. increasing the quantity of money.
   b. lowering the interest rate.
   c. decreasing government expenditure.
   d. decreasing needs-tested spending.
   e. cutting taxes.

9. Discretionary fiscal policy works to close a recessionary gap by shifting the
   a. *AD* curve leftward.
   b. *AS* curve leftward.
   c. *AD* curve leftward and the *AS* curve leftward.
   d. *AD* curve rightward.
   e. potential GDP line leftward.

10. If the economy is at an above full-employment equilibrium, ____ gap exists and discretionary fiscal policy that ____ will return real GDP to potential GDP.
    a. an inflationary; increases aggregate demand
    b. an inflationary; decreases aggregate demand
    c. a recessionary; increases aggregate supply
    d. a recessionary; decreases aggregate supply
    e. a recessionary; decreases aggregate demand

■ **FIGURE 16.1**

Price level (GDP deflator, 2000 = 100)

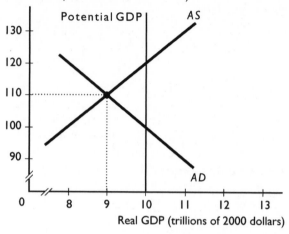

11. The figure above shows an economy with ____ gap and a fiscal policy that can eliminate this gap is ____.
    a. an inflationary; an increase in government expenditures
    b. an inflationary; a tax hike
    c. a recessionary; an increase in the quantity of money
    d. a recessionary; a tax hike
    e. a recessionary; an increase in government expenditures

12. The supply-side effects of a tax cut ____ potential GDP and ____ aggregate supply.
    a. increase; increase
    b. increase; decrease
    c. decrease; increase
    d. decrease; decrease
    e. increases; does not change

13. If a tax cut increases aggregate demand more than aggregate supply, real GDP ____ and the price level ____.
    a. increases; rises
    b. increases; falls
    c. decreases; rises
    d. decreases; falls
    e. increases; does not change

14. Discretionary fiscal policy is handicapped by
    a. law-making time lags, induced taxes, and automatic stabilizers.
    b. law-making time lags, estimation of potential GDP, and economic forecasting.
    c. economic forecasting, law-making time lags, and induced taxes.
    d. automatic stabilizers, law-making time lags, and potential GDP estimation.
    e. automatic stabilizers, the multipliers, and potential GDP estimation.

Complete the graph

■ FIGURE 16.2

Price level (GDP deflator, 2000 = 100)

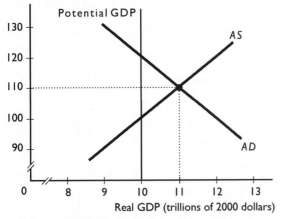

1. Figure 16.2 illustrates the economy.
    a. Is there an inflationary gap or a recessionary gap present?
    b. What type of fiscal policy might be used to restore the economy to full employment?
    c. Ignoring any supply-side effects, in Figure 16.2, illustrate the effect of the policy you suggested in your answer to part (b).

2. Figure 16.3 illustrates the economy. Potential GDP is $11 trillion. Suppose that the government cuts its taxes and that the supply-side effects are larger than the demand-side effects. If the economy moves back to potential GDP, in Figure 16.3, illustrate the effect of this government policy.

■ FIGURE 16.3

Price level (GDP deflator, 2000 = 100)

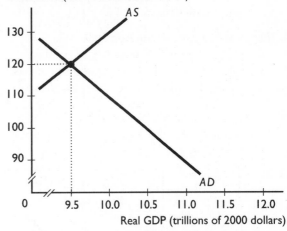

Real GDP (trillions of 2000 dollars)

Short answer and numeric questions

1. What happens to the national debt if the government has a $100 billion budget deficit?

2. How can the government use fiscal policy to eliminate a recessionary gap?

3. What are the demand-side effects of a tax cut? What are the supply-side effects? Why does a tax cut have supply-side effects?

4. It is not easy to determine potential GDP. Why does this fact hamper the use of discretionary fiscal policy?

5. What are automatic stabilizers? Can they eliminate a recession?

CHECKPOINT 16.2

■ Describe the Federal Reserve's monetary policy process and explain the effects of monetary policy.

Quick Review

- *Ripple effects from monetary policy* When the Fed increases the interest rate, three main events follow: investment and consumption expenditure decrease; the price of the dollar rises on the foreign exchange market and net exports decrease;

a multiplier effect induces a further decrease in consumption expenditure and aggregate demand.

Additional Practice Problems 16.2

1. If the Fed increases the quantity of money, explain how each of the following items changes:
   a. Businesses' investment
   b. Households' purchases of new cars and houses
   c. The price of the dollar on foreign exchange markets

2. The figure shows the U.S. economy in 2009.
   a. Will the Fed fear inflation or recession?
   b. What policy should the Fed undertake to avoid what it fears?
   c. In the figure, illustrate the effect of the Fed's policy.
   d. How does this set of answers compare to the answers of Additional Practice Problem 1 in Checkpoint 16.1?

3. What is an advantage that monetary policy has over fiscal policy?

Solutions to Additional Practice Problems 16.2

1a. An increase in the quantity of money lowers the interest rate. The interest rate is the opportunity cost of the funds used to finance investment. When the opportunity cost of investment decreases, businesses increase their purchases of new capital equipment or, in other words, investment increases.

1b. An increase in the quantity of money lowers the interest rate. The interest rate is the opportunity cost of the funds used to finance the purchase of big-ticket consumer items. When the opportunity cost falls, households increase their purchases of new cars and houses.

1c. When the interest rate in the United States falls relative to the interest rate in other countries, people sell dollars and buy other currencies. With fewer dollars demanded and more dollars supplied, the price of the dollar falls on the foreign exchange market.

2a. There is an inflationary gap in the figure and so the Fed fears inflation.

2b. In order to eliminate the potential for inflation, the Fed should decrease the quantity of money. Decreasing the quantity of money decreases aggregate demand and thereby lowers the price level and decreases real GDP, which eliminates the possibility of inflation.

2c. The figure shows the effect of the monetary policy. A decrease in the quantity of money raises the interest rate, which, in turn, decreases consumption expenditure, investment, and 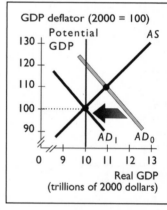 net exports. Aggregate demand decreases and the aggregate demand curve shifts leftward, from AD_0 to AD_1 in the figure. As a result, the price level falls from 110 to 100 and real GDP decreases from $11 trillion back to potential GDP of $10 trillion.

2d. The answers are very similar insofar as in both instances the correct policy was a contractionary policy. Both the contractionary fiscal policy in the earlier Practice Problem and the similarly contractionary monetary policy in this Practice Problem decrease aggregate demand and shift the AD cure leftward.

3. Monetary policy has an advantage over fiscal policy because it cuts out the law-making time lags. The FOMC meets eight times a year and

can conduct telephone meetings between its scheduled meetings. And the actual actions that change the quantity of money are daily actions taken by the New York Fed operating under the guidelines decided by the FOMC. So monetary policy is a continuous policy process and is not subject to a long decision lag.

■ Self Test 16.2

Fill in the blanks

The Beige Book is a ____ (book that outlines the Fed's current monetary policy; report summarizing economic conditions). In the ____ (long; short) run, the Fed has no control over the real interest rate. To raise the interest rate, the FOMC instructs the New York Fed to ____ (purchase; sell) securities in the open market. When the interest rate rises, investment and consumption expenditure ____ (increase; decrease) and net exports ____ (increase; decrease). When the Fed eases to fight recession, the aggregate ____ (demand; supply) curve shifts ____ (leftward; rightward).

True or false

1. The FOMC meets once a year in January to determine the nation's monetary policy.

2. In the short run, when the Fed changes the nominal interest rate, the real interest rate also changes.

3. If the Fed fears a recession, it lowers the interest rate.

4. A change in the interest rate changes net exports.

5. The Fed's monetary policy works by changing aggregate supply.

6. If the Fed's monetary policy raises the interest rate, aggregate demand decreases.

7. To combat a recession, the Fed lowers taxes, which increases aggregate demand and shifts the aggregate demand curve rightward.

8. Monetary policy is a perfect stabilization tool because it does not have law-making time lags.

Multiple choice

1. The FOMC is the
   a. report the Fed gives to Congress twice a year.
   b. group within the Fed that makes the monetary policy decisions.
   c. report that summarizes the economy across Fed districts.
   d. name of the meeting the Fed has with Congress twice a year.
   e. interest rate the Fed most directly influences.

2. The Fed affects aggregate demand through monetary policy by changing
   a. the quantity of money and influencing the interest rate.
   b. tax rates and influencing disposable income.
   c. the quantity of money and determining government expenditure.
   d. government expenditures and so influencing the budget balance.
   e. tax rates on only interest income and so influencing disposable income.

3. If the Fed sells government securities, in the short run the nominal interest rate ____ and the real interest rate ____.
   a. rises; rises
   b. does not change; rises
   c. falls; falls
   d. rises; does not change
   e. rises; falls

4. When the Fed increases the nominal interest rate, the real interest rate
   a. temporarily rises.
   b. permanently rises.
   c. temporarily falls.
   d. permanently falls.
   e. does not change.

5. In the long run, the Fed's policies can influence
   a. the real interest rate.
   b. the inflation rate.
   c. induced taxes.
   d. income taxes.
   e. the size of the tax multiplier.

6. If the Fed decreases the interest rate, which of the following occurs?
   a. Investment increases.
   b. Consumption expenditure decreases.
   c. The price of the dollar on the foreign exchange market increases.
   d. Net exports decreases.
   e. Government expenditures on goods and services increases.

7. If the Fed increases the interest rate, which of the following occur?
   a. The price of the dollar on the foreign exchange market increases.
   b. Investment increases.
   c. Aggregate demand increases.
   d. Net exports increases.
   e. Consumption expenditure increases.

8. The Fed increases the interest rate when it
   a. fears recession.
   b. wants to increase the quantity of money.
   c. fears inflation.
   d. wants to encourage bank lending.
   e. cannot change the quantity of money.

9. Decreasing the quantity of money shifts the aggregate demand curve ____, so that real GDP ____ and the price level ____.
   a. rightward; increases; rises
   b. leftward; decreases; rises
   c. rightward; increases; falls
   d. leftward; decreases; falls
   e. leftward; increases; rises

10. To fight a recession, the Fed can
    a. lower the interest rate by buying securities.
    b. lower the interest rate by selling securities.
    c. raise the interest rate by buying securities.
    d. raise the interest rate by selling securities.
    e. lower income taxes on interest income.

11. When the economy is in a recession, the Fed can ____ the interest rate, which ____ aggregate demand and ____ real GDP.
    a. lower; increases; decreases
    b. raise; decreases; increases
    c. lower; increases; increases
    d. raise; increases; decreases
    e. lower; decreases; decreases

12. An advantage monetary policy has over fiscal policy is that monetary policy
    a. can be quickly changed and implemented.
    b. is coordinated with fiscal policy.
    c. is approved by the president of the United States.
    d. affects consumption expenditure and investment without impacting international trade.
    e. has no multiplier effects.

Complete the graph

■ **FIGURE 16.4**

Price level (GDP deflator, 2000 = 100)

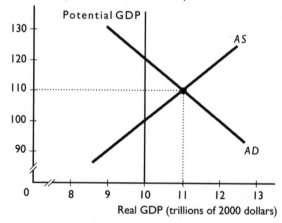

1. Figure 16.4 illustrates the economy.
   a. What type of monetary policy is used to restore the economy to full employment?
   b. In Figure 16.4, illustrate the effect of the policy you suggested in your answer to part (a).
   c. In the Complete the Graph question 1 from Checkpoint 16.1, you answered a similar question about fiscal policy. Compared to using fiscal policy, what is an ad-

vantage of using monetary policy to restore the economy to potential GDP? Compared to monetary policy, what is an advantage of using fiscal policy?

Short answer and numeric questions

1. How does the Fed keep the public informed about the state of the economy and its monetary policy decisions?

2. In the short run, how does the Fed affect the real interest rate? In the long run, how does the Fed affect the real interest rate?

3. Suppose the Fed increases the quantity of money. In the short run, what is the effect on the interest rate? On investment? On aggregate demand?

4. How does monetary policy affect the price of the dollar on the foreign exchange market? In your answer, explain the case in which the Fed raises the interest rate.

5. Suppose the Fed is concerned that the economy is entering a recession. What policy can the Fed pursue and what is the effect of the policy on real GDP and the price level?

SELF TEST ANSWERS

■ CHECKPOINT 16.1

Fill in the blanks

The national debt is <u>the total amount of debt outstanding that arises from past budget deficits</u>. <u>Discretionary</u> fiscal policy is a fiscal policy action that is initiated by an act of Congress; <u>automatic</u> fiscal policy is a fiscal policy action triggered by the state of the economy. The government expenditure multiplier is the magnification of a change in government expenditures on aggregate <u>demand</u>. A tax cut <u>increases</u> aggregate supply and shifts the *AS* curve <u>rightward</u>. One limitation of discretionary fiscal policy is the <u>law-making time lag</u>.

True or false

1. False; page 406
2. True; page 409
3. False; page 409
4. True; page 409
5. False; page 409
6. True; page 411
7. False; pages 412-414
8. True; page 416

Multiple choice

1. c; page 406
2. c; page 406
3. d; page 406
4. c; page 406
5. d; page 406
6. a; page 409
7. c; page 409
8. e; page 410
9. d; page 410
10. b; page 411
11. e; page 410
12. a; page 413
13. a; page 414
14. b; page 415

Complete the graph

1. a. There is an inflationary gap because real GDP exceeds potential GDP; page 411.

■ FIGURE 16.5

Price level (GDP deflator, 2000 = 100)

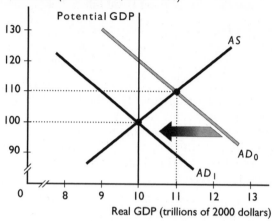

b. The economy will return to full employment with a tax hike or a decrease in government expenditures; page 411.

c. Figure 16.5 shows the results of the suggested policy. Aggregate demand decreases and the *AD* curve shifts leftward from AD_0 to AD_1. Real GDP decreases from $11 trillion to $10 trillion and the price level falls from 110 to 100; page 411.

■ FIGURE 16.6

Price level (GDP deflator, 2000 = 100)

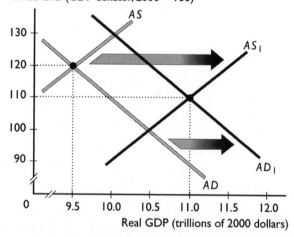

2. The tax cut increases both aggregate demand and aggregate supply, so in Figure 16.6, the aggregate demand curve shifts rightward

from *AD* to *AD*1 and the aggregate supply curve shifts rightward from *AS* to *AS*1. Because the effect on aggregate supply exceeds the effect on aggregate demand, the shift of the *AS* curve is larger than the shift of the *AD* curve. As a result, real GDP increases and the price level falls. The exact fall of the price level depends on the precise sizes of the shifts but in the figure it falls to 100; page 414.

Short answer and numeric questions

1. If the government has a $100 billion budget deficit, the national debt increases by $100 billion; page 406.

2. A recessionary gap exists when real GDP is less than potential GDP. The government can eliminate the recessionary gap by using expansionary fiscal policy to increase aggregate demand. The government can increase aggregate demand by increasing its expenditures on goods and services or by cutting taxes; page 410.

3. A tax cut increases disposable income, which increases consumption expenditure and aggregate demand. A tax cut creates an incentive to work and save. So a tax cut increases the supply of labor and the supply of saving. An increase in the supply of labor increases the equilibrium quantity of labor employed. An increase in the supply of saving increases the equilibrium quantity of investment and capital. With larger quantities of labor and capital, potential GDP increases and so does aggregate supply. So a decrease in taxes increases aggregate supply; pages 412-413.

4. It is not easy to tell whether real GDP is below, above, or at potential GDP. So a discretionary fiscal action can move real GDP *away* from potential GDP instead of toward it; page 416.

5. Automatic stabilizers are features of fiscal policy that stabilize real GDP without explicit action by the government. Automatic stabilizers include induced taxes and needs-tested spending. Induced taxes and needs-tested spending decrease the multiplier effect of a change in autonomous expenditure. So they moderate both expansions and recessions and make real GDP more stable. But they cannot eliminate a recession; page 416.

■ CHECKPOINT 16.2

Fill in the blanks

The Beige Book is a report summarizing economic conditions. In the long run, the Fed has no control over the real interest rate. To raise the interest rate, the FOMC instructs the New York Fed to sell securities in the open market. When the interest rate rises, investment and consumption expenditure decrease and net exports decrease. When the Fed eases to fight recession, the aggregate demand curve shifts rightward.

True or false

1. False; page 418
2. True; page 419
3. True; page 420
4. True; page 421
5. False; page 423
6. True; page 423
7. False; page 424
8. False; page 425

Multiple choice

1. b; page 418
2. a; page 419
3. a; page 419
4. a; page 419
5. b; page 419
6. a; page 421
7. a; page 421
8. c; page 423
9. d; page 423
10. a; page 424
11. c; page 424
12. a; page 425

Complete the graph

■ FIGURE 16.7

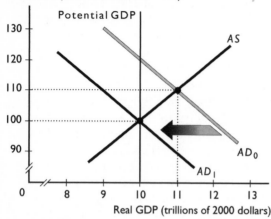

Price level (GDP deflator, 2000 = 100)

1. a. The economy will return to full employment with a decrease in the quantity of money; page 423.

   b. Figure 16.7 shows the results of the decrease in the quantity of money. Aggregate demand decreases and the AD curve shifts leftward from AD_0 to AD_1. Real GDP decreases from \$11 trillion to potential GDP of \$10 trillion and the price level falls from 110 to 100; page 423.

   c. The advantage of using monetary policy is that there is no law-making lag. The actions that change the quantity of money are taken each day. The advantage of using fiscal policy is that the impact on aggregate demand is direct. The effects of monetary policy are indirect and depend on how private decisions respond to a change in the interest rate. These responses are hard to forecast and vary from one situation to another in unpredictable ways; page 425.

Short answer and numeric questions

1. To keep the public informed about the state of the economy, the Fed makes available the Beige Book, which is a report that summarizes the current economic conditions in each Federal Reserve district and each sector of the economy. After each FOMC meeting the FOMC announces its decisions and describes its view of the likelihood that its goals of price stability and sustainable economic growth will be achieved. The minutes of the FOMC meeting are released only after the next meeting. The Fed is required to report twice a year to the House of Representatives Committee on Financial Services, at which time the Fed chairman testifies before the committee; page 418.

2. In the short run, the Fed can determine the nominal interest rate by changing the quantity of money in circulation. In the short run, the expected inflation rate is determined by recent monetary policy and inflation experience. So when the Fed changes the nominal interest rate, the real interest rate also changes, temporarily.

   In the long run, saving supply and investment demand determine the real interest rate in global financial markets. So in the long run, the Fed influences the nominal interest rate by the effects of its policies on the inflation rate. But it does not directly control the nominal interest rate, and it has no control over the real interest rate; page 419.

3. If the Fed increases the quantity of money, the interest rate falls and investment increases. Aggregate demand increases because investment increases and because consumption expenditure and net exports also increase; pages 420-421.

4. If the U.S. interest rate rises relative to the interest rate in other countries, some people will want to move funds into the United States from other countries to take advantage of the higher interest rate they can now earn on U.S. bank deposits and bonds. To move money into the United States, people must buy dollars and sell other currencies. With more dollars demanded, the price of the dollar rises on the foreign exchange market; page 421.

5. When the Fed is concerned that the economy is entering a recession, it makes an open market purchase of government securities.

Banks' reserves increase and the quantity of money increases. The interest rate falls. As a result, the quantity of investment and other interest-sensitive expenditure increases. Net exports also increases. With the increase in aggregate expenditure, the multiplier effect increases aggregate demand by even more. With the increase in aggregate demand, real GDP increases and the price level rises; page 424.

The Short-Run Policy Tradeoff

Chapter 17

Chapter 17 discusses the relationship between inflation and unemployment in the short run and the relationship between the long-run Phillips curve and the short-run Phillips curve. It also discusses how the Fed can influence the expected inflation rate.

■ **Describe the short-run tradeoff between inflation and unemployment.**

The short-run Phillips curve shows the relationship between the inflation rate and the unemployment rate when the natural unemployment rate and expected inflation rate remain constant. The downward-sloping short-run Phillips curve indicates a tradeoff between inflation and unemployment: lower unemployment can be attained but at the cost of higher inflation. The short-run Phillips curve is another way of looking at the upward-sloping aggregate supply curve, because a change in real GDP also changes the unemployment rate and a change in the price level also changes the inflation rate. So moving up the aggregate supply curve, the higher price level corresponds to higher inflation and the larger real GDP corresponds to lower unemployment. The relationship between output and unemployment is called Okun's Law. Okun's Law states that for each percentage point that the unemployment rate is above the natural unemployment rate, there is a 2 percent gap between real GDP and potential GDP.

■ **Distinguish between the short-run and the long-run Phillips curves and describe the shifting tradeoff between inflation and unemployment.**

The long-run Phillips curve is a vertical line that shows the relationship between inflation and unemployment when the economy is at full employment. At full employment, the unemployment rate is the natural unemployment rate, but the inflation rate can take on any value. So along the long-run Phillips curve, there is no long-run tradeoff between inflation and unemployment. The short-run Phillips curve intersects the long-run Phillips at the expected inflation rate. If the expected inflation rate changes, the short-run Phillips curve shifts upward or downward to intersect the long-run Phillips curve at the new expected inflation rate. The natural rate hypothesis is the proposition that when the money growth rate changes, the unemployment rate changes temporarily and eventually returns to the natural unemployment rate. If the natural unemployment rate changes, both the long-run Phillips curve and the short-run Phillips curve shift rightward (if it increases) or leftward (if it decreases).

■ **Explain how the Fed can influence the expected inflation rate and how expected inflation influences the short-run tradeoff.**

The expected inflation rate helps set the money wage rate and other money prices. To forecast inflation, people use data about past inflation and other relevant variables, as well as economic science. If the Fed pursues a surprise inflation reduction, inflation slows but at the cost of recession. If the Fed pursues a credible announced inflation reduction, the expected inflation rate falls along with the inflation rate and there is no accompanying loss of output or increase in unemployment.

CHECKPOINT 17.1

■ **Describe the short-run tradeoff between inflation and unemployment.**

Quick Review

- *Short-run Phillips curve* A curve that shows the relationship between the inflation rate and the unemployment rate when the natural unemployment rate and the expected inflation rate remain constant.
- *Okun's Law* For each percentage point that the unemployment rate is above the natural unemployment rate, there is a 2 percent gap between real GDP and potential GDP.

Additional Practice Problems 17.1

1. The table describes five possible situations that might arise in 2007, depending on the level of aggregate demand in that year. Po-

	Price level (2006 = 100)	Unemployment rate (percentage)
A	101.5	9
B	104.0	6
C	105.0	5
D	106.5	4
E	109.0	3

tential GDP is $7 trillion, and the natural unemployment rate is 5 percent.

  a. Calculate the inflation rate for each possible outcome.

  b. Use Okun's Law to find the real GDP associated with each unemployment rate in the table.

  c. Plot the short-run Phillips curve for 2007.

  d. Plot the aggregate supply curve for 2007.

  e. Mark the points A, B, C, D, and E on each curve that correspond to the data provided in the table and the data that you have calculated.

2. In the Practice Problem, what is the role played the aggregate demand curve? In the figure you have drawn with the aggregate supply curve, show an aggregate demand curve that would create an inflation rate of 5 percent. To what point on the Phillips curve does this aggregate demand/aggregate supply equilibrium correspond?

Solutions to Additional Practice Problems 17.1

1a. The inflation rate equals the change in the price level divided by the initial price level, all multiplied by 100. So, for row A, the inflation rate equals $\frac{101.5 - 100.0}{100.0} \times 100$, or 1.5

	Inflation rate (percent per year)
A	1.5
B	4.0
C	5.0
D	6.5
E	9.0

percent. The rest of the inflation rates are calculated similarly.

1b. Okun's Law states that for each percentage point that the unemployment rate is above the natural unemployment rate, there is a 2 percent gap between real GDP and potential GDP. In row A the unemployment rate is 9 percent. The natural unemployment rate is 5 percent, so the unemployment rate is 4 percentage points above the natural unemployment rate. So real GDP is (2) × (4 percent) = 8 percent below potential GDP. Potential GDP is $7 trillion, so real GDP is (8 percent) × ($7 trillion) = $0.56 trillion dollars below potential GDP. Real GDP equals $7 trillion minus $0.56 trillion, which is $6.44 trillion, as shown in the table. The rest of the real GDP calculations are similar.

	Real GDP (trillions of 2002 dollars)
A	6.44
B	6.86
C	7.00
D	7.14
E	7.28

1c. The short-run Phillips curve for 2007 shows the relationship between the inflation rate and the unemployment rate. The unemployment rates are given in the

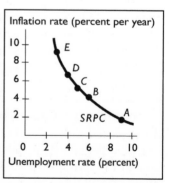

table in the problem and the associated inflation rates are given in the answer to part (a). The figure plots the resulting Phillips curve.

1d. The aggregate supply curve for 2007 is plotted in the figure. The price levels are given in the problem and the corresponding real GDPs are calculated from Okun's Law in part (b).

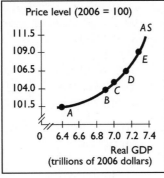

Price level (2006 = 100)

1e. The figures in part (e) and part (f) have the points labeled.

2. When aggregate demand increases, everything else remaining the same, there is a movement up along the aggregate supply curve. Real GDP increases and the price level rises. At the same time, the unemployment rate decreases and the inflation rate rises. There is a movement up along the short-run Phillips curve.

When aggregate demand decreases, everything else remaining the same, there is a movement down along the aggregate supply curve. Real GDP decreases and the price level falls. At the same time, the unemployment rate increases and the inflation rate falls. There is a movement down along the short-run Phillips curve.

Because the current price level is 100, to create an inflation rate of 5 percent, the aggregate demand curve must intersect the aggregate supply at a price level of 105. The figure shows this

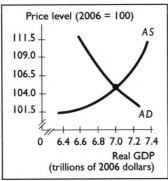

Price level (2006 = 100)

aggregate demand curve. This price level corresponds to point *C* and so this aggregate demand/aggregate supply equilibrium corresponds to point *C* on the short-run Phillips curve

■ Self Test 17.1

Fill in the blanks

The short-run Phillips curve is the curve that shows the relationship between the ____ (price level; inflation rate; nominal interest rate) and the ____ (quantity of real GDP supplied; unemployment rate; real interest rate) when the natural unemployment rate and expected inflation rate remain constant. The short-run Phillips curve is ____ (downward; upward) sloping. Okun's Law states that for each percentage point that the unemployment rate is above the natural unemployment rate, there is a ____ (2; 6) percent gap between real GDP and potential GDP. A change in aggregate demand that leads to a movement along the aggregate supply curve also leads to a ____ (shift in; movement along) the short-run Phillips curve.

True or false

1. The short-run Phillips curve shows the tradeoff between the natural unemployment rate and the expected inflation rate.

2. Moving along a short-run Phillips curve, the price of a lower unemployment rate is a higher inflation rate.

3. Okun's Law states that for each percentage point that real GDP is less than potential GDP, there is a 2 percent gap between the unemployment rate and the natural unemployment rate.

4. Points on the short-run Phillips curve correspond to points on the aggregate supply curve.

5. Aggregate demand fluctuations bring movements along the aggregate supply curve and along the short-run Phillips curve.

Multiple choice

1. The short-run Phillips curve shows the relationship between
   a. the inflation rate and the interest rate.
   b. real GDP and the inflation rate.
   c. the unemployment rate and the interest rate.
   d. the inflation rate and the unemployment rate.
   e. real GDP and the price level.

2. The short-run Phillips curve is
   a. vertical at the natural unemployment rate.
   b. upward sloping.
   c. downward sloping.
   d. horizontal at the expected inflation rate.
   e. U-shaped.

3. Moving along the short-run Phillips curve, as the unemployment rate increases the inflation rate
   a. decreases.
   b. increases.
   c. remains unchanged.
   d. initially decreases and then increases.
   e. initially increases and then decreases.

4. If real GDP exceeds potential GDP, then employment is ____ full employment and the unemployment rate is ____ the natural unemployment rate.
   a. below; above
   b. equal to; below
   c. above; below
   d. above; above
   e. equal to; equal to

5. Okun's Law states that for every percentage point that the unemployment rate is above the natural unemployment rate, there is a ____ percent gap between real GDP and potential GDP.
   a. 1
   b. 1.5
   c. 2
   d. 2.5
   e. 5

6. According to Okun's Law, if the natural unemployment rate is 5 percent, the actual unemployment rate is 4 percent, and potential GDP is $10 trillion, then actual real GDP is
   a. $12 trillion.
   b. $11 trillion.
   c. $9.6 trillion.
   d. $10.4 trillion.
   e. $10.2 trillion.

7. When a movement up along the aggregate supply curve occurs, there is also
   a. a movement down along the short-run Phillips curve.
   b. a movement up along the short-run Phillips curve.
   c. a rightward shift of the short-run Phillips curve.
   d. a leftward shift of the short-run Phillips curve.
   e. no movement along and no shift in the short-run Phillips curve.

8. When aggregate demand increases, there is a movement ____ along the *AS* curve and ____
   a. up; a movement up along the short-run Phillips curve.
   b. up; a movement down along the short-run Phillips curve.
   c. up; an upward shift of the short-run Phillips curve.
   d. down; a downward shift of the short-run Phillips curve.
   e. down; a movement down along the short-run Phillips curve.

9. By looking at the data on inflation and un-employment for the United Kingdom and the United States, we see
   a. a neat, tight tradeoff between the variables in both countries.
   b. a positive relationship between the variables in both countries.
   c. no neat, tight tradeoff between the variables in both countries.
   d. that the relationship in the United States is positive and in the United Kingdom the relationship is negative.
   e. that the relationship in the United States is negative and in the United Kingdom the relationship is positive.

Complete the graph

Inflation rate (percent per year)	Unemployment rate (percentage)
2	12
3	8
4	5
5	3
6	2

■ **FIGURE 17.1**

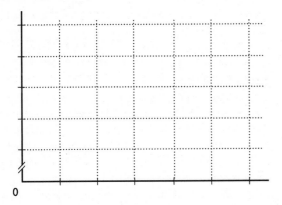

0

1. The table above has data on the inflation rate and the unemployment rate.
   a. Using the data, label the axes and plot the short-run Phillips curve in Figure 17.1. Label the curve *SRPC*.
   b. What is the effect of a decrease in the unemployment rate from 8 percent to 5 percent? Show the effect in Figure 17.1.

c. How does your answer to question (b) indicate the presence of a tradeoff?

Short answer and numeric questions

1. What does the slope of the short-run Phillips curve indicate about the tradeoff between inflation and unemployment?

Unemployment rate (percentage)	Real GDP (trillions of 2000 dollars)
4	___
5	___
6	___
7	___

2. The table above gives data for an economy. Suppose that for this economy the natural unemployment rate is 5 percent and potential GDP is $8 trillion.
   a. What is Okun's Law?
   b. Using Okun's Law, complete the table by calculating real GDP for each unemployment rate.

3. What is the effect on the aggregate supply curve and on the short-run Phillips curve of an increase in aggregate demand?

CHECKPOINT 17.2

■ **Distinguish between the short-run and the long-run Phillips curves and describe the shifting tradeoff between inflation and unemployment.**

Quick Review

- *Long-run Phillips curve* The long-run Phillips curve is the vertical line that shows the relationship between inflation and unemployment when the economy is at full employment.

- *Factor that shifts the long-run Phillips curve* An increase (decrease) in the natural unemployment rate shifts the long-run (and short-run) Phillips curve rightward (leftward).

Additional Practice Problems 17.2

1. The figure shows a short-run Phillips curve and a long-run Phillips curve.

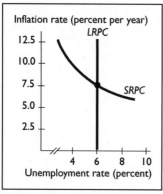

   a. What is the expected inflation rate?

   b. What is the natural unemployment rate?

   c. If the expected inflation rate falls to 2.5 percent a year, show the new short-run and long-run Phillips curves.

   d. If the natural unemployment rate decreases to 4 percent but the expected inflation rate does not change from what it is in the figure above, show the new short-run and long-run Phillips curves.

2. Explain how the inflation rate and unemployment rate might simultaneously increase.

Solutions to Additional Practice Problems 17.2

1a. The expected inflation rate is the inflation rate where the short-run Phillips curve and the long-run Phillips curve intersect. The expected inflation rate is 7.5 percent a year.

1b. The long-run Phillips curve is vertical at the natural unemployment rate. The natural unemployment rate is 6 percent.

1c. When the expected inflation rate decreases to 2.5 percent a year, the short-run Phillips curve shifts downward but the long-run Phillips curve does not shift. The new short-run Phillips curve intersects the long-run Phillips curve at the new expected inflation rate. The figure shows that the short-run

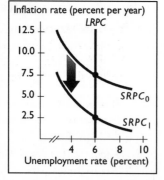

Phillips curve shifts downward from $SRPC_0$ to $SRPC_1$.

1d. A decrease in the natural unemployment rate shifts *both* the short-run Phillips curve and the long-run Phillips curve leftward. In the figure the long-run Phillips curve shifts

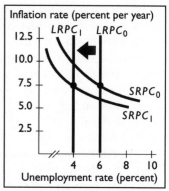

leftward from $LRPC_0$ to $LRPC_1$ and the short-run Phillips curve shifts leftward from $SRPC_0$ to $SRPC_1$. The new short-run Phillips curve intersects the new long-run Phillips curve at the expected inflation rate.

2. If the natural unemployment rate increases, the short-run Phillips curves shifts rightward. If simultaneously the inflation rate rises, it is possible to move from a point on its old short-run Phillips

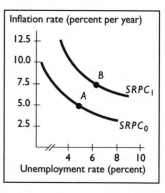

curve to a point on the new short-run Phillips curve such that both the inflation rate and the unemployment rate increase. For instance, in the figure the short-run Phillips curve shifts and the inflation rate rises from 5.0 percent to 7.5 percent. The movement from point A on the initial short-run Phillips curve $SRPC_0$ to point B on the new short-run Phillips curve $SRPC_1$ shows how both the unemployment rate and inflation rate can simultaneously increase.

■ Self Test 17.2

Fill in the blanks

The long-run Phillips curve is a ____ (vertical; horizontal) line that shows the relationship between inflation and unemployment when the economy is at full employment. The long-run Phillips curve tells us that ____ (any; only one) inflation rate is possible at the natural unemployment rate. A change in the expected inflation rate ____ (shifts; does not shift) the long-run Phillips curve and ____ (shifts; does not shift) the short-run Phillips curve. The ____ (natural rate hypothesis; constant natural unemployment rate theory) is the proposition that when the growth rate of the quantity of money changes, the unemployment rate ____ (permanently; temporarily) changes. A change in the natural unemployment rate ____ (shifts; does not shift) the long-run Phillips curve and also ____ (shifts; does not shift) the short-run Phillips curve.

True or false

1. The long-run Phillips curve is horizontal because it shows that at the expected inflation rate, any unemployment rate might occur.

2. An increase in the expected inflation rate shifts the long-run Phillips curve.

3. An increase in the expected inflation rate shifts the short-run Phillips curve.

4. The natural rate hypothesis states that an increase in the growth rate of the quantity of money temporarily decreases the unemployment rate.

5. A change in the natural unemployment rate shifts both the short-run and long-run Phillips curves.

Multiple choice

1. The long-run Phillips curve is the relationship between
   a. unemployment and the price level at full employment.
   b. unemployment and the rate of inflation at the expected price level.
   c. inflation and real GDP at full employment.
   d. inflation and unemployment when the economy is at full employment.
   e. inflation and the expected inflation rate.

2. The long-run Phillips curve is
   a. upward sloping.
   b. downward sloping.
   c. horizontal.
   d. vertical.
   e. upside-down U-shaped.

3. The inflation rate that is used to set the money wage rate and other money prices is the
   a. natural inflation rate.
   b. actual inflation rate.
   c. expected inflation rate.
   d. cost of living inflation rate.
   e. wage inflation rate.

4. Burger King is paying $8 an hour to its servers. If the expected inflation rate is 10 percent a year, then to keep the real wage rate constant in a year the money wage rate must
   a. rise to $8.80 an hour.
   b. fall to $7.20 an hour.
   c. stay at $8.00 an hour.
   d. rise to $8.10 an hour.
   e. rise to $8.40 an hour.

5. When the expected inflation rate ____, the short-run Phillips curve shifts ____.
   a. falls; upward
   b. rises; upward
   c. rises; downward
   d. None of the above because a change in the expected inflation rate leads to a movement along the short-run Phillips curve but does not shift the short-run Phillips curve.
   e. None of the above because a change in the expected inflation rate only shifts the long-run Phillips curve and has no effect on the short-run Phillips curve.

■ **FIGURE 17.2**

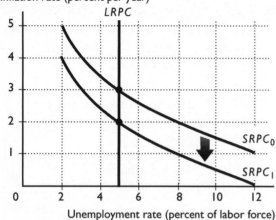

6. The shift in Figure 17.2 is the result of
   a. an increase in the expected inflation rate.
   b. a decrease in the expected inflation rate.
   c. an increase in the natural unemployment rate.
   d. a decrease in the natural unemployment rate.
   e. an increase in the inflation rate.

7. The natural rate hypothesis states that
   a. only natural economic policies can bring a permanent reduction in the unemployment rate.
   b. changes in the growth rate of the quantity of money temporarily change the unemployment rate.
   c. it is natural for the unemployment rate to exceed the inflation rate.
   d. it is natural for the unemployment rate to be less than the natural unemployment rate.
   e. changes in the growth rate of the quantity of money temporarily change the natural unemployment rate.

8. If the natural unemployment rate decreases, then the short-run Phillips curve ____ and the long-run Phillips curve ____.
   a. does not shift; shifts leftward
   b. shifts leftward; shifts leftward
   c. shifts rightward; shifts leftward
   d. shifts rightward; shifts rightward
   e. shifts leftward; does not shift

9. The natural unemployment rate
   a. changes because of changes in frictional and structural unemployment.
   b. never changes.
   c. always increases.
   d. decreases when the inflation rate rises.
   e. increases when the expected inflation rate rises.

Complete the graph

Inflation rate (percent per year)	Unemployment rate (percentage)
2	12
3	8
4	5
5	3
6	2

■ **FIGURE 17.3**

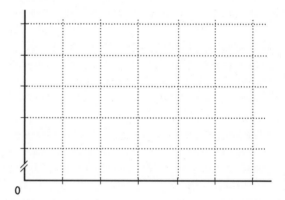

1. The table above has data on a nation's short-run Phillips curve. In this nation, the natural unemployment rate equals 5 percent.
   a. Label the axes and then draw both the short-run Phillips curve and long-run Phillips curve in Figure 17.3.
   b. What is the expected inflation rate?
   c. Suppose the expected inflation rate falls by 1 percentage point. Show the effect of this change on the short-run Phillips curve and long-run Phillips curve in Figure 17.3.

■ **FIGURE 17.4**

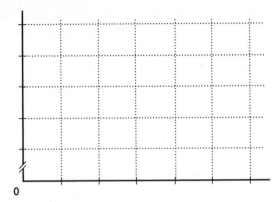

2. In Figure 17.4, redraw your initial short-run and long-run Phillips curves from Figure 17.3. Suppose that the natural unemployment rate falls to 3 percent and the expected inflation rate does not change. In Figure 17.4, show the effect of this change.

Short answer and numeric questions

1. In the *AS-AD* model, does the aggregate demand curve, the aggregate supply curve, or the potential GDP line best correspond to the long-run Phillips curve?

2. What are the key points about the long-run Phillips curve and the relationship between the long-run Phillips curve and the short-run Phillips curve?

3. How does an increase in the expected inflation rate change the short-run and long-run Phillips curves?

4. What is the natural rate hypothesis?

5. How does an increase in the natural unemployment rate change the short-run and long-run Phillips curves?

CHECKPOINT 17.3

■ **Explain how the Fed can influence the expected inflation rate and how expected inflation influences the short-run tradeoff.**

Quick Review

- *Surprise inflation reduction* A surprise inflation reduction slows inflation but at the cost of recession.

- *Credible announced inflation reduction* A credible announced inflation reduction lowers the inflation rate but with no accompanying loss of output or increase in unemployment.

Additional Practice Problem 17.3

1. The figure shows the short-run and long-run Phillips curves. The current inflation rate is 7.5 percent a year and the current unemployment rate is the natural unemployment rate, 5 percent.

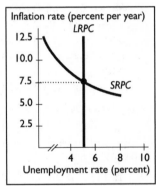

a. Suppose that the Fed announces that it will slow the money growth rate such that inflation will fall to 5 percent a year and everyone believes the Fed. Explain the effect of the Fed's action on inflation and unemployment next year.

b. Suppose that the Fed announces that it will slow the money growth rate such that inflation will fall to 5 percent a year and no one believes the Fed. The Fed actually carries out its policy. Explain the effect of the Fed's action on inflation and unemployment next year.

c. Based on your answers to this question, should the Fed be concerned about its credibility?

Solution to Additional Practice Problem 17.3

1a. If the Fed's announcement is credible, the expected inflation rate falls. The short-run Phillips curve shifts downward as illustrated in the figure. The economy moves from point A to point B. The inflation rate falls to 5 percent a year and the unemployment rate remains at 5 percent. In this case the reduction in the inflation rate had no effect on the unemployment rate.

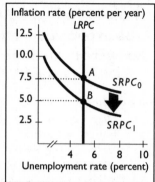

1b. Because no one expected the Fed's action, the expected inflation rate does not change and the short-run Phillips curve does not shift. The economy moves along its short-run Phillips curve from point A to point B. As the inflation rate falls to 5 percent, the unemployment rate rises to 8 percent.

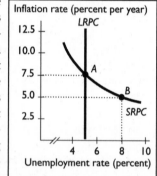

1c. The Fed should be concerned about its credibility. *Only* if the Fed has credibility can it make an announcement about reducing inflation that reduces the inflation rate without an increase in the unemployment rate.

■ Self Test 17.3

Fill in the blanks

When all the relevant data and economic science are used to forecast inflation, the forecast is called ____ (an accurate prediction; a rational expectation; an accurate expectation). A surprise inflation reduction will result in a temporarily ____ (higher; lower) unemployment rate than a credible announced inflation reduction.

True or false

1. The expected inflation rate never changes.
2. One factor that can be used to predict inflation are data on past inflation and money growth.
3. A surprise inflation reduction does not increase the unemployment rate.
4. A credible announced inflation reduction leads to a large increase in the unemployment rate.
5. When the Fed slowed inflation in 1981, the consequence was recession.

Multiple choice

1. A rational expectation of the inflation rate is
   a. a forecast based on the forecasted actions of the Fed and other relevant determinant factors.
   b. an expected inflation rate between 1 percent and 5 percent.
   c. a forecast based only on the historical evolution of inflation over the last 100 years.
   d. an expected inflation rate between 5 percent and 10 percent.
   e. always correct.

2. Because money supply growth is a major component determining the inflation rate, in order to forecast inflation we should forecast actions by the
   a. Office of the Treasury.
   b. president.
   c. Congress.
   d. Fed.
   e. U.S. Mint.

3. If the economy begins at its natural unemployment rate and the Fed provides a surprise slowing of the inflation rate more than expected, there is a
   a. rightward shift of the long-run Phillips curve.
   b. movement upward along the short-run Phillips curve.
   c. leftward shift of the long-run Phillips curve.
   d. movement downward along the short-run Phillips curve.
   e. movement downward along the long-run Phillips curve.

4. A surprise reduction of inflation will come at the expense of
   a. a higher expected inflation rate.
   b. an increase in real GDP.
   c. recession.
   d. a decrease in the natural unemployment rate.
   e. a downward shift in the short-run Phillips curve.

5. A "credible announced" inflation reduction policy is one that
   a. has monetary policy slowly increasing the money supply.
   b. the public is told about *after* the policy change has occurred.
   c. the public is told about before policy changes have occurred and that is believed by the public.
   d. depends only on fiscal policy changes that have been publicly debated and implemented.
   e. the public is never told about.

6. If the Fed makes a credible announcement that its policy aims to reduce inflation, the
   a. long-run Phillips curve shifts downward.
   b. short-run Phillips curve shifts downward.
   c. long-run Phillips curve shifts upward.
   d. short-run Phillips curve shifts upward.
   e. long-run Phillips curve shifts rightward.

7. A credible announced inflation reduction results in _____ natural unemployment rate and _____ shift in the short-run Phillips curve.
   a. a higher; an upward
   b. a lower; an upward
   c. no change in the; an upward
   d. no change in the; a downward
   e. no change in the; no

8. In 1981, the Fed
   a. created a surprise inflation reduction policy and created an expansion.
   b. created a surprise inflation reduction policy and created a recession.
   c. credibly announced an inflation reduction policy and created a recession.
   d. credibly announced an inflation reduction policy and created an expansion.
   e. took no action so that the inflation rate skyrocketed.

Complete the graph

■ **FIGURE 17.5**

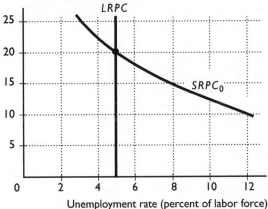

1. Figure 17.5 shows a nation's short-run and long-run Phillips curves. In this nation, the natural unemployment rate equals 5 percent and the actual and expected inflation rate is 20 percent. The nation's government decides to take actions to lower the inflation rate to 10 percent.
   a. Suppose the government announces that the inflation rate will be lowered to 10

percent but no one believes this policy will be carried out. The government, however, actually does lower the inflation rate to 10 percent. In the figure draw any new Phillips curve you need and indicate the new inflation rate and unemployment rate by labeling it *A*.

b. Returning to the initial situation of 5 percent unemployment and 20 percent inflation, suppose that when the government announces that the inflation rate will be lowered to 10 percent everyone believes this policy will be carried out. The government then follows through by lowering the inflation rate to 10 percent. In the figure draw any new Phillips curve you need and indicate the new inflation rate and unemployment rate by labeling it *B*.

c. Returning to the initial situation of 5 percent unemployment and 20 percent inflation, suppose that when the government announces that the inflation rate will be lowered to 10 percent one half of the people believe the announcement and the other half do not. The government follows through by lowering the inflation rate to 10 percent. In the figure draw any new Phillips curve you need and indicate the new inflation rate and unemployment rate by labeling it *C*.

d. How does the number of people that believe the government's announcement affect the unemployment rate that results?

Short answer and numeric questions

1. What short-run effects does a surprise inflation reduction have on the short-run and long-run Phillips curves and the unemployment rate? What long-run effects does it have?

2. What short-run effects does a credible announced inflation reduction have on the short-run and long-run Phillips curves and the unemployment rate? What long-run effects does it have?

3. How do the long-run effects of a surprise inflation reduction compare to the effects of a credible announced inflation reduction?

SELF TEST ANSWERS

■ CHECKPOINT 17.1

Fill in the blanks

The short-run Phillips curve is the curve that shows the relationship between the <u>inflation rate</u> and the <u>unemployment rate</u> when the natural unemployment rate and expected inflation rate remain constant. The short-run Phillips curve is <u>downward</u> sloping. Okun's Law states that for each percentage point that the unemployment rate is above the natural unemployment rate, there is a <u>2</u> percent gap between real GDP and potential GDP. A change in aggregate demand that leads to a movement along the aggregate supply curve also leads to a <u>movement along</u> the short-run Phillips curve.

True or false

1. False; page 432
2. True; page 432
3. False; page 433
4. True; page 434
5. True; page 435

Multiple choice

1. d; page 432
2. c; page 432
3. a; page 432
4. c; page 433
5. c; page 433
6. e; page 433
7. b; page 434
8. a; page 435
9. c; pages 435-436

Complete the graph

1. a. Figure 17.6 plots the short-run Phillips curve, labeled *SRPC*; page 432.
   b. The decrease in the unemployment rate brings a rise in the inflation rate. There is a movement along the short-run Phillips curve, as indicated by the movement from point *A* to point *B*; page 432.

■ FIGURE 17.6

Inflation rate (percent per year)

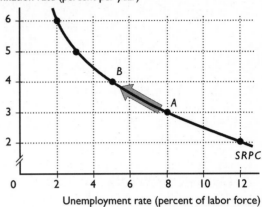

Unemployment rate (percent of labor force)

c. The movement indicates a tradeoff because a decrease in the unemployment rate has a rise in the inflation rate as the price; page 432.

Short answer and numeric questions

1. The slope of the short-run Phillips curve is negative, which indicates that as the unemployment rate decreases, the inflation rate increases. So the price of a lower unemployment rate is a higher inflation rate; page 432.

2. a. Okun's Law states that for each percentage point that the unemployment rate is above the natural unemployment rate, there is a 2 percent gap between real GDP and potential GDP; page 433.

Unemployment rate (percentage)	Real GDP (trillions of 2000 dollars)
4	<u>8.16</u>
5	<u>8.00</u>
6	<u>7.84</u>
7	<u>7.68</u>

b. The completed table is above. When the unemployment rate is 7 percent, it is 2 percentage points above the natural unemployment rate. According to Okun's Law, real GDP is (2) × (2 percent) or 4 percent below potential GDP. So real GDP is (4 percent) × ($8 trillion) or $0.32 trillion

below potential GDP. Real GDP is $8 tril-
lion minus $0.32 trillion, which is $7.68
trillion; page 433.

3. When aggregate demand increases, the aggregate demand curve shifts rightward and
there is a movement up along the aggregate
supply curve. The price level rises and real
GDP increases. As the price level rises the inflation rate rises and as real GDP increases
the unemployment rate decreases. There is a
movement up along the short-run Phillips
curve; page 435.

■ CHECKPOINT 17.2

Fill in the blanks

The long-run Phillips curve is a <u>vertical</u> line
that shows the relationship between inflation
and unemployment when the economy is at full
employment. The long-run Phillips curve tells
us that <u>any</u> inflation rate is possible at the natural unemployment rate. A change in the expected inflation rate <u>does not shift</u> the long-run
Phillips curve and <u>shifts</u> the short-run Phillips
curve. The <u>natural rate hypothesis</u> is the proposition that when the growth rate of the quantity
of money changes, the unemployment rate <u>tem-
porarily</u> changes. A change in the natural unemployment rate <u>shifts</u> the long-run Phillips
curve and also <u>shifts</u> the short-run Phillips
curve.

True or false

1. False; page 438
2. False; page 440
3. True; page 440
4. True; page 441
5. True; pages 442-443

Multiple choice

1. d; page 438
2. d; page 438
3. c; page 440
4. a; page 440
5. b; page 440
6. b; page 440

7. b; page 441
8. b; pages 442-443
9. a; page 443

Complete the graph

■ FIGURE 17.7

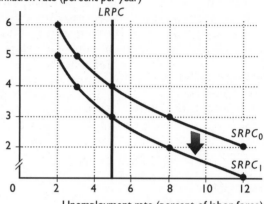

1. a. Figure 17.7 plots the short-run Phillips
   curve, labeled $SRPC_0$ and the long-run
   Phillips curve, labeled $LRPC$; page 438.

   b. The expected inflation rate is 4 percent a
   year because that is the inflation rate at
   which the short-run Phillips curve intersects the long-run Phillips curve; page 440.

   c. The new short-run Phillips curve is illustrated as $SRPC_1$; page 440.

■ FIGURE 17.8

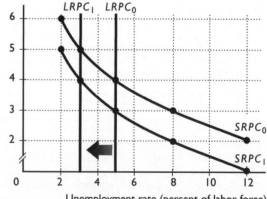

2. The initial short-run Phillips curve is labeled

SRPC0 and the initial long-run Phillips curve is labeled LRPC0 in Figure 17.8. The decrease in the natural unemployment rate by 2 percentage points shifts both the long-run Phillips curve leftward from LRPC0 to LRPC1 and the short-run Phillips curve leftward from SRPC0 to SRPC1. The new short-run Phillips curve and the new long-run Phillips curve intersect at the expected inflation rate; pages 442-443.

Short answer and numeric questions

1. The potential GDP line best corresponds to the long-run Phillips curve. The potential GDP line shows that a change in the price level does not change potential GDP and has no effect on the natural unemployment rate. The long-run Phillips curve shows that a change in the inflation rate does not change the natural unemployment rate; pages 438-439.

2. There are several key points: First, the long-run Phillips curve is vertical at the natural unemployment rate. Next, the short-run Phillips curve intersects the long-run Phillips curve at the expected inflation rate. Finally, changes in the expected inflation rate shift only the short-run Phillips curve, and changes in the natural unemployment rate shift both the short-run and long-run Phillips curves; pages 438, 440, 442.

3. An increase in the expected inflation rate shifts the short-run Phillips curve upward but does not change the long-run Phillips curve; page 440.

4. The natural rate hypothesis is the proposition that when the money supply growth rate changes (so that the growth rate of aggregate demand changes), the unemployment rate changes temporarily and eventually returns to the natural unemployment rate. An increase in the money supply growth rate increases the inflation rate and temporarily lowers the unemployment rate but eventually the unemployment rate returns to the natural unemployment rate. The

fall in the unemployment rate was only temporary; page 441.

5. An increase in the natural unemployment rate shifts *both* the long-run and short-run Phillips curves rightward; pages 442-443.

■ CHECKPOINT 17.3

Fill in the blanks

When all the relevant data and economic science are used to forecast inflation, the forecast is called <u>a rational expectation</u>. A surprise inflation reduction will result in a temporarily <u>higher</u> unemployment rate than a credible announced inflation reduction.

True or false

1. False; page 447
2. True; page 447
3. False; page 448
4. False; page 449
5. True; page 449

Multiple choice

1. a; page 447
2. d; page 447
3. d; page 448
4. c; page 448
5. c; page 449
6. b; page 449
7. d; page 449
8. b; page 449

Complete the graph

■ FIGURE 17.9

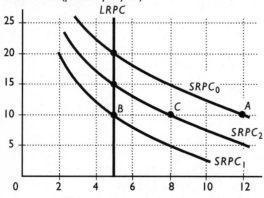

Inflation rate (percent per year)

1. a. Because people do not believe the government's announcement, the actual fall in inflation is a surprise. People's expectations about the inflation rate have not changed, so the fall in inflation does not change the short-run Phillips curve. With the surprise fall in inflation, the economy moves along its initial short-run Phillips curve $SRPC_0$ to point A in Figure 17.9. The inflation rate is 10 percent and the unemployment rate is 12 percent; page 447.

   b. Because people believe the government's announcement, the expected inflation rate falls to 10 percent. With the fall in the expected inflation rate, the short-run Phillips curve shifts downward, in the figure to $SRPC_1$. It intersects the long-run Phillips curve at the new expected inflation rate. The credible announcement by the government means that the economy moves down its long-run Phillips curve to point B. The inflation rate is 10 percent and the unemployment rate is 5 percent; pages 447-448.

   c. Because one half the people believe the government's announcement, so their expected inflation rate is 10 percent, and the other half do not believe the announcement, so their expected inflation rate remains 20 percent, overall the expected inflation rate is 15 percent. With this fall in the expected inflation rate, the short-run Phillips curve shifts downward in the figure to $SRPC_2$. This Phillips curve intersects the long-run Phillips curve at the expected inflation rate, 15 percent. The inflation rate falls to 10 percent and the economy moves along its short-run Phillips curve $SRPC_2$ to point C. The inflation rate is 10 percent and the unemployment rate is 8 percent; pages 447-448.

   d. The more people who believe the government's announcement, the more the expected inflation rate falls and the smaller the resulting increase in unemployment. When no one believes the announcement, the fall in inflation is a surprise and the unemployment rate rises to 12 percent; when half the people believe the announcement, the unemployment rate rises to 8 percent; and when the announcement is credible so that everyone believes it, the unemployment rate remains equal to 5 percent; pages 447-448.

Short answer and numeric questions

1. In the short run, a surprise inflation reduction does not change the short-run or long-run Phillips curve. The economy moves down along the short-run Phillips curve. The inflation rate falls and the unemployment rate rises. In the long run, the inflation reduction is no longer a surprise. The short-run Phillips curve shifts downward. The long-run Phillips curve does not change. The inflation rate falls and the unemployment rate returns to the natural unemployment rate; page 448.

2. In the short run, a credible announced inflation reduction shifts the short-run Phillips curve downward. It has no effect on the long-run Phillips curve. Because the announcement is credible, the inflation rate falls and the unemployment rate does not change. The long-run effects are identical to the short-run effects; page 449.

3. The long-run effects of a surprise inflation reduction are the same as the short-run effects of a credible announced inflation reduction. In both cases the short-run Phillips curve shifts downward and the inflation rate falls with no change in the unemployment rate. The reason for the similarity is that in both instances people revise the expected inflation rate downward. In the case of the surprise inflation reduction, the expected inflation rate is revised downward because of the actual experience with lower inflation. In the case of the credible announcement, the expected inflation rate is revised downward because people are aware in advance of the Fed's policy; pages 448-449.

Fiscal and Monetary Policy Debates

Chapter
18

Chapter 18 discusses the relative strength of fiscal policy and monetary policy, whether they should be used to help stabilize the economy, and if they are used, what they should target.

■ **Discuss whether fiscal policy or monetary policy is the better stabilization tool.**

A change in the quantity of money changes the interest rate, which influences interest-sensitive components of aggregate expenditure. If a change in the quantity of money brings a large change in the interest rate because the demand for money is relatively insensitive to the interest rate and aggregate expenditure is highly sensitive to the interest rate, monetary policy is powerful. The more predictable the demand for money and investment demand, the more predictable is the effect of monetary policy. An increase in government expenditures or a tax cut increases aggregate demand and real GDP, which increases the demand for money and raises the interest rate. The higher interest rate decreases investment, which counteracts the effects of the initial increase in aggregate expenditure. If the interest rate rise is small and a given change in the interest rate has a small effect on aggregate expenditure, the crowding-out effect is small and fiscal policy is powerful. Discretionary fiscal policy actions create policy goal conflicts because it is not clear which of the many spending programs or tax laws should be changed. Monetary policy has fewer policy goal conflicts than fiscal policy and is more flexible.

■ **Explain the rules-versus-discretion debate and compare Keynesian and monetarist policy rules.**

Three broad approaches to the Fed's monetary policy are discretionary policy, which is policy based on the judgments of policymakers, fixed-rule policy, which is policy that is pursued independently of the state of the economy, and feedback-rule policy, which is policy that responds to changes in the economy. For an aggregate demand shock under a fixed-rule policy, in which the quantity of money remains constant, the economy returns to potential GDP when aggregate supply changes. A feedback rule offsets the initial change in aggregate demand. Feedback-rule policies are difficult to use if potential GDP is uncertain, if there are policy lags that exceed forecast horizons, or if the policy creates uncertainty. Aggregate supply shocks, which are changes to aggregate supply, result in larger changes in the price level with a feedback rule that targets real GDP.

■ **Assess whether policy should target the price level rather than real GDP.**

Two possible targets for monetary policy are stabilizing real GDP and the price level. If aggregate demand shocks were the only shocks to affect the economy, then stabilizing aggregate demand would stabilize both the price level and real GDP. But in the face of aggregate supply shocks, stabilizing real GDP means destabilizing the price level and stabilizing the price level means destabilizing real GDP. Inflation targeting is a monetary policy framework that combines an announced target for the inflation rate with publication of the central bank's economic forecasts.

CHECKPOINT 18.1

■ **Discuss whether fiscal policy or monetary policy is the better stabilization tool.**

Quick Review

- *Strength of monetary policy* The more insensitive the quantity of money demanded to a change in the interest rate, and the more sensitive investment demand and other components of aggregate expenditure are to a change in the interest rate, the more powerful is monetary policy.

- *Strength of fiscal policy* The power of fiscal policy depends on the strength of the crowding-out effects that counteract it.

Additional Practice Problems 18.1

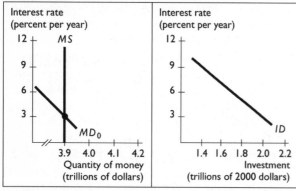

1. The left figure above shows the initial money market equilibrium and the right figure above shows the investment demand curve. Suppose the government increases its expenditures, which increase real GDP, which then, in turn, increases the demand for money by $0.2 trillion at every interest rate.

   a. Before the government's fiscal policy, in the money market figure show the equilibrium interest rate. Show the effect in the money market from the fiscal policy. What is the new equilibrium interest rate?

   b. Before the government's fiscal policy, using the investment demand curve show the equilibrium quantity of investment? After the fiscal policy, show the new equi-

librium quantity of investment? How much investment was crowded out?

2. When is fiscal policy powerful? Why? When is monetary policy powerful? What is the relationship between the conditions that make these policies either stronger or weaker?

Solutions to Additional Practice Problems 18.1

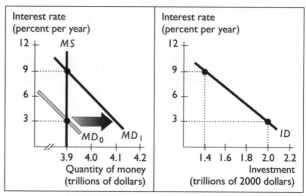

1a. In the left figure, before the fiscal policy the equilibrium interest rate was 3 percent, determined by the intersection of the demand for money curve, MD_0 and the supply of money curve, MS. The increase in real GDP increases the demand for money and shifts the demand for money curve to MD_1. The equilibrium interest rate rises to 9 percent.

1b. Before the fiscal policy, the equilibrium interest rate was 3 percent. The top right figure shows that at this interest rate the equilibrium quantity of investment is $2.0 trillion. When the interest rate rises to 9 percent, the equilibrium quantity of investment decreases to $1.4 trillion. $0.6 trillion of investment is crowded out.

2. Fiscal policy is powerful when the demand for money is sensitive to the interest rate and investment demand is insensitive to the interest rate. In these cases the crowding-out effect is smaller.

   Monetary policy is powerful when the demand for money is insensitive to the interest rate and investment demand is sensitive to the interest rate.

   Both policy tools affect aggregate demand, but

the size of the change in aggregate demand depends on the demand for money and investment demand. Fiscal policy is powerful when monetary policy is weak and monetary policy is powerful when fiscal policy is weak.

■ Self Test 18.1

Fill in the blanks

If the demand for money is not sensitive to the interest rate, monetary policy is ____ (less; more) powerful. If investment demand is not sensitive to the interest rate, fiscal policy is ____ (less; more) powerful. In a liquidity trap, monetary policy ____ (is very powerful; has no effect) and fiscal policy ____ (is very powerful; has no effect). Discretionary fiscal policy ____ (is; is not) subject to goal conflicts. Monetary policy has ____ (more; fewer) goal conflicts than discretionary fiscal policy. (Fiscal policy; Monetary policy; Neither fiscal policy nor monetary policy) is clearly the best stabilization policy.

True or false

1. Monetary policy is more powerful the more sensitive investment demand is to the interest rate.

2. Fiscal policy is more powerful the less sensitive investment demand is to the interest rate.

3. In a liquidity trap, monetary policy is extremely powerful.

4. A major reason fiscal policy suffers from goal conflicts is because there are only a few spending programs and tax laws that can be changed.

5. Monetary policy can be undertaken more rapidly than fiscal policy.

Multiple choice

1. When the Fed implements monetary policy, it changes ____ which changes ____ which changes ____.
   a. the supply of money; the interest rate; investment
   b. the supply of money; investment; the interest rate
   c. the interest rate; investment; the supply of money
   d. investment; the supply of money; the interest rate
   e. the interest rate; investment; government expenditure

2. One of the factors that determines the power of monetary policy is the responsiveness of
   a. the supply of money to the interest rate.
   b. the demand for money to the interest rate.
   c. investment to the level of potential GDP.
   d. the unemployment rate to the natural unemployment rate.
   e. inflation to the interest rate.

3. In which case is fiscal policy the strongest?
   a. There is a large crowding-out effect.
   b. The multiplier is large.
   c. Aggregate expenditure is very sensitive to a change in the interest rate.
   d. A change in real GDP results in a large change in money demand.
   e. Real GDP is a fixed amount.

4. If the demand for money is not sensitive to the interest rate and investment is sensitive to the interest rate, fiscal policy is ____ and monetary policy is ____.
   a. powerful; powerful
   b. powerful; weak
   c. weak; powerful
   d. weak; weak
   e. completely ineffective; completely ineffective

5. The term "goal conflicts" refers to the situation in which
   a. fiscal and monetary policy conflict in their goals.
   b. stabilization policy can have side effects that conflict with other goals.
   c. the announcement of policy goals is in conflict with the reality of their actions.
   d. goals are not made clear by either monetary or fiscal policy authorities.
   e. fiscal policy attempts to stabilize the price level and monetary policy attempts to stabilize the inflation rate.

6. The three main goals of monetary policy are
   a. price level stability, real GDP stability, and income redistribution.
   b. price level stability, real GDP stability, and financial market stability.
   c. real GDP stability, financial market stability, and income redistribution.
   d. provision of goods and services, financial market stability, and price level stability.
   e. price level stability, potential GDP stability, and interest rate stability.

7. Discretionary fiscal policy is
   a. volatile, because it responds to rapidly changing political agendas.
   b. flexible, because discretionary fiscal policy is passed quickly through Congress.
   c. coherent, because the Fed dictates it according to its monetary policy.
   d. inflexible, because fiscal policy is political in nature.
   e. completely ineffective because it cannot change real GDP.

8. To deal with normal fluctuations in the economy,
   a. there is no clear winner between monetary policy and fiscal policy.
   b. monetary policy is more flexible and therefore preferred.
   c. fiscal policy is superior with its use of automatic stabilizers and discretionary action.
   d. fiscal policy is better understood by the public and therefore should be used more often than monetary policy.
   e. neither fiscal policy nor monetary policy can do anything to dampen these common occurrences.

Complete the graph

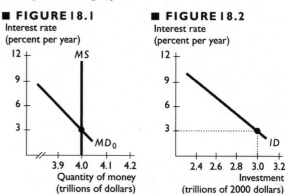

■ **FIGURE 18.1**

■ **FIGURE 18.2**

1. Figures 18.1 and 18.2 show the money market and the investment demand curve.
   a. The government increases its expenditures. What is the effect on real GDP and the price level?
   b. What happens to the demand for money when government expenditures are increased? Suppose the change is $0.1 trillion at each interest rate. Use Figure 18.1 to illustrate the effect.
   c. What is the effect of this fiscal policy on investment? Use Figure 18.2 to illustrate the effect.
   d. Relate your answer to part (c) to the crowding-out effect. How does the size of the crowding-out effect relate to the strength of the fiscal policy?

■ **FIGURE 18.3**

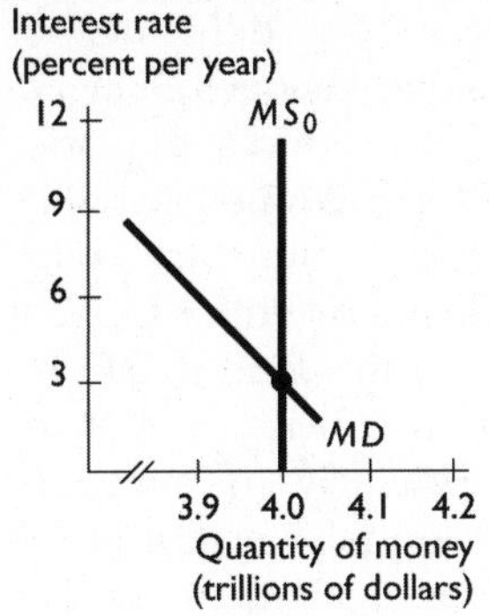

Interest rate
(percent per year)
12
9
6
3
MS_0
MD
3.9 4.0 4.1 4.2
Quantity of money
(trillions of dollars)

■ **FIGURE 18.4**

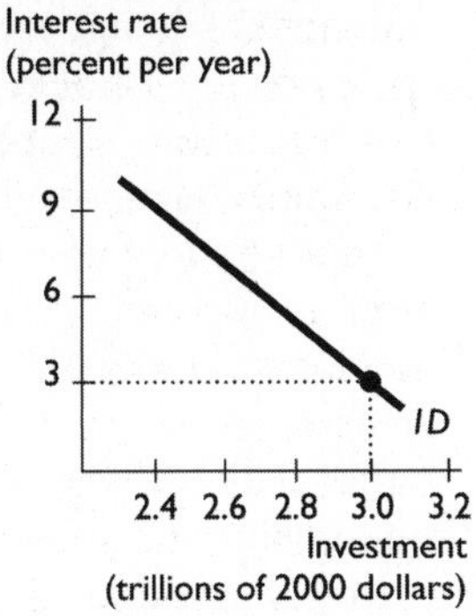

Interest rate
(percent per year)
12
9
6
3
ID
2.4 2.6 2.8 3.0 3.2
Investment
(trillions of 2000 dollars)

2. Figures 18.3 and 18.4 show the money market and the investment demand curve.
   a. The Fed decreases the quantity of money by $0.1 trillion. Use Figure 18.3 to illustrate the effect of this decrease on the interest rate.
   b. Use Figure 18.4 to illustrate the effect of this monetary policy on investment. Will this policy increase real GDP or decrease real GDP?

Short answer and numeric questions

1. Explain why monetary policy is more powerful if the quantity of money demanded is insensitive to the interest rate.
2. What is a liquidity trap? What is the relationship between a liquidity trap and monetary policy?
3. What are the three main fiscal policy goals? How might stabilization lead to a goal conflict?
4. Why is monetary policy considered more flexible than fiscal policy?
5. Is fiscal policy or monetary policy best for handling the normal fluctuations in economic activity? Why?

CHECKPOINT 18.2

■ Explain the rules-versus-discretion debate and compare Keynesian and monetarist policy rules.

Quick Review

- *Fixed-rule policy* A fixed-rule policy is a policy that is pursued independently of the state of the economy. A fixed-rule monetary policy is to keep the quantity of money constant.

a. *Flexible-rule policy* A flexible-rule policy is a policy that specifies how policy actions respond to changes in the state of the economy. A flexible-rule monetary policy is to increase the quantity of money when aggregate demand decreases and decrease the quantity of money when aggregate demand increases.

Additional Practice Problems 18.2

1. The economy shown in the figure is initially on aggregate supply curve *AS*0 and aggregate demand curve *AD*. Then aggregate supply decreases, and the aggregate supply curve shifts leftward to *AS*1.

Price level (GDP deflator)
140
130
120
110
AS_1
AS_0
AD
0 10.0 10.5 11.0 11.5 12.5
Real GDP
(trillions of 2000 dollars)

   a. What are the initial equilibrium real GDP and price level?
   b. If the Fed adopts a fixed-rule policy, over time what happens to real GDP and the price level?
   c. If the Fed adopts a feedback-rule policy that targets real GDP, over time what happens to real GDP and the price level?
2. Can monetary policy offset fluctuations in aggregate supply so that neither the price level nor real GDP changes? Explain your answer.

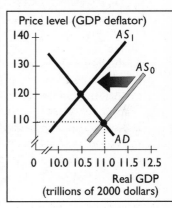

Solutions to Additional Practice Problems 18.2

1a. The initial equilibrium is where the aggregate demand curve intersects the aggregate supply curve. As the figure shows, equilibrium real GDP is $11.0 trillion and the equilibrium price level is 110.

1b. In the short run, real GDP and the price level move to the intersection of AS_1 and AD, so the price level rises to 120 and real GDP decreases to $10.5 trillion. If the Fed is

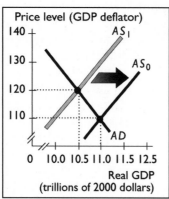

using a fixed-rule policy, the changes in the price level and real GDP do not bring any change in policy. With real GDP equal to only $10.5 trillion, there is a recessionary gap so that eventually the money wage rate falls. When this occurs aggregate supply increases and the aggregate supply curve shifts back to AS_0. The price level and real GDP return to their original values of 110 and $11.0 trillion.

1c. In the short run, the price level rises to 120 and real GDP decreases to $10.5 trillion. The Fed increases the quantity of money to restore real GDP back to

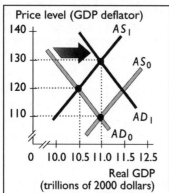

$11.0 trillion. As a result aggregate demand increases and the AD curve shifts to AD_1. Real GDP increases to $11.0 trillion and the price level rises to 130. The feedback rule has restored real GDP but the price level is permanently higher.

2. It is not possible for monetary policy to offset fluctuations in aggregate supply so that neither the price level nor real GDP changes. A negative aggregate supply shock raises the price level and decreases real GDP. Monetary policy changes aggregate demand. If monetary policy aims to restore real GDP to potential GDP, it increases aggregate demand. Real GDP increases, as desired, but the price level rises more than otherwise. Similarly, if monetary policy aims to offset the initial increase in the price level, it decreases aggregate demand. The price level falls, as desired, but real GDP decreases more than otherwise.

■ Self Test 18.2

Fill in the blanks

A policy that is pursued independently of the state of the economy is a ____ (fixed-rule; feedback-rule) policy and a policy that specifies how policy actions respond to changes in the state of the economy is a ____ (fixed-rule; feedback-rule) policy. A monetarist favors ____ (fixed-rule; feedback-rule) policies and a Keynesian activist favors ____ (fixed-rule; feedback-rule) policies. When faced with a recessionary gap, a fixed-rule policy ____ (increases; decreases; does not change) the quantity of money while a feedback-rule policy ____ (increases; decreases; does not change) the quantity of money. The fact that there is uncertainty about potential GDP favors ____ (fixed-rule; feedback-rule) policies. After being hit by a negative aggregate supply shock, in the long run the price level is higher when using a ____ (fixed-rule; feedback-rule) policy.

True or false

1. An example of a feedback-rule policy is to keep the quantity of money growing at a constant rate to make the average inflation rate equal to zero.

2. Advocates of fixed rules propose that the Fed increase the quantity of money when aggregate demand decreases.

3. A feedback-rule policy attempts to pull the economy out of a recessionary gap by using a policy action.

4. Because it is difficult to forecast future economic conditions, feedback-rule policies are better than fixed-rule policies.

5. Feedback-rule policies react only to aggregate demand shocks and not to aggregate supply shocks.

Multiple choice

1. Monetary policy that is based on the judgments of the policymakers about current needs of the economy is called ____ monetary policy.
   a. fixed-rule
   b. sure-thing
   c. feedback-rule
   d. discretionary
   e. judgemental

2. A fixed-rule policy is policy
   a. determined by policymakers who use their own judgment to decide what is needed.
   b. that is determined by a preset list of rules.
   c. that is followed regardless of the state of the economy.
   d. determined by the unemployment rate.
   e. that responds to the state of the economy in a fixed way.

3. Economists who believe fluctuations in the quantity of money are the main source of economic fluctuations are
   a. Keynesians.
   b. monetarists.
   c. feedback advocates.
   d. fiscalists.
   e. quantists.

4. To eliminate a recessionary gap with a fixed-rule monetary policy, the Fed will
   a. increase the supply of money.
   b. decrease the supply of money.
   c. not change the supply of money.
   d. cut income tax rates.
   e. lower the interest rate.

5. A Keynesian activist is likely to prefer a ____ policy.
   a. rigid-rule
   b. fixed-rule
   c. feedback-rule
   d. directed-rule
   e. wait-and-see

6. Reasons given to support a fixed-rule monetary policy include all of the following EXCEPT
   a. potential GDP is not known.
   b. the price level is not known.
   c. policy lags are longer than the forecast horizon.
   d. feedback rules are less predictable than fixed-rule policies.
   e. aggregate supply fluctuations are the source of most fluctuations of the economy.

7. When an economy experiences a negative aggregate supply shock, the policy rule that waits for real wage rates to change and move the economy back to potential GDP is the ____ policy.
   a. fixed-rule
   b. discretionary
   c. feedback-rule
   d. directed-rule
   e. wait-and-see

8. To eliminate a recessionary gap that is the result of a supply shock, a feedback-rule monetary policy that targets real GDP will
   a. decrease the quantity of money.
   b. increase the quantity of money.
   c. increase government expenditures.
   d. decrease government expenditures.
   e. decrease taxes.

Complete the graph

■ FIGURE 18.5

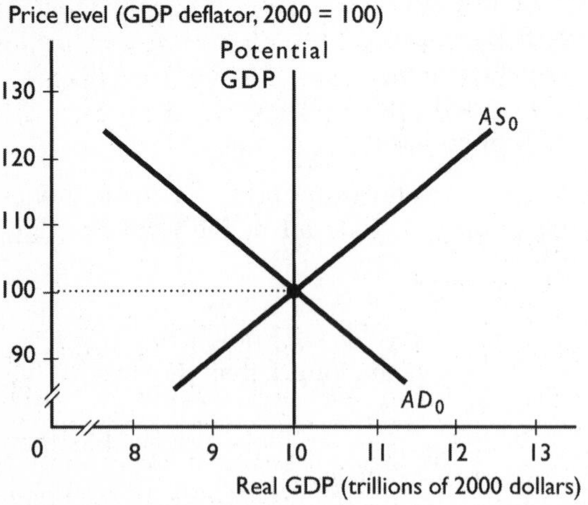

Price level (GDP deflator, 2000 = 100)

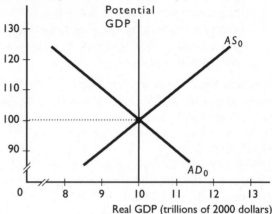

1. Figure 18.5 shows the economy in its initial equilibrium with real GDP equal to potential GDP of $10 trillion and the price level equal to 100.

   a. Suppose a negative aggregate demand shock hits so that in the short run, the new equilibrium price level is 90. In Figure 18.5, illustrate the effect of this aggregate demand shock. What is equilibrium real GDP?

   b. Suppose that monetary policy follows a feedback-rule policy that moves real GDP back to potential GDP. In Figure 18.5, illustrate the effect of the monetary policy. What is the equilibrium price level?

2. Figure 18.6 (at the top of the next column) shows the economy in its initial equilibrium with real GDP equal to potential GDP of $10 trillion and the price level equal to 100.

   a. Suppose a negative aggregate supply shock hits so that in the short run, the new equilibrium price level is 110. In Figure 18.6, illustrate the effect of this aggregate supply shock. What is equilibrium real GDP?

   b. Suppose that monetary policy follows a feedback-rule policy that moves real GDP back to potential GDP. In Figure 18.6, illustrate the effect of the monetary policy. What is the equilibrium price level?

■ FIGURE 18.6

Price level (GDP deflator, 2000 = 100)

Short answer and numeric questions

1. What are the three general approaches to monetary policy that the Fed can follow?

2. If the Fed is following a fixed-rule policy, how does it respond to a decrease in aggregate demand? To a decrease in aggregate supply?

3. If the Fed is following a feedback-rule policy, how does it respond to a decrease in aggregate demand?

4. Suppose it takes two years for monetary policy to have an effect and recessions last for only one year. What implication does this have for monetary policy?

CHECKPOINT 18.3

■ Assess whether policy should target the price level rather than real GDP.

Quick Review

- *Real GDP target* If monetary policy targets real GDP, an increase in aggregate supply is met with a decrease in aggregate demand and the price level falls; and a decrease in aggregate supply is met with an increase in aggregate demand and the price level rises.

- *Price level target* If monetary policy targets the price level, an increase in aggregate supply is met with an in increase in aggregate demand and the real GDP increases; and a decrease in aggregate supply is met with a decrease in aggregate demand and real GDP decreases.

Additional Practice Problems 18.3

1. Suppose that in 2007, the inflation rate is 4 percent a year and potential GDP is $13 trillion. Oil prices then increase so that aggregate supply decreases. If the Fed decides that it wants to keep the inflation rate between 1 percent and 7 percent a year and to keep real GDP within the range $12.9 trillion to $13.1 trillion.
    a. Is the Fed placing more weight on inflation or on real GDP?
    b. What actions will the Fed take?

2. Suppose in Practice Problem 1, the Fed now wants to keep the inflation rate between 3.8 percent a year and 4.2 percent a year and is willing to allow real GDP to range between $11 trillion to $15 trillion. How will this change in targets affect the Fed's monetary policy?

3. What general conclusion can you draw from your answers to Practice Problems 1 and 2?

Solutions to Additional Practice Problems 18.3

1a. The Fed is placing more weight on real GDP. The Fed will accept a decrease in real GDP of $0.1 trillion from potential GDP, which is less than 1 percent. The Fed is willing to accept a 3 percentage point deviation from the midpoint of 4 percent a year, which is a deviation of 75 percent.

1b. The decrease in aggregate supply raises the price level and decreases real GDP. The Fed is more concerned with the decrease in real GDP, so it increases the supply of money. Aggregate demand increases. The price level rises and real GDP moves to its target range.

2. The Fed is now placing more weight on the inflation rate and less weight on real GDP. Now when confronted with a decrease in aggregate supply, the Fed will *decrease* the quantity of money to decrease aggregate demand and keep the inflation rate within its acceptable range. The change in the Fed's targets changes its monetary policy.

3. If the Fed stabilizes real GDP, as it does in Practice Problem 1, it destabilizes the price level and inflation rate. If the Fed stabilizes the inflation rate, as it does in Practice Problem 2, it destabilizes real GDP.

■ Self Test 18.3

Fill in the blanks

Targeting ____ (real GDP; the price level) is equivalent to targeting the unemployment rate. If policy targets real GDP, aggregate supply shocks result in the policy destabilizing ____ (real GDP; the price level). If monetary policy targets the price level, an increase in aggregate supply is met with ____ (an increase; a decrease) in the quantity of money. One part of inflation targeting is for the central bank to ____ (publicize its inflation target; keep its inflation target secret).

True or false

1. The only possible target for stabilization policy is real GDP.

2. If monetary policy targets real GDP, it attempts to offset aggregate supply shocks.

3. If there are aggregate supply shocks and monetary policy targets real GDP, then the monetary policy destabilizes the price level.

4. Aggregate supply shocks mean that the Fed can simultaneously stabilize real GDP and the price level.

5. Inflation targeting aims to keep the inflation rate within an announced target range.

Multiple choice

1. Targeting real GDP is equivalent to targeting
    a. inflation.
    b. unemployment.
    c. labor supply.
    d. the tax rate.
    e. the price level.

2. Two possible targets for monetary policy are
   a. real GDP and the price level.
   b. real GDP and potential GDP.
   c. low taxes and low inflation.
   d. low taxes and zero inflation.
   e. the unemployment rate and real GDP.

3. Targeting real GDP works best when the source of shocks to the economy come from
   a. the aggregate demand side.
   b. the aggregate supply side.
   c. changes in the natural rate of unemployment.
   d. changes in potential GDP.
   e. changes in the price of oil.

4. If monetary policy targets real GDP, an increase in aggregate supply is met by ____ in the quantity of money and ____ in aggregate demand.
   a. an increase; an increase
   b. an increase; a decrease
   c. a decrease; an increase
   d. a decrease; a decrease
   e. no change; no change

5. If the Fed targets real GDP and the economy experiences an aggregate supply shock, then
   a. monetary policy will not move the economy toward potential GDP.
   b. the price level will fluctuate.
   c. the price level will be effectively stabilized.
   d. both real GDP and the price level will be stabilized.
   e. there is nothing the Fed can do to move the economy back to potential GDP.

6. If the Fed decides to stabilize real GDP by using a real GDP target, then aggregate supply shocks mean that the
   a. Fed actually stabilizes both real GDP and the price level.
   b. price level becomes destabilized.
   c. Fed must fail so that real GDP becomes destabilized.
   d. Fed must increase the quantity of money if the price level falls.
   e. Fed must ignore all aggregate supply shocks.

7. If the Fed targets the price level, an increase in aggregate supply means that the Fed takes actions to
   a. increase aggregate demand but not aggregate supply.
   b. decrease aggregate demand but not aggregate supply.
   c. increase aggregate supply but not aggregate demand.
   d. decrease both aggregate demand and aggregate supply.
   e. increase both aggregate demand and aggregate supply.

8. If monetary policy targets the price level, then an increase in aggregate supply is countered with an action by the Fed that
   a. decreases aggregate supply.
   b. increases potential GDP.
   c. decreases aggregate demand.
   d. increases aggregate demand.
   e. decreases potential GDP.

Short answer and numeric questions

1. Does it matter whether the Fed targets real GDP or the price level when faced with a decrease in aggregate demand? Does it matter which the Fed targets if it is faced with a decrease in aggregate supply?

2. What is inflation targeting? Why does the central bank announce its inflation rate targets?

SELF TEST ANSWERS

■ CHECKPOINT 18.1

Fill in the blanks

If the demand for money is not sensitive to the interest rate, monetary policy is <u>more</u> powerful. If investment demand is not sensitive to the interest rate, fiscal policy is <u>more</u> powerful. In a liquidity trap, monetary policy <u>has no effect</u> and fiscal policy <u>is very powerful</u>. Discretionary fiscal policy <u>is</u> subject to goal conflicts. Monetary policy has <u>fewer</u> goal conflicts than discretionary fiscal policy. <u>Neither fiscal policy nor monetary policy</u> is clearly the best stabilization policy.

True or false

1. True; pages 456-457
2. True; page 458
3. False; page 459
4. False; page 459
5. True; page 460

Multiple choice

1. a; page 456
2. b; pages 456-457
3. b; page 458
4. c; pages 456-458
5. b; page 459
6. b; page 460
7. d; page 460
8. b; page 460

Complete the graph

1. a. The increase in government expenditures increases real GDP and raises the price level; page 458.
   b. The increase in real GDP increases the demand for money and the demand for money curve shifts rightward. Figure 18.7 illustrates a rightward shift in the demand for money curve. The interest rate rises; page 458.
   c. The rise in the interest rate decreases investment. In Figure 18.8 there is a movement up along the investment demand curve; page 458.

■ **FIGURE 18.7**

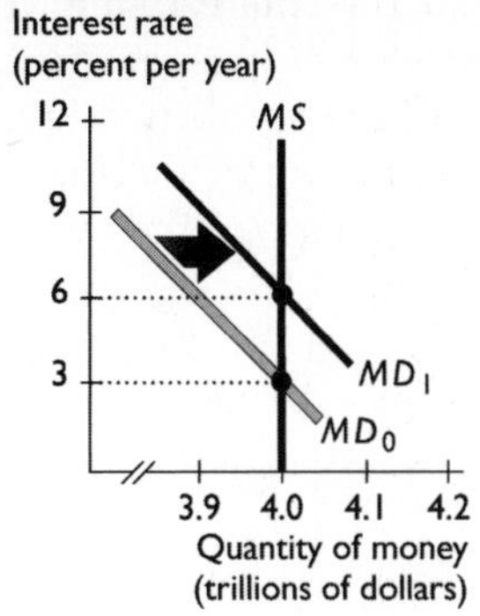

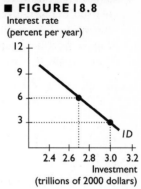

■ **FIGURE 18.8**

d. The increase in government expenditures decreases investment. The decrease in investment is the crowding-out effect. The larger the crowding-out effect, that is, the greater the decrease in investment, the weaker the effect of the fiscal policy. So the more the interest rate rises and the more sensitive investment is to the rise in the interest rate, the weaker is fiscal policy; page 458.

■ **FIGURE 18.9**

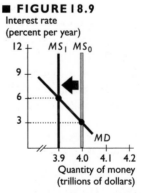

■ **FIGURE 18.10**

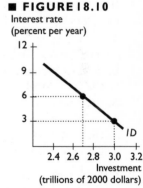

2. a. The decrease in the quantity of money raises the interest rate to 6 percent, as illustrated in Figure 18.9; page 457.
   b. As Figure 18.10 shows, the increase in the interest rate decreases investment to $2.6 trillion. Real GDP will decrease because investment decreases (as well as other interest-sensitive components) so aggregate demand decreases; pages 456-457.

Short answer and numeric questions

1. When the quantity of money demanded is relatively insensitive to the interest rate, a change in the interest rate brings a small change in the quantity of money demanded. Then, when the quantity of money increases by a given amount, the decrease in the interest rate is large. The larger the decrease in the interest rate, the larger is the change in investment and aggregate expenditure, and the more powerful the monetary policy; pages 456-457.

2. A liquidity trap is an interest rate at which people are willing to hold any quantity of money. In a liquidity trap, a change in the quantity of money has no effect on the interest rate. So a change in the quantity of money has no effect on aggregate expenditure. Monetary policy has no effect; page 459.

3. The three fiscal policy goals are to provide public goods and services, to redistribute income, and to stabilize aggregate demand. The main source of conflict that arises from stabilization is the very large number of spending programs and tax laws in place and the difficulty of changing all of them to balance the costs and benefits of one against the costs and benefits of others; page 459.

4. Monetary policy is more flexible than fiscal policy. The Fed and its policy committee, the FOMC, can quickly take policy actions. Every day, the Fed monitors the financial markets and watches for signs that its policy needs to be tweaked to keep the economy on course; page 460.

5. Monetary policy is best for handling the normal fluctuations in economic activity because it can be changed quickly; page 460.

■ CHECKPOINT 18.2

Fill in the blanks

A policy that is pursued independently of the state of the economy is a <u>fixed-rule</u> policy and a policy that specifies how policy actions respond to changes in the state of the economy is a <u>feedback-rule</u> policy. A monetarist favors <u>fixed-rule</u> policies and a Keynesian activist favors <u>feedback-rule</u> policies. When faced with a recessionary gap, a fixed-rule policy <u>does not change</u> the quantity of money while a feedback-rule policy <u>increases</u> the quantity of money. The fact that there is uncertainty about potential GDP favors <u>fixed-rule</u> policies. After being hit by a negative aggregate supply shock, in the long run the price level is higher when using a <u>feedback-rule</u> policy.

True or false

1. False; page 462
2. False; page 464
3. True; page 465
4. False; pages 465-466
5. False; page 468

Multiple choice

1. d; page 462
2. c; page 462
3. b; page 464
4. c; page 464
5. c; page 465
6. b; page 465-466
7. a; page 468
8. b; page 468

Complete the graph

■ FIGURE 18.11

Price level (GDP deflator, 2000 = 100)

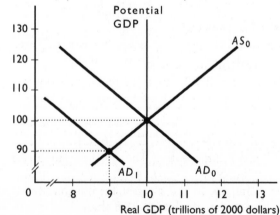

1. a. The negative aggregate demand shock de-

creases aggregate demand and shifts the aggregate demand curve leftward from AD_0 to AD_1. Figure 18.11 shows that the price level falls to 90 and real GDP decreases to $9 trillion; page 463.

b. If the Fed follows a feedback-rule policy that restores real GDP back to potential GDP, it increases the quantity of money, which increases aggregate demand. In Figure 18.11, the aggregate demand curve shifts rightward, from AD_1 back to AD_0. Real GDP returns to equal potential GDP of $10 trillion and the price level rises to return to 100; pages 464-465.

■ FIGURE 18.12

Price level (GDP deflator, 2000 = 100)

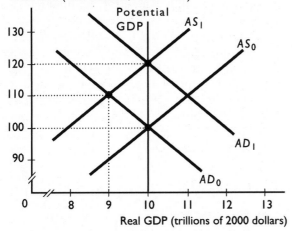

Real GDP (trillions of 2000 dollars)

2. a. The negative aggregate supply shock decreases aggregate supply and shifts the aggregate supply curve leftward from AS_0 to AS_1. Figure 18.12 shows that the price level rises to 110 and real GDP decreases to $9 trillion; page 467.

b. If the Fed follows a feedback-rule policy that restores real GDP back to potential GDP, it increases the quantity of money, which increases aggregate demand. In Figure 18.12, the aggregate demand curve shifts rightward, from AD_0 to AD_1. Real GDP equals potential GDP of $10 trillion and the price level rises to 120; page 468.

Short answer and numeric questions

1. The Fed can follow discretionary monetary policy (in which the policy is based on the judgments of policy makers about the current needs of the economy), a fixed-rule policy (in which the policy is pursued independently of the state of the economy), or a feedback-rule policy (in which the policy actions respond to changes in the economy); page 462.

2. If the Fed is following a fixed-rule policy, in the face of a decrease in aggregate demand it does nothing. And it does nothing in the face of a decrease in aggregate supply. A fixed-rule policy does *not* respond to the current state of the economy; pages 464, 468.

3. If the Fed is following a feedback-rule policy, in the face of a decrease in aggregate demand the Fed increases the quantity of money and lowers the interest rate, which increases aggregate demand; page 465.

4. If it takes two years for monetary policy to have an effect and recessions last for only one year, a feedback-rule policy will be difficult. If the Fed's feedback-rule policy increases the quantity of money when the economy is in a recession then in two years when aggregate demand responds by increasing, the economy will be out of the recession and in an expansion. So monetary policy based on feedback rules might increase aggregate demand when aggregate demand is increasing strongly already. Monetary policy runs the risk of boosting the inflation rate rather than fighting the recession; page 466.

■ CHECKPOINT 18.3

Fill in the blanks

Targeting <u>real GDP</u> is equivalent to targeting the unemployment rate. If policy targets real GDP, aggregate supply shocks result in the policy destabilizing <u>the price level</u>. If monetary policy targets the price level, an increase in aggregate supply is met with <u>an increase</u> in the quantity of money. One part of inflation targeting is for the central bank to <u>publicize its inflation target</u>.

True or false

1. False; page 470
2. True; page 470
3. True; page 471
4. False; page 471
5. True; page 472

Multiple choice

1. b; page 470
2. a; page 470
3. a; page 470
4. d; page 470
5. b; pages 470-471
6. b; page 471
7. a; page 471
8. d; page 471

Short answer and numeric questions

1. A decrease in aggregate demand lowers the price level and decreases real GDP. Regardless of the Fed's target, the appropriate feedback monetary policy is to increase the quantity of money, which increases aggregate demand. An increase in aggregate demand can return real GDP and the price level back to their original levels.

   If the Fed is faced with a decrease in aggregate supply and is using a feedback policy, the choice of target is important. If the Fed is targeting real GDP, the appropriate monetary policy is to increase the quantity of money, which can return real GDP to its original level but with a rise in the price level. Or if the Fed is targeting the price level, the appropriate monetary policy is to decrease the quantity of money, which can return the price level to its original level but with a decrease in real GDP; pages 470-471.

2. Inflation targeting is a monetary policy framework in which the central bank announces a target range for the inflation rate and publicizes its economic forecasts and analysis. The central bank attempts to stabilize real GDP and unemployment while keeping the inflation rate within its target zone. The target is announced because the announcement gives the people and businesses an anchor for their inflation expectations, which can help stabilize aggregate supply; page 472.

International Trade

Chapter

19

In Chapter 19 we see that all countries can benefit from free trade but, despite this fact, countries nevertheless restrict trade.

- **Describe the patterns and trends in international trade.**

The goods and services that we buy from people in other countries are called imports. The goods and services that we sell to people in other countries are called exports. In 2004 manufactured goods were 54 percent of U.S. exports and 66 percent of U.S. imports. Goods comprise 70 percent of U.S. exports and 83 percent of U.S. imports. The rest of U.S. international trade is in services. Trade has grown over time. Between 1960 and 2005 exports grew from 5 percent of total output to 10.5 percent, and imports grew from 4 percent to 16 percent. The biggest U.S. trading partner is Canada. The balance of trade is the value of exports minus the value of imports. In 2005, the United States had a trade deficit.

- **Explain why nations engage in international trade and why trade benefits all nations.**

Comparative advantage enables countries to gain from trade. A nation has a comparative advantage in producing a good if it can produce that good at a lower opportunity cost than another country. In this case, the domestic no-trade price is lower than the world price. To achieve the gains from trade, a nation specializes in the production of the goods and services in which it has a comparative advantage and then trades with other nations. By specializing and trading, a nation can consume at a point beyond its production possibilities frontier, which is the gains from trade. Offshoring occurs when a U.S. firm either produces in another country or buys finished goods or services from firms in other countries. Offshoring increased in the 1990s because telecommunication prices fell.

- **Explain how trade barriers reduce international trade.**

A tariff is a tax on a good that is imposed by the importing country when an imported good crosses its international boundary. A tariff on a good reduces imports of that good, increases domestic production of the good, yields revenue for the government, and reduces the gains from trade. A quota is a specified maximum amount of a good that may be imported in a given period of time.

- **Explain the arguments used to justify trade barriers and show why these arguments are incorrect but also why some barriers are hard to remove.**

The three main arguments for protection and restriction of trade are the national security argument, the infant-industry argument, and the dumping argument. Each of these arguments is flawed. Other flawed arguments for protection are that protection saves jobs, allows us to compete with cheap foreign labor, brings diversity and stability, penalizes lax environmental standards, and protects national culture. Tariffs are imposed in some nations to gain revenue for the government. In addition, trade is restricted is because of rent seeking from those who benefit from trade restrictions.

CHECKPOINT 19.1

■ **Describe the patterns and trends in international trade.**

Quick Review
  • *Imports* The goods and services that we buy from people in other countries are called imports.
  • *Exports* The goods and services that we sell to people in other countries are called exports.

Additional Practice Problems 19.1

1. The London School of Economics in the United Kingdom buys 100 copies of Windows that were produced in the United States. Describe how the United States and the United Kingdom categorize these goods.

2. A U.S. contractor in Seattle buys 1 ton of lumber from Canada in order to build homes in the state of Washington.

3. Citibank, an American firm, provides financial services to firms in France. Describe how the United States and France categorize these financial services.

Solutions to Additional Practice Problems 19.1

1. For the United States, the copies of Windows are exports to the United Kingdom. For the United Kingdom, the copies of Windows are imports from the United States.

2. For the United States, the lumber is an import from Canada. For Canada, the lumber is an export to the United States.

3. For the United States, the services rendered by Citibank are exports to France. For France, the services rendered by Citibank are imports from the United States.

■ **Self Test 19.1**

Fill in the blanks

Manufactured goods account for ____ (8; 28; 54) percent of U.S. imports. ____ (Canada; Mexico; The United Kingdom; Japan) is the United States' biggest trading partner. The United States ____ (is; is not) a member of NAFTA, the North American Free Trade Agreement. In the United States between 1960 and 2005, trade ____ (decreased; increased) as a fraction of total output.

True or false

1. The United States exports more services than goods.

2. In 2005, 1 percent of total U.S. output was exported.

3. The United Kingdom is the biggest U.S. trading partner.

4. In 2005, the United States imported a larger value of goods and services than it exported.

Multiple choice

1. Goods and services that we buy from people in other countries are called our
   a. imports.
   b. exports.
   c. inputs.
   d. raw materials.
   e. obligations.

2. The largest fraction of U.S. imports is ____ and the largest fraction of U.S. exports ____.
   a. industrial materials; industrial materials
   b. industrial materials; manufactured goods
   c. manufactured goods; industrial materials
   d. manufactured goods; manufactured goods
   e. raw materials; food

3. Goods account for about ____ percent of U.S. exports and services account for about ____ percent of U.S. exports.
   a. 51; 49
   b. 70; 30
   c. 30; 70
   d. 100; 0
   e. 85; 15

4. The largest U.S. trading partner is
   a. Canada.
   b. Mexico.
   c. Japan.
   d. Spain.
   e. Korea.

5. If a college student from North Carolina State University travels to Germany, the money spent on hotels and sight-seeing in Germany is counted as services ____ America and ____ Germany.
    a. exported to; imported from
    b. imported from; imported from
    c. imported from; exported to
    d. exported to; exported to
    e. neither exported to nor imported from; imported from

6. The balance of trade equals
    a. the value of imports minus the value of exports.
    b. the value of exports minus the value of imports.
    c. the value of imports.
    d. the value of exports.
    e. the value of exports divided by the value of imports.

Short answer and numeric questions

1. French cheese is flown to the United States abroad a United Airlines plane. Classify these transactions from the vantage point of the United States and from the vantage point of France.

2. How has the amount of international trade changed in the United States between 1960 and 2005?

3. What is NAFTA? What is its goal?

CHECKPOINT 19.2

■ **Explain why nations engage in international trade and why trade benefits all nations.**

Quick Review

 • *Comparative advantage* A nation has a comparative advantage in a good when its opportunity cost of producing the good is lower than another nation's opportunity cost of producing the good.

Additional Practice Problems 19.2

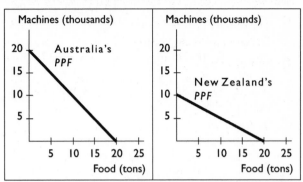

1. Suppose that Australia and New Zealand do not trade with each other. The figure above to the left shows Australia's production possibilities frontier and the figure to the right shows New Zealand's production possibilities frontier.
    a. What was the opportunity cost of 1 ton of food in Australia?
    b. What was the opportunity cost of 1 ton of food in New Zealand?
    c. What was the opportunity cost of 1 machine Australia?
    d. What was the opportunity cost of 1 machine in New Zealand?
    e. Which country has a comparative advantage in producing food? In machines? Why?
    f. If trade between the two countries opens, which good does Australia import from New Zealand? Which good does New Zealand import from Australia?
    g. Does Australia gain from this trade? Explain why or why not.
    h. Does New Zealand gain from this trade? Explain why or why not.

2. In Practice Problem 19.1, suppose that new technology becomes available so that the production of machines doubles in Australia and New Zealand. Now which good does Australia import from New Zealand?

Solution to Additional Practice Problem 19.2a

1a. In Australia, when 20 tons of food are produced, 20,000 machines are forgone. The opportunity cost of 1 ton of food is (20,000 machines) ÷ (20 tons of food), which is 1,000 machines per ton of food.

1b. In New Zealand, when 20 tons of food are produced, 10,000 machines are forgone. The opportunity cost of 1 ton of food is (10,000 machines) ÷ (20 tons of food), which is 500 machines per ton of food.

1c. In Australia, when 20,000 machines are produced, 20 tons of food are forgone. The opportunity cost of 1 machine is (20 tons of food) ÷ (20,000 machines), which is 1/1,000 of a ton of food per machine.

1d. In New Zealand, when 10,000 machines are produced, 20 tons of food are forgone. The opportunity cost of 1 machine is (20 tons of food) ÷ (10,000 machines), which is 1/500 of a ton of food per machine.

1e. New Zealand has the comparative advantage in producing food because its opportunity cost, 500 machines per ton of food, is less than the opportunity cost in Australia. Australia has the comparative advantage in producing machines because its opportunity cost, 1/1,000 of a ton of food per machine, is less than the opportunity cost in New Zealand.

1f. Australia will import food from New Zealand because the cost of imported food is only 500 machines per ton whereas the cost of domestically produced food is 1,000 machines per ton. New Zealand will import machines from Australia because the cost of imported machines is only 1/1,000 of a ton of food per machine whereas the cost of domestically produced machines is 1/500 of a ton of food per machine.

1g. Yes, Australia gains from this trade. Australia can buy food cheaper from New Zealand than Australia can produce.

1h. New Zealand also gains from this trade. New Zealand can buy machines from Australia at a lower cost than New Zealand can produce. When the opportunity costs between countries diverge, comparative advantage enables countries to gain from international trade.

2. Australia still has the comparative advantage in machines. New Zealand still has the comparative advantage in food. So Australia continues to import food from New Zealand.

■ Self Test 19.2
Fill in the blanks
A country has a comparative advantage in producing a good if it can produce the good at ____ (higher; lower) opportunity cost than another country. If the world price of clothing is less than the price in the United States with no international trade and the United States imports clothing from Asia, U.S. buyers of clothing ____ (gain; lose) and Asian producers of clothing ____ (gain; lose). Trade ____ (allows; does not allow) a nation to produce at a point beyond its production possibilities frontier. Trade ____ (allows; does not allow) a nation to consume at a point beyond its production possibilities frontier.

True or false
1. The United States has a comparative advantage in the production of a good if the opportunity cost of producing that good is higher in the United States than in most other countries.

2. Only the exporting country gains from free international trade because it has a comparative advantage.

3. If Intel produces chips in Taiwan rather than California, Intel has offshored its production of chips.

4. There are no gains from trade when services are offshored.

Multiple choice
1. The fundamental force that drives trade between nations is
   a. the government.
   b. NAFTA.
   c. absolute advantage.
   d. comparative advantage.
   e. legal treaties.

2. A nation will import a good if its
   a. no-trade, domestic price is equal to the world price.
   b. no-trade, domestic price is less than the world price.
   c. no-trade, domestic price is greater than the world price.
   d. no-trade, domestic quantity is less than the world quantity.
   e. no-trade, domestic quantity is greater than the world quantity.

3. When Italy buys Boeing jets, the price Italy pays is ____ if it produced their own jets and the price Boeing receives is ____ than it could receive from an additional U.S. buyer.
   a. lower than; lower
   b. higher than; higher
   c. lower than; higher
   d. higher than; lower
   e. the same as; higher

4. When a good is imported, the domestic production ____ and the domestic consumption ____.
   a. increases; increases
   b. increases; decreases
   c. decreases; increases
   d. decreases; decreases
   e. increases; does not change

5. The United States can use all its resources to produce 250 DVDs or 500 shoes. China can use all of its resources to produce 30 DVDs or 300 shoes. The opportunity cost of producing a DVD in the United States is
   a. 2 shoes.
   b. 1/2 of a shoe.
   c. 20 shoes.
   d. 500 shoes.
   e. 1 DVD.

6. The United States can use all its resources to produce 250 DVDs or 500 shoes. China can use all of its resources to produce 30 DVDs or 300 shoes. In this example,
   a. China has a comparative advantage in DVDs.
   b. China has a comparative advantage in shoes.
   c. China has a comparative advantage in the production of both goods.
   d. China has a comparative advantage in neither good.
   e. The United States has a comparative advantage in the production of both goods.

7. Specialization and trade make a country better off because with trade the country can consume at a point
   a. outside its production possibilities frontier.
   b. inside its production possibilities frontier.
   c. on its production possibilities frontier.
   d. on its trading partner's production possibilities frontier.
   e. inside its trading partner's production possibilities frontier.

8. Which of the following is correct?
   i. Offshoring moves an estimated 1.2 million jobs per year away from the United States and into other countries.
   ii. A U.S. firm is offshoring if it hires foreign labor and produces in another country.
   iii. Offshoring of services increased in the last decade.
   a. i only.
   b. iii only.
   c. i and ii.
   d. ii and iii.
   e. i, ii, and iii.

Complete the graph

■ FIGURE 19.1

Price (dollars per bushel)

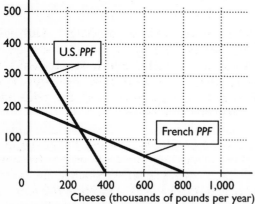

Quantity (millions of bushels per year)

1. Figure 19.1 shows the U.S. demand and supply curves for wheat.

   a. In the absence of international trade, what is the price of a bushel of wheat in the United States?

   b. If the world price of a bushel of wheat is $6 a bushel, will the United States import or export wheat? Above what world price for wheat will the United States export wheat? Below what world price for wheat will the United States import wheat?

■ FIGURE 19.2

Computer chips (thousands per year)

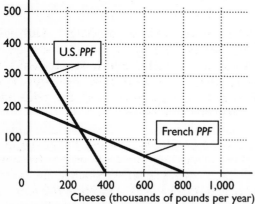

Cheese (thousands of pounds per year)

2. Figure 19.2 has the U.S. and French *PPF*s.

   a. What is the opportunity cost of a computer chip in the United States? In France?

Who has the comparative advantage in producing computer chips?

   b. What is the opportunity cost of a pound of cheese in the United States? In France? Who has the comparative advantage in producing cheese?

   c. When the United States and France trade, who exports chips and who exports cheese?

   d. The United States produced 200,000 computer chips and 200,000 pounds of cheese before trade. France produced 100,000 computer chips and 400,000 pounds of cheese. Label as point *A* the point that shows the total chip and cheese production before trade.

   e. The United States and France both specialize according to comparative advantage after trade. Label as point *B* the point that shows the total chip and cheese production after trade. How does point *B* compare to point *A*?

Short answer and numeric questions

Price (dollars per ton)	Quantity supplied (tons per year)	Quantity demanded (tons per year)
400	38	58
500	42	52
600	46	46
700	50	40
800	54	34
900	58	28

1. The table above has the U.S. demand and supply schedules for potatoes.

   a. If there is no international trade, what is the equilibrium price and quantity?

   b. If the world price of potatoes is $800 a ton, what is the quantity supplied and the quantity demanded in the United States? Does the United States import or export potatoes? What quantity?

   c. If the world price of potatoes rises to $900 a ton, what is the quantity supplied and the quantity demanded in the United States? Does the United States import or export potatoes? What quantity?

d. Would the United States ever import pota-toes?

2. Suppose the United States and France pro-duce only ice cream and cheese. The United States can produce 50 tons of ice cream or 100 tons of cheese and France can produce 20 tons of ice cream or 120 tons of cheese.

a. What is the opportunity cost of a ton of ice cream in France? In the United States? Which nation has the comparative advan-tage in producing ice cream?

b. What is the opportunity cost of a ton of cheese in France? In the United States? Which nation has the comparative advan-tage in producing cheese?

c. If France and the United States trade, what does the United States import? What does it export?

d. Before trade the United States produced 25 tons of ice cream and 50 tons of cheese and France produced 10 tons of ice cream and 60 tons of cheese. What is the total production of ice cream? Of cheese?

e. After trade, France and the United States specialize according to comparative ad-vantage. What is the total amount of ice cream produced? Of cheese?

f. Compare your answers to (d) and (e).

3. What are the gains from trade? How do countries obtain the gains from trade?

4. What is offshoring? Why is it controversial? Are there any gains from trade with offshor-ing?

CHECKPOINT 19.3

■ **Explain how trade barriers reduce international trade.**

Quick Review

- *Tariff* A tariff is a tax on a good that is imposed by the importing country when an imported good crosses its interna-tional boundary.

- *Quota* A quota is a specified maximum amount of a good that may be imported in a given period of time.

Additional Practice Problems 19.3

Price (dollars per ton of plywood)	U.S. quantity supplied (tons per month)	U.S. quantity demanded (tons per month)
1,000	600	1,400
750	500	1,600
500	300	1,800
250	100	2,000

1. The table above shows the U.S. supply and demand schedules for plywood. The United States also can buy plywood from Canada at the world price of $500 per ton.

a. If there are no tariffs or nontariff barriers, what is the price of a ton of plywood in the United States? How much plywood is produced in the United States and how much is consumed? How much plywood is imported from Canada?

b. Suppose that the United States imposes a $250 per ton tariff on all plywood im-ported into the country. What now is the price of a ton of plywood in the United States? How much plywood is produced in the United States and how much is con-sumed? How much plywood is imported from Canada?

c. Who has gained from the tariff and who has lost?

2. For many years Japan conducted extremely slow, detailed, and costly safety inspections of *all* U.S. cars imported into Japan. In terms of trade, what was the effect of this inspection? How did the inspection affect the price and quantity of cars in Japan?

Solutions to Additional Practice Problems 19.3

1a. With no tariffs or nontariff barriers, the price of a ton of plywood is equal to the world price, $500 per ton. At this price, 300 tons per month are produced in the United States and 1,800 tons per month are consumed. The dif-ference between the quantity consumed and the quantity produced, which is 1,500 tons per month, is imported from Canada.

1b. If a $250 per ton tariff is imposed, the price in the United States rises to $750 per ton. At this price, 500 tons per month are produced in the United States and 1,600 tons per month are consumed. The difference between the quantity consumed and the quantity produced, which is 1,100 tons per month, is imported from Canada.

1c. Gainers from the tariff are U.S. producers of plywood, who have a higher price for plywood and therefore increase their production, and the U.S. government, which gains tariff revenue. Losers are U.S. consumers, who consume less plywood with the tariff, and Canadian producers of plywood, who wind up exporting less plywood to the United States.

2. Japan's safety inspection (which has since been eliminated) was an example of a nontariff barrier to trade. It served a role similar to tariffs and quotas. The safety inspection added to the cost of selling cars in Japan. It raised the price of U.S. produced cars in Japan and decreased the quantity of U.S. cars sold. The Japanese government, however, received no tariff revenue.

■ Self Test 19.3

Fill in the blanks

A tax on a good that is imposed by the importing country when an imported good crosses its international boundary is a ____ (quota; tariff) and a specified maximum amount of a good that may be imported in a given period of time is a ____ (quota; tariff). A tariff ____ (raises; lowers) the price paid by domestic consumers and ____ (increases; decreases) the quantity produced by domestic producers. A quota ____ (raises; lowers) the price paid by domestic consumers and ____ (increases; decreases) the quantity produced by domestic producers.

True or false

1. If the United States imposes a tariff, the price paid by U.S. consumers does not change.

2. If a country imposes a tariff on rice imports, domestic production of rice will increase and domestic consumption of rice will decrease.

3. A tariff increases the gains from trade for the exporting country.

4. A quota on imports of a particular good specifies the minimum quantity of that good that can be imported in a given period.

Multiple choice

1. A tax on a good that is imposed by the importing country when an imported good crosses its international boundary is a
   a. quota.
   b. nontariff barrier.
   c. tariff.
   d. sanction.
   e. border tax.

2. The average U.S. tariff was highest in the
   a. 1930s.
   b. 1940s.
   c. 1970s.
   d. 1980s.
   e. 1990s.

3. Suppose the world price of a shirt is $10. If the United States imposes a tariff of $5 a shirt, then the price of a shirt in the
   a. United States falls to $5.
   b. United States rises to $15.
   c. world falls to $5.
   d. world rises to $5.
   e. world rises to $15.

4. When a tariff is imposed on a good, the ____ increases.
   a. domestic quantity purchased
   b. domestic quantity produced
   c. quantity imported
   d. quantity exported
   e. world price

5. When a tariff is imposed on a good, domestic consumers of the good ____ and domestic producers of the good ____.
   a. win; lose
   b. lose; win
   c. win; win
   d. lose; lose
   e. lose; neither win nor lose

6. Which of the following parties benefits from a quota but not from a tariff?
   a. the domestic government
   b. domestic producers
   c. domestic consumers
   d. the person with the right to import the good
   e. the foreign government

Complete the graph

■ **FIGURE 19.3**

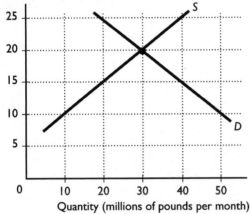

1. Figure 19.3 shows the supply of and demand for sugar in the United States.
   a. If the world price of sugar is 10¢ a pound, draw the world price line in the figure. What is the quantity consumed in the United States, the quantity produced in the United States, and the quantity imported?
   b. Suppose the government imposes a 5¢ a pound tariff on sugar. Show the effect of the tariff in Figure 19.3. After the tariff, what is the quantity consumed in the United States, the quantity produced in the United States, and the quantity imported?

Short answer and numeric questions

Price (dollars per ton of steel)	U.S. quantity supplied (tons per month)	U.S. quantity demanded (tons per month)
1,000	20,000	20,000
750	17,000	22,000
500	14,000	24,000
250	11,000	26,000

1. The table above gives the U.S. supply and the U.S. demand schedules for steel. Suppose the world price of steel is $500 per ton.
   a. If there are no tariffs or nontariff barriers, what is the price of steel in the United States, the quantity of steel consumed in the United States, the quantity produced in the United States, and the quantity imported into the United States?
   b. If the U.S. government imposes a tariff of $250 per ton of steel, what is the price of steel in the United States, the quantity of steel consumed in the United States, the quantity produced in the United States, and the quantity imported into the United States?
   c. Instead of a tariff, if the U.S. government imposes a quota of 5,000 tons of steel per month, what is the price of steel in the United States, the quantity of steel consumed in the United States, the quantity produced in the United States, and the quantity imported into the United States?
   d. Comparing your answers to parts (b) and (c), are U.S. consumers better off with the tariff or the quota? Are U.S. producers better off with the tariff or the quota? Is the U.S. government better off with the tariff or the quota?

2. Suppose the U.S. government imposes a tariff on sugar. How does the tariff affect the price of sugar? How does it affect U.S. sugar consumers? U.S. sugar producers?

3. Suppose the U.S. government imposes a quota on sugar. How does the quota affect the price of sugar? How does it affect U.S. sugar consumers? U.S. sugar producers?

4. Why do consumers lose from a tariff?

CHECKPOINT 19.4

■ **Explain the arguments used to justify trade barriers and show why these arguments are incorrect but also why some barriers are hard to remove.**

Quick Review

- *Rent seeking* Lobbying and other political activity that seeks to capture the gains from trade.

Additional Practice Problems 19.4

1. Canada has limits on the amount of U.S. television shows that can be broadcast in Canada. What are Canada's arguments for restricting imports of U.S. television shows? Are these arguments correct? Who loses from this restriction of trade?

2. The United States has, from time to time, limited imports of lumber from Canada. What is the argument that the United States has used to justify this quota? Who wins from this restriction? Who loses?

3. In each of the first two Practice Problems, identify who is rent seeking.

Solutions to Additional Practice Problems 19.4

1. Canada has used a number of arguments, but they are all incorrect. Canada has argued that Canadian television shows are of a higher quality than U.S. shows, but if Canadian consumers can detect a quality difference, they can watch Canadian shows rather than U.S. shows. Canada also has argued that these limitations are necessary to save Canadian culture, but if Canadian consumers want to protect this part of their heritage, they can watch exclusively Canadian shows rather than U.S. shows. The major losers from the Canadian limitations are Canadian consumers who can watch only a limited number of popular U.S. television shows.

2. In past decades, the United States asserted that the lumber industry was needed because it played a major role in national defense. With the use of more exotic materials in defense armaments, the national defense argument has passed into history. More recently, the United States has set quotas and tariffs allegedly for environmental reasons and allegedly because the Canadian government was subsidizing the production of lumber. Both of these arguments are likely not the true reason for the quotas. The quotas and limitations are the result of political lobbying by lumber producers and lumber workers. The winners from the quotas and tariffs are the lumber producers and lumber workers. The losers are all U.S. lumber consumers.

3. Rent seeking is lobbying and other political activity that seeks to capture the gains from trade. In Practice Problem 1, the Canadian producers of television shows are rent seeking. In Practice Problem 2, the U.S. lumber producers and U.S. lumber workers are rent seeking. It is important to keep in mind that free trade promotes prosperity for all countries. Protection reduces the potential gains from trade

■ Self Test 19.4

Fill in the blanks

The assertion that it is necessary to protect a new industry to enable it to grow into a mature industry that can compete in world markets is the ____ (infant-industry; maturing-industry) argument. Dumping occurs when ____ (U.S. jobs are lost to cheap foreign labor; a foreign firm sells its exports at a lower price than its cost of production). Protection ____ (is; is not) necessary to bring diversity and stability to our economy. Protection ____ (is; is not) necessary to penalize countries with lax environmental standards. The major reason why international trade is restricted is because ____ (foreign countries protect their industries; of rent seeking).

True or false

1. The national security argument is the only valid argument for protection.

2. Dumping by a foreign producer is easy to detect.

3. Protection saves U.S. jobs at no cost.

4. International trade is an attractive base for tax collection in developing countries

Multiple choice

1. The national security argument is used by those who assert they want to
   a. increase imports as a way of strengthening their country.
   b. increase exports as a way of earning money to strengthen their country.
   c. limit imports that compete with domestic producers important for national defense.
   d. limit exports to control the flow of technology to third world nations.
   e. limit all imports.

2. The argument that it is necessary to protect a new industry to enable it to grow into a mature industry that can compete in world markets is the
   a. national security argument.
   b. diversity argument.
   c. infant-industry argument.
   d. environmental protection argument.
   e. national youth protection argument.

3. _____ occurs when a foreign firm sells its exports at a lower price than its cost of production.
   a. Dumping
   b. The trickle-down effect
   c. Rent seeking
   d. Tariff avoidance
   e. Nontariff barrier protection

4. The United States
   a. needs tariffs to allow us to compete with cheap foreign labor.
   b. does not need tariffs to allow us to compete with cheap foreign labor.
   d. should not trade with countries that have cheap labor.
   d. will not benefit from trade with countries that have cheap labor.
   e. avoids trading with countries that have cheap labor.

5. Why do governments in less-developed nations impose tariffs on imported goods and services?
   a. The government gains revenue from the tariff.
   b. The government's low-paid workers are protected from high-paid foreign workers.
   c. The nation's total income is increased.
   d. The national security of the country definitely is improved.
   e. The government protects its national culture.

6. What is a major reason international trade is restricted?
   a. rent seeking
   b. to allow competition with cheap foreign labor
   c. to save jobs
   d. to prevent dumping
   e. to protect national culture

Short answer and numeric questions

1. What is the dumping argument for protection? What is its flaw?

2. How do you respond to a speaker who says that we need to limit auto imports from Japan in order to save U.S. jobs?

3. Why is it incorrect to assert that trade with countries that have lax environmental standards needs to be restricted?

SELF TEST ANSWERS

■ CHECKPOINT 19.1

Fill in the blanks

Manufactured goods account for <u>54</u> percent of U.S. imports. <u>Canada</u> is the United States' biggest trading partner. The United States <u>is</u> a member of NAFTA, the North American Free Trade Agreement. In the United States between 1960 and 2005, trade <u>increased</u> as a fraction of total output.

True or false

1. False; page 480
2. False; page 480
3. False; page 482
4. True; page 483

Multiple choice

1. a; page 480
2. d; page 480
3. b; page 480
4. a; page 482
5. a; page 480
6. b; page 483

Short answer and numeric questions

1. From the U.S. vantage, the cheese is an imported good and the air transportation is an exported service. From the French vantage, the cheese is an exported good and the air transportation is an imported service; page 480.

2. Between 1960 and 2005, international trade in the United States expanded. In 1960, U.S. exports were 5 percent of total output and in 2005, exports were 10.5 percent of total output. In 1960, U.S. imports were 4 percent of the goods and services purchased and in 2005, imports were 16 percent of the goods and services purchased; page 480.

3. NAFTA is the North American Free Trade Agreement. It is an agreement among Canada, the United States, and Mexico with the goal of making trade among the three nations easier and freer; page 482.

■ CHECKPOINT 19.2

Fill in the blanks

A country has a comparative advantage in producing a good if it can produce the good at <u>lower</u> opportunity cost than another country. If the world price of clothing is less than the price in the United States with no international trade and the United States imports clothing from Asia, U.S. buyers of clothing <u>gain</u> and Asian producers of clothing <u>gain</u>. Trade <u>does not allow</u> a nation to produce at a point beyond its production possibilities frontier. Trade <u>allows</u> a nation to consume at a point beyond its production possibilities frontier.

True or false

1. False; pages 484-485
2. False; page 490
3. True; page 491
4. False; page 492

Multiple choice

1. d; page 484
2. c; pages 485-486
3. c; pages 484-487
4. c; page 486
5. a; page 487
6. b; pages 487-488
7. a; pages 489-490
8. d; pages 491-492

Complete the graph

1. a. In the absence of international trade, the equilibrium price of a bushel of wheat in the United States is $4; pages 484-485.
   b. If the world price of a bushel of wheat is $6 a bushel, the United States will export wheat because the world price exceeds the no-trade price. If the price of wheat exceeds $4 a bushel, the United States will export wheat. If the price of wheat is less than $4 a bushel, the United States will import wheat; pages 484-485.

2. a. The opportunity cost of a computer chip in the United States is 1 pound of cheese. In France, the opportunity cost of a computer chip is 4 pounds of cheese. The United States has the comparative advantage in chips; pages 487-488.

b. The opportunity cost of a pound of cheese in the United States is 1 computer chip. In France, the opportunity cost is of a pound of cheese 1/4 of a computer chip. France has the comparative advantage in cheese; pages 487-488.

c. The United States has the comparative advantage in chips, so it will specialize in producing chips and export chips to France. France will specialize in cheese and export cheese to the United States; page 489.

■ FIGURE 19.4

Computer chips (thousands per year)

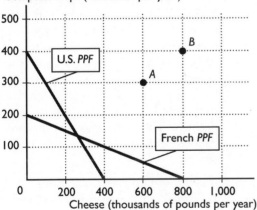

d. The point is labeled in Figure 19.4; page 490.

e. The United States produces 400,000 chips and no cheese and France produces 800,000 pounds of cheese and no chips. The total production is 400,000 chips and 800,000 pounds of cheese, labeled as point *B* in Figure 19.4. More chips *and* more cheese are produced at point *B* after trade than are produced at point *A* before trade; page 490.

Short answer and numeric questions

1. a. In the absence of international trade, the equilibrium price is $600 a ton and the equilibrium quantity is 46 tons; pages 484-485.

b. In the United States, the quantity supplied is 54 tons and the quantity demanded is 34 tons. The United States exports 20 tons of potatoes; pages 484-485.

c. In the United States, the quantity supplied is 58 tons and the quantity demanded is 28 tons. The United States exports 30 tons of potatoes; pages 484-485.

d. The United States would import potatoes if the world price is less than $600 a ton; pages 486-487.

2. a. In France, the opportunity cost of a ton of ice cream is 6 tons of cheese; in the United States, the opportunity cost of a ton of ice cream is 2 tons of cheese. The United States has the comparative advantage in producing ice cream; pages 487-488.

b. In France, the opportunity cost of a ton of cheese is 1/6 of a ton of ice cream; in the United States, the opportunity cost of a ton of cheese is 1/2 of a ton of ice cream. France has the comparative advantage in producing cheese; pages 487-488.

c. The United States imports cheese and exports ice cream; page 488.

d. 35 tons of ice cream are produced and 110 tons of cheese are produced; pages 488-490.

e. 50 tons of ice cream are produced in the United States and 120 tons of cheese are produced in France; pages 488-490.

f. The world production of ice cream *and* cheese increased, which demonstrates the gains from trade; pages 489-490.

3. The gains from trade occur because after specialization and trade, a country can increase its consumption so that it can consume at a point beyond its production possibilities frontier. To obtain the gains from trade a country must specialize and trade; pages 489-490.

4. Offshoring occurs when a U.S. firm either hires labor and produces in other countries or when it buys goods and services produced in other countries. Offshoring is controversial because some observers assert that it is "exporting America." There are gains from offshoring exactly as there are gains from all international trade. In particular, by specializing in producing the goods and services in which it has a comparative advantage (and not producing or "offshoring" the goods in which it does not have a comparative advantage) and trading with other countries, the nation can consume more of all goods and services ; pages 491-492.

■ CHECKPOINT 19.3

Fill in the blanks

A tax on a good that is imposed by the importing country when an imported good enters its boundary is called a <u>tariff</u> and a specified maximum amount of a good that may be imported is called a <u>quota</u>. A tariff <u>raises</u> the price paid by domestic consumers and <u>increases</u> the quantity produced by domestic producers. A quota <u>raises</u> the price paid by domestic consumers and <u>increases</u> the quantity produced by domestic producers.

True or false

1. False; pages 495
2. True; pages 496
3. False; pages 496
4. False; page 496

Multiple choice

1. c; page 494
2. a; page 494
3. b; page 495
4. b; pages 495-496
5. b; pages 495-496
6. d; pages 496-497

Complete the graph

■ FIGURE 19.5

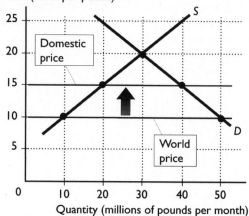

1. a. The world price line is shown in Figure 19.5. 50 million pounds of sugar are consumed in the United States, 10 million pounds are produced in the United States, and 40 million pounds are imported into the United States; pages 495-496.

   b. The tariff increases the domestic price, as shown in the figure. The quantity consumed in the United States decreases to 40 million pounds, the quantity produced in the United States increases to 20 million pounds, and the amount imported decreases to 20 million pounds; pages 495-496.

Short answer and numeric questions

1. a. The price is the world price, $500 per ton. At this price, the quantity consumed in the United States is 24,000 tons per month, the quantity produced in the United States is 14,000 tons per month, and the quantity imported is the difference, 10,000 tons per month; page 495.

   b. With a $250 per ton tariff, the price is $750 per ton. At this price, the quantity consumed in the United States is 22,000 tons per month, the quantity produced in the United States is 17,000 tons per month, and the quantity imported is the difference, 5,000 tons per month; page 495.

c. With a quota of 5,000 tons per month, the total supply schedule equals the U.S. supply schedule plus 5,000 tons per month. The price of steel is $750 per ton because this is the price that sets the U.S. quantity demanded (22,000 tons) equal to the U.S. quantity supplied (17,000 tons) plus the quantity that can be imported (5,000 tons). At this price, the quantity consumed in the United States is 22,000 tons per month and the quantity produced in the United States is 17,000 tons per month; page 497.

d. U.S. consumers are no better off or worse off with the tariff or the quota because both raise the price to $750 per ton and decrease the quantity consumed to 22,000 tons. U.S. producers are no better off or worse off with the tariff or the quota because both raise the price to $750 per ton and increase the quantity produced to 17,000 tons. The U.S. government is better off with the tariff because it receives revenue with the tariff and nothing with the quota; pages 495-497.

2. The tariff raises the price of sugar. U.S. sugar consumers decrease the quantity they purchase and U.S. sugar producers increase the quantity they produce; pages 495-496.

3. The quota has the same effects as the tariff in the previous question. The quota raises the price of sugar. U.S. sugar consumers decrease the quantity purchased and U.S. sugar producers increase the quantity produced; pages 496-497.

4. Consumers lose from a tariff because the tariff raises the price they pay and the quantity bought decreases. The tariff makes people pay more than the opportunity cost of the good; page 496.

■ CHECKPOINT 19.4

Fill in the blanks

The assertion that it is necessary to protect a new industry to enable it to grow into a mature industry that can compete in world markets is the <u>infant-industry</u> argument. Dumping occurs when <u>a foreign firm sells its exports at a lower price than its cost of production</u>. Protection <u>is not</u> necessary to bring diversity and stability to our economy. Protection <u>is not</u> necessary to penalize countries with lax environmental standards. The major reason why international trade is restricted is because <u>of rent seeking</u>.

True or false

1. False; page 499
2. False; page 8500
3. False; pages 500-501
4. True; page 503

Multiple choice

1. c; page 499
2. c; page 499
3. a; page 500
4. b; page 501
5. a; page 503
6. a; page 504

Short answer and numeric questions

1. Dumping occurs when a foreign firm sells its exports at a lower price than its cost of production. The dumping argument is flawed for the following reasons. First, it is virtually impossible to detect dumping because it is hard to determine a firm's costs and the fair market price. Second, it is hard to think of a good that is produced by a global natural monopoly. Third, if a firm truly was a global natural monopoly, the best way to deal with it would be by regulation; page 500.

2. Saving jobs is one of the oldest arguments in favor of protection. It is also incorrect. Protecting a particular industry will likely save jobs in that industry but will cost many other jobs in other industries. The cost to consumers of saving a job is many times the wage rate of the job saved; pages 500-501.

3. The assertion that trade with developing countries that have lax environmental standards should be restricted to "punish" the nation for its lower standards is weak. Everyone wants a clean environment, but not

every country can afford to devote resources toward this goal. The rich nations can afford this expenditure of resources, but for many poor nations protecting the environment takes second place to more pressing problems such as feeding their people. These nations must develop and grow economically in order to be able to afford to protect their environment. One important way to help these nations grow is by trading with them. Through trade these nations' incomes will increase and with this increase will also increase their ability and willingness to protect the environment; page 502.

International Finance

Chapter

20

Chapter 20 studies how nations keep their international accounts, what determines the balance of payments, and how the value of the dollar is determined in the foreign exchange market.

- **Describe a country's balance of payments accounts and explain what determines the amount of international borrowing and lending.**

There are three balance of payments accounts, which are the current account, the capital account, and the official settlements account. The current account balance equals exports minus imports, plus net interest and transfers received from abroad. The capital account is a record of foreign investment in the United States minus U.S. investment abroad. The official settlements account is a record of the change in U.S. official reserves. The sum of the balances on the three accounts always equals zero. We pay for imports that exceed the value of our exports by borrowing from the rest of the world. A net borrower is a country that is borrowing more from the rest of the world than it is lending to the rest of the world, and a net lender is a country that is lending more to the rest of the world than it is borrowing from the rest of the world. A debtor nation is a country that during its entire history has borrowed more from the rest of the world than it has lent to it, and a creditor nation is a country that during its entire history has invested more in the rest of the world than other countries have invested in it. Net exports equals the sum of the private sector balance and the government sector balance.

- **Explain how the exchange rate is determined and why it fluctuates.**

Foreign currency is needed to buy goods or invest in another country. The foreign exchange rate is the price at which one currency exchanges for another and is determined by demand and supply in the foreign exchange market. The quantity of dollars demanded increases when the exchange rate falls. The demand for dollars changes and the demand curve for dollars shifts if the U.S. interest rate differential or the expected future exchange rate changes. A rise in either increases the demand for dollars. The quantity of dollars supplied increases when the exchange rate rises. The supply of dollars changes and the supply curve of dollars shifts if the U.S. interest rate differential or the expected future exchange rate changes. A rise in either decreases the supply of dollars. At the equilibrium exchange rate, the quantity of dollars demanded equals the quantity of dollars supplied. The exchange rate is volatile because factors that change the demand also change the supply. Exchange rate expectations are influenced by purchasing power parity, a situation in which money buys the same amount of goods and services in different currencies, and interest rate parity, a situation in which the interest rate in one currency equals the interest rate in another currency once exchange rate changes are taken into account. The Fed and other central banks can intervene directly in the foreign exchange market by pegging the exchange rate. If the peg overvalues the exchange rate, the central bank runs out of foreign reserves; if the peg undervalues the exchange rate, the central bank accumulates foreign reserves.

CHECKPOINT 20.1

■ **Describe a country's balance of payments accounts and explain what determines the amount of international borrowing and lending.**

Quick Review

- *Current account balance* The current account balance equals net exports plus net interest plus net transfers received from abroad.
- *Capital account balance* The capital account balance equals foreign investment in the United States minus U.S. investment abroad.

Additional Practice Problems 20.1

In 2002 the U.S. economy recorded the following transactions:

Imports of goods and services, $1,418 billion; net interest, –$25 billion; net transfers –$52 billion; increase in U.S. official reserves, $7 billion; exports of goods and services, $975 billion; statistical discrepancy $198 billion; foreign investment in the United States, $885 billion; and, U.S. investment abroad, $556 billion.

  a. Calculate the current account balance.

  b. Calculate the capital account balance.

  c. Calculate the official settlements account balance.

  d. To what do these balances sum?

  e. Was the United States a debtor or a creditor nation in 2002?

2. Suppose the official settlements account equals zero. In this case, what is the relationship between the current account and the capital account? Why does this relationship exist?

Solutions to Additional Practice Problems 20.1

1a. The current account balance equals exports plus net interest plus net transfers minus imports. So the current account balance equals $975 billion + (–$25 billion) +(–$52 billion) – $1,418 billion = –$520 billion.

1b. The capital account balance equals foreign investment in the United States minus U.S. investment abroad plus any statistical discrepancy. So the capital account balance equals $885 billion – $556 billion + $198 billion = $527 billion.

1c. The official settlements account balance is the negative of the change in U.S. official reserves. When reserves increase by $7 billion, the official settlements account balance is –$7 billion.

1d. Keep in mind that the sum of the current account, capital account, and official settlements account is zero. So, if the previous answers are correct, they will sum to zero. Fortunately, they do: –$520 billion + $527 billion –$7 billion = $0.

1e. Interest payments reflect the value of outstanding debts. The United States is a debtor nation because the value of interest payments received from the rest of the world is less than the value of interest payments made to the rest of the world.

2. If the official settlements account equals zero, then the deficit in the current account equals the surplus in the capital account. Or, if the official settlements account equals zero, then the surplus in the current account equals the deficit in the capital account. This relationship exists because the sum of the current account, capital account, and the official settlements account equals zero. If the official settlements account equals zero, the current account balance must equal the negative of the capital account balance.

■ **Self Test 20.1**

Fill in the blanks

The ____ (current; capital; official settlements) account records payments for the imports of goods and services. The ____ (current; capital; official settlements) account records foreign investment in the United States minus U.S. investment abroad. The sum of the balances on current account, capital account, and the official settlements account always equals ____ (zero;

100 percent). The United States is a ____ (debtor; creditor) nation. The United States is borrowing for ____ (consumption; investment).

True or false

1. If foreign investment in the United States increases, and U.S. investment in the rest of the world decreases, the current account shows an increase in exports and a decrease in imports.

2. The official settlements account balance is negative if U.S. official reserves increase.

3. The United States has a current account deficit.

4. If the United States has a surplus in its capital account and a deficit in its current account, the balance in its official settlements account is zero.

5. The United States is a net lender and a debtor nation.

6. If the United States started to run a current account surplus that continued indefinitely, it would immediately become a net lender and would eventually become a creditor nation.

7. Net exports equals the private sector balance minus the government sector balance.

8. In 2004, U.S. borrowing from abroad financed investment.

Multiple choice

1. A country's balance of payments accounts records its
   a. tax receipts and expenditures.
   b. tariffs and nontariff revenue and government purchases.
   c. international trading, borrowing, and lending.
   d. its tariff receipts and what it pays in tariffs to other nations.
   e. international exports and imports and nothing else.

2. Which of the following are balance of payments accounts?
   i. capital account.
   ii. tariff account.
   iii. current account.
   a. i only.
   b. ii only.
   c. iii only.
   d. i and iii.
   e. ii and iii.

3. Which balance of payments account records payments for imports and receipts from exports?
   a. current account
   b. capital account
   c. official settlements account
   d. reserves account
   e. trade account

4. The current account balance is equal to
   a. imports − exports + net interest + net transfers.
   b. imports − exports + net interest − net transfers.
   c. exports − imports − net interest + net transfers.
   d. exports − imports + net interest + net transfers.
   e. exports − imports − net interest − net transfers.

5. If an investment of $100 million from the United Kingdom is made in the United States, the $100 million is listed as a ____ entry in the ____ account.
   a. positive; current
   b. negative; capital
   c. positive; capital
   d. negative; current
   e. positive; official settlements

6. If the United States receives $200 billion of foreign investment and at the same time invests a total of $160 billion abroad, then the U.S.
   a. capital account balance increases by $40 billion.
   b. current account must be in surplus.
   c. balance of payments must be negative.
   d. capital account balance decreases by $40 billion.
   e. official settlements account balance increases by $40 billion.

7. In the balance of payments accounts, changes in U.S. official reserves are recorded in the
   a. current account.
   b. capital account.
   c. official settlements account.
   d. international currency account.
   e. international reserves account.

8. If a country has a current account balance of $100 billion and the official settlements account balance is zero, then the country's capital account balance must be
   a. equal to $100 billion.
   b. positive but not necessarily equal to $100 billion.
   c. equal to –$100 billion.
   d. negative but not necessarily equal to –$100 billion.
   e. zero.

9. A country that is borrowing more from the rest of the world than it is lending is called a
   a. net lender.
   b. net borrower.
   c. net debtor.
   d. net creditor.
   e. net loaner country.

10. A debtor nation is a country that
    a. borrows more from the rest of the world than it lends to it.
    b. lends more to the rest of the world than it borrows from it.
    c. during its entire history has invested more in the rest of the world than other countries have invested in it.
    d. during its entire history has borrowed more from the rest of the world than it has lent to it.
    e. during its entire history has consistently run a capital account deficit.

11. Comparing the U.S. balance of payments in 2004 to the rest of the world, we see that the
    a. United States has the largest current account surplus.
    b. U.S. current account is similar in size to most developed nations.
    c. United States has the largest capital account deficit.
    d. United States has the largest current account deficit.
    e. U.S. current account is similar in size to most developed nations and has a deficit.

12. According to the U.S. balance of payments accounts in 2004, U.S. international borrowing is used for
    a. private and public investment.
    b. private consumption.
    c. government expenditure.
    d. private and public saving.
    e. private saving and public consumption.

Short answer and numeric questions

1. What is recorded in the U.S. current account? In its capital account? In its official settlements account?

2. If its official settlements account equals zero, what will a country's capital account equal if it has a $350 billion current account deficit?

Item	(billions of dollars)
U.S. investment abroad	400
Exports of goods and services	1,000
Net transfers	0
Change in official reserves	10
Net interest	0
Foreign investment in the United States	800

3. The table above has balance of payment data for the United States.
   a. What is the capital account balance?
   b. What is the official settlements balance?
   c. What is the current account balance?
   d. What is the value of imports of goods and services?

4. What is a net borrower? A debtor nation? Is it possible for a nation to be net borrower and yet not be a debtor nation?

Item	(billions of dollars)
Saving	1,600
Investment	1,900
Government expenditures	1,300
Net taxes	1,400

5. The table above has data for the United States.
   a. What is the private sector balance?
   b. What is the government sector balance?
   c. What is net exports?

CHECKPOINT 20.2

■ **Explain how the exchange rate is determined and why it fluctuates.**

Quick Review

- *U.S. interest rate differential* On the foreign exchange market, an increase in the U.S. interest rate differential increases the demand for dollars and decreases the supply of dollars.
- *Expected future exchange rate* On the foreign exchange market, a rise in the expected future exchange rate increases the demand for dollars and decreases the supply of dollars.

Additional Practice Problems 20.2

1. The figure shows the supply and demand curves for dollars in the foreign exchange market.

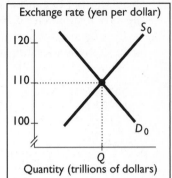

   a. What is the equilibrium exchange rate?
   b. Suppose the U.S. interest rate rises so that the U.S. interest rate differential increases. Assume that the effect on the supply is the same as the effect on the demand. In the figure, show the effect of this change. Does the equilibrium exchange rate rise or fall? Does the equilibrium quantity of dollars exchanged increase or decrease?

2. How and why does an increase in the expected future exchange rate change the demand for U.S. dollars and the demand curve for dollars? How and why does an increase in the expected future exchange rate change the supply of U.S. dollars and the supply curve of dollars? What is the effect on the equilibrium exchange rate?

Solutions to Additional Practice Problems 20.2

1a. The figure shows that the initial equilibrium exchange rate is 110 yen per dollar.

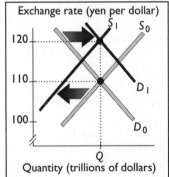

1b. The increase in the U.S. interest rate differential increases the demand for U.S. dollars and simultaneously decreases the supply of U.S. dollars. As a result the demand curve for dollars shifts rightward, from D_0 to D_1 and the supply curve of dollars shifts leftward, from S_0 to S_1. The exchange rate rises. In the figure the exchange rate rises to 120 yen per dollar. Because the effect on the demand is the same as the effect on the supply, the curves shift by the same amount, so the equilibrium quantity of dollars exchanged does not change.

2. An increase in the expected future exchange rate increases the demand for U.S. dollars and shifts the demand curve rightward. The demand for U.S. dollars increases because at the current exchange rate people want to buy U.S. dollars now and sell them in the future at the higher expected exchange rate. An increase in the expected future exchange rate decreases the supply of U.S. dollars and shifts the supply curve leftward. The supply of U.S. dollars decreases because people would rather keep the dollars until they can sell them in the future at the higher expected exchange rate. Because the demand for dollars increases and the supply of dollars decreases, the current equilibrium exchange rate rises.

■ Self Test 20.2

Fill in the blanks

The price at which one currency exchanges for another is called a foreign _____ (exchange rate; interest rate). If the dollar falls in value against the Mexican peso, the dollar has _____ (appreciated; depreciated). A rise in exchange rate _____ (decreases; increases) the quantity of U.S. dollars demanded. An increase in the demand for dollars shifts the demand curve for dollars _____ (leftward; rightward) and an increase in the supply of dollars shifts the supply curve of dollars _____ (leftward; rightward). The exchange rate is volatile because an influence that changes the demand for dollars often _____ (changes; does not change) the supply of dollars. An increase in the expected future exchange rate _____ (raises; lowers) the equilibrium exchange rate. Purchasing power parity is equal value of _____ (interest rates; money). If the Fed buys dollars on the foreign exchange market, the exchange rate _____ (rises; falls).

True or false

1. The U.S. foreign exchange rate changes infrequently.

2. If the exchange rate increases from 90 yen per dollar to 110 yen per dollar, the dollar has appreciated.

3. The larger the value of U.S. exports, the larger is the quantity of U.S. dollars demanded.

4. An increase in the U.S. exchange rate increases the supply of U.S. dollars and shifts the supply curve of dollars rightward.

5. A rise in the expected future exchange rate increases the demand for dollars and also the supply of dollars and might raise or lower the exchange rate.

6. The equilibrium U.S. exchange rate is the exchange rate that sets the quantity of dollars demanded equal to the quantity of dollars supplied.

7. An increase in the U.S. interest rate differential raises the U.S. exchange rate.

8. To prevent the price of the euro from falling, the European Central Bank might sell euros on the foreign exchange market.

Multiple choice

1. The foreign exchange market is the market in which
   a. all international transactions occur.
   b. currencies are exchanged solely by governments.
   c. goods and services are exchanged between governments.
   d. the currency of one country is exchanged for the currency of another.
   e. the world's governments collect their tariff revenue.

2. When Del Monte, an American company, purchases Mexican tomatoes, Del Monte pays for the tomatoes with
   a. Canadian dollars.
   b. Mexican pesos.
   c. gold.
   d. Mexican goods and services.
   e. yen.

3. If today the exchange rate is 100 yen per dollar and tomorrow the exchange rate is 98 yen per dollar, then the dollar ____ and the yen ____.
   a. appreciated; appreciated
   b. appreciated; depreciated
   c. depreciated; appreciated
   d. depreciated; depreciated
   e. depreciated; did not change

4. In the foreign exchange market, as the U.S. exchange rate rises, other things remaining the same, the
   a. quantity of dollars demanded increases.
   b. demand curve for dollars shifts rightward.
   c. demand curve for dollars shifts leftward.
   d. quantity of dollars demanded decreases.
   e. supply curve of dollars shifts rightward.

5. In the foreign exchange market, the demand for dollars increases and the demand curve for dollars shifts rightward if the
   a. U.S. interest rate differential increases.
   b. expected future exchange rate falls.
   c. foreign interest rate rises.
   d. U.S. interest rate falls.
   e. exchange rate falls.

6. As the exchange rate ____, the quantity supplied of U.S. dollars ____.
   a. rises; increases
   b. falls; increases
   c. falls; remains the same
   d. rises; decreases
   e. rises; remains the same

7. In the foreign exchange market, the supply curve of dollars is
   a. upward sloping.
   b. downward sloping.
   c. vertical.
   d. horizontal.
   e. identical to the demand curve for dollars.

8. Everything else remaining the same, in the foreign exchange market which of the following will increase the supply of U.S. dollars?
   a. The Japanese interest rate rises.
   b. The expected future exchange rate rises.
   c. The U.S. interest rate rises.
   d. The U.S. interest rate differential increases.
   e. The exchange rate falls.

9. When there is a shortage of dollars in the foreign exchange market, the
   a. demand curve for dollars shifts leftward to restore the equilibrium.
   b. U.S. exchange rate will appreciate.
   c. U.S. exchange rate will depreciate.
   d. supply curve of dollars shifts leftward to restore the equilibrium.
   e. supply curve of dollars shifts rightward to restore the equilibrium.

10. In the foreign exchange market, when the U.S. interest rate rises, the supply of dollars ____ and the foreign exchange rate ____.
    a. increases; rises
    b. increases; falls
    c. decreases; rises
    d. decreases; falls
    e. increases; does not change

11. A situation in which money buys the same amount of goods and services in different currencies is called
    a. exchange rate equilibrium.
    b. purchasing power parity.
    c. exchange rate surplus.
    d. exchange rate balance.
    e. a fixed exchange rate.

12. Interest rate parity occurs when
   a. the interest rate in one currency equals the interest rate in another currency when exchange rate changes are taken into account.
   b. interest rate differentials are always maintained across nations.
   c. interest rates are equal across nations.
   d. prices are equal across nations when exchange rates are taken into account.
   e. interest rates no longer affect the exchange rate.

Complete the graph

■ **FIGURE 20.1**

Exchange rate (yen per dollar)

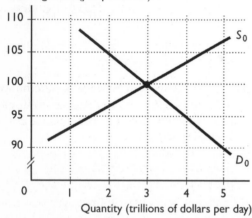

1. Figure 20.1 shows the foreign exchange market for U.S. dollars.
   a. What is the equilibrium exchange rate?
   b. The U.S. interest rate differential rises. In Figure 20.1, illustrate the effect of this change. What happens to the exchange rate?

2. Figure 20.2 shows the foreign exchange market for U.S. dollars. Suppose people expect that the future exchange rate will be lower. In Figure 20.2, illustrate the effect of this change. What happens to the exchange rate? Has the exchange rate appreciated or depreciated?

■ **FIGURE 20.2**

Exchange rate (yen per dollar)

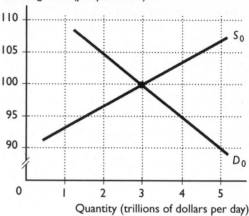

Quantity (trillions of dollars per day)

Short answer and numeric questions

1. If the exchange rate rises from 90 yen per dollar to 100 yen per dollar, has the dollar appreciated or depreciated? Has the yen appreciated or depreciated?

2. What is the relationship between the value of U.S. exports and the quantity of U.S. dollars demanded? Why does this relationship exist?

3. What is the relationship between the value of U.S. imports and the quantity of U.S. dollars supplied? Why does this relationship exist?

4. Everything else remaining the same, how will a rise in the Japanese interest rate affect the demand for dollars, the supply of dollars, and the U.S. exchange rate?

5. If the Fed believes the exchange rate is too low and wants to raise it, what action does the Fed undertake in the foreign exchange market? What limits the extent to which the Fed can undertake this action?

■ CHECKPOINT 20.1

Fill in the blanks

The <u>current</u> account records payments for the imports of goods and services. The <u>capital</u> account records foreign investment in the United States minus U.S. investment abroad. The sum of the balances on current account, capital account, and the official settlements account always equals <u>zero</u>. The United States is a <u>debtor</u> nation. The United States is borrowing for <u>investment</u>.

True or false

1. False; page 512
2. True; page 512
3. True; page 512
4. False; page 512
5. False; page 514
6. True; page 515
7. False; pages 516-517
8. True; page 517

Multiple choice

1. c; page 512
2. d; page 512
3. a; page 512
4. d; page 512
5. c; page 512
6. a; page 512
7. c; page 512
8. c; page 512
9. b; page 514
10. d; page 514
11. d; page 517
12. a; page 517

Short answer and numeric questions

1. The current account records payments for imports, receipts from exports, net interest and net transfers received from abroad. The capital account records foreign investment in the United States minus U.S. investments abroad. The official settlements account records changes in U.S. official reserves, the government's holding of foreign currency; page 512.

2. The current account balance plus the capital account balance plus official settlements account balance sums to zero. So if the official settlements account equals zero, a $350 billion current account deficit means there is a $350 billion capital account surplus; page 512.

3. a. The capital account balance equals foreign investment in the United States minus U.S. investment abroad, which is $400 billion; page 512.

   b. The official settlements balance is the negative of the change in official reserves, or –$10 billion; page 512.

   c. The sum of the current account balance, the capital account balance, and the official settlements account balance is zero. The capital account balance is $400 billion and the official settlements account balance is –$10 billion, so the current account balance is –$390 billion; page 512.

   d. The current account balance equals exports minus imports plus net interest plus net transfers received from abroad. Net interest and net transfers are given as zero. The current account balance is –$390 billion and exports are $1,000 billion, so imports equal $1,390 billion; page 512.

4. A net borrower is a country that is borrowing more from the rest of the world than it is lending to the rest of the world. A debtor nation is a country that during its entire history has borrowed more from the rest of the world than it has lent to it. It is possible for a nation to be a net borrower but not be a debtor nation. A country can be a creditor nation and a net borrower. This situation occurs if a creditor nation is, during a particular year, borrowing more from the rest of the world than it is lending to the rest of the world; page 514.

5. a. The private sector balance equals saving minus investment, so the private sector balance is –$300 billion; page 516.

   b. The government sector balance equals net taxes minus government expenditures on goods and services, so the government sector balance is $100 billion; page 516.

   c. The sum of the private sector balance plus the government sector balance equals net exports, so net exports equals –$200 billion; pages 516-517.

■ CHECKPOINT 20.2

Fill in the blanks

The price at which one currency exchanges for another is called a foreign <u>exchange rate</u>. If the dollar falls in value against the Mexican peso, the dollar has <u>depreciated</u>. A rise in the exchange rate <u>decreases</u> the quantity of U.S. dollars demanded. An increase in the demand for dollars shifts the demand curve for dollars <u>rightward</u> and an increase in the supply of dollars shifts the supply curve of dollars <u>rightward</u>. The exchange rate is volatile because an influence that changes the demand for dollars often <u>changes</u> the supply of dollars. An increase in the expected future exchange rate <u>raises</u> the equilibrium exchange rate. Purchasing power parity is equal value of <u>money</u>. If the Fed buys dollars on the foreign exchange market, the exchange rate <u>rises</u>.

True or false

1. False; page 519
2. True; page 520
3. True; page 520
4. False; page 524
5. False; pages 522, 525
6. True; page 526
7. True; page 527
8. False; pages 530-531

Multiple choice

1. d; page 519
2. b; page 519
3. c; pages 519-520
4. d; page 520
5. a; page 522
6. a; pages 523-524
7. a; page 524
8. a; page 525
9. b; page 526
10. c; pages 525, 527
11. b; page 528
12. a; page 530

Complete the graph

■ FIGURE 20.3

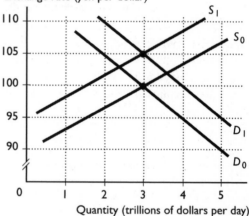

Exchange rate (yen per dollar)

1. a. The equilibrium exchange rate is 100 yen per dollar; page 526.

   b. The increase in the U.S. interest rate differential increases the demand for dollars and shifts the demand curve from D_0 to D_1 in Figure 20.3. The increase in the U.S. interest rate differential also decreases the supply of dollars and shifts the supply curve from S_0 to S_1. The exchange rate rises. In the figure, the exchange rate rises to 105 yen per dollar; page 527.

■ FIGURE 20.4

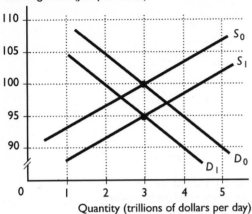

Exchange rate (yen per dollar)

2. The fall in the expected future exchange rate decreases the demand for dollars and increases the supply of dollars. The demand curve shifts leftward from D_0 to D_1 and the supply curve shifts rightward from S_0 to S_1. The exchange falls from 100 yen per dollar to 95 yen per dollar in Figure 20.4. The exchange rate depreciates; page 527.

Short answer and numeric questions

1. When the exchange rate rises from 90 yen per dollar to 100 yen per dollar, the dollar appreciates because the dollar buys more yen. The yen depreciates because it now takes 100 yen to buy a dollar instead of 90 yen to buy a dollar; pages 519-520.

2. The larger the value of U.S. exports, the larger is the quantity of U.S. dollars demanded. This relationship exists because U.S. firms want to be paid for their goods and services in dollars; page 520.

3. The larger the value of U.S. imports, the larger the quantity of U.S. dollars supplied. This relationship exists because U.S. consumers must pay for their imports in foreign currency. To obtain foreign currency, U.S. consumers supply dollars; page 523.

4. An increase in the Japanese interest rate decreases the U.S. interest rate differential. The smaller the U.S. interest rate differential, the smaller is the demand for U.S. assets and the smaller the demand for dollars. And the smaller the U.S. interest rate differential, the greater is the demand for foreign assets and the greater is the supply of dollars. So when the Japanese interest rate rises, the demand for dollars decreases, the supply of dollars increases, and the equilibrium exchange rate falls; page 528.

5. If the Fed wants to raise the exchange rate, it will buy dollars. The Fed would have to sell U.S. official reserves to buy dollars. The Fed is limited by its quantity of official reserves. If the Fed persisted in this action, eventually it would run out of reserves and would be forced to stop buying dollars; page 530.